AF862196

Themis
Bar Review

Multistate Essay Exam
Lecture Handouts

Agency
Conflict of Laws
Corporations
Family Law
Partnerships
Secured Transactions
Trusts
Wills and Decedents' Estates

Essay Writing Workshops

Some lecture handouts may not be included in this volume due to the timing of the lecture tapings. All handouts, including any omitted from this book, may be downloaded from the Themis learning portal.

ISBN 978-1-949634-59-4

Themis
Bar Review

Agency

Themis
Bar Review

AGENCY

PROFESSOR WILLIAM BIRDTHISTLE

CHICAGO–KENT COLLEGE OF LAW

CHAPTER 1: THE AGENCY RELATIONSHIP

A. Overview

- Every agency relationship must have a ____________________ and an ____________________.
- Generally, an ____________________ does things on behalf of the ____________________ and the ____________________ typically directs the ____________________'s acts.
- Why create an agency relationship?
    - To extend the principal's ____________________ reach
    - To acquire the agent's expertise
    - To make money
- Common examples of principal-agent relationships:
    - Employee-Employer
    - Named agents (e.g., talent agent, governmental agents, etc.)
    - Partner-Partnership
    - Officer/Director-Corporation
- Whether an agency relationship exists matters because there is a legal consequence to valid agency relationships; when one exists, a principal can be held ____________________ for acts of agents.
- When might a principal be liable to third parties for the actions of the agent?
    - In contracts
    - In torts

B. Components of Creating an Agency Relationship

- Three components of an agency relationship (ABC):
    - A____________________: This requires that both parties ____________________ to work with one another
    - B____________________: The agent agrees to work for the ____________________

- C____________________________: The agent agrees to work subject to the ____________________________ of the principal

- There is no requirement of ____________________________ to create an agency relationship.

  Example 1: *You ask your new roommate to sign up your apartment for electricity. The roommate orders the electricity. When the bill arrives, will you be liable for payment?*

  Answer: ____

  Example 2: *You ask your roommate to move your car for you for street cleaning. Your roommate says "Roger that." When your roommate moves the car, he hits someone. Are you liable?*

  Answer: ____

  Exam Tip 1: The parties are not going to always say, or even think, that they are in an agency relationship. As long as the essential elements are there, an agency relationship exists.

- When one or more parties disclaim the creation of an agency relationship, courts will look to ____ of ____________________________, which can range from a formal letter, to spoken words, to physical actions.

CHAPTER 2: PRINCIPALS AND AGENTS

A. Who Can Be a Principal?

- Almost any person or entity that has ____________________________________ can be a principal.
  - This excludes: _________________ and anyone incapacitated by illness or intoxication.
- Types of entities that can be principals:
  - Employer
  - Corporation; LLC
  - Partnership; LLP
- Employers typically exert a great amount of control over employees. This includes a significant amount of control over the ____________________________________ activities of the employees, including:
  - Giving the employees ________________ to work at the workplace;
  - Paying employees on a structured ________________; and
  - Directing the ways in which employees should finish and perform the tasks.

- While most entities can be principals, ______________________________ associations cannot because they lack ______________________________.

  Example 3: *A book group, a bird-watching group, or a collection of folks who like to hang out at coffee shops do not have legal capacity.*

B. Who Can Be an Agent?

- Any person or entity who has ______________________________ capacity
  - A ______________________________ may serve as an agent.
- To have minimal capacity, an agent must be able to:
  - ______________________________ to the agency relationship;
  - Perform the tasks on behalf of the principal; and
  - Be subject to the principal's ______________________________.
- Generally, any type of business entity may serve as an agent.

C. Formalities for Creating an Agency Relationship

- Agency formation simply requires: (i) assent, (ii) benefit, and (iii) control.
- No ______________________________ is required to form an agency relationship; service may be gratuitous.
- No evidence in writing is necessary.

D. Types of Agents

- **Servants/employees:** The employer has the right to control the agent's ______________________________ conduct of ______________.
- **Independent contractors:** The principal does not control or have the right to control the agent's ______________________________ conduct of ______________.
  - Characteristics of an independent contractor:
    - Maintain a high level of ______________________________
    - Free to work for other people
    - Paid on a ______________________________
    - Typically owns his own ______________

    Example 4: *Law firm big wig tells an associate to drive him to a meeting downtown. That will be an employer/employee relationship. Now contrast that with the lawyer hailing a cab and telling the cab driver to drive him downtown.*

    What are the differences?

    ____

    ____

This is relevant because principals are more ________________ when they have more control; they are more legally responsible.

- Terminating an agency relationship: ________________________________ can terminate an agency relationship ________________________________.

CHAPTER 3: SPECIFIC LIABILITY OF PRINCIPALS TO THIRD PARTIES

A. Introduction

- When you encounter an agency problem on the bar, the fact pattern will include:
    1) Activity that arguably constitutes the formation of an agency relationship between the principal and the agent;
    2) The agent will do the work, either by entering into a contract on behalf of the principal or by doing a task in which the agent commits a tort; and
    3) The principal is going to be sued by the third party—a contractual third-party or tort victim.

B. Contract Liability

- When is a principal liable for contracts that an agent enters on behalf of the principal? The principal is bound on a contract when:
    - The principal ________________________________ the agent to enter into the contract; and
    - The agent acted with ________________________________
- There are four types of legal authority:
    - ________________________________ authority
    - ________________________________ authority
    - ________________________________ authority
    - Ratification

> **Exam Tip 2:** As a general rule, when you are trying to discern between actual authority and apparent authority, look to the communication. When the principal is communicating with the agent, there is actual authority; when the principal is communicating with the third party, there is apparent authority.

CHAPTER 4: ACTUAL AUTHORITY

A. Actual Express Authority

- Look to communication between agent and principal.
- The principal creates actual express authority by using ________________, ________________ or ________________ to convey authority to the agent.

> ***Example 5:*** *You whisper in the ear of your roommate to have your car washed. Or you write something down on paper to tell your roommate to have the car washed, but then you burn the paper. When you receive a bill from the car wash, who is liable to pay? Why?*
>
> *Answer: The ______________________________ is bound to pay. An agency relationship existed. The agent had actual express authority to act on the principal's behalf.*

1. Requisite Intent

- **Subjective intent:** The agent must ________________ that he is doing what the principal ________________ him to do.
- **Objective intent:** The belief must be objectively ________________________________.

2. Termination by Death

- Upon the death of the principal, actual express authority ____________________________ when the agent has ________________________________ of the principal's death.
- Actual express authority terminates ________________________________ upon the death of the agent.

B. Actual Implied Authority

- Look to communication between ________________ and ________________________.
- A principal creates actual implied authority by using words, written or spoken, or ________________________________ to convey authority to the agent to take whatever steps are ________________________________ to achieve the principal's objectives.
- The agent has actual implied authority (absent express instructions to the contrary) to act within the accepted ____ or general ____.

> ***Example 6:*** *You tell your roommate, who happens to be a talent agent, to get you a role in the new Aquaman film. In an attempt to do this, your roommate takes the producer of the film out to dinner and tells the waiter to send the bill to you. Are you bound by the bill?*
>
> *Answer: ________________. The agent had actual implied authority to do whatever was necessary, under accepted business custom or trade usage, to secure the role for the principal.*

Example 7: *A barista has been signing invoices for cups without receiving instructions from the restaurant's owner. The owner has seen this take place several times. One morning, a delivery of cups arrives and the barista signs for the delivery without first receiving authorization from the owner. The owner, seeing this take place, does not object. Will the owner be liable for deliveries signed by the barista?*

Answer: Yes, because the owner saw and did not object.

CHAPTER 5: APPARENT AUTHORITY AND RATIFICATION

A. Apparent Authority

- Look to communication between the ________________________ and the ________________________.
- The principal creates apparent authority by words, written or spoken, that cause the ________________________ to reasonably believe that the principal ______________ to have acts done on the principal's behalf, by the ____________.
- Is the third party's belief reasonable? Have the principal and the third party had similar dealings before?

Example 8: *I tell the wine store that my butler has the authority to buy my wine for me. The butler has ________________________.*

If I send a letter to the wine store instead, would I, as principal, be bound by the butler's actions? ____________.

I tell the wine store the same thing, but I tell the butler that I can't stand the German stuff, and not to order any. The butler does it anyway. Am I bound to pay? ____________.

What if I fire the butler, but he still occasionally orders things and puts it on my bill, am I still liable? ____________*, until the apparent authority is revoked. The principal must tell the store that he is no longer bound.*

B. Ratification

- There's no pre-act communication to consider.
- Ratification requires that (i) the principal has knowledge of the material terms of the contract and (ii) the principal then ________________________ the contract's ________________________.

Example 9: *I have said nothing to my butler about wine, and I have said nothing to the store. I just hired the butler yesterday. The butler, to cheer me up, goes down to the store on the very first day of employment and orders me a huge crate of wine; I have not authorized him and I have not said anything to the store. He brings the crate of wine back and gently drops it at my feet.*

If I reject the wine, I am bound to pay the bill?

Answer: _______________

If I accept the wine, knowing the contract he entered to buy it for me, I am bound to pay the bill?

Answer: _______________

Exam Tip 3: Remember that regardless of whether the principal is liable, the agent may still be liable for violating a contract or committing a tort, regardless of his status as an agent. In other words, it is possible for both the agent and the principal to be liable.

CHAPTER 6: DISCLOSURE OF PRINCIPALS

- Three types of principals:

  1) Principals can be **disclosed**. The third party knows: (i) the agent is acting on behalf of a _______________ and (ii) the principal's _______________.

     - In these scenarios, the parties to the contract are the third party and the principal.

  2) Sometimes, the principal is **partially disclosed.** The third party knows that the agent is working on behalf of a principal, but not the _______________ of the principal.

     - In these scenarios, the parties to the contract are the third party, the principal, and the agent.

  Note 1: The two scenarios above assume that the agent had the proper authority to bind the principal to a contract. Note that disclosed and partially disclosed principals only become parties to a contract if (i) the agent had authority to bind the principal to the contract, or (ii) the principal ratified the contract.

  3) The principal can also be **undisclosed**. The third party knows neither agent's status as an agent nor the principal's identity.

     - In these scenarios, the parties to the contract are the _______________ and the _______________.
     - Whether an undisclosed principal is also party to the contract depends on whether the agent had the _______________ to bind the principal to the contract.

CHAPTER 7: PRINCIPALS' LIABILITY FOR TORTS

A. Vicarious Liability

- Vicarious liability, or respondeat superior: A principal may be liable for the tortious acts of his agent.
- Requirements for respondeat superior to apply:
    1) The principal has sufficient ______________________ over the agent's ______________________ such that the agency relationship is employer-employee; and
    2) The tort committed by the agent was committed while the agent was acting within the ____________ of his ______________________.
- **Sufficient control**: A principal who controls, or has the right to control, the ______________________ (manner and means) of the agent's performance of work is in the higher category of employer-employee status.
- A principal does NOT have vicarious liability for torts committed by an independent contractor.
    - Exceptions:
        - The task is ______________________ dangerous.

          Example 10: *You hire an independent contractor to remove your spent uranium from your bedroom.*

        - The principal was negligent in ______________________ the independent contractor.

          Example 11: *If you just picked a name out of a hat for your uranium removal, you could be liable.*

        - The principal retains control over certain ____________ and the tort occurs within those ____________.
- To determine scope of employment, ask:
    - Did the agent intend to ____________ the principal?
    - Was the agent's conduct of the kind that the agent was ____________ to perform?
    - Did the tort occur "______________________?"
- Look for **frolic** and **detour**:
    - **Frolic**: A ______________________ deviation from an assigned path; outside scope of employment

      Example 12: *A UPS driver, while making a delivery, stops to play basketball and commits a tort against one of the other players. There is no liability to the principal because the tort was outside the scope of employment.*

- Detour: A ______________________ deviation from an assigned path; within scope of employment

  Example 13: *A UPS driver takes a shortcut and gets in an accident with another driver. The principal is probably liable because the tort was within the scope of employment.*

  Example 14: *A UPS driver comes back to the office and dribbles a basketball around the office while waiting to load the trucks. The principal is probably liable because the tort was within the scope of employment.*

B. Intentional Torts

- Generally, intentional torts are ______________________ the scope of employment. Therefore, there would not be liability for the ______________________.
- Exceptions in which a principal may be held vicariously liable for intentional torts:
  - The conduct occurred within the general ______________ and ______________ limits of employment.
  - The agent was motivated in some part to ______________________ the principal.
  - The act is of a kind that the agent was hired to perform.

    Example 15: *A pitcher is warming up at the ballgame in the bullpen, and a fan is mouthing off to him. The pitcher beans the fan in the head with one of the balls.*

    Example 16: *A salesperson intentionally lies about a product.*

CHAPTER 8: FIDUCIARY DUTIES

- Three duties that all agents owe to principals—even if the agent is unpaid:
  1) Duty to exercise reasonable ______________
  2) Duty to ______________ reasonable instructions
  3) Duty of loyalty

A. Duty of Loyalty

- The agent cannot ______________ a business opportunity.

  Example 17: *A machinist is working for a company and has the opportunity to moonlight or do some separate work on the side; he cannot do it.*

- The agent cannot take in ______________________.

Example 18: *If a soldier, in uniform, uses the uniform to help smugglers get supplies past a military checkpoint, then those are secret profits that should have been disgorged to the soldier's boss.*

- The agent cannot compete in competing businesses with the principal.

Example 19: *A cleaner who leaves the employ of a cleaning company and takes the customer list.*

[END OF HANDOUT]

Themis
Bar Review

Conflict of Laws

Themis
Bar Review

CONFLICT OF LAWS

PROFESSOR DAVID L. FRANKLIN

DEPAUL UNIVERSITY COLLEGE OF LAW

CHAPTER 1: INTRODUCTION; DOMICILE; CHOICE OF LAW

A. Introduction

- **Three Concepts:**
  - Domicile;
  - Choice of Law; and
  - Recognition and Enforcement of Judgments

> **Exam Tip 1:** Conflicts is a popular subject on the Multistate Essay Exam.
>
> **Exam Tip 2:** Never tested on its own—often tested with family law
>
> **Exam Tip 3:** Not subtle or hidden—usually easy to recognize, but there are often no clear right or wrong answers

B. Domicile

- The most important way in which the law connects a ________________________ with a particular ______________________________.
- Person can have ____ domicile
- Domicile can be acquired in two ways:

  1) By ________________________—a person must:
     - ___________________________________ her previous domicile;
     - Establish a ____ in the chosen domicile; and
     - Have an ____ for an indefinite time
       - Shown by the person's actions and statements taken as a whole
       - Relevant facts: owning real estate, voting, paying taxes, setting up a bank account, registering a vehicle

Example 1: *A farmer decides to move from West Virginia to Pennsylvania. But he doesn't move very far. He is going to live on a family farm, most of which is in West Virginia. The small farmhouse where he's planning to live is in Pennsylvania. He gets to the small farmhouse, unloads his goods, and sets loose his livestock to graze. Then he falls ill and goes back to West Virginia, to recuperate. While there, he dies. What was his domicile at the time of death?*

____

____

____

2) By ____________________

- For people who do not have the legal capacity to choose their domicile
- A child takes the domicile of ______________________________.
    - o Takes the domicile of the custodial parent if parents are in different states
    - o An emancipated minor can choose her own domicile.

- Corporations—Generally the state where it is ______________________________
    - o Other contacts (e.g., the principal place of business) may prove relevant.

C. Choice of Law—In General

- A choice-of-law issue exists whenever the law of more than one jurisdiction arguably applies to ______________________________.

1. Terminology

- o The state in which the lawsuit is brought: ______________________________
- o The law of that state: ______________________________
- o The law of another jurisdiction is called ______________________________

Note 1: Do not confuse choice of law with jurisdiction! Jurisdiction is whether the court can decide a case. Choice of law is which law is used.

2. Approaches to Choice of Law

- o State court will look to ____________________ to determine which choice of law rules to apply
- o General Approaches:

3) ______________________________ approach (First Restatement)

4) ______________________________Interest Analysis

5) Most Significant ____________________ (Second Restatement)

Exam Tip 4: The exam will typically tell you which approach a forum state follows. If it does not, you should briefly discuss all three approaches.

D. Traditional Approach

- o Territorial—each state determines the legal effect of events that occur within its ______________________________
- o As soon as a legally significant event occurs, a ______________________________ becomes ____________________ under the laws of the state where it occurred.

- Generally, a court need only determine where the legal right vested and apply the law of that place.
- A right vests when the ______________________ takes place that is necessary to give the plaintiff a ______________________.

Example 2: *David and Victoria are a married couple who live in the state of Tinnsylvania. One day David and Victoria are driving with their three sons in the state of West Carolina. While checking himself out in the mirror, David negligently drives into a ditch, and Victoria is injured. She sues David for negligence in Tinnsylvania state court. West Carolina law contains a rule of spousal immunity; wives cannot sue their husbands in tort. Tinnsylvania law contains no such rule. Their courts have adopted the traditional approach to choice of law. Should David be able to assert the defense of spousal immunity?*

____

____

____

____

CHAPTER 2: CHOICE OF LAW (CONT.)

A. Governmental Interest Analysis

- A law applies to a set of facts if its application to those facts would promote the underlying ______________________ of the law.
- If the law of a state applies, the state is said to be ______________________ in the case.

1. Determine Which States are Interested

- If only one state is truly interested, there is a ______________________.
  - Court should apply the law of the ______________________
- If more than one state is interested, there is a ______________________.
  - Court should apply the law of the ______________________

Note 2: In the governmental interest approach, the court is NOT supposed to balance the interests of different states.

- If neither is interested (unprovided-for case), a court should apply the law of the ______________________.

2. The Key to the Interest Analysis Approach

- Distinguish between ______________________ laws and ______________________ laws.

- **Conduct-regulating laws**—designed to regulate conduct (i.e., declare some conduct as wrongful)
- **Loss-shifting laws**—determine who can or cannot be liable (e.g., immunity, vicarious liability, etc.)

  - States have an interest in applying a ***conduct-regulating*** law when the wrongful conduct occurs ______________________________, or when a state domiciliary is injured (regardless of where).
  - States have an interest in applying a ***loss-shifting*** law when doing so would ______________ a state domiciliary.

> ***Example 3:*** *Recall that David and Victoria are a married couple who live in Tinnsylvania. They're involved in a car accident in West Carolina in which Victoria is injured. She sues David for negligence in Tinnsylvania state court. West Carolina law contains a rule of spousal immunity; wives cannot sue their husbands in tort. Tinnsylvania law contains no such rule. Tinnsylvania courts have adopted the governmental interest analysis to choice of law. Should David be allowed to assert the defense of spousal immunity?* ______________
> ______________________________
> ______________________________
> ______________________________

B. Most Significant Relationship Analysis (Second Restatement)

- Apply the law of the state with the ______________________________ to the particular issue in question.
- Significant relationship—based on seven guiding principles
- **Three guiding principles clusters:**

  1) Promoting the relevant ______________ of the forum and other interested states;

  2) ______________ interests;

     - Certainty, uniformity, ______________________, and simplicity

  3) Protecting the ______________________________ of the parties

     - Applies to ______________ transactions (e.g., contracts, trusts, real property)

> **Exam Tip 5: Introductory Language for Second Restatement Answers:**
>
> *The court must determine which state has the most significant relationship to the issue in question. In making this determination, the court should strive to promote the relevant policies of the forum and other interested states, advance systemic interests such as certainty, uniformity, predictability, and simplicity, and protect justified expectations of the parties.*

- For each type of issue (tort, contract, etc.) there is a list of ____________________ that courts should consider in applying the guiding principles
  - These are facts that connect the issue to a particular state.
- There are presumptions based on the type of issue.

Exam Tip 6: If no state has a more significant relationship, courts will apply ______________________________ as a tie-breaker.

Example 4: *Recall that David and Victoria are a married couple who live in Tinnsylvania. They're involved in a car accident in West Carolina in which Victoria is injured. She sues David for negligence in Tinnsylvania state court. West Carolina law contains a rule of spousal immunity; wives cannot sue their husbands in tort. Tinnsylvania law contains no such rule. Tinnsylvania courts have adopted the Second Restatement approach to choice of law. Should David be allowed to assert the defense of spousal immunity?* ________________

____

____

____

C. Recurring Issues

1. Depeçage

Application of different states' laws to ____ within the same case

2. Renvoi

- When a court applies the law of another state, it applies the ______________________ of that state, including the state's ____.
  - Applying the other state's choice-of-law rules is called _________________________ the renvoi
  - Ignoring the other state's choice-of-law rules is called ___________________________ the renvoi

Note 3: Accepting renvoi can lead to an infinite loop: If a North Dakota court applies South Dakota law, including its choice-of-law rules, those rules might point back to North Dakota law, including its choice-of-law rules, etc.

- All three approaches to choice-of-law generally ___________________ the renvoi
  - **Except**—for issues involving property rights in ______________ courts generally accept the renvoi

CHAPTER 3: TORTS AND CONTRACTS

A. Torts

1. Traditional Approach

- Governed by the law of the place where ______________________________
  - The last event necessary to create a tort is the ____________________
- Apply the law of the place of ____________________

Example 5: *A car is defectively manufactured in Michigan. It is then negligently repaired in Georgia. Finally, it breaks down and crashes in Florida, causing injury to the plaintiff. As a result of his injuries, the plaintiff misses out on a lucrative business opportunity in California. He sues the Michigan manufacturer and the Georgia repair shop in Florida state court. Florida follows the traditional (First Restatement) approach to choice of law. Which state's tort law should the court apply?* ______________________________

____

2. Governmental Interest Analysis Approach

- No special rules for particular areas of law
- Courts examine the purpose and policies that underlie the competing states' laws to determine whether those states are truly ______________________________.
- Distinguish between conduct-regulating vs. loss-shifting laws
  - **Conduct-regulating laws**—states have an interest when the wrongful conduct:
    a) Occurs within ______________________________;
    b) Causes ____________________ within the territory; or
    c) Injures a ______________________________ of the state.
  - **Loss shifting laws**—states have an interest when it would ____________________ a domiciliary.

Example 6: *Thelma and Louise are domiciled in California. They drive together to Texas, where Thelma negligently drives off the road, injuring Louise. Louise sues Thelma in California. Thelma raises the defense that Texas has enacted a so-called "guest statute," which immunizes drivers against lawsuits by passengers. The purpose of the statute is to protect drivers' insurance companies from fraudulent claims. Thelma's car is licensed in California, and that is where she bought her auto liability insurance. California has no guest statute and follows interest analysis. Will the California court apply Texas's guest statute?* ______________________________

____

____

3. The Second Restatement

- Courts apply the law of the state with the ______________________________________ ______________________________________ to the issue, considering the seven guiding principles.
- Contains a list of contacts to be balanced in tort cases:
  1) The place where ______________________________________ occurred;
  2) The place where the conduct ____________________________ the injury took place;
  3) The ______________________, residence, or place of ________________________, of the parties; and
  4) The place where the ____________________________ between the parties is centered
- **Presumption:** The law of the place of __________________ will usually be applied, but can be overcome if another state has a more significant relationship

B. Contracts

1. Choice of Law Clause

- Parties are free to choose the law that will govern their ______________________.
- Choice of law provisions are generally enforceable (i.e., "party autonomy").

> ***Example 7:*** *A movie producer and a movie director are on location in Utah, discussing their upcoming Western movie. They decide to make the movie together and they execute a contract in Utah. The contract states that the director shall do "all shooting in person on request." Because both parties (and their lawyers) are familiar with the ways of Hollywood, the contract states that it shall be interpreted according to the rules of California contract law. During the filming of the climactic shootout, the producer insists that the director fire the gun himself. The director refuses and storms off the set, arguing that the phrase "all shooting" in the contract was limited to shooting with the camera. The producer sues the director in Utah state court for breach of contract. Utah follows the Second Restatement. Which state's law will the Utah court apply?*
>
> ____
>
> ____

- **Exception**—________________________ of a contract cannot be resolved solely by the parties' choice of law
  - Validity issues include: illegal subject matter, incapacity, and absence of formalities

a. Contract Validity (Second Restatement)

- Parties can choose the law that will apply to contract validity if:

- The chosen state has a ________________________________ relationship to the parties or transaction; or
- There is some other ____ for the choice.

▪ Choice will be ignored if application of the chosen law would be contrary to a ____ of the state with the most significant relationship to the issue.

Example 8: *Jimmy the Greek and Timmy the Geek are both citizens of New Jersey. They want to bet $10,000 on the Super Bowl. Gambling contracts are unenforceable in New Jersey, so they specify in the contract that the law of Nevada will govern the agreement. Gambling contracts are enforceable in Nevada. They place the bet in New Jersey. Timmy picks the Detroit Lions to win the game. However, the Lions are not in the Super Bowl, so Timmy loses. But Timmy refuses to pay. Jimmy sues him for breach of contract in New Jersey court. New Jersey follows the Second Restatement approach to conflicts of law. What law should the court apply?* _______________________________

____

____

____

Note 4: If the parties do not have an effective choice-of-law provision in the contract, turn to the general approaches for choice-of-law.

2. Traditional Approach

- The place of ______________________________ will govern issues of contract formation, interpretation, and validity
- Place of contracting—where the _________________________ necessary to create a contractual right occurred (generally the place of _________________________________)

Example 9: *Brittney is a former singing superstar who has fallen on hard times. She lives in Georgia. Lady Gaga is an up-and-coming superstar who lives in New York. Brittney calls Gaga on the telephone in an attempt to sell her schoolgirl outfit from the "Hit Me Baby One More Time" video. Gaga says "I'll give you $500." Brittney says "Sold." But then Brittney refuses to deliver the outfit and Gaga sues her for breach of contract in Georgia, a traditional approach (First Restatement) state. Under Georgia law, contracts like this one must be in writing and signed by the parties in order to be valid. Under New York law, the oral contract would be valid. Who wins?* ________________

____

____

- Issues related to the performance of the contract are governed by the place of ____.

- Performance issues include: the manner of performance, sufficiency, and excuse

3. The Second Restatement

- Determine which state has the ______________________________ ______________________________ to the contract using the seven guiding principles.
- In addition, three contacts to be taken into account:
  1) The place of contracting, ______________________________, and performance;
  2) The place where the ______________________________ of the contract is located; and
  3) The location of the parties' ____________________, residences, places of incorporation, or places of ____________________.
- Presumption: If the location of ______________________________ and ______________________________ are the same, the law of that state usually applies.

> **Note 5:** Presumptions for specific kinds of contracts are listed in the Outline. Remember that these presumptions can be overcome if a state is found to have a more significant relationship to the issue.

CHAPTER 4: PROPERTY, CORPORATIONS, AND FAMILY LAW

A. Property

1. Two Types of Property

1) ______________________________
2) ______________________________

a. Immovables

- Includes: ____________________ and ____________________ in land
- Under all three approaches, governed by the law of the place where the property ______________________________
  - **Second Restatement**—still requires consideration of the seven guiding principles
    - Most important principle: the justified ______________________________ of the parties
    - Strong presumption in favor of the law of the ______________
- Court applies the ____________________ law of the state, including the state's choice of law rules (renvoi generally accepted)

b. Movables

- Divided into ______________________ and ________________________ property

1) Tangibles

- Most issues governed by the ____________________
  - Allows parties to choose the applicable law
- If the UCC does not apply, turn to the general approaches
  - First and Second Restatement: Apply the law of the state where the ________________________ was located at the time of the transaction.
  - Second Restatement still requires the seven guiding principles

2) Intangibles

- **First Restatement—**Apply the law of the state in which the intangible property was _______________________________.
- **Second Restatement**—Look to the seven guiding factors

2. Succession of Property at Death

- **First and Second Restatements**—issues concerning distribution of **immovable** property at death are governed by the law of the ______________________________.
- **First and Second Restatements**—issues concerning distribution of **moveable** property at death are governed by the law of the ____ at the time of __________________.
- **Exceptions**:
  - Many states will enforce a ____________________________ clause in a will or trust.
  - Preference in favor of _____________________________
    - If a will or trust is ______________ under the law of the place where it was made, courts will generally enforce it.

B. Corporations

- Divided into: ____ and ____
- **Internal Affairs**—concern the rights and obligations of the participants in the venture
  - Governed by the law of ____
- **External Affairs**—involve transactions with third parties outside the corporate venture.
  - Corporation is treated like ____
  - Second Restatement contacts: the place of incorporation and principle place of business are potentially relevant

C. Family Law

1. Marriage

Exam Tip 7: Marriage is frequently tested.

a. Traditional Approach

- Validity is governed by the law of the place where the marriage was

  ____

  Example 10: *If California permits common law marriages, then all other states should recognize a common law marriage entered into in California.*

- **Exception**—If the marriage violates a particularly strong ______________________ ________________ of the domicile of either party, the court __________ refuse to recognize it.

  Example 11: *A state statute or constitutional provision may outlaw particular forms of marriage like polygamy or incestuous marriage.*

  Note 6: The public policy exception is often enforced when the parties married in another state in order to evade restrictive laws in their state of domicile.

  Example 12: *Suppose that Arizona outlaws incestuous marriage between second cousins, but Utah allows it. Arizona will probably recognize the validity of a marriage celebrated in Utah between two Arizona domiciliaries who are second cousins. On the other hand, Arizona would probably refuse to recognize a marriage between siblings because that marriage is a more serious violation of Arizona's public policy.*

b. First Restatement

- Makes a distinction between validity of marriage and the incidents of marriage
- Incidents of marriage—rights that come from marital status
  - Determined by the law of the place where they are ______________________ ____
- State may recognize some incidents of marriage but not others, or refuse the validity of a marriage but enforce the incidents

  Example 13: *In one case, California enforced a will that divided the property of a foreign decedent to his multiple wives, even though California did not recognize polygamous marriages.*

c. Second Restatement

- A marriage that is valid where celebrated will be valid ______________________.

- **Unless** it violates the public policy of the state with the ______________________ ______________________ with the parties at the time of marriage

2. **Marital Property**

   - Any interest in property that one spouse acquires in the property of the other spouse by virtue of marriage other than an expectation of inheritance
   - **Immovable property**—governed by the law of the state where the ______________________ ______________________
   - **Movable property**—governed by the law of the state where the couple ______________ ______________ at the time of ______________________
     - Community property remains community property, even if moved to a non-community property state.
     - If marital funds or property are used by one spouse to acquire property in another state, the acquired property has the same ______________________ as the ______________ or ______________ used to acquire it.

     Example 14: *If a wife in a community property state purchases a house in a separate property state using community funds, the house is community property.*

CHAPTER 5: PROOF OF FOREIGN LAW AND DEFENSES

A. Pleading

- **Traditional approach**—laws of another state or country were not considered law at all
  - Considered ______________ to be proven in court
  - If party failed to plead and prove foreign law, the court would apply ______________ law or ______________ the case
- **Modern approach**—most states allow courts to take ______________________ ______________ of the laws of other states.
- Federal courts must take judicial notice of the laws of ______________, but they require pleading and proof of ______________________ law.

B. Defenses

1. **Penal Law Exception**
   - Under all three general approaches—court ______________ enforce the ______________ laws of another state
   - Laws that provide for ______________ recovery are not considered penal laws.
   - Tax laws ______________ penal laws.

2. Public Policy Exception

- First and Second Restatements—court may refuse to apply foreign law if that law violates a ______________________ and ______________________ public policy of the forum state
- This is a narrow defense; applies only if enforcement of foreign law would violate the forum's principles of justice or deep-rooted morals or traditions
- If successful, the result is ______________________ ______________________
- Can be used to reject a foreign cause of action, but not a foreign ______________________.

Example 15: *During the Nazi era, a German-Jewish employee brought a wrongful discharge claim in New York court against his German employer. The employer defended against the claim by pointing out that Nazi law required him to fire all of his Jewish employees. The New York court found this defense to be against public policy, but allowed the defense.*

3. Substance v. Procedure Distinction

- ______________________ always governs procedural.

Example 16: *The plaintiff is suing on a Mississippi contract in an Alabama state court. Alabama requires briefs to be bound, but Mississippi allows staples. Alabama follows the First Restatement of conflicts. Must the briefs be bound?*

____

- **General principle**—substantive laws regulate people's behavior ______________________ court, and procedural laws regulate people's behavior ______________________ court

a. Parol Evidence Rule

- A ______________________ rule
- Purpose—make sure that people reduce their contracts to writing
- Governed by the law of the state that governs the issue of contract validity

b. Evidentiary Privileges

- **First Restatement**—the existence and validity of a privilege are considered ______________________ issues.
  - Governed by ______________________ law
- **Second Restatement**—the law of the state with the most significant relationship with the communication should apply.
  - Strong presumption in favor of the law that would ______________________ admission of the evidence

c. Damages

Example 17: Damages Cap: A law that states no more than $250,000 in punitive damages may be recovered on a medical malpractice claim.

- **First Restatement**—treats the measure and type of damages as a ____________________ issue
  - Statutory limits on damages are considered ____________________.
- **Second Restatement**—governed by the law of the state with the most ____________________ to the issue
  - A damage cap is a ____________________ rule to protect defendants.
  - Under interest analysis and the Second Restatement, a state will generally apply its own damage caps only to protect a defendant domiciled in that state.

d. Statute of Limitations

- **First Restatement**—considered ____________________
  - Exception: the statute of limitations is inextricably bound up with a ____________________, in which case it is considered ____________________

Example 18: A wrongful death statute contains a limitations period from the place of the injury. The period is treated as substantive.

- **Second Restatement**—generally, forum applies its own statute of limitations if it would ____________________ the claim
  - If the forum statute of limitations would permit the claim, it should apply unless:
    - Maintenance of the claim would serve ____________________ of the forum; and
    - The claim would be barred under the statute of limitations of a state having a ____________________ with the issue.

4. Borrowing Statutes

- Bar suits on foreign causes of action that are precluded under the shorter of:
  - The ____________________ statute of limitations; or
  - The statute of limitations of the place where the cause of action arose.

CHAPTER 6: CONSTITUTIONAL LIMITATIONS ON CHOICE OF LAW

- A state may apply its own **substantive** law to an issue **only if** the state has a significant ____________________ or ________________________________ of contacts with the issue such that application of its own law is neither ______________________ nor ____.
    - The choice of law analysis is different from the personal jurisdiction analysis.
    - This rule enforces both the ____________________________________ Clause and the ____ Clause.
    - The forum state is entitled to apply its own ______________________________ law to any issue that is traditionally viewed as ______________________________.

__Example 19:__ Willie is married to Minnie. They live in Wisconsin. Willie commutes to work every day in Minnesota. Willie is killed in an auto accident in Wisconsin. The driver of the other car was also a Wisconsin resident. After his death, his widow Minnie moves to Minnesota and sues Willie's insurance company seeking damages from the accident. The insurance company does business in all 50 states. Can the Minnesota court constitutionally apply its own substantive law to the case? ________________________________
____
____

__Example 20:__ A class action is brought in Kansas state court on behalf of 28,000 class members alleging that they are entitled to delayed royalty payments from natural gas leases. Fewer than 1,000 of the class members are Kansas residents, and less than one percent of the leases are located in Kansas. Can the Kansas court constitutionally apply the substantive law of Kansas to all the claims? ____
____
____

__Example 21:__ On the same facts as the last example, can the Kansas court apply its own statute of limitations to all 28,000 claims? ____________________
____

- Under the Full Faith and Credit Clause, a state may not refuse to entertain claims under another state's law simply because that law ____.

CHAPTER 7: STATE LAW IN FEDERAL COURT

A. In General

- Federal courts exercising federal question jurisdiction always apply ____.

- ***Erie* Doctrine**—Federal courts exercising diversity jurisdiction must apply the substantive law of ______________________________ as the law has been interpreted by the highest state court.

  > ***Example 22:*** *Pete from Pennsylvania sues Della from Delaware to recover for an alleged tort that took place in Delaware. He sues her in the federal district court for the Eastern District of Pennsylvania under federal diversity jurisdiction. What law should the Pennsylvania federal court apply to this tort case?*
  >
  > ______________________________

  - The federal court generally looks to rulings of the state's highest court
  - If state substantive law is unclear the federal court must look to other court decisions to determine how the highest court would rule on the issue.

B. Substantive Laws vs. Procedural Laws under Erie

- **Substantive law**—any state law that defines the ______________________________ and ______________________________ of the parties
  - E.g., the elements of a claim, elements of a defense, burdens of proof
- **Procedural law**—applies only in ______________ court, not ______________ court

  > **Note 7:** The substance v. procedure analysis for choice-of-law is different than the analysis for the Erie doctrine.

- Statutes of limitations:
  - Under traditional choice of law analysis—______________________________
  - For *Erie* purposes—______________________________
- Purpose of *Erie*—to prevent plaintiffs from forum shopping

  > ***Example 23:*** *Recall the facts from the last example. Imagine that Pete has not sued Della yet, and the Pennsylvania statute of limitations has already run. If federal judges were free to apply a more lenient rule, Pete's case might still be live in federal court.*

- A state statute is substantive under *Erie* if it is ______________________________ ______________________________ (in a direct and certain enough way that it encourages forum shopping between state and federal court).
- **Wrinkle 1**—A state law that is ______________________________ substantive (i.e., outcome determinative without defining rights or obligations of the parties)
  - May apply judge-made federal common law after a balancing test

  > ***Example 24:*** *The facts of Pete's tort action against Della would be decided by a judge in Pennsylvania state court, but would be decided by a jury in a federal court. If Pete files in a Pennsylvania federal court under diversity jurisdiction,*

will the facts be decided by a jury?__________, because even though the state rule is outcome determinative, the federal interest in providing jury trials supersedes the state rule.

- **Wrinkle 2**—A ____, such as a federal rule of civil procedure or evidence, applies directly to the issue in question
  - The federal rule ______________________ be applied in federal court.

  Example 25: *Pennsylvania state law requires Pete to serve Della with service in person. Federal Rule of Civil Procedure 4 allows plaintiff to serve defendants by mail. Pete, as always, files a diversity action against Della in federal district court in Pennsylvania. Must he serve her in person?* ____________________

  ____

C. The Klaxon Rule

- A federal district court in a diversity case must apply the choice-of-law rules of ______________ ____.

  Example 26: *Pete is suing Della in federal court in Pennsylvania for a tort that happened in Delaware. Suppose Pennsylvania follows the First Restatement of Conflicts, while Delaware has adopted the most significant relationship approach. Which state's tort law should the federal court apply?* __________

  ____

  ____

  ____

- **Exception**—If a diversity case was properly filed in a federal court in one state, but then transferred to a federal court in another state pursuant to the Federal venue statute, then the ______________________________________ choice-of-law rules apply.

CHAPTER 8: RECOGNITION OF FOREIGN JUDGMENTS

- Terminology for this chapter:
  - First state in which judgment was rendered—rendering state
  - Second state in which enforcement is sought—enforcement state

A. Full Faith and Credit

- A judgment from another state ______________________ be given the __________________ effect that it would be given by the courts of the rendering state.
- All kinds of judgments are protected by the Full Faith and Credit Clause.

1. Preclusion

- Claim Preclusion (____)

- Issue Preclusion (____)
- Judgment must be ____________________, ____________________, and __________ ______________________________
- There is no public policy ________________________ to enforcing sister state judgments.

  Example 27: *Imagine Mississippi law makes it a crime to enter into gambling contracts and makes such contracts void. Two Mississippi residents nonetheless enter into such a contract in Mississippi. The winner of the bet then sues the loser on the contract in Missouri, having somehow obtained personal jurisdiction over the defendant. The Missouri court purports to apply Mississippi law, but it completely ignores the fact that Mississippi law makes the contract illegal and void. The Missouri court awards a judgment to the plaintiff. The plaintiff brings the judgment back to Mississippi for enforcement. Must it be enforced?* ____
  ____

2. Last in Time Rule

- Arises when a valid, final judgment is inconsistent with another valid, final judgment
- The ________________________________ judgment is entitled to full faith and credit.

  Example 28: *The winner of the bet sues the loser first in Mississippi. Naturally, he loses, since the contract is void under Mississippi law. Now he goes to Missouri and sues again. The Missouri court ignores the contrary judgment and awards a judgment to the plaintiff. The plaintiff brings the Missouri judgment back to Mississippi for enforcement. Must it be enforced?* ______________
  ____
  ____

3. Judgment Requirements

- **Valid**—rendered by a court with proper ____
  - A judgment by a court without jurisdiction ________________ entitled to full faith and credit.
    - Exception applies only if the issue of jurisdiction ____________________________ ______________________________ in the original action
  - __________________________ fraud—i.e., bribing the judge
    - Judgments that are the result of extrinsic fraud ____________________ entitled to full faith and credit.
- **Final**—No outstanding appeals; the judgment is not ______________________________
- **On the Merits**—Substantive issues were decided by a court

- Includes: judgment after trial, summary judgment, dismissal on the merits, and a default judgment
- Excludes: dismissals for lack of jurisdiction and dismissals without prejudice

B. Special Categories of Judgments

1. Workers' Compensation

- If an employee gets an award in State A, he can still get a supplemental award in State B, unless the law of State A bars additional recovery using ______________________________ ______________________________.
- Administered by state agencies of limited jurisdiction, so an award does not normally preclude additional recovery

2. Divorce Decrees

- A divorce is a judgment.
- At least one spouse must be ______________________________ in that state.
- If court has ______________________________ over both spouses, the divorce judgment is called a "__________________ divorce decree."
  - Entitled to full faith and credit
- If the court has personal jurisdiction over only one party and not the other, it is called an __________________________ divorce.
  - The party seeking ex parte divorce must establish _________________________ in the forum state.
    - Most states also add a durational residency requirement.
  - Entitled to full faith and credit, even though there was no personal jurisdiction over the absent spouse.
    - The enforcing state does not have to give full faith and credit to the divorcing state's determination of ________________________.
    - Applies only to the divorce decree itself; orders other than the dissolution of marital status are valid only if the court had personal jurisdiction over _________________ _________________________
      - Orders related to the divorce include decrees affecting property, alimony, child custody, and child support
      - Known as the "Divisible Divorce Doctrine"

3. Child Custody and Support Decrees

- Uniform Child Custody Jurisdiction and Enforcement Act ("UCCJEA")—One state gets exclusive jurisdiction to make the _______________________ custody decision

- Usually the child's "home state" or state of domicile
- All other states must give full faith and credit to that decision.

- Can only be modified by a new state if:
  - The original state no longer has a ____ ______________________________ to the child or parents; and
  - The new court meets the test for exclusive jurisdiction

4. Foreign Country Judgments

- Not subject to full faith and credit
- Usually enforced as a matter of ____________________ (mutual respect among sovereigns)
- In some cases, American courts have refused to enforce foreign country judgments where the underlying law was _________________________________ to the forum's public policy.
- Uniform Foreign Money Judgment Recognition Act (adopted in most states)
  - Foreign __________________ judgments are enforceable in the same manner as sister state judgments
  - Foreign ____________________________ judgments are not covered by the statute but are usually enforced under comity

GOOD LUCK ON THE EXAM!

[END OF HANDOUT]

Themis
Bar Review

Corporations

Themis
Bar Review

CORPORATIONS

PROFESSOR WILLIAM A. BIRDTHISTLE

CHICAGO – KENT COLLEGE OF LAW

CHAPTER 1: INTRODUCTION AND FORMATION OF CORPORATIONS

A. Introduction

1. Corporations Generally

- **Definition:** A distinct ______________________________ that can conduct business in its own right by buying, selling, and holding property or by *suing or being sued*, and by lasting forever.
- Why form a corporation?
  - Limited ______________________________; and
  - Promoting investment.
- **Corporate law:** Set of state laws governing the ______________________________ of corporations and the rights and responsibilities of the participants in corporations.

2. The People Involved in a Corporation

- ______________________________: Investors, ultimate owners of a residuary interest in a corporation;
- ______________________________: Elected by shareholders, responsible for major corporate decisions, appoint officers;
- ______________________________: Run the corporation on a daily basis.

CHAPTER 2: FORMATION—PRE-INCORPORATION TRANSACTIONS

Who is liable?

A. Promoters

- Try to find investors who are willing to invest in the corporation
- Enter into ______________________________ on behalf of the corporation (even before it exists)
- Promoters are ______________________________ of the corporation—they cannot make **secret profits**.

B. General Rule

- Corporation is ______________________________ for pre-incorporation agreements.

- Promoters are ______________________________ for any contracts entered into *before* the corporation exists.

C. Exception

- ______________________________: Special agreement that alters the default rule; it shifts liability from the promoter to the corporation.
- An agreement between the promoter, the corporation, and the third party
- Corporation is substituted for the promoter under the agreement.

CHAPTER 3: FORMATION—ARTICLES OF INCORPORATION

A. Incorporation

1. Incorporators

- Must ______________________________ and ______________________________ the articles of incorporation, pay a fee
- Incorporators are ______________________________ for contracts formed by promoters.

2. Articles of Incorporation

- Like a contract between the corporation and the shareholders—establishes their basic rights
- Also like a contract between the state and the corporation
- Must include:
  - The ______________________________ of the corporation, which must include: "Corporation," "Company," "Incorporated," "Limited", or an abbreviation of these words;
  - The ______________________________ of the corporation (name and address within the state of incorporation);
  - The names and addresses of the ______________________________;
  - The ______________________________ of the corporation (most are perpetual);
  - The ______________________________ of the corporation; and
    - **Ultra vires:** Acts beyond the powers of the corporation.
    - If the corporation acts outside of its stated purpose, the acts will be held unenforceable.
    - ______________________________ can sue to enjoin an ultra vires action.
    - Corporation can take action against ultra vires directors or officers.
    - ______________________________ can initiate proceedings to enjoin such actions.
    - Today: The purpose is usually stated as "to engage in any lawful activity."
      - As a result, ultra vires claims are not as common.
  - Authorized ______________________________.

- Must state the maximum number of shares of each class of stock that the corporation is authorized to issue

CHAPTER 4: TIMING OF INCORPORATION

- Moment of incorporation is when limited liability begins.
- **Rule:** When the Secretary of State ______________________________ and ______________________________ the articles, the corporate existence begins.

A. Bylaws

- NO obligation to file bylaws—almost every corporation does have them.
- Bylaws set forth the day-to-day rules regarding the operation and management of the corporation.
- Could be put in the articles but most companies do not—why?
    - Bylaws are easier to ______________________________.
    - Board can typically change bylaws; articles can only be amended by the shareholders.
- If the bylaws and the articles of incorporation **conflict**, the ______________________________ always win.
- When all of the statutory requirements for incorporation have been satisfied, a **de jure corporation** is created.

B. Defective (De Facto) Corporations

- **Issue:** What if the corporation is not properly formed, but nevertheless enters into obligations after it was supposedly formed?
- **Rule**: Corporation will still be treated as a corporation, with limited liability, if the organizers:
    - Made a ______________________________ effort to comply with the incorporation process; and
    - Have no ______________________________ of a defect in the corporate status.

CHAPTER 5: VEIL PIERCING

- **General rule:** Shareholders are NOT personally liable for the debts of a corporation, but only liable for the amount invested into the corporation, except a court may "pierce the veil" of limited liability to avoid ______________________________ or ______________________________.
- **Three factors** in deciding whether to pierce the veil:
    - ______________________________: The investor or shareholder has failed to observe any corporate formalities between the person and the corporation—treated the company just like itself;

Example 1: *Personal funds intermingled with the company's funds; not holding separate meetings or taking separate minutes.*

- ______________________________: Failure to maintain funds sufficient to cover foreseeable liabilities; and
- ______________________________: The parties engaged in fraud or fraud-like behavior.

- Courts are more likely to pierce the veil in tort situations rather than contractual situations; more likely in small, closely held corporations.

> **Exam Tip 1:** If you're doing a question on corporations on the bar, veil piercing is a very popular topic. Remember, the basic rule is that corporations enjoy limited liability, but there may be circumstances in which a court is willing to pierce the veil to get assets from shareholders.

CHAPTER 6: INVESTING IN THE CORPORATION

A. Stock and Dividends

1. Stock

- Ownership is represented by shares of stock.
- Carries voting attributes and ______________________________ rights.
- Traditionally, ownership was demonstrated by stock certificates.
- Today, ownership is generally demonstrated electronically.

2. Debt and Equity

- ______________________________—hold the debt of a corporation.
  - Entitled ONLY to repayment of their loan plus interest
- ______________________________ (equity holders)—entitled to ALL the value that remains in a corporation after the debts have been paid.

3. Preferred Stock

- Has preference over ______________________________ with respect to:
  - Dividends (payments to shareholders); and
  - ______________________________.

> **Note 1:** Upon liquidation, a secured creditor will generally take priority over even preferred shareholders.

4. Classes of Stock

- Most corporations have one class of stock.
- Can have as many as they choose, with different voting and economic rights

Example 2: *Family-owned business—retain control by creating different classes of equity ownership (different voting rights and economic rights).*

CHAPTER 7: ISSUANCE OF STOCK (PART 1)

The sale of stock from the corporation to the investing public

1. **Four Concepts**

   a. ______________________________ **Shares**

   - Maximum number of shares that the directors of a corporation can sell
   - Set in the articles of incorporation and need shareholder approval to sell more

   b. ______________________________ **Shares**

   - Number of shares from the authorized pool that the directors have actually sold

   c. ______________________________ **Shares**

   - Shares that were once issued to shareholders and still remain in the possession of the shareholders
   - NOT reacquired by corporation

   d. ______________________________ **Shares**

   - Stock previously issued to shareholders, but then reacquired by the corporation.

Note 2: Usually, only outstanding shares are voted.

Example 3: *A corporation's articles of incorporation authorize one million shares of stock, and it has sold 400,000 shares to the public. Subsequently, the corporation has reacquired 25,000 shares.*

Authorized Shares: ______________________________;

Issued Shares: ______________________________;

Outstanding Shares: ______________________________;

Treasury Shares: ______________________________.

Exam Tip 2: If the word or concept of "outstanding shares" comes up, that's particularly important for determining who can vote. Remember, it's only outstanding shares whose vote is important.

CHAPTER 8: ISSUANCE OF STOCK (PART 2)

A. Par Value Stock

- A corporation may, but is not required to, issue stock at a par value.
- If it does, it must sell the shares for at least the minimum par value amount.

> ***Example 4:*** *If a corporation sells 10,000 shares of $2 par stock, how much must it receive? At least $__________.*

- Today, par is typically NOT required.
  - If it is required, it will usually be set at a ______________________________ value.

1. Valuation of Consideration

- Corporation can receive **any valid consideration** that the board of directors deems adequate (e.g., labor, IP rights, etc.).
- Directors have discretion.

2. ______________________________ Stock

- The corporation sets a par value amount and sells the stock for less than the stated amount.

> ***Example 5:*** *A corporation sells 10,000 of its $2 par stock for $15,000 instead of $20,000. Who is liable?*
>
> *The ______________________________ who bought the below par value stock (watered stock) are liable to the creditors of the corporation.*

> **Exam Tip 3:** If the word "par" or "par value" comes up, it will almost certainly going to involve a question of watered stock, so keep those concepts together.

CHAPTER 9: ISSUANCE OF STOCK (PART 3)

A. Stock Subscriptions

- Ask people to agree in advance to buy stock before the corporation is formed.
- **Prior to incorporation:** Subscription agreements are **irrevocable** for ______________________________.

B. Preemptive Rights

- Right to acquire stock to **maintain the percentage of ownership** any time new shares are issued

> ***Example 6:*** *Darjeeling Corporation has 2000 shares outstanding. You own 500 of the shares (25%). If the corporation wishes to make more money and issue another 8000 shares, preemptive rights allow you to buy a proportional amount (2000 additional shares) to maintain your percentage of ownership (25%).*

- Default rule in most jurisdictions: Shareholders ______________________________ preemptive rights unless negotiated or included in the articles.

CHAPTER 10: GETTING MONEY OUT OF THE CORPORATION (DISTRIBUTION)

A. Two Ways

- Board can declare a ______________________________ (usually cash).
- Board can buy back shares of the corporation.

B. Directors' Authority and Liability

- Power to authorize dividends lies with **the board of directors**.
- ______________________________ have NO right to dividends.
- Board CANNOT declare dividends under two circumstances:
  - If the corporation is ______________________________; or
  - If, by issuing the dividend, the corporation would become insolvent.
- Directors who vote to authorize an unlawful dividend are ______________________________, jointly and severally, to the corporation for the amount in excess of the lawful amount.
  - **Defense:** A director will NOT be liable if he relied **in good faith** on financial statements.

CHAPTER 11: PRIORITY OF DISTRIBUTION

Example 7: *If a corporation declares a $500,000 dividend, who will receive what portion of that dividend?*

1. 100,000 shares of outstanding common stock—then each common stock share receives a $__________ dividend.

2. 100,000 shares of common stock and 50,000 preferred shares with a $4 dividend preference—the preferred shares receive a total dividend of $__________. The corporation is left with $__________ to be divided among the 100,000 common shares. Thus, each common share receives $__________ dividend per share.

3. 100,000 shares of common stock and 50,000 "participating" preferred shares with a $4 dividend preference. So, first the 50,000 participating preferred shares are paid their $4 dividend to equal $__________, leaving $__________. "Participating" means you collect as preferred and then participate with the common shares. The common shares and participating preferred shares are combined to equal 150,000 shares. Third, the $300,000 is divided among those combined shares. Thus, the common stock holders get $__________ per share, and the participating preferred stock holders get $4 for the preferred dividend *and $__________ per share as part of its participation, for a total of $6 per share.*

4. 100,000 common shares and 50,000 "cumulative" preferred shares with a $4 dividend preference and last year, no dividend was paid. Each cumulative preferred share receives $4 for this year, which equals $200,000, and collects $4 for last year because the shares are cumulative. Thus, the cumulative preferred shareholders get $__________ per share. The corporation is left with $100,000 to be divided among the common shares. Thus, each common share receives $__________ per share.

> **Exam Tip 4:** If the fact pattern mentions the size of the dividend being paid out, then keep a close track of where that money is going to be going.

CHAPTER 12: POTENTIAL ILLEGALITIES WITH THE SALE OF SECURITIES

- Generally, shareholders can sell shares to anyone at ______________________________ time for ______________________________ price.
- Two major exceptions: Closely held corporations and federal restrictions

A. Closely Held Corporations (______________________________ Restrictions on the Sale of Securities)

- To prevent ______________________________ from becoming involved in the corporation
- So the initial shareholders can retain ______________________________ over the shares

1. Restriction Must Be ______________________________ Noted

- The stock certificate must contain either a full and ______________________________ statement of what the restriction is or a statement that says that there are restrictions, which will be provided upon request.

2. Enforceability

- Generally, restrictions are enforceable.
- Even a lawful restriction may not be used against someone with no ______________________________ of it.
  - Unless the restriction is certified and conspicuous.

3. Types of Restrictions

- ______________________________ prohibition on transfers
- Requires company's ______________________________
- Company has an ______________________________ to buy
- Company has a ______________________________

4. **Challenge to Restrictions**

   - Usually made on the basis of restraint on ______________________________;
   - Test is one of ______________________________.
     - It is reasonable to restrict to maintain ______________________________ (e.g., an S Corp).

5. **Who is Bound?**

   - Anyone who agrees: Almost any shareholder in a closely held corporation agrees to these restrictions.

CHAPTER 13: FEDERAL CAUSES OF ACTION

A. Rule 10b-5

- Fraudulent purchase or sale of stock or other securities (like bonds or options)
- For a ______________________________ to pursue a 10b-5 action, the following must be met:
  - Plaintiff has to have purchased or sold the security;
  - Transaction involves interstate ______________________________;
  - Defendant engaged in fraudulent or ______________________________ conduct;
  - Conduct related to material information;
  - Defendant acted with ______________________________;

> **Editorial Note 1:** A defendant is **not liable** for **negligently** making a false or misleading statement. Instead, the defendant must make the statement **intentionally or recklessly**.

  - Plaintiff ______________________________ on defendant's conduct;
  - Plaintiff suffered harm.

1. **Fraudulent or Deceptive Conduct**

   - Making an ______________________________ of a material fact
   - Failing to state a material fact that is necessary to prevent statements already made from being misleading
   - **Exception:** Opinions and ______________________________ do not count as untrue statements of material fact.

2. **Materiality**

   - Material if a reasonable investor would find that fact important in deciding to purchase or sell the security.

3. **Scienter**
    - Statements must be made ______________________________ or ______________________________

4. **Harm**
    - A causal connection between the conduct and the harm

5. **Computing Damages**
    - ______________________________: The difference between the stock's value and the price the plaintiff paid or received
    - No ______________________________ damages are allowed

CHAPTER 14: SECTION 16(B) (INSIDER TRADING)

- A corporate insider can be forced to return short-swing profits to the corporation.
- The reason for buying or selling or having non-public information is irrelevant.
- Necessary elements:
    - Applicable companies—only the following:
        - Corporations with securities traded on a national ______________________________ exchange; or
        - Corporations with assets of more than $__________ million and more than __________ shareholders
    - Corporate insiders:
        - Directors, officers, or shareholders who hold more than 10% of any class of stock
        - Officers—president, vice president, secretary, treasurer, comptroller, etc.
    - Transactions made ______________________________ someone becomes a corporate insider are generally not subject to short-swing issues; transactions made after a corporate insider leaves office may be.
- Short-swing profits: During any ______________________________, a corporate insider who both buys and sells the corporation's stock is liable to the corporation for ______________________________ made on those transactions.
- Reporting: Corporate insiders must report changes in stock ownership to the SEC.

CHAPTER 15: SHAREHOLDER MEETINGS

A. In General

- Most important duty—elect the ______________________________
- Vote on major decisions that affect fundamental changes in the corporation

B. Meetings

1. Annual Meeting

Every corporation **must** hold an annual meeting to elect ______________________________ and conduct other shareholder business.

2. Special Meetings

- May be called to vote upon ______________________________ (e.g., dissolution, merger)
- State laws typically specify who may call special meetings (e.g., board of directors, senior officer, a certain percentage of shareholders or shares, etc.).

3. Notice

- Shareholders must be given notice of either type of meeting (annual or special) no fewer than __________ days, but no more than __________ days, before the meeting.
- Must include the ______________________________, ______________________________, and ______________________________ of the meeting.
- **Special meeting:** Notice must include the ______________________________ of the meeting.
- Insufficient notice can allow a shareholder to challenge any actions taken at the meeting.
  - **Waiver of notice:** Notice can be waived by ______________________________.

4. Record Date

- Used to determine which shareholders are eligible to vote
- The ______________________________ must fix a record date.
- Must be no more than 70 days before the meeting
- ONLY shareholders who actually own shares on the record date are entitled to vote.

> ***Example 8:*** *Pekoe Corporation's record date is 45 days before its annual shareholder meeting. Three months ago, A sold her stock to B. One month ago, B sold the stock to C. One week ago, C sold the stock to D, and D holds the stock at the time of the meeting. Which shareholder is entitled to vote? Shareholder ____________________________ was the only shareholder who owned the shares on the record date and is, therefore, the ONLY shareholder entitled to vote at the meeting.*

CHAPTER 16: SHAREHOLDER MEETINGS (CONT'D): MEETING ALTERNATIVES

- All shareholders may take any action without a meeting by unanimous ______________________________ consent.

A. Proxy

- Allows large corporations to deal with meeting logistics—shareholders rarely attend the meeting in person
- Authorizes others to vote shares in accordance with the wishes of the shareholder
- To be legally effective, a proxy must:
    - Be in writing;
    - Be signed by the shareholder as of ______________________________;
    - Be sent to the ______________________________ of the corporation;
    - State that it authorizes another to vote the shareholder's shares; and
    - Cannot be valid for more than ______________________________, unless otherwise specified.

CHAPTER 17: VOTING

A. Issues

- Shareholders typically vote on:
    - Election of directors;
    - Mergers;
    - Share exchanges;
    - Amendments to the articles of incorporation;
    - Sales of all or substantially all of its assets; or
    - Dissolution.

B. Shareholder Approval

1. Quorum

- For the vote to be effective, a quorum of the corporation's ______________________________ (NOT shareholders) must be represented at the meeting, in person or via proxy.
- A quorum is a **majority** of the corporation's ______________________________ shares represented **at the start of the meeting**.

> ***Example 9:*** *Earl Grey Corporation has 10 million authorized shares. So far, the board has issued 7.5 million, and of those, 7.2 million are outstanding. 950 shareholders hold the outstanding shares. What constitutes a quorum? ____________ shares (7.2 mil / 2 + 1).*

2. Necessary Vote

- If a quorum is present, a shareholder vote is effective if the votes cast ______________________________ of the proposal exceed the votes cast ______________________________ the proposal.

  Example 10: *Earl Grey Corporation has 7.2 million outstanding shares. Four million shares are present at the meeting, and only one million are voting on an issue. How many shares must vote in favor for it to pass? ______________ shares.*

CHAPTER 18: CUMULATIVE VOTING, INSPECTION RIGHTS

A. Cumulative Voting

- Applies only to the election of directors
- Protects shareholders' right to elect directors
- Corporations can choose to permit cumulative voting in the articles.
- Shareholders are given a number of votes that is equal to the number of ______________________________, multiplied by the number of ______________________________ positions being voted on.
- Votes can be spread around or put on one director.

  Example 11: *If you own 10,000 shares of a corporation and there are nine director positions up for election, you will be able to cast ______________ votes instead of 10,000 votes.*

B. Shareholder Inspection Rights

- A shareholder may inspect the corporation's records in person or through an agent as long as the shareholder states a ______________________________.
- Must be a shareholder and have a proper purpose—related to the shareholder's financial interest in the corporation.
- Improper purpose—designed to harass the corporate officers.

CHAPTER 19: SHAREHOLDER LITIGATION

A. Direct Lawsuits

- Shareholder is suing **in the shareholder's own name** for damages and the damages go directly to the shareholder.
- A shareholder can sue directly if the shareholder has been harmed directly, including:
  - Interference in voting rights or dividends, misinformation about important issues, and tort injury.

B. Derivative Lawsuits

- Shareholder is **suing on behalf of the corporation**
- Alleged harm harms the corporation, principally
- Harm to corporation—bad business decisions (e.g., disloyalty)
- Claim must be made in the ________________________________ and any recovery belongs to the ________________________________

1. Standing

- Must maintain contemporaneous ________________________________
- Requirements:
  - Must have been a shareholder at the time of ________________________________;
  - Must hold the shares throughout the litigation; and
  - Must fairly and adequately represent the interests of the corporation.

2. Demand Requirement

- The plaintiff shareholder is generally required to first demand that the board of directors bring the lawsuit in the corporation's name *before* the shareholder can bring the suit.
- Demand ________________________________—demand is not required if it would be futile (e.g., directors have been named as the potential defendants).

> **Note 3:** Although the futility exception is recognized in some states, it is not recognized in states that have adopted the RMBCA.

3. Recovery

- Any recovery goes to the corporation, NOT the shareholder.
- Attorney's fees: If the litigation produces a "________________________________" to the corporation, the plaintiff's attorneys are entitled to have their fees paid by the corporation.

CHAPTER 20: SHAREHOLDERS' DUTIES TO OTHER SHAREHOLDERS

Shareholders do NOT owe a duty to fellow shareholders in the corporation.

A. Duties of a Controlling Shareholder

- An exception to the general rule pertains to controlling shareholders.
- A controlling shareholder MAY owe a fiduciary duty to ________________________________ shareholders in two circumstances:

1. Sale of Stock to an Outsider/Looter

- A controlling shareholder may be liable for damages caused to other shareholders when the controlling shareholder sells stock to an outsider if the stock was sold to an outsider intent on ________________________________ or destroying the company.

- **Classic red flags include:** The looter had done this before or the looter had given some indication that this is what they intended to do.

2. **Controlling Shareholder Transacts with the Corporation**

   - A controlling shareholder who receives a special distribution or otherwise conducts major business transactions to his own benefit owes a duty of loyalty.

B. Who is a Controlling Shareholder?

- Easy case—those who own 50% plus one, or more
- Less than 50% plus one—look to the nature of the ownership of the company

> ***Example 12:*** *A widely held corporation with an average investment stake of 0.1%. A shareholder who owns 15% or 20% could be a controlling shareholder based on the nature of ownership of the company.*

CHAPTER 21: MANAGEMENT OF THE CORPORATION

A. Board of Directors

1. **In General**

   - The board of directors manages and directs the management of a corporation's ______________________________.
   - Main tasks:
     - Appoint officers;
     - Oversee officers; and
     - Make high-level corporate decisions.
   - Directors may (and usually do) receive compensation.

2. **Number and Qualifications**

   - A corporation must have at least ______________________________.
   - Directors must be natural persons.

3. **Term and Selection**

   - Elected by shareholders
   - Serve for a limited term—usually ______________________________

4. **Removal and Replacement**

   - Shareholders may remove directors **with or without cause**.
   - There is an **important exception: Staggered board**
     - Classes of directors are elected at different times—e.g., nine directors: Three elected in year one, three elected in year two, and three elected in year three;

  - May only be **removed for cause, only if the articles provide**; and
  - Different classes of shareholders may elect different directors—only directors elected by a particular class may be removed by that class.

- Vacancy or size of the board has increased—new director(s) can be chosen by the ______________________________ at a special meeting OR by the ______________________________.

CHAPTER 22: BOARD MEETINGS

- Boards are relatively small and meet regularly.
- Directors must be given notice for ______________________________ meetings, but not for ______________________________ meetings.
- ______________________________ waives notice, unless the director promptly objects at the meeting.
- Directors CANNOT vote by proxy or enter into voting agreements.

A. Voting Requirements

1. Quorum

- A **majority of the total number of the directors**, unless the ______________________________ specify a higher or lower number.

2. Affirmative Vote

- As long as a quorum is present, a resolution of the board will pass upon a majority vote of those ______________________________.

> ***Example 13:*** *A corporation has 13 directors. To have a quorum, at least seven directors must attend the meeting. If seven directors are present, how many must vote in the affirmative to pass a resolution?*
> ______________________________ *directors.*

3. Unanimous Written Consent

- The board may approve a proposal and avoid a meeting, if agreed upon by unanimous written consent.

B. Dissent

- To avoid potential liability for a board decision with which a director disagrees, the director must dissent by:
  - Entering dissent in the ______________________________;
  - File written dissent before the meeting is adjourned; or

- Provide written dissent by certified or registered mail to the corporation's ______________________________ immediately following the adjournment of the meeting.

CHAPTER 23: OFFICERS

- Officers are selected by the ______________________________.
- Run the corporation on a daily basis
- Typically consist of a president, secretary, and treasurer
- **Duties:** Owe fiduciary duties of ______________________________ and ______________________________

A. Duty of Care

Directors and officers owe a fiduciary duty of care to the corporation.

1. ______________________________ Rule

- Directors and officers are protected from legal liability under the business judgment rule.
- **Rule:** In the absence of ______________________________, ______________________________, or ______________________________, courts will not disturb good-faith business decisions.

> **Editorial Note 2:** See § V.H.1.c.1) of the Corporations outline for information about overcoming the business judgment rule.

2. Standard of Care

- Act with the care that a **person in a like position would reasonably believe appropriate under similar circumstances.**
- Special skills are expected to be used (i.e., accounting background, legal background).

3. Reliance Defense

- A director or officer is entitled to rely on the expertise of officers and other employees, outside experts, and ______________________________ of the board.

> **Exam Tip 5:** Corporation's most important rule is the Business Judgment Rule, which is: In the absence of fraud, illegality, or self-dealing, a court will not disturb an honest business judgment.

CHAPTER 24: DUTY OF LOYALTY

A. General Rule

- May not receive an unfair benefit to the detriment of the corporation without effective ______________________________ and ratification

B. _______________________________ Transactions

- A transaction in which the director, officer, or their relative receives a substantial benefit directly from the corporation (e.g., a salary).

C. Corporate Opportunity Doctrine

- Usurping or stealing a corporate opportunity

D. Insulation from Liability/Ratification

- A self-interested transaction may be upheld if it is disclosed and ratified by:
  - A majority of disinterested _______________________________; or
  - A majority of disinterested _______________________________.
- Ratification doesn't always win the case—it might only shift the burden.

E. Fairness

- If a director or officer can demonstrate that the transaction was fair, then they will win.

CHAPTER 25: INDEMNIFICATION

- The practice of corporations paying for the costs of a director's or officer's defense in litigation, usually by purchasing insurance.

A. Required or Mandatory Indemnification

- The corporation is ALWAYS required to pay the costs of defense if the director or officer _______________________________ the case.

B. Prohibited Indemnification

- The corporation CANNOT indemnify a director or officer who is liable for receiving an _______________________________ from the corporation or otherwise loses a lawsuit.

C. Permissive Indemnification

- The corporation may, but is NOT required, to indemnify a director or officer for the costs of a suit if the director or officer:
  - Acted in _______________________________ with no intent to harm the corporation; or
  - Had no reasonable cause to believe the conduct was illegal.

CHAPTER 26: FUNDAMENTAL CHANGES TO A CORPORATION

A. Required Approval

- BOTH the shareholders and directors must approve fundamental changes.

B. Merger and Consolidation

- **Merger:** The combination of two or more corporations where one corporation survives and assumes the ______________________________ and the ______________________________ of the other corporation.
- **Consolidation:** The combination in which neither of the two corporations survives.
  - New entity is created;
  - New entity assumes the assets and liabilities of both corporations.

C. Dissolution

1. Definition

- The existence of a corporation is extinguished either ______________________________ by the shareholders and the directors or ______________________________ by disgruntled parties.

2. Involuntary Dissolution

- A corporation may be dissolved involuntarily by creditors if the creditors show the corporation is not paying its debts.
- Shareholders can have a corporation dissolved if the shareholders can show:
  - The corporate assets are being wasted;
  - The directors are acting fraudulently; or
  - The directors and shareholders are deadlocked.

D. Process

- The board must **adopt a resolution** proposing the change;
- ______________________________ must be sent to the shareholders of the special meeting; and
- A ______________________________ of the shareholders casting a vote must vote in favor of the fundamental change.

CHAPTER 27: DISSENTERS' RIGHTS OR APPRAISAL RIGHTS

A. General Rights

- If a shareholder does not wish to participate in a duly authorized merger, asset sale, share exchange, or amendment of the articles, the shareholder is entitled to dissenters' or appraisal rights.
- Entitled to have their shares purchased from them by the corporation at a ______________________________ determined by the court.

B. Procedural Requirements

- To invoke dissenters' rights:

- The shareholder must send ______________________________ to the corporation prior to the vote of her intent to dissent;
- At the meeting, the shareholder must ______________________________ or vote "no" (dissent) at the meeting; and
- The shareholder must make prompt ______________________________ for fair market value after the action has been approved.

C. Fair Market Value Determination

- If the shareholder and the corporation disagree as to fair market value, a court can appoint an ______________________________ to issue a binding appraisal of the value.

CHAPTER 28: CLOSE CORPORATIONS, LLCS, AND OTHER CORPORATE ENTITIES

A. Close Corporations

1. "Close corporation" (or "closely held corporation")

- Term used to describe a corporation with few ______________________________

2. Characteristics

- Shareholders are often also directors and officers.
- Typically NOT publicly traded
- Relaxation of rigid rules for corporations—it is hard to get out due to the lack of a market to sell the shares.

3. Voting Agreements

- Can form voting agreements
- Different from regular corporations (where it is not permitted)

4. Preemptive Rights

- The default rule prohibiting preemptive rights may be relaxed.

B. S Corporation

- An S Corp is really just a corporation for state corporate law purposes, but it gets special treatment for tax purposes.
- Only taxed ______________________________, like a partnership
- NOT taxed at entity level—allows "pass-through" taxation
- An S Corp is limited in the number of shareholders it may have.

C. Limited Liability Company (LLC)

1. In General

- The LLC combines the limited liability of corporations with the tax treatment of a partnership.

- Generally no limitations on the number of shareholders, no residency requirements, and no natural person requirements (more flexible than an S Corp).

2. **Key Characteristics**

- An LLC files articles of organization and **an operating agreement** with the state.
- The owners are called ______________________________, rather than shareholders.
- An LLC is presumed to be managed by ALL of its members.

3. **Comparison to Corporations**

- Legally, LLCs are generally treated like corporations.
- There is a difference in terminology and taxing features, but otherwise, analyze LLCs under general corporate law principles.

CHAPTER 29: COMMONLY TESTED TOPICS

A. Fiduciary Duties

1. **Business Judgment Rule**

- In the absence of fraud, illegality, or self-dealing, a court will not disturb the good-faith judgment of the directors or officers.

2. **Duty of Care**

- Directors and officers must use the care a person in a like position would reasonably believe appropriate under similar circumstances.
- Did the officer or director have special skills? If so, she is obligated to use them.
- An officer or director is entitled to rely on the expertise and the reports of:
    - Officers and other employees;
    - Outside experts; and
    - A committee of the board of directors.

3. **Duty of Loyalty**

- Directors and officers cannot receive unfair benefits to the detriment of the corporation unless they effectively disclose and obtain ratification of those benefits.
- **Self-dealing transaction:** When the director or officer (or a relative) receives compensation directly from the corporation.
- **Corporate opportunity:** When the director or officer prevents money from coming into the corporation.
- **Avoiding liability:** (i) approval by the disinterested board members; (ii) approval by the disinterested shareholders; or (iii) a court concludes the transaction was fair

B. Shareholder Voting

1. Annual Meetings

- Every corporation is required to hold an annual meeting at which the shareholders elect directors and conduct other shareholder business.

2. Special Meetings

- A special meeting may be called to vote on fundamental corporate changes.
  - Fundamental changes include mergers and dissolutions.
  - Typically, a special meeting may be called by some percentage of the board, by the president or some number of officers or directors, or by a specified group of the shareholders.
  - Adequate notice must be given to the shareholders before the meeting:
    - No fewer than 10 days but no more than 60 days;
    - The notice must give the date, time, location, and purpose of the meeting; and
    - Anyone who attends the meeting or participates in the meeting waives the notice requirement.

3. Record Date

- To determine which shareholders are eligible to vote, the directors fix a record date no more than 70 days before the meeting.
- Only the shareholders who actually hold the shares on that date are entitled to come to the meeting, even if they subsequently sold their shares.

4. Absence of a Shareholder Meeting

- Business may be conducted by shareholders by unanimous written consent.

5. Voting Proxies

- There are several requirements that are necessary for a proxy to be used. A proxy must be:
  - In writing;
  - Signed by the shareholder;
  - Sent to the secretary of the corporation;
  - An authorization by the shareholder to vote the shares; and
  - Valid for no more than 11 months, unless otherwise specified.

C. Distributions by the Board of Directors

1. Distribution

- When a corporation removes profit from the corporation and gives it to the shareholders

2. Authorization

- The power to authorize a dividend lies with the board of directors. A board cannot declare a dividend if:
  - The corporation is insolvent; or
  - Declaring the dividend would make the corporation insolvent.

3. Liability

- Directors who vote to authorize an unlawful dividend in violation of their fiduciary duties are personally liable, jointly and severally, to the corporation in the amount in excess of the lawful amount.

[END OF HANDOUT]

Themis
Bar Review

Family Law

Themis
Bar Review

FAMILY LAW

PROFESSOR DAVID SCHOTT

UNIVERSITY OF DENVER STURM COLLEGE OF LAW

CHAPTER 1: INTRODUCTION AND GETTING MARRIED

Exam Tip 1: Historically, Family Law is frequently tested on the MEE.

A. Terminology

- "Irretrievably broken"—relates to a petition for divorce
- "Equitable"—applies to the division of ________________________ and marital property

Note 1: "Equitable" does not mean "________________________."

- "Best interest of the child" or "best interest and ________________________ of the child"—the foundational standard that courts employ when dealing with issues surrounding a child

B. Getting Married

- Marriage is a civil ________________________ between two parties.
  - Both parties need to be legally capable of ________________________.
  - There must be an exchange of ____:
    - Mutual promises that you make;
    - Imposition of the rights and obligations that go along with the marriage
- No longer a civil contract that is limited to only a man and a woman
- A marriage contract CANNOT be modified or terminated without _____________ intervention.

C. Ceremonial Marriage—requires a license and solemnization

1. Licensing

a. Age restriction

- All U.S. jurisdictions impose a minimum age requirement.
- Almost all states require parental ________________________ if one of the parties is under 18 years old.
- Most jurisdictions allow a marriage if a party is under 18, if that party gets parental consent.

Editorial Note 1: The professor misspoke. **Most** jurisdictions permit individuals under the age of 18 to marry with parental consent.

b. **Waiting period**—most states require a waiting period between the date of the marriage license and the date of marriage _______________________________.

c. **Premarital medical testing** (some states)

A state can require you to get the test; the results cannot be one of the conditions upon which the ________________________________ of the marital license relies.

> ***Example 1:*** *A Utah statute prohibited an HIV-positive individual from marrying. That was declared to be invalid.*

d. **Expiration of license**—varies from ______________ to ______________ days

2. When Will a License NOT be issued?

- If a party is ______________________________ to someone else;
- If the parties are too closely related, as defined by statute (marriage of consanguinity);
- If the marriage is a sham;
- If the parties are incapable of understanding the act of the marriage (e.g., substances render a party incapable or a lack of consent due to __________________ or ________________)

3. Same-Sex Marriages

- Same-sex couples may marry in all states.
- All states and the federal government must ______________________________ a same-sex marriage legally entered into in another state.

4. Solemnization

- Most states require at least ____.
- Most states require an officiant (e.g., judge, person of the clergy, political official)
- Marriage license must be ____________________ with the appropriate government office
- Some states allow for a ________________, so long as the parties provide ______________________________ authorization.

D. Common-Law Marriage

1. **In General**

- **Definition:**
  - The parties agree that they are married;
  - They ________________________ as spouses; and
  - They hold themselves out in ________________________ as being married.
- No ____________________________ and no ________________________
- NOT valid if either party was married to someone else at the time that the common-law marriage was entered into

2. Recognition

- Most states have abolished common-law marriages.
- Some states allow common-law marriages that occurred before a certain date.

- ALMOST ALL states recognize common-law marriages from states that allow for common-law marriages to occur.

> **Editorial Note 2:** The professor misspoke. **Almost** all states recognize out-of-state common law marriages.

  - A state need not recognize a common-law marriage if it violates a strong ______________________________ of the state.

Example 2: *Jack and Jill live in a state that recognizes common-law marriage but they only live there for a very short time. Then they move to a state that does not recognize common-law marriage. Some states will still recognize this common-law marriage.*

  - Some states require the parties to be ______________________ in the permitting state for a period of time.

> **Exam Tip 2:** On the bar exam, assume that the jurisdiction has abolished common-law marriages unless the question states otherwise.
>
> **Editorial Note 3:** The professor misspoke. You should assume that the jurisdiction has abolished common-law ***marriages***.

3. Legal and mental capacity

- Both parties must have the mental capacity to enter into the common-law marriage;
- They must be old enough; and
- They must not be too closely ____________________

4. Intent

The parties must produce ______________________ that they intended to enter the marriage and the words must be in the ____________________ tense.

E. Heartbalm Actions

- No longer recognized

> **Exam Tip 3:** On the bar exam, assume that heartbalm actions have been abolished unless the question states otherwise.

- **Definition**—if the marriage fails to take place, a jilted party is entitled to bring a civil suit for money damages for damage to their ______________________ after the engagement was broken.

F. The Marriage Relationship

- A marriage brings many _______________ and responsibilities, as well as _______________ and obligations.
- These include constitutional ______________________ issues.

CHAPTER 2: ENDING A MARRIAGE

A valid marriage can only be terminated in one of three ways:

- ____;
- ________________________ (Dissolution);
- ________________________

A. Annulment

- Voids a marriage
- The impediment must exist at the ________________________ of the marriage.

1. Void Marriage—"as if it never happened"

- Does not require judicial dissolve; will not be legally recognized for ____________ purpose
- Any party may seek an annulment for a void marriage (e.g., parent, guardian, party).

a. A prior existing marriage

> ***Example 3:*** *Marge and Homer get married, but Homer was previously married and was still in that valid, legal marriage at the time that he and Marge tried to get married.*

- The ________________________ marriage will be void.
- The burden is on the person who is trying to prove the __________________ marriage.
- **Exception:** Some states allow that once the impediment is removed, then the second marriage becomes valid ("Enoch Arden" rule)

b. Incest

- Must prove marriage or sexual relations within a prohibited degree of ______________
- All states restrict marriages within a specified degree of consanguinity:
  - 50% of states bar marriages between _____________________________________;
  - Most states prohibit marriages between relatives of half-blood;
  - Many states prohibit marriages of relationship by __________________________.

c. Mental incapacity

- Must be _____________________ for the moment of contract
- Must be able to understand the duties and the responsibilities to which they are engaging

> ***Example 4:*** *Temporary insanity would lead to a void marriage.*

2. Voidable Marriage

- A _____________________ marriage until a spouse seeks annulment
- Requires a __________________________________ decree

a. **Age**

- Any party who is under the age of ________________________ and who did not seek their parents' consent can ask for an annulment.
- The ________________________ of the minor child can also seek an annulment.

Example 5: *If Romeo is 18 and Juliet is 14, Juliet can ask for an annulment, and Mr. and Mrs. Capulet can also ask for an annulment.*

- The overage party ________________________ seek an annulment if he was of the age of majority at that time.
- Once the underage party reaches the age of majority and continues to ________________________, can no longer seek an annulment

b. **Impotence**

- One party is naturally and ________________________________ impotent
- **Exception:** One of the parties knew about the impotence prior to the marriage

c. **Intoxication**

- If either party was incapable of contracting due to alcohol or drugs
- **Exception:** The parties continue to live together ____________________ the marriage (ratification)

d. **Fraud, misrepresentation, duress, coercion, force**

- Marriage may be annulled if it is the result of fraud that goes to the ________________________ of the marriage
- The fraud must be present at the time of the marriage; it cannot be about __________ facts.
- The parties must immediately cease living together once the fraud is ____.
- **Insufficient grounds:** spouse has low morals, bad habits, a bad ___________________, or claim certain financial status

Note 2: Jurisdictions differ as to whether a false claim that a woman is pregnant amounts to fraud that justifies an annulment.

e. **Lack of intent**

- If the marriage is _________________________________, then it cannot be annulled.
- Marriage of limited purpose—parties agree to only ____________________ of the conventional aspects of a marriage

3. **Effect of Annulment**

- A party can still ask for ________________________ support
- Can still ask for an ___________________________________ distribution of property

- Can also seek child support if a child was born within the now-annulled marriage
- Courts try to place the parties in the same position as before the marriage.
- **Children**—children of an annulled marriage are considered ____________________ children.

4. Defenses to an annulment action:

- Deny the impediment
- Other party can still pursue a dissolution (divorce) action

5. Putative marriage (spouse) doctrine

- Someone is __________________________ to be the spouse
- Most jurisdictions have adopted the putative marriage doctrine.
- Purpose—to protect the party that is __________________________ of the impediment
- The unknowing party may use the state's divorce provisions, even if the marriage is found to be void.

B. Divorce and Separation

- Divorce—a __________________________ dissolution of a marriage
- Most states have a _______________________________________ requirement:
  - One party must be a resident of the state.
  - The length of the residency requirement varies. **Factors:**
    - Was the couple married in that state?
    - Did the grounds for the divorce happen in that state?
- Grounds:
  - Most states recognize __________________________ and ______________________ divorce.
  - All states recognize __________________________ divorce.
  - A substantial minority of states recognize **only** __________________________ divorce.

1. No-Fault Divorce

- Two grounds:
  - "Irretrievably broken" ("irreconcilable differences")—most commonly used terminology
  - "Incapacity"
- Half of states require the parties to be _________________________________ for a particular period of time before they can file for the dissolution of marriage.
- One spouse who desires to ______________________________ does not bar the dissolution.
- Most states have abolished the traditional ____________________________ to divorce.

> **Note 3:** A court may deny a dissolution if it is based on the wrong basis. However, that will not prevent the divorce.

2. Fault-Based Divorce

- Most jurisdictions retain some fault-based grounds, but some have removed it completely.
- Mainly used to determine maintenance (alimony)

a. Grounds for fault-based divorce

1) Adultery

- Voluntary sexual intercourse with someone other than your spouse
- The charging spouse has to show ______________________________ and inclination by the other spouse.
- May be proven through circumstantial evidence

2) Cruelty or inhumane treatment

- There has to be a _________________ of conduct; it cannot be just a one-time incident.
- It has to be harmful to either the _______________________ or _____________________ health; **and**
- It makes cohabitation unsafe or improper

Editorial Note 4: To prevail on the grounds of cruelty or inhumane treatment, most jurisdictions require that the plaintiff demonstrate a course of conduct by the other party that is harmful to the plaintiff's physical or mental health **and** that makes the continued cohabitation between the parties unsafe or improper.

- The majority of jurisdictions allow for divorce to be based on ________________________ abuse.
- Only some allow for divorce based on emotional abuse or cruelty.

3) Desertion (abandonment)

- One spouse voluntarily leaves the marital home without _________________ or ____________________ from the other spouse.
- The intent has to be to remain apart ______________________________.
- Some jurisdictions also find desertion when a spouse forces the other spouse out, **and** there is fear of harm if they return.

Editorial Note 5: The lecturer inadvertently reads the word "and" in the above rule as "or." Note that the rule is stated correctly in your handout.

4) Habitual Drunkenness (in some states)

- The frequent habit of getting drunk that causes _______________________ in the marriage
- Alcoholism is not a requirement
- **Defense:** Assumption of the risk by the party now claiming an at-fault basis

5) Bigamy

- One party knowingly entered into a __________________ legal marriage before entering into the current marriage.
- Most jurisdictions—grounds for annulment and grounds for divorce

6) Imprisonment

- Imprisonment of one of the parties in the marriage may be grounds for an at-fault divorce if the imprisonment period is for a specified period of ________________.

7) Indignity

- When one spouse exhibits negative behavior to the other that renders that spouse's condition intolerable and their life ____.

Example 6: *Vulgarity, habitual laziness, manifest disdain, malignant ridicule, violence, sexually deviant behavior, etc.*

- The majority of states do not recognize indignity as a basis for at-fault divorces.

8) Institutionalization

- If a spouse's insanity or serious mental condition results in the spouse being _____________________________ to a mental institution for a specified time, prior to the commencement of the divorce, and there is no reasonable prospect of discharge or rehabilitation.

3. Defenses to Divorce

- Only apply to fault-based divorces
- Must be affirmatively pleaded when asserted

a. Recrimination and unclean hands

1) Recrimination—both spouses commit a marital wrongful act of like conduct

Example 7: *Since both parties have committed adultery, the court cannot grant the at-fault divorce.*

2) Unclean hands—a common defense to an at-fault divorce when the plaintiff's own __________________________________ is in question

b. Connivance—the complaining spouse has given ________________________ to participate in the marital wrong

c. Condonation

- ___________________________ for whatever wrongful act in which they were engaged
- The forgiving spouse must have _______________________________ and must resume marital relations after having that knowledge.

- At common law, once that misconduct is forgiven, it cannot be used as a ground for at-fault divorce.

d. **Collusion**—both parties have conspired to ______________________ grounds for divorce

e. **Provocation**—the misconduct of the respondent is due to something the other spouse is doing

f. **Insanity**—one spouse does not know the difference between right and wrong and lacks the ability to understand the act is wrongful

g. **Consent**—consent to desertion or adultery

h. **Justification**—one spouse leaves the home because of the other spouse's misconduct

i. **Religion**—challenges to a divorce on religious grounds will __________ in all jurisdictions

4. Limited Divorce

- Widely recognized but rarely used
- If the parties live apart, the courts can still determine support and property.

5. **Separate Maintenance**—when a party is asking for a decree to be provided for support of a party that does not authorize the parties to live apart.

6. Finalizing Divorces—once a dissolution is granted, many states do not finalize until a certain period has elapsed (______________________________ decree)

7. Mediation

- Requires a neutral court-appointed mediator who is ____________________ who does not engage in any collusion with one party or the other
- Mediators can assist with child support, custody, visitation, parenting time, etc.
- The parties will agree on a separation agreement and they will submit that to the court along with a ____________________ plan, and the court approves it.

CHAPTER 3: DIVISION OF PROPERTY

A. Overview

1. Community Property

- Marriage is a ______________________; an equal distribution of property is merited
- Only nine states currently use community property standards.

2. Equitable Distribution

- Most states follow this approach.
- "________________" distribution

Exam Tip 4: "Equitable" does not mean "equal" distribution.

B. What is Marital Property?

1. In General

- All property acquired __________________________ the marriage is considered marital property (with exceptions).
- Much depends on whether it remains ____________________________ during the marriage.

2. Increases in Non-Marital Property

- Increases in non-marital property resulting from either spouse's efforts is considered marital property.
- Improvement due to marital funds is also considered marital property.

Example 8: *Pensions, insurance funds, and other things that accrue*

Example 9: *Jack has a robust pension worth $100,000 when he gets married. Then, it accumulates another $50,000 during the course of the marriage. Jill would have a right to make a claim to some portion of the $50,000 increase.*

Example 10: *Jack owns a house and then marries. Both spouses start contributing to the mortgage. Jill would be entitled to an equitable value in the increase in value of the home.*

Note 4: Titling is not material.

Example 11: *If Jill moves into the house and starts contributing to the mortgage, even if the title stays in Jack's name, courts do not care. He does not get to claim that it is all his; it is now marital property (the increase in value).*

3. Gifts Between Spouses—Marital property

4. Burden of Proof

- The party who is claiming that something is nonmarital property has the burden of proving that it is separate property.

Editorial Note 6: The professor misspoke. The above bullet point is an accurate statement of the law (i.e., the burden is on the party claiming that an asset is **nonmarital** property).

C. Exceptions to Marital Property

- Property acquired __________________________ the marriage
- Property that is excluded pursuant to a valid agreement
- Property acquired by gift or ______________________________________, unless those gifts are between spouses
- Property that a party has sold or granted or conveyed for __________________________ in good faith before the date of the final separation

Example 12: Jack has a car (marital property) and he sells it prior to the date of final separation. Jill cannot claim that the car is marital property.

- Property that was mortgaged or incumbered in ____________________________ before the final separation
- An award or settlement payment that was received for any cause that occurred before the marriage

Example 13: Jill got into a car accident before the marriage and they get married and a month later, she gets an award or settlement payment. That would be considered to be non-marital.

Exam Tip 5: Watch for this scenario: If a husband owned a house prior to the marriage, the house is not necessarily marital property. The increase in value could be marital property. However, if the husband titles it in both parties' names, then there is a presumption that the home is going to be marital property. The husband would have the burden to show that it was not a gift.

D. Distribution of Marital Property—Factors

- How ____________________ was the marriage?
- Were there prior marriages?
- What are the ________________________________ circumstances of each spouse:
  - How old are they?
  - How is their _________________________?
  - How close are they to retirement?
  - What are their earnings and earning ____________________________________?
  - What are the needs of the spouses?
- Contributions to the education or _________________________ of the other spouse;

Example 14: Jill helped pay for Jack to go to medical school, and now they are getting divorced.

- Their needs for future acquisitions;
- Income, medical needs, retirement of both spouses;
- Increases in marital property, including ________________________________ and child-rearing services;
- What is the value of the separate property?
- Was there a reduction in value in marital property by one spouse?
- Standard of _________________________;
- Economic circumstance of each spouse at divorce; and
- Custodianship of any minor children
- Dissipation of _________________________ can also be a factor

Note 5: In states that recognize fault-based divorce, the fault is not a factor in the distribution of property. However, dissipation of assets can be considered.

E. Treatment of Specific Types of Marital Property

1. Professional License or Degree

- Majority: Not distributable property (future earnings are ______________________________)
- May affect alimony, ____________________________________, or distribution of marital assets
- Spousal reimbursement: A court may reimburse a spouse for amounts that spouse contributed to the other spouse's ______________________________ ("cost-value approach")

2. Retirement or Pension Benefits

- Considered marital property and subject to equitable distribution
- Court looks at the ____________________________ value of the pension, not the future value

Exam Tip 6: Watch the timing of pension benefits. Often, it is both marital property and non-marital property because it started prior to the marriage. The portion that accrued prior to the marriage is non-marital property.

Example 15: *Jack worked for 15 years at the nuclear plant and then gets married. He has a fairly robust pension plan. He is married for 10 years. The first 15 years of the pension is non-marital property. The subsequent 10 years after he is married is marital property.*

3. Personal Injury Claim Proceeds

- "Marital property" approach—if the cause of action occurred during the marriage, then it is marital property, even if the proceeds are received __________________________ the divorce

  Example 16: *Jack and Jill are married. Jack gets in a car accident while they are married. For two years, Jill has to help him and care for him. They get divorced and two months later, Jack gets a large settlement. That is considered to be marital property because Jill was sacrificing and contributing to his well-being in helping him get better.*

- "Separate and marital allocation" approach—depends on the nature of the award:
  - Lost wages, income, medical expenses—__________________________________ property
  - Pain and suffering, disability award—__________________________________ property
  - Consortium claims—separate property of the non-injured spouse

4. Goodwill

- Considered marital property if it is developed during the marriage
- Intangible (e.g., the ____ of a business)
- It must be independent of the individual.

Example 17: *If Jack and Jill owned a dry cleaner and built up goodwill, that goodwill is marital property.*

Example 18: Jack is a fortune teller. The goodwill of the fortune-telling business is attributable just to him; the court will say that is not marital property.

5. **Accumulated Sick and Vacation Days**—split jurisdictions:
   - Option 1—They are marital property;
   - Option 2—They are not marital property;
   - Option 3—Only those that ________________ during the marriage are marital property.
6. **Future Interest—**a possible future inheritance ______________________ distributable.
7. **Social Security Benefits**—______________________ to equitable distribution
8. **Post-Separation Property**
   - Applies when a spouse acquires property after the separation but before the divorce
   - **Most states**—It is still marital property if it is ______________________ the divorce
   - Some states—separate property if acquired after the separation but before the divorce
   - Other states—depends on the date of the filing
9. **Stock Options**—if acquired during the marriage, then it is marital property, even if the stock options will not be ______________________________ until after the divorce

F. Tax Consequences

Example 19: Jill gets half of Jack's stock options from equitable distribution during a divorce.

- Such distributions ______________________ taxed as regular income at the time of transfer.

G. Modification of a Property Division Award

- Once a property division occurs, it is ____.
- Changes in circumstances after divorce are not considered once the award is entered.

CHAPTER 4: FINANCIAL SUPPORT OF SPOUSES (PART 1)

A. Spousal Support Generally

- The obligation of one spouse to provide support to the other in the form of _______________
- Arises when one spouse cannot support themselves with their own ___________________________________
- Can occur at any time after or even during a marriage
- Can last any length of time
- Cannot be _________________________ in bankruptcy
- Can be waived for other consideration (e.g., waive maintenance in exchange for the house)

B. Factors in Determining the Amount of Support

- ____________________________ resources of both parties, and the ability of the payor to pay (e.g., assets, non-marital assets, inheritances, _____________, child support, earning potential)
- Standard of living during the marriage
- Time to find a __________________ or to complete education
- Length of the marriage:
  - Short term—up to seven years
  - Moderate term—seven years to 15 or 16 years
  - Long term—16 or 17 years or more
- Contributions to the marriage—particularly if a spouse ________________________ the earning potential of the other spouse (e.g., homemaking, child care, etc.)
- Age and health of the parties
- Marital misconduct—many jurisdictions ___________________ marital misconduct as a factor
  - In some jurisdictions, adultery can be considered in a support determination.
- Children—future responsibilities for the children (i.e., who is going to be taking care of them)
- Sources of income—____________ sources of income can be considered
- Tax treatment and consequences of the alimony and maintenance

C. Types of Support

Note 6: Marital home—the use or possession of the marital home may be ordered as a form of alimony or child support.

1. Lump sum

- The spouse gets it all at once.
- Cannot be modified later, unless ________________________ is shown

2. Permanent alimony

- Most likely in a ______________________________ marriage
- Alimony for remainder of the payee's (receiver's) life
- Usually to compensate for lost earning capacity or benefits conferred during the marriage (e.g., child rearing)

3. Durational alimony (limited duration)

- Usually only awarded if ________________________ of the other categories are suitable
- Only for a short period:
  - Following a short- or moderate-term marriage
  - Only for a long-term marriage if there is no need for permanent support
- Typically cannot ________________________ the length of the marriage

4. **Rehabilitative alimony**

- For a limited time to help the spouse re-establish themselves

  Example 20: *A spouse pays for their soon-to-be ex-spouse's four years of college and their living expenses to help them get back on their feet.*

- Purpose—to help improve their earning ________________________ so they can become independent
- Automatically _____________________________ at the end of the period

5. **Reimbursement maintenance**

- To compensate for the spouse who made __________________________ sacrifices which resulted in their lower standard of living

  Example 21: *Spouse 1 goes to law school and does not work; Spouse 2 is doing all the working. Now, Spouse 1 is going to have an enhanced standard of living now that Spouse 1 has a professional degree. Spouse 2 helped Spouse 1 get the professional degree. The court will take this into consideration.*

- Some jurisdictions handle this reimbursement in property division.

6. **Palimony** (*Marvin v. Marvin*, 1976)

- Only recognized in a few states
- Applies to __________________________ couples who are cohabitants whose relationship has ended
- The relationship must have been long and stable, and sex was not part of the contractual _______________________________________.
- Need not be in writing

CHAPTER 5: FINANCIAL SUPPORT OF SPOUSES (PART 2)

A. Modification of Spousal Support

1. Generally

- Maintenance may be modified, even if it was originally ______________________________.
- Cannot seek to modify a support order if no original maintenance was awarded or reserved.
- The movant has the burden to show ____ in circumstances:
  - In either the needs of the recipient; or
  - In the financial abilities of the ____________________.
- Voluntary income reduction does not reduce the payor's support obligation.

2. Factors That May Affect Modification

a. Death

- Support usually continues until the death of the spouse.
- The payor's obligation usually is not included as an obligation of the ________________, unless specified by the court.

Example 22: Marge cannot pursue Homer's estate for maintenance after he dies, unless it was part of the agreement or part of the court's order.

b. Remarriage

- If the payor remarries, the court may __________________________ support.
- If the recipient remarries, the court may ________________________________ support.

> **Note 7:** If the second marriage is annulled, the support obligation is not revived.

c. Cohabitation

- If the recipient lives with a non-family member, support may be modified or terminated.
- Does not ____ end maintenance
- Factors:
  - How long has the recipient lived with the other person?
  - Have they held themselves out to be ________________________ and for how long?
  - Do both jointly contribute to the property or real estate in which they are living?
  - Did they both support the __________________________ of the other?
  - How much do they support each other (financially or services)?

> **Note 8:** Cohabitation does not terminate **alimony pendente lite**, which is alimony that is paid during the pendency of the divorce litigation.

d. Voluntary retirement

- Some jurisdictions deny modification (should have addressed it in the ________________________________).
- Some jurisdictions will modify on that basis.

B. Jurisdiction of the Court

- Courts must have _________________________ jurisdiction and __________________________ _______________ jurisdiction.

1. Duration of Residency

- Most states require some residency for subject-matter jurisdiction (generally ____________________________ to ______________________________).
- Full faith and credit will apply if one spouse is a resident for that length of time.
- Powers—matrimonial courts have full __________________________ powers, including:

- Division of property;
- Divorce or annulment;
- __________________________ of the children;
- Support and alimony;
- Award attorney's fees;
- Enforce _____________________________________ agreements; and
- Many other matters.

2. Divisible and Ex Parte Divorces

- The court has PJ over one party but ______________________ have PJ over the other party.
- The court can grant the __________________________ but it cannot ___________________ on property, alimony, or child support.

> ***Example 23:*** *Marge moves to Alaska; Homer stays in Springfield, OR. Alaska has personal jurisdiction over Marge; it does not have personal jurisdiction over Homer. The court can grant the divorce, but that is it. For all other issues, the court would have to get personal jurisdiction over Homer.*

3. Collateral Attack on Jurisdiction

- The defendant/respondent may attack such an ex parte order for lack of jurisdiction.
- Can show that the plaintiff was not _____________________________ in the divorcing state

4. Indigent Parties

- Courts cannot require an indigent party to pay _____________ and ___________________.
- But, there is no right to legal ____________________________, so the court can award attorney's fees and costs if one of the parties is indigent.

CHAPTER 6: CHILD SUPPORT (PART 1)

A. Generally

- Both parents are legally required to support their minor children.
- They have __________________________ responsibility, unless circumstances dictate otherwise.
- Based on the child's ____________________, not the parents' ______________________ to pay
- Typically, support is paid until the child reaches the age of ____________ years old; **Exceptions:**
    - Can be required until the child is _____________ years old, if working full-time on obtaining a high school diploma;
    - Extended if there is a physical or mental condition which ____________________ the child;
    - Sometimes, it will be extended through a __________________________ degree.

> **Note 9:** Child support is entirely separate from visitation rights. Visitation cannot be denied because the payor is failing to pay child support.

- The right to child support belongs to the _______________; parents cannot bargain it away.
- Parents can agree regarding __________________________.

B. Nonmarital Children

- Historically—nonmarital children were not entitled to child support
- Now—nonmarital children cannot be denied child support, government benefits, or death benefits
- Paternity needs to be proved before the father dies.
- When nonmarital kids can become marital kids:
  - If the parents marry __________________________ the birth of the nonmarital child;
  - If the father consents to putting his name on the child's ______________________________ ________________________________;
  - If the father holds himself out to be the father; or
  - By judicial __________________________.

C. Paternity

- Paternity actions are not available to the __________________________.
- Once paternity is established:
  - The rights to __________________________ and visitation attach; and
  - The duty to __________________________ also attaches.

1. Blood Test

- The court may order a paternity test (if the father is indigent, the court will pay).
- If there is no paternity, then any child support case filed against that individual is _________________________________.

2. Other Evidence

- Prior statements by ____________________________ family members
- Medical testimony based on the probability of conception
- The defendant's own knowledge of paternity
- The ___________________________________ between the child and the defendant

3. Time Limit on Paternity Petition

- No time limit on the filing a paternity claim—violates the ____________________________ ____________________________ Clause of the U.S. Constitution
- The nonmarital child or the child's mother can bring the suit.
- Burden of proof varies by jurisdiction

4. Marital Presumption

- A child born to a married woman is presumed to belong to the woman's _______________.

    - Presumption applies in cases of artificial insemination, provided the father ________________________ to the procedure and it was performed by a doctor
  - When can a wife deny that her husband is the father?
    - Some states—a wife is ____________________ from denying the husband's paternity
    - Half of the states—allow for a wife to present evidence that her husband is not the father of the child (e.g., if the husband is impotent, sterile, or not accessible)
    - Some states—allow the court to ________________________ evidence of the mother's rebuttal, if it is not in the best interest of the child

5. Estoppel

  - A husband who is not the biological father may be required to pay child support:
    - When the husband said he'd pay it;
    - The wife ________________________ on it; and
    - The wife would suffer economic ___________________________ from relying on that
  - Usually only allowed to estop the husband from not paying child support
  - Cannot be used to block the biological father of his rights
  - Some states—non-father husbands are being allowed to show that they are not the father and thus, they do not owe child support

D. Personal Jurisdiction over an Out-of-State Parent

- Long-arm provision—Uniform Interstate Family Support Act (UIFSA)
- Adopted in every state
- Obtaining PJ over the out-of-state parent:
  - Personal ________________________ on the defendant-parent;
  - ________________________ of the defendant-parent (e.g., entering an appearance);
  - Past ____________________________________ with the child in the state;
  - Past residency in the state, not with the child, but they provided support;
  - Defendant directed the child to reside in the state (or the child was ________________________ to reside there due to the defendant's actions);
  - Defendant engaged in the act of conception in that state that resulted in the child;
  - Defendant asserted parentage via the putative father ________________________ maintained by the state;
  - Any other basis consistent with the federal and state constitution for exercising PJ

CHAPTER 7: CHILD SUPPORT (PART 2)

A. Amount of Support

- All jurisdictions have adopted some form of guidelines

- Any source of income can be factored into calculating child support:
  - ________________________;
  - Dividends;
  - Interest;
  - Capital ________________________;
  - Rental income;
  - Retirement benefits;
  - Social security income
- Three public policy principles that guide child support:
  - Parents have a fundamental obligation to ________________________ their children.
  - The combined income is what is important; as if the home were intact
  - To minimize litigation (i.e., a fair and ____________________________ settlement)
- Both parents must file an ________________________ regarding their net income, and a child support guidelines ____________________________.

1. **Calculating Support**

   a. **"Income shares" model**—employed in ______________________ jurisdictions

   - **Method:**
     - Add both incomes.
     - Determine the amount of child support.
     - Allocate responsibility respective to each person's ____________________ income.

   Example 24: *If mom 1 makes 2/3 of the income and mom 2 makes 1/3 of the income, then mom 1 would be responsible for 2/3 of the child support obligation and mom 2 would be responsible for 1/3 of the child support obligation.*

   b. **"Percentage-of-income" model—**some jurisdictions

   - Uses a percentage of the non-custodial parent's income
   - Determined by the ________________________ of children who are being supported

   c. **Deviations from child support guidelines**

   - Court must specify ______________ it is deviating (e.g., imputing income to an underemployed parent)

   Example 25: *Mom 2 has gone to part time work, earning only half of what she used to make. The court can deviate from the child support guidelines and impute income to her as if she were fully employed.*

  - The payor is not permitted to monitor how that money is ___________________.

2. **Other Considerations**

- Age of the child when determining child support;
- Unusual needs (e.g., _________________________ education);
- Support obligations of the parties themselves;
- _________________________ of the parties;
- Medical expenses outside of ________________________________ coverage;
- Relative standard of living;
- Duration of the marriage (particularly for spousal support or alimony pendente lite);
- **Best interest of the child**

3. **Medical Insurance**

- Most jurisdictions include medical expenses in a child support award.
- Premium costs of insurance will be ___________________________ from the net income of the parent who pays for the insurance.

B. Modification of Child Support

- Can modify child support if the _________________________ circumstances change or the _________________________ circumstances change

1. **"Substantial Change" in the Parent's Circumstances**

> ***Example 26:*** *Change in occupation; increase in income; decrease in health; remarriage that creates additional obligations*

- "Substantial change"— _______________% change or more in the amount owed

> ***Example 27:*** *Mom 1 owes $1,500 per month to Mom 2. Mom 1 loses her job or experiences a decrease in health. Mom 1 calculates that she now owes $1,000 per month, based on her new income. This is more than a 10% change in what she owed. The courts would deem that, in most jurisdictions, to be a substantial change.*

- Burden—on the party _________________________ the modification
- Change is retroactive to the date of service of the motion for modification
- A party cannot ___________________________________ reduce income and then seek a modification; courts ______________________ an income amount on that parent.

> ***Example 28:*** *A chiropractor decided to quit their job and paint nature scenes, making far less income. The court will impute the chiropractic salary.*

> **Exam Tip 7:** Be aware of a fact pattern where the obligor (payor) quits a job voluntarily. Child support may not be reduced. Courts will still impute income to the obligor based on age, health, physical condition, etc.

  - **Exception:** If the change was made in _____________________________________ and there is no hardship to the child

2. Termination of Child Support

- Automatically ends when the child reaches the age of majority (typically, 18 years of age)
- Court might order support beyond the age of majority if:
  - The child goes to college (some jurisdictions);
  - The child cannot support himself due to disability; or
  - The child is still in high school

> **Editorial Note 7:** The Professor misspoke. A court might order continued child support beyond the age of majority in the above circumstances.

- Child support can also be terminated in the following circumstances:
  - Child marries;
  - Termination of parental rights;
  - Child emancipation;
  - Child dies;
  - Parent dies (**Note:** Courts can require a life insurance policy).

> **Exam Tip 8:** If the question is about child emancipation, discuss the "totality of the circumstances"; it is a fact-specific situation.

Example 29: *Is the child self-supporting after emancipation? It is not enough for the child simply to have employment.*

> **Note 10:** If the child gives birth, that is not automatic termination of support.

3. Jurisdiction for Modification

- Like child custody orders, there are only two ways to move jurisdiction:
  - By ______________________________ of the parties; or
  - Neither party nor the child lives in the "court of continuing jurisdiction."
- If neither of the above applies, the new state cannot modify the support order.
- Parties may register the order in another tribunal, but if an aspect of the order is non-modifiable in State 1, then it is non-modifiable in State 2.

4. Tax Consequences of Child Support

- The paying parent ____________________ deduct child support; the receiving parent cannot include it as income.

> **Editorial Note 8:** The professor failed to specify that it is **the receiving parent** who cannot include child support as income.

- The custodial parent automatically gets the child dependency exemption (but the parties can agree otherwise).
- The parent who pays medical expenses ____________________ deduct those expenses.

C. Enforcing Child Support Awards

- Civil contempt orders;
- Income withholding (wage ____);
- Withholding tax refunds

1. Civil Contempt

- The payor must violate a court order for failure to pay.
- The court may also levy a fine or order _________________________________ until the amount is paid.
- There is a split in courts whether appointment of counsel is constitutionally required in indigent cases.

2. Criminal Contempt

- The court can impose a jail term.
- Typically, the court must find that the failure to pay by the obligor is "_________________________" beyond a reasonable doubt.

3. Other Sanctions

- Intercept tax refunds;
- Suspend driver's license;
- Suspend _______________________________________ licenses;
- Report to credit bureau;
- Seize _________________________ or assets;
- Order insurance or bond;
- Attorney's fees;
- Order a job search; or
- Seize the _________________________, if more than $5,000 in arrears

4. Enforcement in Other Jurisdictions

- Uniform Interstate Family Support Act (UIFSA)
- Adopted in __________________ states
- Created to simplify the __________________________________ from one state to another
- If the order is registered in the second state, it is enforceable from the first state.
- Only the original state may _________________________ the order.

> ***Example 30:*** *Dad 1 and Junior move to State 2. They have a child-support order. Dad 2 is paying Dad 1 child support every month. Dad 1 registers the enforcement order in State 2, and it is enforceable from State 1. State 2 does not have personal jurisdiction over Dad 2, who is the payor.*

> **Exam Tip 9:** If more than one state is involved in a Family Law question, always discuss the UIFSA.

CHAPTER 8: CHILD CUSTODY (PART 1)

A. Definitions

1. Legal Custody

- The right to make major ________________________ (e.g., health, ______________________________________, religion) vs. everyday decisions
- May be shared

2. Physical Custody

- The right to have the child ________________________ with the parent or guardian
- The obligation to provide routine daily care and control
- May be shared

3. Joint Custody

- Applies to the majority of cases (often statutorily favored)
- Both parents must be willing and able to _______________________________ for the best interest of the child.
- Neither parent has a superior right to make decisions on behalf of the child.
- There is usually a procedure for resolving ________________________ (e.g., PC/DM, Parent Coordinator/Decision Maker).
- Not necessarily 50-50 time-sharing; the child maintains residence at the home of each with ______________________________________ time

B. Uniform Child Custody Jurisdiction and Enforcement Act (UCCJEA)

- Purpose—prevent interstate jurisdictional ________________________ regarding child custody and visitation
- Determines what state can have jurisdiction, change it, or decline it
- Under UCCJEA, the court must possess ___________________________________ jurisdiction.

1. Initial Custody Determination (Home-State Jurisdiction)

- **Home state**—where the child lived with a parent for __________ months (or since birth, if the child is less than six months old)
- If the child has moved, the home state can still have jurisdiction if it was the home state within the past six months and a parent or guardian still lives there.

> **Editorial Note 9:** The professor misspoke regarding the above bullet point. The child's home-state continues to have jurisdiction if it was the child's home state **in the past six months**, and the child is absent from the state, but one of the parents (or guardians) continues to live in the state.

2. Significant-Connection Jurisdiction

- If no other state is the home state;

- The ________________ and ______________________ have "significant connections" to a new state; and
- There is substantial ______________________ in that state concerning the child;
- Then that court has significant-connection jurisdiction.

3. Default Jurisdiction

- There is no court that has home-state jurisdiction.
- There is no court that has significant-connection jurisdiction.
- A court has jurisdiction in a state where the child has "______________________ connections."

4. Exclusive Continuing Jurisdiction

The court that made the initial rulings in the custody case ______________________ to have jurisdiction until:

- The parties no longer reside in the state; or
- The child no longer has a significant connection to the state and no substantial ______________________ of the child's condition continues to be available in the state.

5. When Courts can Decline Jurisdiction

The new home state or a court of exclusive continuing jurisdiction can decline to exercise jurisdiction when the forum is no longer ______________________, per the factors below:

> ***Example 31:*** *State 2 has been asked to preside, but State 1 has jurisdiction. When can State 1 say, "Hey, State 2, you can take this"?*

- When domestic ______________________ occurred and is likely to continue in State 1;
- The length of time the child has resided ______________________ of the jurisdiction;
- The ______________________ between the competing jurisdictions;
- The parties' relative ______________________ circumstances;
- Agreement of the parties;
- The nature and location of evidence that is ______________________ in the case;
- Each court's ability to decide the issues expeditiously and the procedures necessary to present the evidence;
- The familiarity of each state court with the facts and issues

6. Temporary Emergency Jurisdiction

- A court can assume emergency jurisdiction if:
  - The child is in ______________________; and
  - The child requires immediate protection.
- If a prior custody order is in existence, the new court must allow time for the parties to return to that prior court to argue the issues.

- If there is no prior custody order in place, then the emergency order stays in place until the ________________________ state changes it.

7. Enforcement of Another State's Orders

a. Registration of order

- Get a ______________________________ copy of the order.
- Register it with the new court.
- The new court can then grant relief under that order.

b. Expedited enforcement of a child custody determination

The respondent must appear the very next judicial day after being served with an order, or else the petitioner will be awarded immediate physical possession; unless:

a) The custody order was not registered and one of the following exists:

   - The court did not have jurisdiction;
   - The order had been stayed or ________________________; or
   - Notice was improper; or

b) The order was registered but stayed, vacated, or modified.

c. Warrant for child custody (physical possession)

A court may issue a warrant upon a petitioner's request to take physical possession of the child if the child is likely:

- To suffer serious ___________________________ injury; or
- Wrongfully be __________________________ from the state.

d. Law enforcement

Allows law enforcement officials to obtain return of the child or enforce an order if:

- The official believes the person holding the child violated a ______________________ statute; or
- If such action is requested by the court.

8. Uniform Deployed Parents Custody and Visitation Act (UDPCVA)

- Applies the UCCJEA to parents serving in the military
- If there is not imminent deployment, then the courts cannot use potential deployment negatively against the military personnel.
- Sets out procedures for temporary ______________________ and out-of-court agreements
- Prohibits permanent orders before or during _______________________________ (unless the military parent consents)

C. Uniform Child Custody Jurisdiction Act (UCCJA)

- Almost all states have replaced the UCCJA with the UCCJEA
- Goal—to create a ____________________________ system to resolve interstate custody matters
- Did not allow another state to modify a custody order if the original state still had jurisdiction
- It ______________________________ with Congress's Parental Kidnapping Prevention Act (PKPA)
- Did not address ____
- Did not give first priority to the ____________________________ state of the minor child

D. Parental Kidnapping Prevention Act (PKPA)

- Applies to kidnapping cases and to interstate parental responsibility disputes
- PKPA supersedes any conflicting ____________________________ law
- Purpose—to discourage forum shopping
- Allocates the powers and duties between the states regarding child custody disputes; a noncompliant state's order will not get full faith and credit
- International PKPA prohibits children from being taken out of the country
  - The Hague Convention requires return of the child, unless return of the child puts the child in grave ____________________________ (either physical or psychological).

CHAPTER 9: CHILD CUSTODY (PART 2)

A. Best Interest and Welfare of the Child Standard

- The standard for determining child custody
- Unless the parent is deemed to be ______________________, a parent is determined to be in the best position to care for the child.
- There is no longer a presumption for custody in favor of the ____________________________.

1. Primary Factor to be Considered

Who was the primary caretaker during the marriage and separation, prior to the ______________________________?

> **Exam Tip 10:** For any fact pattern involving children, be sure to discuss the "best interest and welfare of the child" in determining parental responsibility and time-sharing.

2. Other Factors to be Considered

a. Race & Religion

- Race cannot be used as a factor.
- Religion is typically not a factor.

b. Past sexual conduct

- A parent's past sexual conduct is typically not considered in most jurisdictions

- Unless, it has a ______________________________ impact on the child

c. **Third-party rights**

- Legal parents presumptively get parental responsibility, unless:
  - They are deemed unfit;
  - It is detrimental to the child; or
  - The parent has ____ those rights.
- A parent is presumptively entitled over a grandparent or a stepparent (but a stepparent has priority over a ______________________).
- **Exception:** Parent by estoppel (de facto parent)—the child was living with a third party for an extended period
- Some jurisdictions use the "best interest" standard in ____________ custody cases even if it is between a parent and a third party

d. **The child's preference**

- May be considered in determining custody, but only if the child is of sufficient maturity
- Typically a child in contested cases will never be brought into court, unless ordered by the court (and that must be based on "____________________________________").

e. **Guardian ad litem**

- In highly contested cases, may be appointed by the court to act for the child
- Duty is to ____________________________ on behalf of the child

f. **Siblings**

- Courts avoid ____________________________________ siblings
- Unless, keeping them together would not be in the best interest and welfare of the child

g. **Domestic violence**

- Nearly every jurisdiction requires courts to consider domestic violence
- The presumption in favor of the nonabusive parent is ____________________________.

B. **Visitation (Parenting Time)**

- Generally, parents have a constitutional right to see their child.
- Visitation must be in the best interest of the child.
- Typically, parents create an agreement as to the time, ________________, and circumstances.
- Denying non-custodial visitation is very unusual; only if it would "seriously ________________________" the child
- Can restrict overnights or require ________________________________ visitation

1. **Third Party Visitation**

   - May apply to stepparents, ______________________________, or nonbiological co-parents

- Typically, only granted in cases of in loco parentis prior to the divorce
- No protected ______________________ for ongoing visitation after the divorce

a. "Special weight" to a fit parent's decision

- A fit parent has a ______________________________ right to care for and control their child.
- Must be given "special weight" in their decision to deny a nonparent visitation

b. Grandparent visitation

- The majority of states have a statute regarding grandparent visitation.
- No states "____________________________" grandparent visitation.
- When a grandparent requests visitation that has been denied, the courts will look at: (1) the fit parent's decision; (2) the ______________________; and (3) the best interest of the child.

c. Unwed biological father

- An unwed biological father has a right to substantive ________________________.
- The father must demonstrate a commitment to parenting responsibilities.
- If the mother is married to another man and refuses to join in a paternity action, the state may __________________________ the biological father's paternity petition.

2. Sexual Relationship or Cohabitation

- Courts are ______________________ to restrict visitation by a parent due to a sexual relationship or cohabitation by that parent
- Unless, it adversely affects or impacts the child

3. HIV/AIDS

Courts ______________________ deny a parent's rights of visitation due to HIV or AIDS.

4. Interference

> ***Example 32:*** *Mom is the custodial parent. She is trying to deny Dad any visitation. She is interfering with the visitation order.*

Interference or refusal to comply with a visitation order may be remedied by a change in custody or ______________________ proceedings.

C. Enforcement, Modification, and Termination of Parental Responsibility Order

1. Enforcement

- Potential remedies:
  - Compensatory visitation—order additional time;
  - Award attorney's fees and court costs;
  - Impose a fine or order jail time;

- Tort damages for lost time with the child.

- The court cannot deny visitation for failure to pay ____________________.

a. Habeas Corpus Proceedings

- Generally not available for custody or visitation disputes
- If a parent has ____________ custody but not ____________ custody, they can request Habeas proceedings.

Note 11: Often, the court will revisit the issue of custody and what is in the best interest of the child.

- Better option—a less limiting action is a suit in ____________

b. Enforcement of Foreign Decrees

- The Full Faith and Credit Clause allows for custody and visitation orders to be enforced, if the original order was ____________ in the second state.
- Generally, the new court ____________ modify the order, unless:
  - The prior court ____________ jurisdiction; and
  - The out-of-state party is given sufficient notice.

2. Modification

- Most jurisdictions use the "change in circumstances" standard.
- The change in circumstances must be substantial and ____________ at the time the final judgment was entered.
- Modification must be in the best interest of the child and promote ____________
- The original state retains subject-matter jurisdiction.
- Some states impose a time barrier if there is no immediate danger to the child.
- Violation of the visitation order does not ____________ change the custodial parent.
- Failure to pay child support ____________ a basis to deny visitation or to modify a visitation order.

Example 33: *A custodial parent is proposing to relocate the child out-of-state, and that will "significantly impair" the other parent's visitation. That is a "substantial change," and a modification of visitation will be required.*

a. Relocation

- Some states place most weight on the best interest of the child.
- Some states apply the presumptive right to the ____________ parent, so long as the child's welfare is not prejudiced.
- The relocating parent has the burden to demonstrate a "____________ and reasonable purpose."

- Some states place the burden on the _______________ parent to show that relocation is not in the best interest of the child or will harm the child.

- Trend—allow a parent to relocate, provided there is a legitimate reason
- An application should be filed _______________ relocation.
- Factors:
  - Potential involvement of the non-relocating parent with the child;
  - Age and needs of the child (and special needs);
  - Ability to preserve the _______________ with the nonmoving parent;
  - Child's preference;
  - Movant's history of promoting parenting time;
  - Enhancing effect on the child's life;
  - Each parent's _______________;
  - Any other factor that affects the best interest of the child.

Note 12: If joint custody, then it is harder to relocate; courts protect the non-moving parent more.

b. Cohabitation

- Some states permit a hearing to modify if the custodial parent is living with a nonmarital partner.
- A change in custody is generally not granted, unless it is shown that cohabitation has an adverse _______________ on the child.

3. Termination

The parental responsibility order terminates upon the death of the parent or the child reaching the age of majority.

D. Parental Consent

1. Medical Procedures

- A doctor who performs without parental consent is liable in _______________.
- Exceptions (i.e., when consent is not needed):
  - An emergency;
  - The child is older and _______________; or
  - Public health issues

2. Religious Beliefs

- Religious beliefs may contradict the best interest of the child.
- The court can intervene and declare the child neglected.
- Some states allow exemptions for emergencies without finding the parent was neglectful.

3. **Upbringing**—A parent generally has a right to raise the child as he or she sees fit.

CHAPTER 10: MARITAL AGREEMENTS

A. Types of Marital Agreements

1. Premarital Agreements ("pre-nuptial" or "ante-nuptial" agreements)

- It is a ________________________
- Terms relate to property, spousal support in the case of death or divorce, etc.
- A valid marriage is the ____.
- Many jurisdictions require an express statement in the agreement that it applies to ________________________.
- Not enforceable with regard to ____ or ________________________ support terms
- Uniform Premarital Agreement Act (UPAA)—adopted in 26 states with lots of amendments
- Uniform Premarital **and Marital** Agreements Act (UPMAA)—adopted in two states
- Choice of law—most courts use the state with the "most ____________________________ relationship" to the agreement and the marriage.

2. Separation Agreements

- Can decide: property division, child support, spousal maintenance, custody, visitation, etc.
- Made between spouses planning for divorce
- Enforceable so long as there is no ________________________ or unconscionable aspect
- Modifiable regarding child support and ________________________, if it is in the best interest of the child
- Usually merged into the final decree of divorce

> **Editorial Note 10:** The professor misspoke. When the separation agreement is merged into the final divorce decree, enforcement is accomplished through enforcement of the judgment. **When no merger occurs,** enforcement is based on contract law rather than judicial enforcement.

3. Property Settlement Agreements

- Purpose—settle the ___________________________ issues of the marital estate
- Entered into _________________________ the divorce decree is issued
- Enforceable so long as there is no ________________________ and no unconscionability

B. Validity of Marital Agreements

1. Requirements:

- Full ____________________________________ of assets;
- Fair and reasonable;
- Voluntary;

- In ________________________; and
- Signed

2. **To enforce**

- Disclosure, voluntariness, and fair and reasonable terms are required in all jurisdictions.
- In states where the UPAA is not adopted, other grounds may be used to validate.

3. **To invalidate**

- Must prove the agreement is invalid by clear and convincing evidence.
- To invalidate, the UPAA requires:
  - The agreement was involuntary; or
  - It was ______________________________________ when executed:
    - Spouse did not waive fair and reasonable disclosure; and
    - Spouse did not have or could not have had adequate knowledge of the other's assets and ____.
- If the marriage is ________________________, the premarital contract is enforceable only if it will avoid an inequitable result.

4. **Full Disclosure**

The parties must fully disclose their financial status, including: income, assets, and ___________________________________.

5. **Fair and Reasonable**

- Courts consider wealth, age, and ________________________
- Courts also consider if the agreement was procedurally and substantively fair.
- It is not procedurally fair if by fraud, duress, ________________________, or undue influence, or if there was _____________________________ misconduct.
- Most courts look at the fairness of the document at the time of _________________________________ (vs. time of enforcement).
- Current trend: A court will enforce an agreement as long as there was full disclosure, even if it is not necessarily ________________________.

6. **Voluntary**

Courts consider: time pressure, previous business experience of the party, and whether the party is represented by __________________________

> **Note 13:** Insisting on the agreement as a condition to marriage is not duress.
>
> **Exam Tip 11:** Discuss **procedural fairness** if one party was not independently represented by counsel, and **voluntariness** by asking whether a party was informed of the right to and given an opportunity to consult with counsel.

7. Impoverished Spouse

A court may invalidate the agreement if it leaves one spouse woefully impoverished and he becomes ______________________________ on the state.

8. Modification of Marital Agreements

- Courts will uphold a "cannot modify" provision.
- BUT, courts can and will override such a provision regarding ______________ support.

C. Agreements Between Unmarried Cohabitants

1. Cohabitation Agreements

- Contracts between unmarried persons which consider full-time companionship (or other support) in exchange for ____________________ support
- Enforceable, but not if the only consideration is sexual relations
- Courts are less likely to enforce an implied cohabitation agreement.

2. Property Division Between Unmarried Cohabitants

When there is no express contract, courts turn to ____________________ distribution of property to avoid unjust enrichment.

CHAPTER 11: THE RELATIONSHIP BETWEEN FAMILY AND STATE

A. Adoption

- The previous parent-child relationship is ______________________, and a new parent-child relationship is created.
- The child is adopted for all purposes (e.g., inheritance, rights, privileges)
- Records are __________________, **except** birth parents' medical records
- Most states have residency requirements.
- The law prohibits __________________ to the natural parent for the adoption.

1. Termination of the Natural Parent's Rights

Before adoption may occur, the ______________________ parents' rights must be terminated.

a. Voluntary Termination

Biological parents may voluntarily give up their rights and ____________ to adoption.

1) Consent of unwed fathers

a) Consent by failure to register

- Adoption __________________ exist in some jurisdictions.

- Purposes—determine the identity and location of the putative father and provide ________________________ if the mother puts the child up for adoption
- The putative father must ____________________________.
- Failure to register—waiver of an objection to an adoption and an irrevocable consent to adoption, but only when the father had no relationship with the child

Note 14: If the child is a newborn, the unwed father is constitutionally entitled to an opportunity to develop a relationship with the child.

b) Consent by failing to demonstrate a commitment to the ____ of parenthood

2) Consent of prospective adoptee—if over ____________ years old, the minor child must approve their adoption (some jurisdictions: 12 years old)

3) Withdrawal of consent—can occur prior to the final decree of adoption

b. Involuntary Termination

- Only a ___________________ can involuntarily terminate a parent's constitutional rights.
- Often based on abuse, __________________________, or dependency

1) Requirements

- Standard: ____ evidence
- Bases:
  - Abandonment;
  - Sibling __________________________;
  - Incapacity;
  - Termination of parental rights over a sibling; or
  - Abuse and neglect of the child over time
- Adoption and Safe Families Act—a state can move for termination when the child is outside the home for _________ out of __________ months and not with a relative.

1) Adoption—when the parent abandoned the parent-child relationship

- Objective test—if the parent failed to _________________________ to the child
- Subjective test—if parent ______________________________ to abandon the child

Note 15: "Loss of interest" is not sufficient so show abandonment.

c. Approval of adoption—requires a thorough investigation of the new parents' _____________________ (sometimes waived if a close family member is adopting the child)

2. Legal Effects of Adoption

- The adoptive parents have all the rights and obligations of biological parents.
- The child has all the rights of a __________________________________ child.

- The biological parents have no ______________________________ rights (in most jurisdictions)
- Stepparents can visit (sometimes); it depends on how substantial the relationship was between the stepparent and the child.
- Adoptions may not be ____________________________, except in cases of undisclosed mental or physical illness
  - Courts review the child's needs, parents' motives, and _____________ of the relationship

B. Adoption Alternatives—Uniform Parentage Act (UPA)

- Covers assisted reproduction, surrogacy, and related "frozen embryo" issues that may arise under such circumstances
- Adopted in nine states

C. Domestic Violence

- Domestic violence is typically physical abuse (not emotional or _______________________ abuse).
- Every jurisdiction has a statute for civil relief for victims.

1. Scope of Statute

- Nearly every jurisdiction requires the perpetrator of the violence to be in a ____________________________________ with the victim, or a family or household member.
- Most statutes include: spouses, children, _________________ spouses, household members, ____________________ members, and unmarried parents who have a common child.
- Typically, require a "continuum of behavior," but a single episode may qualify

2. Relief Granted

- An ______________________________________ order is the typical relief.
- "No contact" order usually includes: residence, parenting time, child custody, or support
- Two-step process:
  1) Ex parte order with limited injunctive relief (TRO); and
  2) Notice to defendant, and a ___________________________ for a permanent order (PRO)
- Violation of the order can result in imprisonment or ___________________________.
- Typically last one year to an indefinite period

> **Exam Tip 12:** A typical example of relief obtained by a protective order is that the defendant will not abuse the petitioner and have no contact with them.

D. Rights and Obligations of Children

> ***Example 34:*** *Children can convey property and enter into contracts (but not wills). They have the option to disaffirm at the age of majority.*

1. Right to Consent to Medical Care

- A child's right to make medical decisions varies.

- Parental consent is almost always necessary for ______________________________ medical care (but a risk to life can override that requirement).
- Minors can usually consent to abortions, treatment for STDS, and birth control.

2. Liability for Torts and Criminal Acts

- Torts—children are judged by a more moderate standard
- Criminal acts—generally subject to __________________________ courts and laws
    - The purpose is to provide ____________________________________ and rehabilitation.
    - Degree depends on age

3. Emancipation

- If the child is self-supporting and not living with parents, the child may petition the court for a decree of emancipation:
    - No longer a minor
    - Have duties and obligations of an adult
- The parents no longer have a ____________________ to support the now-emancipated child.
- Typically, a __________________________ minor is considered to be emancipated.

4. Limits on Parental Authority

- Parental authority is not __________________________.

  Example 35: *Child abuse and neglect laws; compulsory school attendance statutes, etc.*

- Courts may terminate parental rights if it is ____ ____.
- Grounds for termination of parental rights can include: abandonment, __________________________, failure to support, inflicting serious harm, etc.

[END OF HANDOUT]

Themis
Bar Review

Partnerships

Themis
Bar Review

PARTNERSHIPS

PROFESSOR WILLIAM BIRDTHISTLE

CHICAGO – KENT COLLEGE OF LAW

CHAPTER 1: FORMING A PARTNERSHIP

A. Partnership Definition

- An association of two or more legal persons who carry on a ______________________________ business as co-owners.
- A partnership may be formed by an individual or a ______________________________.

B. Person

- Anyone or anything that has ______________________________ capacity to contract;
- Not humans who are incapacitated (e.g., minority, inebriation, etc.);
- Includes legal ______________________________, such as corporations, LLCs, etc. in addition to humans.

C. Intent

- No need to have the specific intent to form a partnership, merely to (i) carry on as co-owners, (ii) for ______________________________.

> ***Example 1:*** *You and your roommate decide to sell flowers from your garden at the county fair. Your roommate was given the task of securing space at the fair, and you were in charge of cutting the flowers. You and your roommate verbally agree to split the sales. Is this a partnership?*
>
> ***Answer:*** *Yes. Although there was never a conversation about whether you intended to form a partnership, you and your roommate agreed to split the profits, and both had a degree of control (i.e., ownership). This is a partnership.*

- By contrast, to form a corporation, you must file with the secretary of state, pay fees, write a charter or bylaws, and prepare a large packet of information and take affirmative, concrete steps. That is, you must intend to form a corporation.

D. Co-Ownership

- When two or more persons share profits, there is a ______________________________ of a partnership relationship.
- The presumption does not apply in the following situations:
    - Payment of a ______________________________;
    - Interest payments;
    - Rent;

- ______________________________;
- Goodwill.

E. Sharing Control

- Ask, has there been a sharing of control?

> ***Example 2:*** Fenwick v. The Unemployment Compensation Commission, *132 N.J.L. 185 (N.J. Sup. Ct. 1947). An employer did not want to pay unemployment, so it drew up a partnership agreement and split the profits 80/20, subject to employer's approval. This looked like a partnership; there was a division of profits, but there was no division of control—the employer had all of the control. He alone could decide whether or not to pay the profits.*

CHAPTER 2: CONSEQUENCES OF FORMING A PARTNERSHIP

A. Separate Legal Entity

- The partnership is distinct from each of the ______________________________ inside the partnership.
- The partnership can hold ______________________________ and sue and be sued in its own name.

B. Partnership Liability

- Partners are ______________________________ liable for the partnership's ______________________________.
- No limited liability

C. No Entity-Level Taxation

- Partnerships do not have entity-level taxation.
- With a corporation, there is entity-level taxation.

D. Partnership Agreement

- The partnership agreement is the law of partnerships.
  - There need not be a ______________________________ partnership agreement.
  - If there is no partnership agreement, then state law will govern the partnership with default rules.
  - However, when there is a ______________________________ partnership agreement, it will govern.
  - **Exception:** When the state law is mandatory

> ***Example 3:*** *Partners cannot waive personal liability in the partnership agreement.*

- Which state laws are mandatory?

- Liability to ______________________________;
- You cannot deny partners access to the books and ______________________________;
- ______________________________ duties cannot be eliminated.

> **Exam Tip 1:** Remember: "The partnership agreement is the law of partnerships."

CHAPTER 3: INTERNAL AFFAIRS OF A PARTNERSHIP

A. Fiduciary Duties

- Every partner is a fiduciary of the ______________________________, and owes the fiduciary duties of loyalty and care to the partnership.

B. Duty of Loyalty

- Partners must not:
  - ______________________________ with the partnership business;

    Example 4: *A partner in a civil litigation law firm cannot also have his own civil litigation solo practice. This would be in direct competition.*

  - Advance an interest that is ______________________________ to the partnership;

    Example 5: *If you work for a law firm and you lobby Congress to outlaw law firms, you will be in violation of this duty.*

  - ______________________________ a partnership opportunity.

    Example 6: *If somebody is approaching the law firm for business, you step in front and offer to handle it yourself.*

- Limitations on the Duty of Loyalty
  - As a matter of state law, a partnership cannot ______________________________ the duty of loyalty; but
  - It can limit the duty of loyalty by describing it differently, as long as it is not manifestly ______________________________.

    Example 7: *In a real-estate partnership, the partnership agreement permits certain partners to retain commissions on land that they bought and sold.*

- If you are worried that something may be considered disloyal, there is a safe-harbor option:
  - If a partner makes full ______________________________ of all material facts, then a certain percentage of the other partners may authorize or ______________________________ the transaction.

C. Duty of Care

- Partners must not:
  - Engage in grossly negligent or ______________________________ conduct;
  - Engage in ______________________________ misconduct;
  - Engage in a ______________________________ violation of the law.

  Example 8: *A partner cannot run a Ponzi scheme out of his office.*

- The partnership agreement may not unreasonably reduce the duty of care.

D. Timing of Duties

- The duties of loyalty and care apply only to partners, not to ______________________________ partners or ______________________________ partners.

  Example 9: *A law firm partnership conducts a merger with another business and, as a part of that merger, it eliminates all retirement plans. You do not owe a fiduciary duty to your former partners.*

CHAPTER 4: PROFITS AND LOSSES

A. The division of profits and losses is generally dictated or determined by agreement.

- The division of profits and losses need not be the ______________________________.
- Financial contributions/capital contributions need not have an effect on the division of profits and losses.
- When there is no partnership agreement regarding division of profits and losses, profits are divided ______________________________ and losses follow profits.

B. Distributions

- **Default Rule:** Partners do not have the right to ______________________________ a distribution.
- Partners can agree in advance to allow distributions to be made according to the partnership agreement.

C. Transfer of Partnership Interests

- **Default Rule:** A partner does have the right to transfer their partnership interest.
- In the past (but no longer), if a partner attempted to convey her interest to somebody else, it would ______________________________ the entire partnership.
- Partners may still agree to change the default rule to require a ______________________________ vote of the partners.

D. New Partner

- **Default Rule:** When a new partner is introduced, all existing partners must ______________________________ to the new partner.

CHAPTER 5: MANAGING/GOVERNING RELATIONSHIPS

A. Default Rule: Every partner has equal rights in the ______________________________ and control of the partnership.

- Can be changed by agreement
- A common division is to reflect the partners' ______________________________ contribution(s) rather than an even share.

B. Ordinary and Extraordinary Business Matters

- Ordinary business requires a vote of the ______________________________ of the partners.

  Example 10: *Declaring a distribution*

- Extraordinary business requires a vote of ______________________________ the partners.

  Example 11: *Amending the partnership agreement*

  - Remember that these are default rules that can be changed.

C. Quorums

- There is no default rule regarding partnership quorums for partnership voting.

D. Access to Records

- Access to records must be provided to the partners and their ______________________________.
- This is mandatory and cannot be abridged by the partnership agreement.

CHAPTER 6: DISSOCIATION

- **Dissociation**—when a partner ceases to be associated with the partnership.
- This can be voluntary or involuntary

A. Voluntary Dissociation

- The partner may give ______________________________ to the partnership that the partner wants to withdraw.

B. Involuntary Dissociation

- Any of the following scenarios may constitute involuntary dissociation:
  - There may be an event triggered in the partnership ______________________________;

- They can be ______________________________ pursuant to the partnership agreement;
- It is unlawful for a partnership to carry on business with that partner;
- A court ______________________________ that a partner must be dissociated;
- A partner goes ______________________________;
- A partner dies;
- A partner has become ______________________________;
- One of the entities of the partnership ______________________________.

> **Exam Tip 2:** A partnership cannot prevent a partner from withdrawing, but can require certain restrictions on withdrawal (e.g., written notice, liability for wrongful dissociation, etc.).

C. Consequences of Dissociation

- If a partner is dissociated, the partnership does not necessarily ______________________________.
- Once dissociated, a former partner has no right to participate in management of the partnership, and the partner no longer has any ______________________________ to the partnership.
- If the partnership continues, it must ______________________________ the dissociated partner's interest.

> **Editor's Note 1:** Note that in the case of wrongful dissociation, the wrongfully dissociated partner may not be entitled to payment of the buyout price until the expiration of the term or completion of the undertaking of the partnership. Because the partner will also be liable for damages caused by the wrongful dissociation, if the partner's liability meets or exceeds the buyout value, the partner may not be entitled to receive any buyout price.

CHAPTER 7: LIABILITIES OF A PARTNERSHIP

- Every partner is an ______________________________ of the partnership; this means the partnership may be liable for a partner's contract and tort liabilities.

A. Contract Liability

- Partners can enter contracts for which they have ______________________________.

1. Express Authority—may come from:

- The partnership agreement;
- A ______________________________ of authority filing; or
- An ad hoc authorization by the partners at a meeting.

2. Implied Authority

- Exists based on the partner's ______________________________ belief that an action is ______________________________ to carry out express authority

Example 12: *Hiring Partner, through a delegation of authority from the executive committee or a vote of the partnership, is placed in charge of hiring Associate. A bill for dinner shows up at the law firm. Is the law firm obligated to pay the bill for dinner? Is dinner reasonably necessary to make Associate take the offer?*

Answer: *________________________________, it is part of the custom and ordinary dealings of the trade.*

3. Apparent Authority

- The partnership may be bound based on the partner acting in the ordinary course of dealings.
- Based on interactions between the partnership and third-parties

Example 13: *Junior Partner at a law firm uses the law firm's letterhead to order supplies. He was not expressly authorized by the law firm to order supplies. Is the law firm liable to the third party who fills the order?*

Answer: *________________________________, the use of letterhead is a conveyance of apparent authority from the law firm to the vendor of office supplies.*

Example 14: *One partner tells another partner not to order more supplies. The second partner goes ahead and orders supplies anyway. Will the partnership have to pay?*

Answer: *It depends on what was told to the third party. If the supplier supplies the office supplies, the partner may still be liable through joint and several liability.* Nabisco v. Stroud *(1959).*

- If you don't see revocation of apparent authority, it is likely still in place.

> **Exam Tip 3:** If you see a contract or tort issue regarding a partnership, remember that the rules for authority are similar to those in the context of agency law.

B. Tort Liability

- A partnership is liable in tort for torts that are committed by partners acting within the ________________________________ of their partnership.

Example 15: *If a partner commits malpractice, then the rest of the partnership is bound to pay for the tort.*

C. Consequences of the Flow of Liability

- Partners are ________________________________ liable for the debts or obligations of the partnership.

- A partner is jointly and severally liable for all partnership obligations.
- You can go after any partner for the ______________________________ sum owed by the partnership.
- Generally, the partnership creditor must exhaust the partnership's funds before going after the partners' personal assets.

- An incoming partner is not personally liable for contract or tortious obligations incurred ______________________________ to becoming a partner.
  - The incoming partner will be liable for the partner's capital contribution.
- An outgoing partner may be personally liable for a partnership obligation that occurred ______________________________ dissociation.

CHAPTER 8: TERMINATING A PARTNERSHIP

- Termination of a partnership is a two-step process: Dissolution and ______________________________.

A. Dissolution

- Triggered by the occurrence of an event
- Not the end of the partnership; it is the beginning of the end
- Can be brought about by a partner or by ______________________________ of law.
- **Partnership at Will:** An open-ended partnership with no ______________________________ term tied to time period or undertaking
  - Generally, the partnership at will is dissolved when any partner chooses to dissociate.
- **Partnership for a Term or Undertaking:**
  - The partnership may be dissolved when the term ______________________________ or when the undertaking is ______________________________.
- Either type of partnership may also be dissolved in one of three ways:
  - **Any dissolving event set forth in the partnership agreement**

    Example 16: *A partnership agreement states, "If we make less than $10.00 in sales in any year, the partnership will be dissolved."*

  - **Any event that makes it ______________________________ to continue if not cured within __________ days**

    Example 17: *The partnership does not pay its state taxes or file returns (partnerships do not pay taxes but must typically make state filings). If the partnership is in breach of some law, and if it has not cured that breach within 90 days, it might lead to dissolution.*

- Judicial determination

B. Winding Up

1. Who may wind up?

- Any partner that has not ______________________________ dissociated
- A legal representative of the last ______________________________ partner
- Any partner, legal representative, or transferee may seek judicial ______________________________ of winding up.

2. What power does the person who is winding up have?

- The person winding up a partnership may dispose of and ______________________________ partnership property, and discharge partnership liabilities.
- The person can also preserve partnership business to ______________________________ value as a going concern.

3. Statement of Dissolution

- A filing that gives ______________________________ to third parties that the partnership has been dissolved after ______________________________ days.
- Why file? It limits the partners' apparent authority and ______________________________.

4. Priority of Distributions

- Creditors first, then partners

CHAPTER 9: OTHER TYPES OF PARTNERSHIPS

A. Limited Liability Partnerships (LLPs)

- **Definition:** A partnership in which a partner's personal liability is ______________________________
  - Must file with the state
- **Formation:** To transform a general partnership into an LLP, you must vote authorizing transformation.
- **Name:** Must always end with either:
  - ______________________________ Limited Liability Partnership (RLLP)
  - Limited Liability Partnership (LLP)
- **Liabilities:**
  - Limited partners are NOT personally liable for the obligations of the LLP.
  - Limited partners are personally responsible for ______________________________ personal misconduct or negligence.

- **Terminating LLP Status:**
    - Partners can voluntarily transform and ______________________________ LLP status.
    - The ______________________________ can revoke an LLP's status.

B. Limited Partnerships (LPs)

- **Definition:** A partnership formed by two or more persons that has at least one ______________________________ partner and one limited partner
    - The limited partners have ______________________________ liability; the general partners have ______________________________ liability.
- **Formation:** File a certificate of limited partnership; it must contain:
    - Name of the limited partnership (including LP);
    - In-state ______________________________;
    - Name of an agent in that state;
    - Names and addresses of all ______________________________ partners;
    - Statement of duration;
    - Signed by the general partner.
- When does it come into existence?
    - When filed, or the effective date, if included
    - ______________________________ compliance is sufficient to be effective.

CHAPTER 10: PARTNERS

A. Limited Partners

- **Admission:** May join at the creation of the partnership or with the ______________________________ of all partners
- **Voting:**
    - Allowed only under the partnership agreement
    - **Default rule:** A limited partner does not vote.
- **Right to access records**
- **Liability to third parties:** A limited partner is not personally liable for the obligations of the partnership unless she serves as a general partner or starts to ______________________________ in the partnership.
- The following are things that limited partners **may do without** running the business:
    - Be an officer, a director, or a ______________________________ of the general partner;
    - Consult the general partner on partnership affairs;
    - Act as a ______________________________ of the partnership;

- Request to attend ______________________________ of the partnership;
- Wind up the partnership;
- Propose or ______________________________ of partnership matters.

- **Withdrawing:** The limited partner must give ______________________________ written notice.

B. General Partners

- **Becoming a general partner:** Join at the beginning or be admitted upon ______________________________ of all partners
- **Rights and powers:** Same as in a general partnership without limited partners, or as otherwise suggested in the partnership agreement.
- **Liability to third parties**
  - ______________________________ liable to third parties for obligations of the partnership
  - To protect from liability, many general partners are ______________________________.
- **Termination of status:**
  - A general partner may ______________________________ withdraw;
  - If the general partner tries to assign the partnership interest, the general partner may be removed;
  - If he goes ______________________________ or becomes insolvent may be removed;
  - Death or incapacitation;
  - A business-entity partner is ______________________________.

[END OF HANDOUT]

Themis
Bar Review

Secured Transactions

Themis
Bar Review

SECURED TRANSACTIONS

PROFESSOR KARA BRUCE

UNIVERSITY OF TOLEDO COLLEGE OF LAW

CHAPTER 1: INTRODUCTION

Editorial Note 1: Throughout this lecture, Professor Bruce refers to and uses examples from the Multistate Essay Exam. Because that exam tests common issues that arise in the context of U.C.C. Article 9, these examples are applicable to all jurisdictions that test the subject. The MEE is a trademark of the National Conference of Bar Examiners.

A. In General

- Article ________ of the Uniform Commercial Code (UCC).
- An agreement between a debtor and a creditor that the debtor's ____ will serve as collateral for a loan.

> ***Example 1:*** *If you have ever financed the purchase of a car, you have probably engaged in a secured transaction. You bought the car and you're paying it off over time, and you've probably signed an agreement giving your lender a security interest in the car. If you don't pay the loan back (default), the lender can repossess the car because it has a property interest in the car.*

- If the debtor ______________________________ on the loan, the creditor will have the rights discussed in this lecture to repossess the collateral and use it to satisfy the debt.

B. Roadmap for the Lecture Series

1. **Attachment**: How security interests are created (i.e., the steps necessary for the security interest to be enforceable against the debtor).
2. **Perfection**: Providing notice of a security interest to establish a claim superior to other parties who may wish to claim an interest in the same collateral.
3. **Priority**: Rules for resolving priority disputes between __________________ __________________ to the same collateral. (Who wins and who loses when claimants fight over the same piece of property?)
4. **Enforcement**: Rights and duties of a secured party who enforces its interest in the collateral (repossession).

- How do these topics fit together?
  - Attachment → Enforcement rights (no perfection needed)
  - Attachment + perfection = good standing in a priority dispute.

C. How to Approach a Priority Question

> **Exam Tip 1:** A secured transactions question will frequently ask you to determine "**who has priority**" or "who has a superior claim" to the collateral. Follow the 6-part, step-by-step guide below to get to the answer.
>
> **Exam Tip 2:** Sometimes a secured transactions question will be more limited "Does Creditor have an enforceable interest in the collateral?" which is a question of attachment. "Is Creditor perfected?" which is a question of perfection. "How can Creditor enforce these interests?" With these more particular questions, you can just zero in on the components of this analysis that are relevant.

- **Step 1**—Determine that you have a secured transactions problem.
  (Trigger words = security agreement and/or security interest)
- **Step 2** – Identify and __________________ the property at issue.
  (Hint: Look at the call of the question.)
- **Step 3**—Determine which parties have or claim an interest in the collateral.
- **Step 4**—At least one will be a secured party with a security interest.
  - For each security interest, assess:
    1. __________________: Has that security interest attached? To which collateral? When?
    2. __________________: Has the secured party perfected its security interest? When? How? Has anything happened that might cause the secured party to lose perfection?
- **Step 5**—Use this information to find the appropriate priority rule.
- **Step 6**—Apply the priority rule to the facts and resolve the dispute.

CHAPTER 2: BASIC VOCABULARY AND SCOPE OF ARTICLE 9

A. Basic Vocabulary

1. Security Interest

- An interest in personal property or fixtures that secures __________________ or __________________ of an obligation.

__Example 2:__ Blunder Muffin Paper Company is a paper manufacturer located in Toledo, Ohio. Blunder Muffin gets a loan from a bank and pledges its inventory (paper for sale, raw materials), equipment (manufacturing equipment, office computers, delivery vehicles), and accounts (right to be repaid for paper sold on credit) as collateral for that loan. This is an Article 9 secured transaction. Blunder Muffin has an obligation to pay its loan back to the bank, which is supported by collateral – the bank has property rights in BMs collateral.

__Example 3:__ A customer buys goods on credit, promising to pay for the goods over time. The customer signs an agreement granting the store a security *interest in those goods to secure payment of the purchase price. This is an Article 9 secured transaction. When you buy something on credit (big screen TV), and you promise to pay it over time, you have a monetary obligation that you owe to the store. If the store has taken a security interest in the goods, that's a property interest that secures that repayment.*

2. Security Agreement

- A ________________ that creates a security interest

3. Parties to a Secured Transaction

- ________________: a creditor who obtains a security interest in the debtor's property
- ________________ a party that must pay or perform the obligation that the collateral secures
- ________________ has an interest, other than a security interest, in the collateral (e.g., owner)
  - The debtor and the obligor are often the same person or entity.

    Example 4: *If you get a loan and pledge your car as collateral for the loan, then you are both the debtor and the obligor.*

  - The debtor and the obligor can, however, be **different people**.

    Example 5: *Your friend co-signs a loan to help you start your law practice and offers her car as collateral for the loan. You are the obligor but you are not the debtor because you don't own the collateral. Your friend is both the debtor and an obligor (secondary obligor).*

B. Scope of Article 9

- Article 9 governs transactions, regardless of form, that create a security interest in personal property or fixtures by contract.
  - Secured transactions must be consensual.
  - Secured transactions involve personal property or fixtures (not real estate).
  - "Regardless of form" means that courts will look at the substance of the transaction, not the labels the parties use.

    Example 6: *A seller sells goods to a buyer, but the contract provides that the seller retains title to the goods until the purchase price is paid in full. This is a secured transaction in substance and Article 9 will apply.*

    Exam Tip 3: This issue has been tested on past essay questions.

- **Agricultural Liens**: an interest in ________________ that secures payment or performance of an obligation for:
  - Goods or services furnished with respect to a farming operations; or

- Rent on real property in connection with a farming operation.

- **Sales of Certain Rights to Payment**

  - Why? To facilitate ________________________________ _ that these sales have happened.
  - Treat the ________________ as the secured party and the ________________ as the debtor.
  - Sales of which types of collateral are treated like secured transactions?

    - Chattel paper
    - Promissory notes
    - Accounts
    - Payment intangibles

  - **MNEMONIC**: Cruel Poodles Poking Needles At Peaceful Iguanas.

> **Exam Tip 4:** If your fact pattern shows a buyer purchasing accounts, chattel paper, promissory notes, or payment intangibles, treat them as if they were a secured party taking a security interest in the collateral. Typically, this means that the buyer must *perfect* its interest in the purchased collateral in order to have a superior claim to the collateral.

- Article 9 also governs certain consignments.

CHAPTER 3: CLASSIFYING COLLATERAL

A. In General

- **Collateral**: Property subject to a security interest
- Why is it important to classify collateral?

  - It can affect the validity of a security interest (*i.e.*, whether the security interest has ________________.
  - It can also determine which ________________ rules apply.
  - It will affect which ________________ rules apply.

- To properly classify collateral, look to the debtor's ________________ at the time the security interest is created.

B. Goods

- Anything ________________ at the time a security interest attaches.
- Also includes some collateral that is not technically "moveable":

  - ________________
  - Standing timber
  - Unborn animals
  - Growing or unharvested crops

- Manufactured homes

- **Sub-classify:** There are **four mutually exclusive** sub-categories of goods.
  - **Mnemonic**: <u>C</u>hampion <u>G</u>ecko <u>F</u>acing <u>P</u>oodles; <u>I</u>guanas <u>E</u>scaped

Consumer Goods

- Goods acquired primarily for ________________, ________________, or household purposes.
- E.g., electronics, furniture, boats, and home appliances.

Farm Products

- Crops, livestock, ________________ used (e.g., animal feed, fertilizer) or produced (e.g., eggs, vegetables) in farming operations.
- NOT FARM PRODUCTS: Farming equipment (e.g., tractors and combines).

Inventory

- Goods that are not farm products that are held for ________________ or ________________ (items on the shelf)
- Also includes goods that are furnished under a ________________ contract, ________________ materials, works in progress, or materials used or consumed in business

Equipment

- ________________ is defined as goods that don't fit into any of the other definitions (consumer goods, farm products, or inventory).
- E.g., ________________, delivery vans, office equipment, and farm equipment.

- **Classification can change:** As collateral passes from debtor to debtor, or the principal use changes, the classification of a piece of collateral can change.

Example 7: *Beets on a farm are ________________________________. But when they are purchased by a grocery store and held for sale, they are ________________. If you buy the beets and take them home, they are ________________________________.*

- **Fixtures:** Goods can also qualify as ________________ if they are attached to real property in such a way that an interest arises in them under real property law.

Example 8: *A chandelier could be considered consumer goods, but when it is installed in the home, it becomes a fixture to the house.*

> **Exam Tip 5:** When does a good become a fixture? ***Rule of thumb:*** Once the good is attached to the house, if you're not going to take it with you when you move away, then it's likely a fixture. It's attached to the home in a way that is rather permanent.

C. Rights to Payment

- The right to be repaid money by a third party that the debtor then uses as ________________ for a loan
- Four types of rights to payment: (**Mnemonic**: Impatient Cow pushes Adorable Pony inside.)

1. Instrument

- Examples: promissory notes, ________________, and drafts governed by Article 3 of the UCC.

2. Chattel Paper

- A record (paper or electronic) with two components:
  - A ________________ obligation, and
  - A security interest or a lease

Example 9: *If an Article 9 secured transaction contract is used as collateral for a different loan, that would qualify as chattel paper; similarly, if your landlord uses your apartment lease as collateral for the loan, that would be chattel paper.*

3. Accounts

- A right to payment of a monetary obligation for property that is ________________, leased, or licensed, or for services rendered (includes a company's accounts receivable, the right to be paid under insurance policies, and amounts owing on credit cards).

4. Payment Intangible

- Our "catch-all" of rights to payment. (Caution: "Accounts" is very broad!)

Example 10: *A right to be repaid a loan of money that does not itself qualify as an instrument or chattel paper is a payment intangible. ("Accounts" does not include rights to be repaid loans of money.)*

- **Attack Outline for Rights to Payment**
  - Look for a transaction in which a **third party** (known as an ________________________ __________)
  - Owes money to your debtor, and
  - **Your debtor uses that money** (that right to payment or expectation of repayment) **as collateral** for the loan.

Exam Tip 6: When classifying rights to payment, start first by determining whether it is chattel paper or instruments because those are the easiest to spot. If the collateral is neither of those, chances are it is going to be an account. But, accounts don't encompass the right to be repaid a loan of money. So if you have a loan of money, and you are sure it is not chattel paper or an instrument, then *and only then* consider payment intangibles.

Example 11: *Landlord leases property to lessee. Landlord gives Lender a security interest in Landlord's rights under the lease. The collateral is ______________________________ because it is a right to be paid under a lease.*

Example 12: *A landscaper gets a loan from bank and grants bank a security interest in her right to receive payment from clients for landscaping work. The right to receive payment for landscaping work is probably an ______________because it is a right to be repaid for services rendered.*

Example 13: *Blunder Muffin Paper Company gets a loan from a bank and pledges as collateral its rights to be paid for the paper it has sold on credit. This could also qualify as an ______________ as it is a right to be repaid for goods sold.*

Example 14: *But imagine if Blunder Muffin's form agreement (used when paper are sold on credit) provides that the store retains a security interest in the paper sold until the buyer repays the purchase price. These contracts, when used as collateral for the loan, are classified ______________________ ______ because the contracts include a right to payment plus a security interest.*

Example 15: *A business loans money to many parties and holds numerous promissory notes that represent borrowers' obligations to repay. If the business then uses those promissory notes as collateral for a loan, the notes are classified as ______________.*

Example 16: *Same facts as above, except that borrowers' obligations were not represented by promissory notes. The business has no security interests in the borrowers' property to secure these obligations. If business uses these rights to payment as collateral for a loan from lender, then the collateral does not meet the definition of accounts, chattel paper, or Instruments. The collateral is classified as ______________________________.*

D. Other Types of Collateral

1. Documents

- Documents of title that generally give the holder ownership rights in goods held by a ______________
- **Examples**: Bills of lading or warehouse receipts (someone is holding the goods and there is something called a document or a warehouse receipt or a bill of lading that represents the ownership rights to the goods).

2. Investment Property

- Certificated and uncertificated securities, such as ______________ and bonds.

3. __________________ **Accounts**

- These are bank accounts. Examples: a savings, passbook, time, or demand account made with a bank

> **Exam Tip 7:** Take note of the difference between deposit accounts and accounts: An account is the right to payment for goods sold or services rendered. A deposit account is a bank account.

4. **Commercial Tort Claims**

- Claims possessed by an organization or an individual that arose in the course of the organization or individual's business. Do not include claims for personal injury or death.

5. **Letter of Credit Rights**

- A right to payment or performance under a letter of credit

6. **General Intangibles**

- A residual category
- Anything that doesn't fit in any of the categories above
- Examples: Blueprints, copyrights, trademarks, and software

> **Exam Tip 8:** A lot can happen to collateral over the course of a Bar Exam fact pattern. Be sure to read the fact pattern fully to determine which collateral truly is at issue. Frequently, the call of the question will tell you which collateral the examiners want you to discuss. Use that as a guide as you're reading through the problem.

CHAPTER 4: ATTACHMENT

For a secured party to have a valid interest in the collateral it must first attach.

A. In General

- Attachment is an arrangement **linking** a __________________ to a particular piece of __________________
- Upon attachment, the security interest becomes __________________ against the debtor's collateral. *(The lender has rights to sue the debtor and also seize the property.)*

> ***Example 17:*** *Dwight buys a car on credit, granting the dealership a security interest in the car to secure repayment of the debt. Once the dealership's security interest has __________________ to the car, the dealership has the rights to repossess and sell the car if Dwight later defaults on the car loan.*

B. Three Requirements for Attachment

- **MNEMONIC**: <u>**V**</u>iolet <u>**R**</u>oses <u>**S**</u>mell <u>**A**</u>mazing

  1. __________________ given by the secured party

The debtor must have __________________ in the collateral (some property interest in the collateral).

There must be a ____________________________________ meeting one of the following requirements:

- There is an __________________ security agreement that describes the collateral, OR
- The secured party has __________________ or control of the collateral pursuant to an oral or unauthenticated security agreement.

C. VALUE

- Value can be given by providing the same __________________ needed for a contract.
- No __________________value needs to be given.

> ***Example 18:*** *If Michael loans Dwight $1,000 and Michael later decides he wants a security interest in Dwight's car to secure that loan, he can ask Dwight to sign a security agreement granting Michael a security interest in the car. Michael does not need to give a second loan.*

- A __________________ commitment to extend credit is value

> ***Example 19:*** *If Michael says "I promise to lend Dwight up to $1,000 as Dwight needs it," Michael has given value even if no money has changed hands (i.e., line of credit).*

- A security agreement may provide that the collateral secures __________________ __________________.

D. RIGHTS in the Collateral

- The security interest only attaches to the rights the debtor has in the collateral (e.g., leasehold, joint tenancy, full ownership).
- Thieves cannot grant security interests in stolen goods because they have no rights in the collateral.
- If a debtor has __________________ title but could transfer full title to a good faith purchaser for value, then the debtor can create an enforceable security interest (*i.e.*, a secured party qualifies as a good faith purchaser for value).

> **Exam Tip 9:** Rights in the collateral are most often relevant in the context of **after-acquired property**. Security interests can attach to after-acquired property, but attachment does not occur until the debtor obtains __________________ in the collateral.

E. SECURITY AGREEMENT

1. Usually an __________________ **record** *(e.g., piece of paper signed by the debtor)*
   - Look for three components: **MNEMONIC**: security agreements are **R.A.D**.

- A __________________: Need not be written on paper, but must be stored in a record—something that others can retrieve.

  The record must be __________________ by the debtor.

  > **Exam Tip 10:** Need a signature or other symbol that shows the intent of the debtor to be bound.

  The security agreement must __________________ the collateral.

  > **Exam Tip 11:** Remember to read the security agreement carefully. The security interest will only attach to that collateral that is described in the security agreement (unless the lender has possession/control of additional collateral as described below).

  - The description must __________________ identify the collateral.

  Example 20: *"All of the debtor's inventory," "Cletrac Tractor Serial No. 12345," "Your Mazda," "All of Jeweler's Rolex watches" are all descriptions that reasonably identify the collateral. "Some" or "My Favorite" or not.*

  - **Exception**: For consumer goods and commercial tort claims, the collateral must be identified with more particularity.

  Example 21: *"All my consumer goods" does not reasonably identify the collateral.*

- A ____________________________________ description, such as "all of the debtor's assets" or "all of the debtor's personal property" does not reasonably identify the collateral for attachment.

  > **Exam Tip 12:** Super-generic descriptions will be adequate to *perfect* a security interest when described in a ________________________________, but the security agreement must be more specific.

2. Possession or control of collateral (alternative to authenticated record)

- If there is no authenticated record that describes the collateral, the secured party's __________________ or __________________ of the collateral pursuant to a security agreement can also be sufficient for the "security agreement" requirement of attachment.

a. Attachment by Possession Pursuant to a Security Agreement

- Types of collateral: consumer goods, equipment, farm products, chattel paper, tangible documents, certificated securities, instruments, and money

  > **Exam Tip 13:** If you can hold it in your hands, a creditor can attach by possession.

b. **Attachment by control pursuant to a security agreement**

- Types of collateral: electronic chattel paper, investment property, letter of credit rights, and deposit accounts

> **Exam Tip 14:** If you can't hold it in your hands, a creditor might be able to attach by control.

REMEMBER: Attachment by possession or control must be pursuant to an oral or unauthenticated security agreement.

> ***Example 22:*** *If Erin borrows $10 from Stanley, and they orally agree that Stanley can hold onto Erin's copy of "Finding Nemo" until the loan is repaid, Stanley has possession of the collateral pursuant to an oral agreement. Thus, Stanley has an attached security interest in the movie.*

> ***Example 23:*** *If Erin borrows $10 from Stanley and also lends Stanley her copy of "Finding Nemo" to watch over the weekend, Stanley has no security interest in the movie because Stanley's possession of the movie is not pursuant to a security agreement.*

3. Rights and Duties of the Secured Party in Possession

- The secured party must act with __________________ care with respect to the collateral;
- Must keep the collateral __________________; and
- Must __________________ the collateral once the obligation has been satisfied.
- May charge the debtor for __________________ expenses for storing and maintaining the collateral.

CHAPTER 5: ADVANCED ISSUES OF ATTACHMENT

A. Scope of the Security Interest

1. After-Acquired Property Clause

- Property acquired by the debtor after the security interest __________________.
- Because a security interest only attaches to the collateral described in the security agreement, a creditor that wants to have a security interest in property acquired by the debtor after the agreement is authenticated, the lender must include an after acquired property clause.

> ***Example 24:*** *Typical Language: "all of the debtor's existing and after-acquired [collateral]" or "all of the [collateral] now owned or hereafter acquired."*

- If there is no reference to after-acquired property, the security interest only attaches to the collateral that existed at the time that the security agreement was __________________.

Exception: In most states, if the security agreement describes ________________ or ________________, there is a rebuttable presumption that the description includes after-acquired inventory or accounts.

Example 25: *Inventory at a grocery store that gets sold or has a limited shelf life (cyclical); if an after-acquired property clause is not included in the security agreement, a court may read one in because it is inventory.*

2. Accessions and Commingled Goods

a. Accessions

- Goods that are physically united with other goods so that the identity of the original goods is ________________ lost.

  Example 26: *You have a security interest in a car stereo and that stereo becomes installed in a car. The stereo is now an accession to the car.*

- If collateral becomes an accession, a security interest in that collateral is not lost; the security interest continues in the accession.
- Look to the terms of the security agreement to determine whether a lender with a security interest in property with which the accession is united (in the example above, the car) obtains a security interest in the accession.

  Example 27: *Debtor signed a valid security agreement granting Finance Company a security interest in 25 of Debtor's "delivery trucks" and "any accessories now or hereafter installed." That description will allow the lender's security interest in the truck to also attach to accessions to the truck (such as tires, radios, etc.)*

b. Commingled goods

- Goods that are physically united with other goods to the point that their identity *is* ________________ in a product or mass
- A security interest does not continue in the original goods that have been commingled, but it will attach to the larger ________________ or ________________ that results.

  Example 28: *If creditor 1 has a security interest in flour, creditor 2 has a security interest in eggs, and they are mixed together with other ingredients to make cookies. The security interests will not continue in the flour and eggs as such, but creditors will have a proportional interest in the cookies (i.e., the product that resulted).*

3. Proceeds

- Proceeds are whatever results when collateral is ________________, leased, licensed, exchanged, or otherwise disposed of.

Attachment rule for proceeds: If a security interest attaches to the original collateral, it also attaches to the proceeds ________________ whether or not the security interest states that it covers proceeds.

Example 29: *Michael has a security interest in Dwight's car. If Dwight sells his car for cash, Michael's security interest will attach to the cash because the cash is proceeds of the car. If Dwight then uses the cash to buy a new car, Michael's security interest will attach to that new car because the new car is proceeds of the cash. (Michael's interest may not remain perfected—save that concept for later.)*

Example 30: *If Dwight trades his car for a luxury watch, Michael's security interest will continue in the watch because the watch is proceeds of the car.*

Example 31: *Bank has a security interest in all of Blunder Muffin's inventory. (That inventory includes paper held for sale.) If Blunder Muffin sells paper to a law school on credit, and the law school promises to pay for the paper later, Bank's security interest in inventory will attach to the right to payment [likely an account] because the right to payment is ________________________.*

B. Purchase Money Security Interests (PMSI)

Exam Tip 15: PMSI is tested heavily on the bar exam.

1. In General

- A PMSI is a special type of security interest subject to its own perfection and priority rules.
- A security interest qualifies as a PMSI only if the collateral is ________________________ or ________________________.
- A PMSI has two components:
  1. The value given allows the debtor to **acquire** the goods or software; and
  2. The goods or software acquired **secure** the loan.

2. Classic PMSI Fact Patterns

- **Lender PMSI**—The lender loans money to the debtor so that the debtor can acquire goods.
  - The value is ________________________ used to acquire the goods.
  - The lender takes a security interest in those ________________________ goods to secure the loan.

Example 32: *Bank lends Dwight money to help him buy a new car and takes a security interest in the car that Dwight bought using the funds. Bank has a PMSI in the car.*

Example 33: *If Dwight instead gets the loan from the bank and spends that money to pay some bills and uses his next paycheck to buy the car, the Bank does not have a PMSI in the car because the loan extended by the bank did not go to help the debtor (Dwight) buy the collateral (the car).*

- **Seller PMSI**—Goods bought ______________________

  Example 34: *Dealer sells Dwight a car for $10,000 on credit. Dwight signs a security agreement granting dealer a security interest in the car. That is a PMSI.*

> **REMEMBER:** An Article 9 consignment is treated as a PMSI in ______________________.

3. The Dual-Status Rule

- For Non consumer-goods transactions (e.g., business transactions), ______________________ ______________________ are permitted.

  Example 35: *Finance Company gives Blunder Muffin a loan to buy a new piece of equipment, taking a security interest in the equipment to secure the loan. This is a PMSI. Later, finance company extends a second loan to Blunder Muffin secured by the same piece of equipment. Finance Company has a PMSI in the equipment for the first loan, and a ______________________ security interest for the second loan.*

- The UCC does not specify a rule for consumer-goods transactions, so courts can either apply the dual status rule or conclude that there is no PMSI.

CHAPTER 6: PERFECTION AND PERFECTION BY FILING

A. In General

- Have the security interests been *perfected* properly?
- Think of perfection as notice to other parties who may want to make a loan to the debtor or buy the collateral to which a security interest has already attached.
- Timing of perfection is essential for winning a priority dispute.

B. Attachment v. Perfection

- **STEP ONE is Attachment:** The process by which a security interest becomes ______________________ against the **debtor** with respect to the collateral
  - The focus is on the relationship between the ______________________ and the ______________________

- **STEP TWO is Perfection**: The process that stakes the secured party's claim, so that the secured party might have **priority over a later party**
  - The focus is on the relationship between the creditor and ________________________ else (such as secured parties, buyers, and lien creditors) who may have or claim an interest in that collateral.

> **Exam Tip 16:** For the security interest to be ______________________ it must first ______________________ to the collateral, so be certain to go through the attachment analysis before perfection.

C. SIX Methods of Perfection (ONCE ATTACHED)

- **MNEMONIC**: "**F**amous **P**eople **C**an't **A**void **A**ttention"

1. ________________________ (the most common way to perfect)
2. Possession
3. Control
4. ____ (Sometimes property is subject to separate state legislation. Can be temporary or permanent.)
5. Perfection under a state's certificate of title law (for a car or motorcycle)
6. ________________________ perfection (can be temporary or permanent)

D. Perfection by Filing

- File a financing statement in the ____ of the appropriate state. *(Simple, short form. The actual security agreement between the parties does not have to be filed.)*
- Applicable to perfect security interests in all collateral **except** ________________________ accounts, money, letters of credit, and collateral subject to other perfection methods (like state certificate of title laws).

> **Exam Tip 17:** Of these exceptions, deposit accounts and cars are the most commonly tested. If you see a financing statement filed to perfect a security interest in cars or deposit accounts, it is ineffective. *Small exception: cars that are inventory can be perfected by filing.*

1. Financing Statement

a. Purpose

- ________________________ filing: puts others on notice that there may be a security interest.

b. Where to file

- In the central filing office, often the secretary of state's office in the state where the ________________________ is located.

- A **corporation** is located in its state of ________________________.
- A **business that is not a registered organization** is located in the state in which it ________________________ its business.
  - If multiple states, the state where the chief executive office is located

▪ **Individuals** are located in the state of their ________________________ ________________________.

> **Exam Tip 18:** Be aware of fact pattern that includes multiple states *(i.e.,* business incorporated in Delaware, but does all business in Ohio). If a secured party files in the wrong location, there is no perfection.

- **Exception:** Security interests in real-property-related collateral
- File in the local real property records in the ________________________ where the property is located
- Includes ________________________, as extracted collateral, including oil and gas, and timber to be cut

c. Required information

1. Name of the ____
2. Name of the ____
3. Description of the ____

▪ **Real property-related collateral (additional requirements)**:

a. The financing statement must indicate that a security agreement covers this type of collateral.

b. It must note that it is to be filed in the local real property records.

c. Describe the ____ to which the collateral relates

d. Name the ____ of the real property, if the debtor is not the person who has an interest in the real property

> **NOTE:** Recording the mortgage in the local real property records can satisfy the financing-statement requirements if it contains the information listed above. (It need not note that it is filed in the local real property records).

> **Exam Tip 19:** This required information is **essential** to perfect. If any element is missing, the secured party is ________________________ perfected.

d. Required but non-essential information

▪ A filing office will refuse to accept a financing statement that does not include the following:

- ________________________ for both the debtor and the secured party, and
- An indication of whether the debtor is an individual or an organization.

> **Exam Tip 20:** If a financing statement is accepted without this non-essential information, it is still ______________________ to perfect a security interest.

e. Authorization

- The debtor must ________________________ a financing statement in an authenticated record.
- The debtor does not have to ________________________ the financing statement.
- If the debtor authenticates a security agreement, that authentication authorizes the secured party to file a financing statement.
- Failure to obtain authorization before filing a financing statement can result in the secured party being liable for ________________________ and ________________________ damages.

CHAPTER 7: ADVANCED ISSUES IN PERFECTION BY FIILING

A. The Debtor's Name

The debtor's name is really important for proper notice because parties typically search UCC filings by the debtor's name.

- Financing statement must contain the debtor's ________________________ name.
- If it is a **registered organization debtor**: use the name on the articles of incorporation, or last public organic record filed with the state.
  - Cannot file under the trade names (i.e., no d/b/a)
- For an individual debtor:
  - Majority rule: If the debtor has a non-expired driver's license (or state issued I.D.), use that name. (If debtor does not have a valid state-issued I.D., use legal name.)
  - Minority rule: Driver's license/state I.D. is a safe harbor, but other legal names may be sufficient to perfect.

B. Description of Collateral

- Secured parties have two options for describing collateral:
  - Use the same types of descriptions used for a security agreement
  - Unlike a security agreement, a financing statement can have a ______________________________________ description.
- A statement that the financing statement covers "all assets" or "all personal property" is effective to perfect a security interest.

- Financing statement does not need to mention ________________________ or indicate that it covers after-acquired property or future advances.

> **Exam Tip 21:** Remember that the security interest must ______________________ before it becomes perfected. A common fact pattern involves a security agreement that describes certain collateral and a financing statement that does not completely match up.

WHERE IS THE COLLATERAL DESCRIBED?

Security Agreement (S.A.)	Financing Statement (F.S.)	Result
YES	NO	✓ATTACHED **NOT** perfected
NO	YES	**NOT** attached **NOT** perfected *(Lender has NO enforceable interest in collateral)*
YES	YES	✓ATTACHED ✓PERFECTED

C. Errors in the Financing Statement

- General rule is that minor errors in a financing statement do not affect perfection unless they make the financing statement ____.
- Errors in the debtor's name are **almost always** seriously misleading
- Exception: If the search for the correct name of the debtor would uncover the financing statement with the error, the error is not seriously misleading.

> ***Example 36:*** *If the secured party lists the debtor's name on the financing statement with the wrong middle initial, that error is likely not seriously misleading because many states' UCC search logic ignore middle initials, corporate designations, and punctuation. Thus, a search under the debtor's correct name would likely return the secured party's erroneous financing statement.*

> **Exam Tip 22:** Remember: If the mistake is seriously misleading, then the security interest is **not perfected**.

D. Filing Office Problems

- The filing office ________________________ refuse a financing statement that lacks the information specified in 9-516(b) or if the debtor fails to tender the fee or if the debtor submits the financing statement in an improper manner.
- If the filing office refuses the financing statement and was not justified in doing so, then the financing statement is treated as having been ________________________.
    - **Exception**: It will be ineffective against a purchaser or secured party who gave value in ________________________ reliance upon the absence of the record from the files.
- If the filing office indexes the financing statement incorrectly, that has **no effect** on perfection.

E. Duration of a Financing Statement

- Financing statements lapse _________________________ after the date of filing, unless continued.
- How do you continue a financing statement? By filing a _________________________ statement within _________________________ months before the financing statement lapses.
- If a financing statement lapses, the secured party loses perfection (unless it is perfected by some other means).
  - The secured party may file a new financing statement to re-perfect, but might lose its place in a priority contest.
- When the obligation is paid back, a _________________________ statement voids the financing statement.

CHAPTER 8: OTHER METHODS OF PERFECTION

A. Perfection by Possession

- Security interests in **tangible** collateral may perfected if the secured party takes _________________________ of the collateral.
  - The following collateral can be perfected by possession:
    - _________________________
    - _________________________
    - Instruments
    - _________________________ documents
    - Tangible chattel paper

    Example 37: *Possession is the **only way** to perfect a security interest in _________________________.*

- As soon as the secured party has possession, the interest is perfected.
  - The interest remains perfected as long as the secured party retains possession.
  - Exceptions that allow a secured party to remain temporarily perfected even after it gives up possession.

B. Perfection by Control

1. Generally

- A secured party may perfect a security interest in specific _________________________ collateral by taking control of that collateral.
- The following collateral can be perfected by control:
  - Deposit accounts

- Investment property
- Electronic documents
- ________________________ chattel paper
- Letter of credit rights.

  - Control is the **exclusive** method for perfecting a security interest in both ________________________ accounts and letter of ____.

> **Exam Tip 23:** If a lender files a financing statement to perfect a security interest in a deposit account or letter of credit right, the filing will be ineffective. Treat the lender as ______________________ unless the lender obtains control of the collateral.

2. Deposit Accounts

- Control can be obtained over a deposit account in one of three ways:

  1. The secured party is the bank that has the deposit account (lender and the bank are the same party).
  2. The secured party, the bank and the debtor agree in an authenticated record that the lender (secured party) has control over the deposit account (deposit account control agreement).
  3. The secured party can become the bank's ________________________ with respect to the deposit account.

C. Perfection Under Alternate Perfection Systems

- When another statute (non-Article 9) governs how a security interest is perfected, you must follow the rules of that statute.
- Most likely to be tested: perfection under a state ____ statute
  - Applicable to cars, motorcycles, or other vehicles that have a title
  - Filing, Possession of the car, or possession of the title are insufficient to perfect in most cars.
  - Perfect by ________________________ a security interest on that certificate of title.

> **Exception:** Cars that are ______________________ can be perfected by other means (e.g., if you purchase a new car, that car likely didn't have a title when purchased so there was no title on which to note the lien – so filing works when the cars are ______________________.)

Example 38: *Debtor is a delivery company. Bank takes a security interest in debtor's equipment and inventory. "Bank did not note its security interest on the certificates of title issued for the trucks. However, Bank immediately filed an appropriate financing statement in the proper state office that listed its collateral as 'all Debtor's inventory and equipment, whether now owned or hereafter acquired.'" Under these facts, Bank's financing statement would be* *effective to perfect a security interest in other equipment and inventory, but* ***not*** *the trucks. Although the trucks are equipment, they are subject to the certificate-of-title exception, and the bank must*

____.

D. Automatic Perfection

1. In General

- Some types of collateral will **automatically perfect** when a security interest __________________________, with no filing, possession, or control required.
- The most common example: a ____.

Example 39: *Angela buys a dishwasher on credit from department store for use in her home. She signs an agreement promising to pay over time and granting the store a security interest in the dishwasher. Store does not file a financing statement. Store is nevertheless perfected because the dishwasher is a consumer good and store's purchase money security interest is automatically perfected.*

Exception: If a ____ statute governs, then no automatic perfection.

Example 40: *Angela instead buys a car on credit, granting dealer a purchase money security interest in the car to secure her obligation to repay. This PMSI is not automatically perfected; the secured party must note its interest on the certificate of title.*

Exam Tip 24: Remember, automatic perfection applies only to PMSIs in **consumer goods**. A PMSI in inventory, equipment, or farm products is NOT automatically perfected.

2. Other Automatic Perfection Rules

- Casual or isolated assignments of accounts that do not transfer a significant part of the outstanding accounts receivable
- Sales of payment intangibles or promissory notes

Example 41: *Debtor obtains loan from Bank. To secure the loan, [Debtor] assigned to [Bank] "all rights to payment owed to [Debtor] by Hotel Corporation for the roofing construction project on its Broadway Street Hotel." The Broadway Street Hotel roofing project was by far the largest of [Debtor's] fifteen roofing projects and represented its largest account receivable. Bank files a financing statement listing the debtor's trade name.*

The financing statement is insufficient to perfect (because the lender used the debtor's trade name, not the correct legal name), but the Bank may be automatically perfected if assignment of the Hotel account qualifies as a "casual or isolated" assignment of accounts. Under these facts and others presented in the problem, this assignment is likely too large to qualify for automatic perfection, so Bank is unperfected.

CHAPTER 9: TEMPORARY AUTOMATIC PERFECTION AND POST-FILING CHANGES

A. In General

- The rules in this section apply when something happens to the collateral or to the debtor ________________________ perfection has occurred.
- Article 9 often allows the secured party a window of time to ________________________ that a change has occurred and to preserve its rights by amending the financing statement or re-filing if necessary.

B. Debtor Name Change

- If the name change causes the filed financing statement to become ____, the secured party has a ________________________-month window to discover the change and file an amendment to the financing statement listing the debtor's new name.
- If the secured party fails to amend:
  - o Collateral that is acquired after ____ ________________ is not covered by the financing statement.
  - o Everything before the name change and within four months after the name change ________________________ perfected under the original financing statement.

__Example 42:__ On March 1, Bank takes a security interest in all of Construction Corp.'s existing and after-acquired equipment. Bank's security interest is perfected by filing a financing statement, listing the debtor's name as "Construction Corp.," the company's legal name. The equipment includes a computer and a bulldozer. On April 1, Construction Corp. changes its name to Construction by Charlie, Inc. On May 1, the company acquires another piece of equipment, a backhoe. On October 1, the company acquires another bulldozer. Bank never filed an amended financing statement. In what collateral is Bank perfected?

The bank is perfected in the ____ ________________ The bank is NOT perfected in the ____ because it was acquired more than four months after the name change.

C. Debtor Moves Out of State

- A perfected security interest will remain perfected for ____ after a debtor moves out of state, unless the financing statement lapses earlier.
- The filed financing statement will cover collateral purchased within the four-month window after the move.
- The secured party must _______________________ in the new state within that four-month window to remain continuously perfected.

D. Collateral Moves Out of State

- If the debtor still owns the collateral, no re-filing is necessary.
- If the collateral is transferred to a new debtor who lives out of state, the secured party has _______________________ to file a financing statement listing the new debtor.
- What happens if the secured party fails to file a financing statement within either the four-month or one-year period?
  - The security interest ____ in the collateral.
  - Perfection is lost prospectively, and against another secured party or purchaser for value, the security interest is deemed ____.

E. Secured Party Perfected by Possession Gives the Collateral Back to the Debtor

- The secured party is only perfected so long as it has actual _______________________ possession of the property.

> ***Example 43:*** *Uncle loans Phyllis $300 and they orally agree that Phyllis's bracelet will serve as collateral for the loan. Uncle takes possession of the bracelet. Uncle's security interest has attached and is perfected by possession. If Uncle loans Phyllis the bracelet to wear for a job interview, Uncle has lost perfection. Perfection will not occur again until Uncle regains possession of the collateral. (When we get into the priority rule of first in time, we would use the date of Uncle regaining possession.)*

- **Limited exception:** Temporary automatic perfection—if a security interest is perfected by possession in an instrument, negotiable document, certificated security, or goods stored with a _______________________, the secured party can give the collateral back to the debtor for limited purposes:
  - To _______________________
  - _______________________
  - To enforce the debtor's rights in the collateral
    - The secured party is temporarily perfected for _______________________ days.

- The secured party needs to either file a _______________________ or _______________________ the collateral within this 20-day period to remain continuously perfected.

CHAPTER 10: PERFECTION RULES RELATING TO PROCEEDS

A. In General

- **Defined:** Proceeds arise when collateral is _______________________, leased, licensed, or otherwise disposed of.
- **Attachment:** The security interest attaches to proceeds _______________________, whether or not the security agreement lists proceeds.
- **Perfection:** A security interest in proceeds is initially perfected for 20 days, and may be perfected after the 20-day period in some circumstances (see below).
- **Priority:** A secured party with an interest in proceeds will have priority dating from the time of perfection in the original collateral if the secured party has remained _______________________.

B. Perfection Rules for Proceeds

- **Initially:** Temporary automatic perfection for _______________________ after collateral is sold
- **Beyond 20 Days**: Perfection will lapse unless one of the following circumstances is present:
  1. **Amend:** The secured party takes necessary steps to _______________________ the financing statement (or the original financing statement is _______________________ enough to encompass the proceeds).

     Example 44: *Bank has a security interest in all of Blunder Muffin's inventory, perfected by filing a financing statement listing "inventory" as the collateral. Blunder Muffin sells 300 boxes of paper for cash, and uses the cash to purchase toilet paper for the sales office. The cash is proceeds of the inventory [security interest attaches and is perfected for 20 days] and the toilet paper is now proceeds of the cash [so security interest attaches and is perfected for 20 days]. Since the toilet paper also qualifies as "inventory," and the original financing statement already covers "inventory," Bank _______________________.*

     Example 45: *Assume instead the boxes of paper (the inventory) were sold for cash, and the cash was used to buy a delivery bicycle (equipment). Bank's security interest attached to the cash and then attached to the bicycle because it's from proceeds and the security interest was perfected for 20 days in each. On the 21 day, perfection will lapse, unless Bank does the following: Bank can remain continuously perfected if it amends its financing statement to cover equipment within _______________________ of the bike's purchase.*

2. **Cash Proceeds Rule**: If collateral is sold, licensed, leased, or otherwise disposed of, and generates cash proceeds, perfection continues ______________________ in cash proceeds so long as they are ______________________.

   Example 46: *Bank has a security interest in all of Blunder Muffin's inventory. The inventory is sold, generating cash. Bank has a perfected security interest in that cash forever, so long as it remains identifiable (e.g. in a segregated bank account).*

3. **Same Office Rule:** A security interest in proceeds will be perfected (as long as the original financing statement remains effective) when:

   - The financing statement covers the ______________________ collateral;
   - The proceeds are collateral in which the security interest may be perfected by filing in the ______________________ office as the original financing statement; and
   - The proceeds are not acquired with ______________________ proceeds.

   Exam Tip 25: Look for collateral that can be perfected by filing turning into proceeds that can also be perfected by filing. Typically, this will be when inventory is sold for accounts or chattel paper. Watch out for any time the collateral is purchased with ______________________ proceeds; the Same Office Rule will **not** apply.

   Example 47: *Bank has a security interest in all of Blunder Muffin's inventory. The inventory is sold on credit, generating accounts. The accounts are proceeds of the inventory. As both the inventory and the accounts would be perfected by filing in the ______________________ and the accounts were not acquired with cash proceeds, Bank will be perfected in the accounts without filing a new financing statement.*

   Exam Tip 26: REMEMBER: A financing statement that covers inventory is sufficient to perfect a security interest in accounts.

   Example 48: *If Blunder Muffin had sold the paper for cash, and used the cash to buy a snow blower, the Same Office Rule would not apply due to the introduction of ______________________ proceeds. The Bank instead would have ______________________ days after the purchase of the snow blower to file as to the snow blower, unless the original financing statement was already broad enough to include the snow blower.*

C. Intro to Priority Rules for Proceeds

- Generally, the basic priority rules apply to proceeds.
- If the security interest is perfected in proceeds and has been ______________________ perfected (*i.e.*, no gap in perfection), then measure the secured party's status based on the time of filing or perfection as to the original collateral.

- Exceptions

    1. Proceeds of PMSIs in ________________________ discussed below.
    2. Proceeds of ________________________ collateral

    - If collateral is of the type that is typically perfected other than by filing, priority continues in the proceeds provided that:
        - The security interest in proceeds is perfected; and
        - The proceeds are either cash proceeds or the same type of collateral as the original collateral.

CHAPTER 11: INTRODUCTION TO PRIORITY AND PRIORITY DISPUTES BETWEEN SECURITY INTERESTS

A. Recognizing Potential Claimants to the Collateral

1. **Secured Creditors:** Any priority dispute will feature one or more secured parties. When you see a secured creditor, determine:

    (i) Whether and when their interests have ________________________ to the collateral
    (ii) Whether and when their interests are ________________________
    (iii) Whether they hold a ________________________

2. **Unsecured Creditors:** Creditors without a ________________________ in the debtor's collateral

    - Unsecured creditors have ________________________ against the ***property.***
    - They likely do have ________________________ rights against the ***debtor***.
    - Can obtain rights in the property by either getting a ________________________ or a ________________________ in the collateral.

    Note 1: If you see an unsecured creditor obtain a judgment against the debtor and execute/levy/get a lien on particular property of the debtor, that execution makes that party a lien creditor.

3. **Lien Creditors**

    - Liens can be judicial or ________________________

    Example 49: *Phyllis obtains a judgment against Store and levies on Store's inventory. Phyllis is a judicial lien creditor.*

    Example 50: *Phyllis takes her car in to be repaired. Under her state's mechanics' or artisans' lien statute, her mechanic has a statutory lien on the car and can hold the car until Phyllis pays for the repairs.*

4. **Purchasers of Chattel Paper, Promissory Notes, Accounts, or Payment Intangibles**

    - **MNEMONIC:** <u>C</u>ruel <u>P</u>oodles <u>P</u>oked <u>N</u>eedles <u>A</u>t <u>P</u>eaceful <u>I</u>guanas

REMEMBER: Treat as secured transactions

- Treat the purchaser as a ________________________ party with an attached security interest.
- Look to see whether the purchaser has perfected (and pay attention to automatic perfection rules discussed above).

Exam Tip 27: If the purchaser/SP has not perfected, the seller/debtor has sufficient rights in the collateral to grant a security interest to another party.

5. Buyers or Transferees of Other Collateral

These parties may wish to "take free of" the secured party's security interest.

B. Gearing Up for a Priority Question

- Using the call of the question and the facts presented, identify the priority dispute at issue:
- "[Party] v. [Party] over [collateral]."
  - Perfected Security Interest v. Unperfected Security Interest over equipment.
  - Unperfected Security Interest v. Lien Creditor over inventory.
  - Perfected Security Interest v. Purchaser of Consumer Goods
  - Perfected Security Interest in Deposit Account (Proceeds) v. Security Interest in Deposit Account Perfected by Control.

C. Security Interest v. Security Interest (neither is a PMSI)

First Dispute: Perfected Security Interest v. Perfected Security Interest

- The first in time to ________________________ *or* ________________________ takes priority.

Note 2: This rule rewards an early filer, even if subsequently the competing secured party is first to attach, or even first to perfect.

Second Dispute: Perfected Security Interest v. Unperfected Security Interest

- ________________________ security interest beats an ________________________ security interest.

Third Dispute: Unperfected Security Interest v. Unperfected Security Interest

- The first security interest to ________________________ or become ________________________ takes priority.

Example 51: *Uncle loans Kelly $1000 on March 1 to help her start a clothing line. That same day, Kelly signs a security agreement granting Uncle a security interest in Kelly's existing equipment to secure the loan made.*

____

____

On March 5, Kelly approaches Bank for additional start-up funds. Kelly gives Bank authorization to file a financing statement covering all of her equipment, and Bank files the financing statement listing "all equipment" on March 5. On

____

____

March 10, Uncle files a financing statement listing "equipment" as collateral.

____

On March 15, Bank agrees to loan Kelly the requested funds and Kelly signs a security agreement granting Bank a security interest in all of her equipment.

QUESTION: Who, between Uncle and Bank has priority?

1. The collateral here is ____________________
2. Uncle's interest attached on ____________________ and was perfected on ____________________.
3. Bank's interest does not attach until ____________________. It is perfected on ____________________ as well. (Remember, you cannot perfect until the interest has attached.)

ISSUE: ____________________ security interest v. ____________________ security interest in ____________________.

RULE: First in time to ____________________ or ____________________ takes priority (whichever one comes first).

ANALYSIS: Apply the facts of the problem to that particular rule. Although Uncle was first to perfect, Bank filed the financing statement first.

CONCLUSION: "Under the first to file or perfect rule, ____________________ has priority."

Example 52: *What happens if Bank failed to file a financing statement?*

Bank would be ____________________.

ISSUE: ____________________ security interest v. ____________________ security interest in equipment.

RULE: A ____________________ security interest takes priority over ______________________________ security interest.

ANALYSIS: Uncle perfected his security interest in the equipment on March 10, and Bank never perfected at all.

CONCLUSION: Because a perfected security interest takes priority over an unperfected security interest, Uncle has priority in the equipment.

CHAPTER 12: PRIORITY DISPUTES BETWEEN SECURITY INTEREST AND A JUDICIAL/STATUTORY LIEN

A. Security Interest v. Judicial Lien Creditors

1. Perfected Security Interest v. Lien Creditor

- A ________________________ security interest takes priority over a ____.

2. UNperfected Security Interest v. Lien Creditor

- Lien creditor will take priority over an ________________________ security interest.

Exception: the filed but ______________________ security interest exception:

  - If the debtor has authenticated a security agreement listing the collateral and a financing statement is on file, but the secured party has not yet given ________________________, the secured party will take priority over a lien creditor

Example 53: *On August 1, Blunder Muffin signs a security agreement granting Lender a security interest in the company's inventory. Lender files a financing statement that same day, but does not give value until August 15. Creditor obtains a judicial lien on Blunder Muffin's inventory on August 4. Although Lender is unattached and unperfected at the time the lien arises, Lender's **filed but unattached** security interest will take priority over creditor's lien.*

B. Security Interest v. Statutory Lien

- A **statutory** lien is a lien created by statute, and it has priority over a security interest (even if it is perfected) as long as:
  - The effectiveness of the lien depends on the lienholder's ________________________ of the goods;
  - The lien secures payment or performance of an obligation for services or materials furnished in the ____ of the person's business (mechanic's lien); and
  - The statute doesn't provide otherwise.

Example 54: *Virginia's mechanic's lien statute gives a mechanic a possessory lien over property that the mechanic has serviced, but states that the lien has priority only up to $1000. In this state, a repairperson that serviced the debtor's property in the ordinary course would have a statutory lien with priority over a* *preexisting security interest, but only for the first $1000 in charges. The lien for the remaining charges would rank under the secured party.*

C. Priority Over Future Advances

REMEMBER: A security agreement can provide that future advances are secured by collateral.

1. Secured Party v. Secured Party Over Future Advances

- Article 9 gives priority to the first party to file or perfect with respect to future advances, even if that secured party has ________________________ of the competing security interest when the future advance is made.

__Example 55: Day 1:__ SP1 lends Erin $10,000 and Erin signs a security agreement providing that the collateral (worth $20,000) secures this loan and future advances. SP1 perfects on Day 1.

***Day 10**: SP2 loans debtor $10,000. SP2's security interest attaches to the same collateral. SP2 perfects on Day 10.*

***Day 25**: SP1, with knowledge of SP2's security interest, gives the debtor an additional advance of $10,000.*

Does the second advance rank under or above SP2's interest that arose in the interim? Because SP1 was the first to file and perfect, it will take priority over SP2 with respect to the entire $20,000.

2. Secured Party versus Lien Creditor Over Future Advances

- If a secured party's advance is made within ________________________ of the lien creditor's lien arising, the ________________________ party has priority.
- Advances made more than 45 days after the person becomes a lien creditor are ________________________ to the lien creditor unless:
  - The advance is made without ________________________ of the lien, OR
  - The advance is made pursuant to a commitment entered into without ________________________ of the lien.

Example 56: **Day 1**: *SP lends Erin $10,000 and Erin signs a security agreement providing that the collateral (worth $20,000) secures this loan and future advances. SP perfects on Day 1.*

Day 10: *Lien creditor executes judgment on the same collateral.*

Day 25: *SP lends the debtor an additional $10,000. Who has priority?*

***Who has priority?** Answer: Because SP's advance was made within ________________________ of the lien arising,*

____________________ *priority with respect to the entire $20,000.*

Example 57: *Assume instead that SP had lent Erin an additional $10,000 on Day 75, which is more than 45 days after the lien arose.*

Answer: *SP has priority if it had no ____________________ of the lien. If SP had knowledge of the lien on Day 75, then give priority to the ____________________ over the future advance.*

CHAPTER 13: PRIORITY RULES: SECURED PARTIES V. BUYERS

A. In General

- When you see a dispute between a buyer and a SP, you can phrase the priority question differently: Did the buyer take the collateral ____________________ a security interest or ____________________ a security interest?

B. Buyer v. Perfected Security Interest

- **General rule:** Unless the secured party authorizes the sale free and clear of its security interest, a buyer takes ____________________ a perfected security interest.

Exception 1: Buyer in the ____________________ of business (BIOCB)

- A BIOCB takes free of a security interest created by the buyer's seller even if that security interest is perfected and even if the buyer knows of the existence of the security interest if:
  - The buyer buys goods from a ____________________
  - In the ordinary course of the merchant's ____________________
  - The buyer acts in ____________________ and ____________________ knowledge *that the sale violates the rights of others in the same goods.*
  - The seller is engaged in the business of selling goods of this kind, and the seller is not a ____________________.

Example 58: *Ryan buys a tie from an upscale clothing boutique. Every aspect of the purchase is typical of a retail sale. The boutique's lender has a perfected security interest in all of the boutique's inventory, including the tie that Ryan bought. Ryan will take the tie free of lender's security interest because Ryan is a buyer in the ordinary course of business. (Analysis: Ryan bought goods from a merchant in the ordinary course of the merchant's business, Ryan acted in good faith and without knowledge that the sale violated the rights of others in the same goods, and the boutique was engaged in the business of selling goods of that type and was not a pawnbroker).*

Example 59: What if Ryan had knowledge of the boutique's lender's security interest in inventory? Nothing would change. Ryan still qualifies as a BIOCB and takes free of lender's security interest because he can assume that boutique's lender and the boutique have agreed to allow sales of inventory.

Example 60: What if lender had forbidden boutique from selling ties and Ryan knew that he was violating the terms of the security agreement when he bought the ties? Here, Ryan would not take free because he had knowledge that the sale violates the rights of secured party. (The knowledge element is very narrow.)

- **Exception 2:** The "Garage Sale Exception" (Consumer to Consumer Exception)
  - A buyer of _______________________ goods will take _______________________ of a security interest, even if it is perfected, if:
    - The buyer buys consumer goods for _______________________
    - For their own _______________________, family, or household use
    - From a _______________________ seller and
    - **Without knowledge** of the security interest, and
    - **UNLESS** the secured party has filed a _______________________________________ covering the goods before the purchase occurred.

> **Exam Tip 28:** PMSIs in consumer goods are automatically perfected. This rule allows a purchaser of consumer goods to take free of a security interest if the secured party relies on automatic perfection. *Secured parties can avoid the Garage Sale Exception by filing a financing statement covering the goods.*

Example 61: Retailer sells a piano to Andy on credit and retains a security interest in the piano to secure the purchase price. Andy intends to use the piano as a consumer good. Because Retailer has an automatically perfected PMSI in consumer goods, Retailer does not take any further steps to perfect. Three months later, Andy sells the piano to Erin for $500. Erin intends to use the piano as a consumer good, and has no actual knowledge of Retailer's security interest. Does Erin take free of Retailer's security interest?

ISSUE: Priority dispute is between Buyer v. Perfected Security Interest.

RULE: Generally buyers take subject to perfected security interests.

EXCEPTION (GARAGE SALE/CONSUMER TO CONSUMER) & ANALYSIS: Buyer takes free of the security interest if buyer buys consumer goods for value (here $500), for their own personal, family, or household use (here, Erin intends to use the piano as a consumer good), from a consumer seller (here, Andy used the piano as a consumer good), without knowledge of the security interest (Erin has no knowledge), and there is no financing statement on file.

CONCLUSION: Erin takes ________________________ of the security interest under the consumer to consumer/garage sale exception.

Example 62: *What if Retailer had filed a financing statement covering the piano? Garage sale exception*

____.

Example 63: *What if Erin had knowledge of Retailer's security interest in the piano when she bought it? Garage sale exception*

____.

Example 64: *What if either Andy or Erin used the piano for business purposes? Garage sale exception* ______________________.

- If the garage sale exception (or another exception) does not apply, then apply the general rule: a buyer takes ________________________ a perfected security interest.

C. Buyer v. Unperfected Security Interest

- **General rule:** Unless a secured party authorizes the sale free and clear of the security interest, the buyer takes ________________________ a security interest.
- **EXCEPTION:** A buyer will take free of an unperfected security interest if the buyer:
  - Gives ________________________
  - Receives ________________________ of the collateral, and
  - Without ________________________ of the preexisting interest

Editorial Note 2: The third element is correctly written in the handout as "without" knowledge.

Exam Tip 29: The buyer in the ordinary course of business and consumer-to-consumer exceptions can also apply in disputes involving unperfected security interests.

D. Buyers and Future Advances

- When applies
  - If a buyer takes **subject to** a security interest according to the rules above, and
  - After the sale the secured party makes a future advance to the debtor/seller.
- **RULE**: The buyer will take free of that future advance if:
  - The secured party had knowledge of the buyer's purchase when it made the advance; ***or***
  - The future advance is made 45 days or more after the purchase.

E. Purchasers of Chattel Paper and Instruments

- Remember, sales of chattel paper and promissory notes are treated as secured transactions
  - **Attachment**: (assumed)
  - **Perfection**: Often by possession with this type of collateral.
- Priority rule oversimplification: Purchasers/Secured parties who take _________________________ of the collateral _________________________ knowledge of the competing security interest will often have priority over competing secured parties.

F. Transferees of Money or Funds

- A transferee of money or funds from a deposit account (that person who received money subject to a security interest) takes _________________________ of security interests unless the transferee acts in _________________________ with the debtor to violate the rights of a secured party.

G. Security Interests v. Buyers' and Sellers' Article 2 Security Interests

- If a buyer or seller has a security interest arising under Article 2 of the UCC, that interest has priority over an Article 9 security interest, as long as the buyer or seller retains _________________________ of the goods.

CHAPTER 14: PMSI PRIORITY RULES AND FIXTURE PRIORITY RULES

A. Review of PMSI Perfection Rules

- PMSIs in consumer goods are _________________________ perfected so long as the collateral is not subject to a certificate of title law.
- For all other PMSIs, the secured party must _________________________ a financing statement or take _________________________ of the collateral in order to perfect.

B. PMSI v. Lien Creditor

- Follow the general priority rule for lien creditors v. security interest
- Except that PMSIs have a _________________________ grace period starting when the debtor ____ of the collateral, to perfect.
- If the purchase money secured party perfects within 20 days of the debtor receiving possession of the collateral, the PMSI will **take priority over** a lien that arose during that 20-day period.

> ***Example 65:*** *On August 1, Darryl purchases equipment on credit, giving Store a PMSI in the equipment. He receives delivery the same day. Creditor levies on the equipment on August 10. Although Store's PMSI is unperfected at the time the lien arose, if Store perfects its PMSI within 20 days of Darryl receiving the equipment, then Store's PMSI will take priority.*

C. PMSIs v. Security Interests

1. PMSI Super-Priority for Goods Other Than Inventory

- PMSI in goods other than inventory or livestock takes priority over **all other security interests**, no matter when they are perfected, if the secured party perfects within ________________________ days of the debtor receiving the goods.
- If the purchase money secured party fails to perfect within 20 days, apply the SP v. SP priority rules (e.g., first in time to file or perfect).

> ***Example 66:*** *Blunder Muffin's lender has a security interest in all of the company's existing and after-acquired equipment. Lender perfected in 2015 and remains perfected. Blunder Muffin buys a forklift on credit from Lifts, Inc., granting Lifts, Inc. a security interest in the forklift. If Lifts, Inc. perfects this PMSI within 20 days of Blunder Muffin receiving the forklift, Lifts, Inc. will have ________________________ in the forklift. This is true even though Lender was the first to perfect.*

> **Exam Tip 30:** Because a PMSI in consumer goods is automatically perfected, this 20-day rule will always be met for consumer goods.

2. PMSI Super-Priority for Inventory

- A PMSI in inventory or livestock will have priority over all other security interests in that same inventory if a secured party:
  - Perfects ________________________ the inventory is delivered to the debtor; and
  - Sends an **authenticated** ________________________ of the PMSI to other secured parties. (One notification is effective for 5 years.)

> ***Example 67:*** *Blunder Muffin's lender has a security interest in all of the company's existing and after-acquired inventory. Lender perfected in 2015 and remains perfected. Blunder Muffin's arranges to buy paper from Supplier on credit. Supplier wishes to retain a PMSI in the paper it supplies. In order to have priority over the first-to-file Lender, Supplier must perfect ________________________ the paper is delivered to Blunder Muffin, and send Lender an ____ that it intends to keep a PMSI in the paper supplied. Once the notification is sent, it's effective for 5 years of paper deliveries.*

> **Exam Tip 31:** Remember, for a PMSI that is perfected but does not satisfy these two super-priority rules, apply the basic secured party v. secured party priority rules.

3. PMSI Super-Priority in Proceeds

- If a PMSI has priority over a competing secured party in goods other than inventory, then that super priority **will extend to the proceeds of the collateral**.

- If a PMSI has priority over a competing secured party in inventory, then the priority will only extend to proceeds that are **up-front** ________________________ payments for the inventory sold.

4. PMSIs v. PMSIs

- A ________________________ PMSI beats a ________________________ PMSI.
- Otherwise, apply the first to file or perfect rule.

D. Fixture Priority Rules

1. In General

- A priority dispute may arise between a secured party with an interest in the fixtures and a party with an interest in the real property to which the goods are affixed.
- If there are two competing Article 9 interests in fixtures, apply the general priority rules.

2. Fixtures v. Real Property Interest

- **General rule**: A security interest in fixtures has priority over an interest in real property if the secured party files a ________________________ filing before the real property interest is recorded.
  - Fixture filing: A financing statement filed in the local ________________________ property records.
- **PMSI Rule**: A PMSI in fixtures has priority over a real property interest if:
  - The debtor has an interest of record in the real property or is in possession of the real property; and
  - The security interest is perfected by a fixture filing, either ________________________ the goods become fixtures or within ________________________ days after the goods become fixtures.
- **Exception** (Construction Mortgage v. PMSI):
  - A construction mortgage has priority over any subsequent security interest in fixtures, including PMSIs in fixtures, if it is recorded ________________________ the goods become fixtures and the goods become fixtures before completion of the construction.

CHAPTER 15: LEASES AND CONSIGNMENTS

A. Leases v. Secured Transactions

- **RULE:** Article 9 governs any transaction, regardless of form, that creates a security interest.
  - Article 9 does not apply to a ________________________ lease but it will apply if the ____________________________________ of the transaction is that the transaction is actually a secured transaction.

1. The Bright-Line Test

- The "lessee" of the property is obligated to pay the ________________________ obligation under the lease, whether or not they terminate the lease early (contract may not be terminated early), **AND**
- One of the following outcomes is present (essentially trying to determine whether the lessor gets anything meaningful back at the end of the lease term):
  - The original term of the lease is equal to or greater than the ____ of the goods (i.e., the goods are used up during the lease term. Nothing of value is going back to the lessor).
  - The lessee is bound to ________________________ the lease for the remaining economic life of the goods (i.*e*., the lessee is obligated to extend the lease until the goods are used up. Nothing of value is going back to the lessor).
  - The lessee has the ________________________ to renew the lease for the remaining economic life of the goods for no additional consideration or ________________________ additional consideration (i.*e*., the lessee would be crazy not to renew the lease until the goods are used up).
  - The lessee has the option to become the ________________________ of the goods for no or ________________________ additional consideration (i.e., the lessee would be crazy not to buy the goods at the end of the lease term).
- **Result:** If the bright line test is met, Article 9 will govern these transactions. That means that the lessor will be treated as the ________________________ party and needs to ________________________ or otherwise perfect his interest in the goods.

Example 68: *Printco entered into a signed agreement with Leaseco, a leasing company, pursuant to which Leaseco agreed to purchase a $100,000 printing press and to immediately lease the press to Printco. The agreement provided that Leaseco retained title to the printing press and required Printco to pay Leaseco $2,500 per month for five years for the use of the press. The agreement also provided that it could not be terminated by Printco for any reason. At the conclusion of the five-year lease, Printco was required to return the press to Leaseco or to purchase the press for $10. Under the bright line test, is this a lease or a secured transaction?*

ANALYSIS: Element 1 – The obligations owed under the lease cannot be terminated early. Element 2 is an option at the end of the lease term to return it or purchase it, and the purchase price is so low that it's nominal.

CONCLUSION: Under the bright-line test described above, this is a ________________________ Treat Leaseco, which did not file a financing statement in this fact pattern, as an unperfected secured party.

2. If the Bright-Line Test is Not Met

- Courts will determine whether a "lease" is actually a secured transaction by looking at the ________________________ of the case.

> **Exam Tip 32:** Ask yourself, "Does the lessor get something of value back at the end of the lease?" If the lessee uses up the goods or keeps the goods at the end of the lease term, it is likely to be a secured transaction.

- Practice point: When in doubt, the lessor should file a financing statement.

B. Consignments

- **Consignments Defined:** A party (the consignor) has ________________________ of goods but gives ________________________ of the goods to another party (the consignee) for the purpose of allowing the consignee to ________________________ the goods.
- The **risk** is that a consignee's lenders may be misled into thinking that consigned inventory is actually owned by the consignee, rather than by the consignor. (Don't think of a consignment store. These rules were designed to deal with a regular store selling inventory that it did not buy, but it is selling for someone else.)
- Article 9 treats consignments that carry this risk as Article 9 ____ to facilitate public notice.
  - The consignor is treated as the ________________________ party and must ________________________ its security interest in the consigned inventory.
  - Apply the rules applicable to a PMSI in ________________________. (*I.e.,* consignor will have PMSI super-priority in consigned goods if consignor perfects by filing before consignee receives possession of the items and consignor properly notifies any secured parties with conflicting security interests in consignee's inventory.)

- **Requirements for a consignment to be subject to Article 9** (when consignors have to file a financing statement to protect their interests):
  - The consignor must deliver goods to a ________________________ who deals in goods of the kind, for the merchant to sell;
  - The merchant is not generally known by its creditors to be substantially engaged in the business of selling the goods of others (because if merchant is in that business we don't need financing statements to put parties on notice);
  - The value of the goods must be at least $________________________ in each delivery; and
  - The goods must not be ________________________ goods immediately before the delivery.

> **Exam Tip 33:** This is not your average consignment (wedding dress, baseball cards, etc.). Think of Article 9 consignments as big-ticket consignments of inventory where the consignee (the one holding the goods for sale) could easily be mistaken as owning the collateral.

Example 69: Pursuant to the written consignment agreement, Specialty delivers speakers to Giant, and Giant displays those speakers on its showroom floor and sells them on behalf of Specialty. The speakers are priced at $2,000 each. When a customer buys a pair of speakers, Giant keeps a commission as compensation for Giant's effort and pays the rest of the customer's purchase price to Specialty. At any given time, Giant has about two dozen pairs of Specialty's speakers on hand. Specialty holds title to the speakers until they are sold. However, as far as any third party can discern, the speakers are part of Giant's own inventory. There is no indication that Specialty is the owner of the speakers. Moreover, Giant does not generally engage in the sale of goods for others and is not known by its creditors to do so.

ANALYSIS: Giant is a merchant who deals in goods of this kind, Giant is not generally known by its creditors to be substantially engaged in the business of selling goods of others, the value of the goods is at least $1,000 per delivery since each speaker is priced at $2,000, and the goods are not consumer goods since they are inventory here.

CONCLUSION: This is an Article 9 consignment, so Specialty (consignor) is treated as a purchase money secured party with a securety interest in the speakers that are in Giant's inventory.

CHAPTER 16: DEFAULT AND ENFORCEMENT

A. Overview

> **Exam Tip 34:** Sometimes default and enforcement issues appear as a separate question after you've resolved a priority dispute. However, don't discuss perfection or priority if those are not at issue in a default and enforcement question.

- Attachment is the pre-requisite to repossession rights or rights to enforce a security interest.

B. Default

- Default is not defined in Article 9.
- Refer to the security agreement and applicable contract law to determine what constitutes a default.

Example 70: Failure to keep the collateral ________________________ will often qualify as an "event of default" in a security agreement.

C. Enforcement Rights in General

- Article 9 enforcement rights are triggered by default.

- These rights are ________________________ and may be exercised ________________________.
- The secured party can:
  - Seek ________________________ of tangible collateral and either sell or retain it in satisfaction of the obligation owed.
  - Abandon its Article 9 rights and instead obtain a ________________________ against the debtor or obligor on the obligation.
  - Pursue other courses of action to which the debtor and secured party have ________________________.

D. Repossession of Goods and Other Tangible Collateral

- Once there has been a default, the secured party can ________________________ the collateral in one of **two** ways:
  1. By using the ________________________ process (e.g. by filing a replevin action); or
  2. By using ________________________repossession.
- When using self-help repossession, the secured party cannot ________________________.

BREACH OF THE PEACE		
Examples that breach of the peace	**Examples that DO NOT breach of the peace**	**Circuit split (Whether repossession in the face of an oral protest breaches the peace)**
✓The secured party brings an officer to the repossession, and the officer is not there pursuant to judicial authorization	✗ The repossession agent ________________________ on land	Some courts hold that oral protest does breach the peace ("Don't take it!")
✓The repossession agent breaks into the debtor's ________________________, or commits criminal act	✗ The repossession occurs without a ________________________ (even at night)	Others hold it does not breach the peace absent the threat of violence
✓Some physical confrontations		
✓Some deception or trickery		

- **Repossession of Large Equipment:** Equipment that is hard to repossess can be rendered ________________________ in lieu of repossession (and then can be sold on sight).
- After repossession, the secured party can either ________________________ of the collateral in an Article 9 disposition sale or can ________________________ the collateral in satisfaction of all or part of the obligation.

E. Disposition of Collateral

1. Commercially Reasonable Standard

- Once a secured party takes possession of the collateral after default, that party may sell, lease, license, or otherwise dispose of the collateral, so long as everything about the disposition is **commercially reasonable**.
- A disposition is commercially reasonable as a matter of law if the collateral is:
  - Sold in the usual manner in a recognized market;
  - Sold at the ____ in that market; or
  - Otherwise in conformity with the reasonable commercial practices among dealers in that type of collateral.

> **Exam Tip 35:** Think of these elements as "safe harbors." A disposition that does not fit within any of these safe harbors might still be commercially reasonable. It is a question of fact.

- ___________________________ alone is not determinative of whether a sale is commercially reasonable or unreasonable. A ___________________________________ price however, will trigger increased scrutiny by a court.

2. Details of Disposition

- A disposition sale can be either ___________________________ or ___________________________.
- A secured party can buy the collateral at a public sale but not at a private sale unless the price of the collateral is ___________________________ (e.g., by the New York Stock Exchange) or subject to widely distributed standard price quotes.
- No specific timetables for the sale but every aspect of the timing must be ____ under the circumstances.

3. Notice

- A secured party has to send authenticated notice of the disposition to a ____.
- **Exceptions:** Notice is not required if:
  - The collateral is perishable or threatens to decline speedily in value;
  - The collateral is sold on a recognized market (e.g., NYSE); or
  - Notice is waived after default.
- **Who** must be given notice?
  - ___________________________
  - ___________________________ obligors (*i.e.*, co-signers or guarantors)
  - Other secured parties, and

        - Anyone else from whom the secured party has received notice of a claim or interest in the collateral.
    - **When** must notice be given?
        - Everything about the notice must be ______________________________ (including the timing).
        - Must give the notified party time to act.
        - "Safe harbor" for __________________ transactions: Reasonable if sent at least __________________ days before the disposition sale.
    - **What** must the notice include?
        - The secured party and the debtor's __________________;
        - A description of the __________________;
        - How, when, and where the collateral is to be disposed of; and
        - A statement that the debtor is ______________________________ for the unpaid indebtedness.
            - Additional contents for consumer goods transactions:
                - Describe any liability for the **deficiency**; and
                - __________________________ that the debtor can call to obtain additional information, including the amount they would need to pay to __________________ the collateral.

F. Proceeds of a Disposition

- Cash proceeds of a disposition are distributed in the following order:
    1. Reasonable __________________ for collection and enforcement;
    2. Pay the __________________ to the foreclosing secured party;
    3. Pay __________________ security interests, provided the subordinated party makes a formal demand prior to distribution of the proceeds;
    4. Any __________________ will be returned to the __________________
- Senior (superior) security interests survive the sale (i.e., whoever purchases the collateral takes it subject to the senior, or superior, security interests.)
- If there is not enough money to satisfy the debt, the secured party can seek a deficiency judgment against the __________________ for the remaining amount.

Example 71: *Assume Angela, Bob, and Charles each have perfected security interests in Dwight's collateral (ranking in priority as listed), and Dwight is in default on all obligations. If Bob repossesses and sells the collateral for $10,000, the cash is allocated as follows:*

1. __________________ reasonable expenses in conducting the foreclosure.

2. ________________________ debt

3. ________________________ debt (assuming he has made a demand for a share of the proceeds)

4. Any leftover cash goes back to ________________________; if the proceeds are insufficient to satisfy Bob and Charles's obligations, then ________________________ is liable for the deficiency.

________________________ does not get anything from the sale. Her senior or superior security interest ________________________ in the collateral in the hands of whoever bought, leased, or licensed it in the foreclosure sale.

CHAPTER 17: OTHER METHODS OF ENFORCEMENT AND REMEDIES FOR CREDITOR MISBEHAVIOR

A. Acceptance of Collateral ("Strict Foreclosure")

- A secured party may accept the collateral in ________________________ or ________________________ satisfaction of the debt, so long as certain conditions are met.

1. Full Satisfaction

- The debtor must ________________________ after default to the acceptance in an authenticated record
- Acceptance by ________________________ is permitted if the debtor does not object to the secured party's proposal to accept the collateral within ________________________ days after the proposal is sent.
- Additional requirements for **consumer goods transactions**:
  - The secured party can only accept the collateral in ________________________ satisfaction of the obligation.
  - ________________________% **Rule**: If the goods are consumer goods and the debtor has paid back ________________________% or more of the debt or the value of the collateral, then the goods must be ________________________. Acceptance is not permitted. (A debtor can ________________________ this rule after default in an authenticated record.)

2. Partial Satisfaction

- The debtor must consent after default to the acceptance in an authenticated record.
- Consent by silence is ________________________ permitted.
- Remember, acceptance in partial satisfaction will not work in ________________________.

B. Redemption Rights

- A debtor, secondary obligor, or other secured party may redeem the collateral by paying the ______________________ secured obligation and expenses (including attorney's fees) incurred in repossessing and preparing the collateral for sale.
- Redemption must occur before the secured party has ______________________ the collateral or ______________________ the collateral in satisfaction of the debt.
- The debtor cannot waive her right to redemption before default.

C. Special Enforcement Rules

1. Fixtures

- o If a secured party has priority, the secured party may ______________________ the fixture from the real estate.
- o Secured party will be liable for the cost of repairing ______________________ to the real estate, but not ______________________ resulting from the removal.

2. Accessions

- o The secured party with priority in the accession is allowed to ______________________ the accession from the other goods.

3. Rights to Payment (e.g., accounts, chattel paper, instruments, payment intangibles)

- o The secured party can step into the ______________________ to collect amounts owing to the debtor by third parties (called "account debtors").
  - ▪ Once the account debtor receives ______________________ from the secured party, she cannot discharge her debt by paying the debtor directly (must pay secured party).
  - ▪ The account debtor may raise defenses she had against the debtor against the secured party.
- o If the underlying transaction is a sale of accounts, chattel paper, promissory notes or payment intangibles (treated as Article 9 security interests) then the rules regarding ______________________ do not apply.

D. Remedies for Secured Party's Failure to Comply

- **Injunctive relief:** If the failure to comply is ongoing, the debtor or another secured party can ask the court to ______________________ the improper enforcement activity.
- **Actual damages:** A debtor or secured party can be compensated for ______________________ resulting from the secured party's violations.
- **Statutory Damages:** Minimum damages in ______________________ transactions for specific violations of Article 9.

- When a secured party has violated its obligations under Article 9, the Code may also prevent the Secured party from claiming a ________________________.
    - **Commercial Transactions**: the ____ rule: If the secured party did not sell the goods in a ____ manner, they are not entitled to a deficiency, unless they can prove a sale that complied with Article 9 would have created a ______________________.
    - **Consumer Transactions:** some courts follow an ________________________ rule, which states that a secured party who fails to comply with Article 9 cannot recover a deficiency.
- A secured party that improperly repossesses collateral may be liable for the tort of ________________________.

GOOD LUCK!

[END OF HANDOUT]

Themis
Bar Review

Trusts

Themis
Bar Review

TRUSTS

PROFESSOR ZACHARY A. KRAMER

ARIZONA STATE UNIVERSITY – SANDRA DAY O'CONNOR COLLEGE OF LAW

CHAPTER 1: INTRODUCTION

A. What's What?

- A trust is a ______________________________ device
- Key feature: A ______________________________ transfer
- Trustee owns ______________________________ title and manages the property for the benefit of the ______________________________.

> ***Example 1:*** *T-Bone Taylor transfers his stock portfolio to Hank Mardukas in trust for the benefit of T-Bone's children, Bonnie and Clyde. This is a bifurcated transfer. Hank, as trustee, owns the ______________________________ interest. Bonnie and Clyde, as beneficiaries, own the ______________________________ interest.*

- ______________________________: Original trust property and any increase in value
- ______________________________: Money invested by the trust
- Revocable trust can be revoked at any time during ______________________________ life
- Person who ______________________________ the trust is the settlor
- Irrevocable trust cannot be revoked
  - Under the majority rule, a trust is presumed to be ______________________________, unless the trust documents say otherwise.
  - The Uniform Trust Code (UTC) reverses this presumption; a trust is ______________________________ unless the trust documents say otherwise.

> **Exam Tip 1:** On the MEE, mention both rules if you get this sort of question.

- **Mandatory Trust:** Trustee ______________________________ make distributions from the trust
- ______________________________ **Trust:** Trustee may make distributions in her discretion
- **Remedial Trust:** Is a ______________________________ created by operation of law
  - Often called a "passive trust"
  - Trustee only has one power – to transfer the property
- **Rule Against Perpetuities:**
  - Applies to trusts

- o **"Wait and see" approach:** Wait until an interest vests to determine its validity

B. Who's Who?

- Person who creates trust is the ______________________________.
- Person who manages the trust is the ______________________________.
    - o Holds ______________________________ title to the property
    - o Has power to manage the property (i.e., sell, transfer, invest)
    - o Can be an individual, a bank, or a trust company
    - o A trust ______________________________ fail for lack of trustee
- The person who receives the benefit of the trust is the ______________________________.
    - o Holds ______________________________ title to the property
    - o Has power to ______________________________ the trust instrument
    - o Can have multiple classes of beneficiaries

Example 2: *Husband devises property in trust "to Wife for life, then to Husband's children." Wife is both trustee and income beneficiary. This is valid, because Wife is not the sole beneficiary. Husband's children have a remainder interest. They have standing to bring an action against Wife to enforce her duties as trustee.*

Example 3: *T-Bone Taylor wants to ensure that after his death, his beloved Cockapoo, Robert Downey, Jr., Jr., is able to continue his luxurious lifestyle. He creates a trust naming Hank Mardukas as trustee for the benefit of Robert Downey, Jr., Jr.*

What type of trust is this? ______________________________.

Is it valid? In a majority of jurisdictions, ______________________________.

Example 4: *T-Bone Taylor transfers a substantial sum to his friend, Hank Mardukas, in trust for the benefit of Hank's children. The terms of the trust say that Hank is to give each child $10,000 each year to pay for school until he graduates from college.*

What kind of trust is this? ______________________________.

Who is settlor? ______________________________.

Who is trustee? ______________________________.

Who are beneficiaries? ______________________________.

CHAPTER 2: EXPRESS TRUSTS

A. Express Trusts

- Owner ______________________________ indicates the intent to create a trust.
- May be private or ______________________________.

B. Private Express Trusts

1. Intent

- "Trust words" create a presumption of a trust (e.g., "in trust," "for the benefit of")
- Oral trusts are ______________________________.

  Example 5: *In front of his entire family, T-Bone Taylor declares, "I am giving my savings to my wife, Charlene, in trust, for the benefit of my best friend, Hank Mardukas." This is enough to create a trust. No writing is necessary.*

- **Exceptions**: When trust must be in writing:
  - Statute of Frauds (i.e., conveying real property)
  - A ______________________________ (i.e., trust created in a will)
    - Property is not transferred by the will, but rather by the trust
    - Trust must be in existence at the time the will was made or created simultaneously
    - Trust avoids probate
  - **Minority**: A valid trust ______________________________ be in writing
- Watch out for:
  - ______________________________ language
    - Language that expresses donor's ______________________________ or ______________________________ that the donee use property in a certain way
    - Does **not** create a trust

    Example 6: *T-Bone transfers $10,000 to Hank Mardukas, "My wish being that he will use the money to support his children's educational pursuits." This likely does not create a trust.*

  - Ambiguous language
  - Distinguishing between a trust and a gift

    Exam Tip 2: Intent is tested frequently. Ask yourself, "Who has the beneficial interest?" That should distinguish it from a gift. A gift is a revocable, outright gift. A trust involves a bifurcated transfer – the settlor gives the property to one person for the benefit of another.

2. Trust Res

- There is no trust unless there is some piece of property in it.

- ______________________________ **trust:** A trust without property
- **Exception:** ______________________________ trust
  - Trust terms must be in writing at time will is executed
  - Property need not be in trust at time of will

> **Exam Tip 3:** Make sure you understand the difference between trusts and debts. A debt is an obligation to pay a sum of money. The source you use to pay the money usually does not matter. A trust necessarily involves a segregated source of funds.

3. Trust Purpose

- Valid if not ______________________________ or contrary to public policy

4. Beneficiaries

- There must be an ______________________________ beneficiary
  - Either a specific person or some ______________________________ to determine who the person is

    Example 7: *T-Bone transfers $10,000 to Hank "in trust for the benefit of the members of the Hilly Flats High School marching band." Are there beneficiaries here? ______________________________. Who are they? ______________________________.*

- **Exceptions:**
  - ______________________________ children

    Example 8: *S conveys property to T in trust to benefit A for life, then to A's children. At the time of the trust, A does not have children. First class of beneficiaries: ______________________________. Second class of beneficiaries: ______________________________. This is a valid trust. We do not know who A's children are. However, by the time the life estate ends, we will know who, if anyone, is in the class.*

  - Class gifts
    - The class must be definite.
  - Charitable trusts

C. Charitable Trusts

- Must have a charitable ______________________________, such as:
  - Relief of ______________________________;
  - Advancement of education or religion;
  - Promotion of good health;
  - Governmental or municipal purposes;

- Other purposes benefitting the ______________________________ at large or a particular ______________________________ of the community.

  Example 9: *Richie Rich conveys his estate to the Cure Tay-Sachs Foundation in trust, to care for those suffering from Tay-Sachs disease. This disease is very rare, and strikes very few people. Even though only a small number of people are affected, the trust is still charitable in nature.*

  - Modern trend: To validate a charitable trust

- **Rule Against Perpetuities:** ______________________________ apply!
- ***Cy pres* doctrine:**
  - Court can modify a trust if the trust's charitable purpose is no longer ______________________________.

    Example 10: *Richie Rich conveys to the Hilly Flats School of the Arts in trust to support the school's pottery program. Because of low enrollment, the school replaces the pottery program with a graphic design program. Using* cy pres*, the court can modify Richie Rich's trust to support the new graphic design program.*

  - To modify, you need a ______________________________ charitable purpose
  - Goal is to make the new purpose as close as possible to the ______________________________ purpose
  - RST and Uniform Trust Code presume a general charitable purpose
  - If there is no general charitable purpose, the property goes to a ______________________________ trust

    Example 11: *The settlor created a trust and directed that the remainder go to a charity to end homelessness. This is a charitable purpose. Thirty years later, the charity has closed its doors, and the question is whether the remainder will go to the settlor's estate, or if the probate court can use* cy pres *to substitute a different charity. The settlor did have general charitable purpose, so the court could modify the trust purpose. What facts would you need to suggest that there is no general charitable purpose? We would need the settlor to say that the money is* ***only for a specific purpose****.*

- **Standing:**
  - Attorney General's office has standing to enforce the terms of a charitable trust
  - Uniform Trust Code: Settlor also has standing

D. Creation of Express Trusts

1. Inter vivos transfer: Created during ______________________________ in one of the following ways:

a. **Declaration of trust**

- Settlor declares herself holder of the property in trust for beneficiaries;
- Settlor also serves as ______________________________.

b. **Deed of trust**

- Settlor conveys property to a trustee;
- Settlor is not the ______________________________.

2. **Testamentary transfer:** Created according to the terms of a will

CHAPTER 3: REMEDIAL TRUSTS; CREDITORS' RIGHTS

A. In General

- Not driven by intent
- It is an ______________________________ remedy created by operation of law
- **Key characteristic:** It is ______________________________ in nature
    - Trustee's only duty is to convey the property back to the settlor
- **Two Types:**
    - ______________________________ trust
    - ______________________________ trust

B. Resulting Trusts

- Used when a trust ______________________________;
- Trustee must return property to ______________________________ or ______________________________ estate;

> ***Example 12:*** *Oliver's will passes property in trust to Tony to benefit "Archer for life, then to Archer's children." Archer dies without having children. What happens to the trust property? The trust ______________________________, and a ______________________________ trust is created. Tony's sole duty is to transfer the property to Oliver's estate. Why to Oliver's estate and not Oliver? Because Oliver created the trust by will.*

- Goal is to avoid ______________________________.

1. **Purchase-Money Resulting Trust:**
    - Person One buys the property, but title is taken in Person Two's name
    - If Person Two is not the ______________________________ of Person One's bounty (i.e., not a close friend or relative), a court will create a purchase-money resulting trust

2. Avoiding a Resulting Trust:

Create a ______________________________ clause

> ***Example 13:*** *Oliver's will provides that if Archer dies without children, the remaining trust property is to go to Henry or Henry's heirs. This is a gift-over clause.*

C. Constructive Trusts

- A remedy used to prevent unjust enrichment if a ______________________________ takes advantage of the settlor
- **Key characteristic:** ______________________________ conduct (e.g., fraud, undue influence)
- Wrongful conduct must be conduct ______________________________ the settlor that caused the settlor to create the trust

> ***Example 14:*** *Darcy has been ill for a number of years. She suffers from depression and occasional dementia. Her lawyer convinces her to disinherit her beloved children, who are far away and unable to visit often, and give her entire estate to him. This is ______________________________. The children successfully challenge the will on this ground, and the will is invalidated. As a remedy, the court will impose a constructive trust, making the lawyer a constructive trustee whose job is to the hold the property for the benefit of Darcy's estate and convey it to her estate.*

- Look for:
    - Fraud;
    - Duress;
    - Undue influence;
    - Breach of a duty;
    - Detrimental reliance by a third party.

> ***Example 15:*** *Slayer cases. A killer is barred from benefiting from the victim's estate. The remedy is to create a constructive trust.*

D. Types of Trust Distributions

1. Mandatory Trusts

Trustee has ______________________________ discretion as to whether he will make a distribution

- "Trustee to pay all income"
- "Trustee to distribute $1,000 every month"
- "Trustee to distribute law school tuition for the next three years"

2. Discretionary Trusts

Trustee has ______________________________ discretion as to whether she will make a distribution

- "Trustee to make payments for the health and care of beneficiary"
- "Trustee to make payments, in her discretion, for the education of the beneficiary"

3. Support Trusts

Trustee makes distributions to ______________________________ the beneficiary

- "Trustee to make distributions for the support of the beneficiary"

E. Alienability of Trust Property and Creditors' Ability to Reach

Two basic rules:

- **Rule 1:** A beneficiary's equitable interest in trust property is ______________________________.
    - **Exception:** Trust instrument or a statute limits this right
    - Creditors can reach the beneficiary's ______________________________ interest

> ***Example 16:*** *T-Bone devises his estate to Hank Mardukas, in trust, to make a mandatory payment every month to T-Bone's daughter, Bonnie. Bonnie can transfer this interest. When can Bonnie's creditors reach her interest in the trust? As ______________________________ are made to her.*

- **Rule 2:** A creditor ______________________________ reach trust principal or income until such amounts become ______________________________ to the beneficiary or the beneficiary can ______________________________ it.

> ***Example 17:*** *T-Bone executed a deed of trust, conveying his savings to Hank in trust for the benefit of T-Bone's daughter, Bonnie. The trust gives Hank full discretion in deciding when to make payments to Bonnie. Thus, Bonnie's creditors cannot reach the trust payment until, at the earliest, Hank makes a payment.*

F. Asset Protection Trusts

Goal is to shield beneficiaries from ______________________________ claims

1. Support Trust

- Creditors cannot reach trust property, because the beneficiary cannot ______________________________ payment.
- Creditors can reach when the trustee makes a ______________________________.

2. **Discretionary Trust**

- Creditors cannot reach trust property, because the beneficiary cannot ______________________________ payment.
- Creditors can reach when the trustee makes a ______________________________.

3. **Spendthrift Trust**

- Trust expressly restricts the beneficiary's power to ______________________________ her interest.
- Creditors cannot reach trust property until the trustee makes a payment.

  Example 18: *T-Bone's son, Clyde, loves to play the ponies. He has incurred a significant amount of personal debt. Concerned that Clyde will never be financially secure, T-Bone inserts a spendthrift clause into the trust he created for Clyde's benefit. As a result, Clyde cannot alienate his interest in the trust property. Additionally, Clyde's creditors cannot reach the trust property, until the trustee makes payments to Clyde.*

- **Exceptions:** The following creditors can reach trust property:
  - Spousal or child support;
  - Those providing ______________________________ to the beneficiary;
  - Holders of federal or state tax liens.

CHAPTER 4: TRUST MODIFICATION AND TERMINATION

A. Termination

- **Expiration:** An express trust can ______________________________ at the end of a stated term.

  Example 19: *T-Bone creates a trust for the benefit of his son, Clyde, which terminates when Clyde turns 25. When Clyde turns 25, the trust automatically terminates.*

- **Material purpose:** If the trust has been ______________________________, the trust automatically terminates.

  Example 20: *T-Bone creates a trust to pay for his daughter Rachel's medical school. After Rachel finishes medical school, the trust terminates.*

- **Unfulfilled material purpose doctrine:** *Claflin* Doctrine
  - Say the settlor is no longer alive. The beneficiary wants to terminate the trust prematurely and the trustee ______________________________ termination.

Example 21: *T-Bone creates a trust for the benefit of his son, Clyde, which terminates when Clyde turns 25. On Clyde's 22nd birthday, he notifies Hank that he wants to terminate the trust. Hank opposes the termination. T-Bone is no longer alive.*

- **Rule:** A trustee can block premature termination if the trust is still serving some ______________________________.
  - Discretionary trusts;
  - ______________________________ trusts;
  - Age-dependent trusts (e.g., example immediately above).

  Example 22: *S leaves her estate in trust, "to A for life, then to B." B predeceases A. B leaves A as her sole heir. In this situation, the material purpose of the trust cannot be fulfilled. The material purpose is to provide for B in the future. If A moves to prematurely terminate, a court is likely to allow it.*

- **Settlor's power:**
  - Can unilaterally terminate, if ______________________________ reserved the right to terminate in the trust documents
  - If settlor did not expressly provide for termination, the settlor can still terminate if ______________________________ and all ______________________________ consent

B. Modification

- If settlor is alive:
  - Can ______________________________ modify, if expressly reserved the right in trust document
  - If did not reserve this right, ______________________________ beneficiaries must consent and proposed change must not interfere with primary ______________________________ of the trust
- If settlor is dead, can generally modify in one of two situations:
  - ______________________________ beneficiaries agree to a modification consistent with material purpose of trust; or
  - An unforeseen event has ______________________________ purpose of trust (i.e., equitable deviation)

  Example 23: *Saul Bellowstein created a trust for the benefit of his grandchildren. Due to substantial changes in the tax code since the trust was created, the grandchildren all agree that the terms of the trust should be changed to lower the grandchildren's tax burden. A court would likely approve this modification because it is consistent with the purpose of the trust.*

__Example 24:__ Saul Bellowstein created a trust for the benefit of his daughter. The trust provided that Saul's house was not to be sold until his daughter died. When the trust was created, the neighborhood was lovely. The purpose of this trust is to provide her a place to live. After the local plant closed, the neighborhood crumbled, and it is no longer a safe place to live. The daughter wants to sell the home and move to a new neighborhood. She will argue that the purpose of the trust (to provide her with a safe, decent place to live) is frustrated.

Exam Tip 4: If you see a fact pattern involving unforeseen events on the exam, be very clear about what the purpose of the trust is.

Note 1: A trustee ______________________________ terminate or modify a trust through unilateral action.

C. Removal of a Trustee

- Generally a remedy when the trustee has breached a ______________________________ duty or ______________________________ mismanaged the property
- Removal likely to be granted:
    - Trustee became ______________________________ of performing duties (e.g., in jail, incapacitated, seriously ill);
    - Material breach of a duty;
    - Trustee develops a conflict of ______________________________;
    - A serious conflict between a trustee and a beneficiary;
    - The trust persistently performs poorly as a result of the trustee's action or inaction.
- Trustee can resign with ______________________________, if settlor is alive, to co-trustees and beneficiaries

CHAPTER 5: PRINCIPAL AND INCOME; TRUST ADMINISTRATION

A. Principal vs. Income

- How should the trustee balance the interests of multiple beneficiaries when their interests are different?

__Example 25:__ Lifetime beneficiaries want a quick return, while remainder holders want greater growth over time.

- Consider an example:

__Example 26:__ Saul Bellowstein conveys a sum of money in trust to Tanya for the benefit of Larry during Larry's life, then to Rachel. The trustee's job is to allocate assets received between principal and income.

1. **Old Rule:** Classified income and principal based on nature of money

   - The life beneficiary was entitled to ______________________________.

     Example 27: *Who is entitled to the income of the trust in the example above?*

     ______________________________.

   - The holder of the remainder interest was entitled to the

     ______________________________.

     Example 28: *In the example above, who is entitled to the principal?*

     ______________________________.

2. **Modern Approach:** Less rigid, more wholistic

   - Governed by the Uniform Principal and Income Act (UPAIA)
   - Trustee is to focus on the ______________________________ of the trust portfolio
   - Trustee can re-characterize and reallocate items as necessary to fulfill trust purposes
   - Allocations must be ______________________________.
   - Factors that trustee must balance:
     - ______________________________ of settlor and language of trust instrument;
     - ______________________________, ______________________________, and purpose of trust;
     - Identities and circumstances of ______________________________;
     - Anticipated effect of ______________________________ conditions;
     - Anticipated ______________________________ consequences.

B. Trustee's Powers

- Always look to the trust document first.
  - If the trust documents are silent, then refer to statutory and common-law principles.
- Modern trend is to grant the trustee all those powers ______________________________ to act as a reasonably ______________________________ person, including powers to:
  - Sell or transfer;
  - Lease trust property;
  - Pay taxes;
  - Sever or consolidate trust property.
- Trustee owns legal title and can act as owner.

C. Trustee's Duties

1. **In General**

   - A trustee has two primary duties: a duty of ______________________________ and a duty of ______________________________.

- Designed to ensure the trustee acts in the best interests of the beneficiaries
- ______________________________ beneficiary has standing to enforce these duties.
- **Duty of Loyalty:**
  - **Objective standard:** Did the trustee act ______________________________?
- **Duty of Care:**
  - **Subjective standard:** Did the trustee act **in good faith**?

2. Duty of Loyalty

- Self-dealing is a breach of the duty of loyalty

  Example 29: *T-Bone Taylor serves as the trustee of a trust. T-Bone sells stock from the trust to himself for fair market value. Is he liable for breach of his duty of loyalty?* ______________________________.

  - Governed by the ______________________________ rule
    - If you have established self-dealing, the court does NOT inquire into the reasonableness or good faith
  - Always a per se breach of duty of loyalty

  Example 30: *T-Bone served as the trustee of a trust created by his best friend, Hank Mardukas. T-Bone borrowed money from the trust for his wife to take a wine appreciation class. T-Bone paid the money back plus interest the following week. Under no further inquiry, we do not inquire whether the trust was harmed. This is a per se breach of T-Bone's duty of loyalty.*

  - Even if the trust documents ______________________________ self-dealing, the transaction must still be ______________________________ and fair for the trustee to avoid liability.
- Conflicts of ______________________________ are non-self-dealing transactions that may still breach the duty of loyalty.
  - Assessed under ______________________________ and ______________________________ test

  Example 31: *Mr. T is the trustee for a trust that owns a valuable instrument collection. The trust needs to sell some of its instruments. It contracts with Music Auction Store to sell them. Although Mr. T is not formally affiliated with Music Auction Store, he builds one-of-a-kind guitars, and the store agrees to sell his guitars as well. He is not doing business with himself, but he is in a conflict with himself, because the trust has done a deal with the store, and now the store is going to do a deal with Mr. T. It seems like the store is doing business with the trust to get Mr. T's business.*

3. Duty of Care

> **Editorial Note 1:** This category of trustee duties may also be referred to as duties of prudence.

- The care that a person of ordinary ______________________________ would practice in the care of his own estate
- A trustee should treat the trust property as his own.
- **Special skills:**
  - Trustee must use those special skills
  - Trustee with special skills is held to a ______________________________ standard

a. Delegation

- **Common law:** Trustee ______________________________ delegate authority
- **Modern law:** ______________________________ delegation
  - If it would be unreasonable for settlor to expect trustee to undertake such functions (e.g., investment decisions)
  - Trustee then has a duty to oversee.

b. Investments

- **Old Rule:**
  - Trustees were limited to specific ______________________________ of acceptable investments.
  - A trustee breached by making investments outside the list.
- **Modern Rule:** Prudent Investor Rule
  - A trustee has discretion to invest and manage property as would a prudent investor.
  - Trustee is expected to ______________________________ assets to spread the risk of ______________________________.
  - **Portfolio Approach:** Measure the success of the portfolio ______________________________.

c. Duty of impartiality

- Trustee has a duty to ______________________________ the competing interests of present and future beneficiaries.
- **Old Rule:**
  - Life beneficiary entitled to ______________________________;
  - Remainder holder entitled to ______________________________.

- **Modern Rule:**
  - The allocation between income and principal must be _______________________________ to treat life tenants and remainder holders _______________________________.

Example 32: T-Bone Taylor is the trustee of a trust benefitting Hank Mardukas for life, with the remainder to Bonnie and Clyde. Because of the nature of the trust property, the principal is increasing steadily, but the property is not producing substantial income. The duty of impartiality requires T-Bone to balance Hank's interests with the interests of Bonnie and Clyde.

  - Look at the total return.
  - Trustee can reallocate as long as it is fulfilling the trust purpose.
  - Must be reasonable

D. Administrative Duties

1. Duty to Inform Beneficiaries

- About the nature of the trust property

2. Duty to Account

- For _______________________________ taken on behalf of the trust
- Report on the health of the trust portfolio

CHAPTER 6: FUTURE INTERESTS

A. In General

Key question: Who has the right to possess property?

- Possessory estate holder has right to _______________________________ possession.
- Future interest holder has a present right to _______________________________ possession.

A. Fee Simple Interests

1. Fee Simple Absolute

- Largest estate because it can last _______________________________;

Example 33: O devises property to A and his heirs. The modern presumption is that the grantor conveys as much as she has unless she says otherwise.

- No future interest

2. Defeasible Fee

A fee simple that can be cut short (could go on forever, but might not)

a. Fee simple determinable

- A fee simple for a ______________________________ period

  Example 34: *"O to A and heirs ___________________________ the land is used as a farm." What future interest does O have? A possibility of ___________________________.*

- "So long as," "while," "during which time" are durational terms.
- Possibility of reverter is held by ______________________________.

b. Fee simple subject to condition subsequent

- A fee simple that is terminated upon the happening of an ______________________________ or ______________________________;

  Example 35: *"O to A. But if liquor is ever sold on the premises, O can enter and retake." O has a right of ___________________________.*

- "But if" or "on the condition that" denote a condition subsequent.
- Right of entry must be elected (go to court and evict); does not happen automatically

3. Life Estate

- A present possessory estate that ends at the ______________________________ of the life tenant

  Example 36: *S creates a trust "for the benefit of A for life, then to B." A has an equitable life interest. B has a vested remainder; S has nothing.*

- **Reversion:**
  - A future interest held by the grantor following a life estate
  - Capable of becoming possessory at the natural termination of the grantee's life estate

  Example 37: *"O to A for life." A has a life estate. O has retained the reversion in fee simple absolute. When does O's interest become possessory? When A dies.*

B. Future Interests of Grantor

- Possibility of ______________________________ (associated with fee simple ______________________________)
- Right of ______________________________ (associated with fee simple subject to condition subsequent)
- Reversion (associated with ______________________________)

C. Future Interests of Transferees

1. Remainder

- A future interest capable of becoming possessory at the _______________________ termination of the prior estate
- Must be held by a transferee

a. Vested

Remainderman is _______________________ and there is not a condition _______________________.

Example 38: *"O to A for life, then to B." A has a life estate. B has a remainder. It is capable of becoming possessory the moment A dies.*

Is it vested? _______________________.

Is there a condition precedent? _______________________.

If B dies before A, it goes to _______________________ estate.

b. Vested as a class gift (vested subject to open)

- There is a class of people who are supposed to take;
- At least one member of the class has _______________________.

Example 39: *"O to A for life, then to O's children." O has one child, B. Gift is vested as to B (because B is ascertained and vested). It is open as to any later-born children. O is alive, and can have more children. Every time a child is born to O, that child will partially divest B.*

- **Key question:** When does the class close? _______________________.

c. Contingent

The taker is either _______________________ or is subject to a condition precedent.

Example 40: *"O to A for life, then to B, if B graduates from law school." B has a remainder. This is a contingent remainder, because there is a condition precedent.*

What is the condition precedent? B must _______________________.

In this situation, what does O have? A _______________________.

Example 41: *"O to A for life, then to B's first child." B has no kids. This is a _______________________ remainder, because the future interest holder is not ascertained.*

In this situation, what does O have? A _______________________.

2. Executory Interest

- An interest held by the grantee that will ______________________________ a prior vested interest (cuts short the prior interest)
- **Springing:** Divests the ______________________________.

  Example 42: *"O to A for life, then to B, if B gives A a proper funeral." This cannot be possessory the moment A dies, because B must give A a proper funeral. Because it is not possessory the moment A dies, it cannot be a remainder. When A dies, the property reverts back to O. O holds the property subject to B's executory interest. The moment B gives A a proper funeral, the property will "spring" from O to B.*

  Example 43: *"O to A in one year." A's springing executory interest will vest in one year. In one year, A will divest O.*

- **Shifting:** Divests a prior ______________________________.

  Example 44: *"O to A for life, then to B and her heirs, but if B goes to law school, then to C." Because C has a shifting executory interest, if B goes to law school, C will divest B. B's interest is a vested remainder in fee simple subject to C's executory interest.*

D. Class Gifts and Similar Terms

- Generally, a gift to a group of individuals with an automatic right of ______________________________.
  - On the death of a class member, that member's share is ______________________________ re-divided among the surviving class members.
  - **RST 3rd:** The share of a deceased class member goes to the class member's surviving ______________________________.

- **Prior MEE question:**
  - Facts: Testator creates a trust that says, "Trustee shall distribute support to Son for his life, then to my grandchildren, with the children of any deceased grandchild taking in their parent's place."
  - When does the future interest become possessory? When ______________________________.
  - What if the grandchild dies without issue before Son? Does the interest vest in the predeceasing grandchild's estate, or does it fail?
  - Two approaches:
    - **Minority Common Law:**
      - The survival of a child is ______________________________.
      - The deceased grandchild's estate takes the interest.

Editorial Note 2: Under the majority common law rule, the interest is shared among only those class members alive upon Son's death and the deceased's estate would take nothing.

- **Uniform Probate Code:**
  - Future interests under a trust are contingent on the beneficiary surviving until the ______________________________.

- Here, the distribution is when Son dies, and under the UPC, the grandchild takes nothing (the gift fails).

E. General Tips

- Who is entitled to possession now?
- Who has the future interest?
- When, if ever, will the future interest vest?

Example 45: *Saul Bellowstein executes a deed of trust conveying his estate "to Arnold in trust for Arnold's life, then to Saul's children, Bernie and Claudette."*

Who has the present possessory estate? ______________________________.

Who has the future interest? ______________________________ *have a vested remainder.*

When, if ever, will the future interest vest?

______________________________.

[END OF HANDOUT]

Themis
Bar Review

Wills and Decedents' Estates

Themis
Bar Review

WILLS

PROFESSOR ZACHARY A. KRAMER

ARIZONA STATE UNIVERSITY – SANDRA DAY O'CONNOR COLLEGE OF LAW

CHAPTER 1: TERMINOLOGY; INTESTACY—SPOUSES

A. What's What?

- **Decedent:** Someone who has ______________________________.
- **Will:** Legal document used to dispose of the decedent's property.
  - Testate—decedent dies ______________________________ a will
  - Intestate—decedent dies ______________________________ a will
- **Codicil:** A ______________________________ that either amends or revokes a decedent's will in whole or in part.
- **Probate:** Judicial process for administering and settling a decedent's estate.
- **Intestate Succession:** A ______________________________ estate plan, developed by the legislature, for distributing property when the decedent dies intestate.

B. Who's Who?

- **Heirs:** Individuals entitled to receive property by ______________________________ succession.
- (______________________________ people do not have heirs.)
- **Spouse:** Decedent's ______________________________ partner
- **Issue/Descendants:** Decedent's ______________________________ line (i.e., decedent's kids, their kids, etc.)
- **Ancestors:** Decedent's ______________________________ line (i.e., parents, grandparents, etc.)
- **Collaterals:** Decedent's relatives through an ______________________________ (i.e., siblings, cousins, aunts, uncles)

C. First Substantive Topic: Intestacy!

- A default estate plan developed by the legislature. The decedent's actual intent is ______________________________.
- Individuals entitled to take an intestate share are called the decedent's ______________________________.
- We are particularly interested in the decedent's ______________________________ and ______________________________.

- To take from a decedent, an individual must ______________________ the decedent.
    - **Special Case:** Simultaneous Death
    The Uniform Probate Code ("UPC") follows the Uniform Simultaneous Death Act ("USDA") to control the situation where the decedent and heir die at the same time. If there is insufficient evidence to determine who survived whom, the property will pass as though each had predeceased the other. Under the USDA, an heir must be proven by ______________________ evidence to have survived the decedent by ______________________ hours.

D. Spouse's Share

1. Who qualifies as a spouse?

- A legally-married ______________________
- Excludes: Unmarried ______________________

2. How do we calculate the surviving spouse's share?

- **Case 1:**
    - Decedent is survived by descendants who are also descendants of surviving spouse, and surviving spouse has no other descendants **[Spouse + shared descendants]**
    - Surviving spouse takes the ______________________ estate
- **Case 2:**
    - Decedent is survived by a parent but no descendant **[Spouse + parent]**
    - Surviving spouse takes $300,000 and ______________________% of the remainder of the estate
- **Case 3:**
    - Decedent is survived by descendants who are also descendants of the surviving spouse, and the spouse has other issue **[Spouse + shared descendants +spouse's kids]**
    - Surviving spouse takes $225,000 and ______________________ of the remaining property

    Example 1: *Decedent dies owning $375,000 in property. She is survived by her Wife and their daughter, as well as her Wife's son by an earlier marriage. What is Wife's intestate share?*

    *Answer: $*______________________.
- **Case 4:**
    - Decedent is survived by issue not related to the surviving spouse **[Spouse + non-spousal kids]**

- Surviving spouse takes $150,000 and ______________________________ of the remaining property

- **Case 5:**
  - Decedent is not survived by descendants or parents **[Just spouse]**
  - Surviving spouse takes the ______________________________ estate

3. Without Heirs

If the decedent dies without heirs, the property will ______________________________ to the state.

> ***Example 2:*** *Decedent dies owning $100,000 in property. A miserable person, Decedent has no family or friends, save for a cat that pities him and steals his food. Decedent's estate will escheat to the state.*

CHAPTER 2: INTESTACY—ISSUE

A. Who Qualifies as Issue?

- Decedent's lineal line (i.e., children, grandchildren, great-grandchildren, etc.)
- There must be a ______________________________ relationship.
- Adoptive children inherit from decedent just like biological children. The adoption works to sever the child's relationship with his/her natural parents.
  - Stepparent Adoption:
    - Creates a parent/child relationship between the child and stepparent for purposes of inheritance
    - Adoption ______________________________ prevent the adoptee from inheriting from the other genetic parent
  - Posthumously Born Children:
    - Child is ______________________________ before, but is born after, the death of the mother's husband
    - If the child is born within ______________________________ days of the husband's death, there is a ______________________________ presumption that the child is the husband's and the child will inherit from husband as if child was born before the husband died.

> **Note 1:** If child is born more than 280 days after death, the child will have to prove parentage in order to inherit from the husband.
>
> **Note 2:** The Uniform Parentage Act ("UPA") increases the rebuttable presumption period to ______________________________ days.

B. Calculating the Issue's Share

1. Per Stirpes

- Divides shares ________________________ according to a decedent's lineal line
- Divide shares into the total number of children who ________________________ or leave issue who survive, and then divide by representation
- Allows a surviving child to stand in the place of his deceased parent

Note 3: Issue take in equal shares regardless of whether anyone in that generation survived.

Example 3:

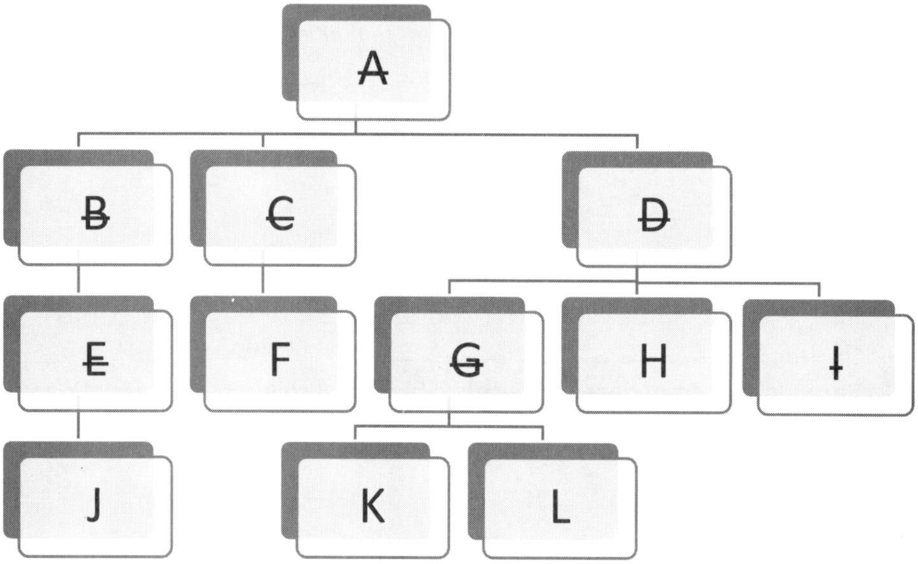

Step 1: *Because A had three children who left surviving issue (B, C, and D), we divide the estate into three shares. Each line takes 1/3.*

Step 2: *Divide by representation. B's 1/3 is passed to J. C's 1/3 is passed to F. D's 1/3 is split between G and H (I doesn't take because I is not survived by issue). K and L split G's 1/6 equally.*

Summary of Distribution to A's Issue:

J = 1/3

F = 1/3

H = 1/6

K and L = 1/12 each

Example 4:

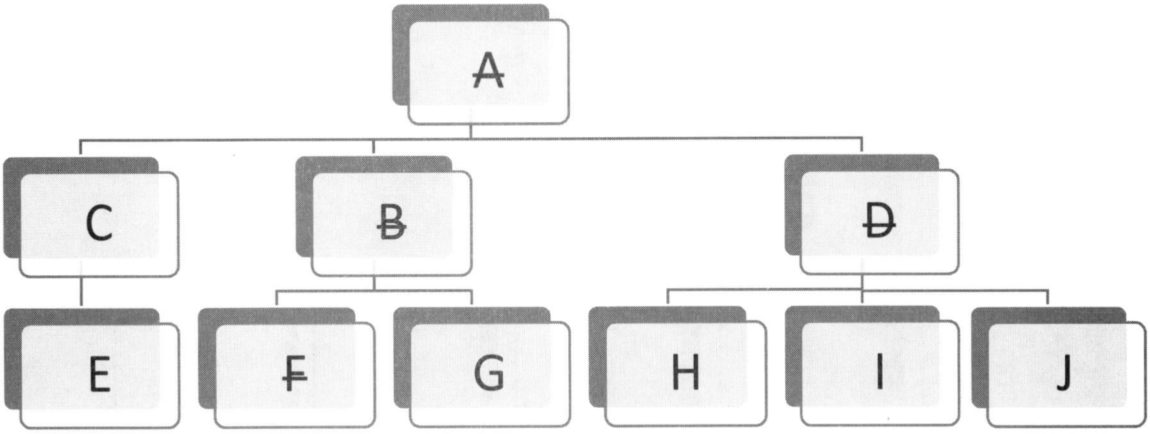

Step 1: *All of A's children who surviving issue. Even though B and D have predeceased, we must account for their shares. Thus, we divide the estate into equal 1/3 shares. C will take a 1/3 share. What about E? E takes nothing.*

Step 2: *We then drop B's and D's shares to their issue. Since B is survived by G, G will stand in B's shoes and take a 1/3 share. Since F has no kids, F takes nothing. Since D is survived by three children, they will divide D's share in equal parts, taking 1/9 each.*

Step 3: *Since each line is survived by living issue, each share is accounted for.*

Summary of Distribution to A's Issue

C = 1/3

G = 1/3

H, I, J = 1/9 each

2. Per Capita with Representation

- Divide the property equally at first generation where a member ______________________________ the decedent.
- If there are deceased members at that first generation, their shares drop down to their surviving issue at the next generation.
- If a deceased member of a generation is not survived by living issue, then that member does not take a share.

Example 5:

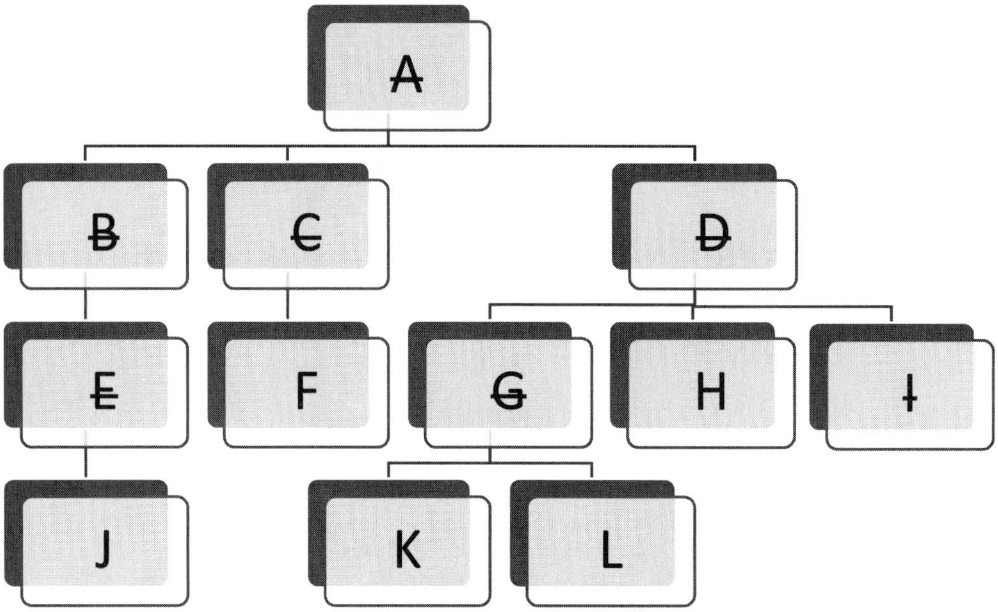

Step 1: *The first level with surviving members is E's generation (A's grandchildren). Although there are only two surviving members at that generation (F and H), we must also account for E's and G's shares, because they are survived by living issue. Thus, we divide the estate into four shares (I doesn't get a share because I is not survived by issue). F and H take 1/4 each.*

Step 2: *E's 1/4 drops down to J. G's 1/4 drops down and is split equally between K and L, giving them 1/8 each.*

Step 3: *As discussed above, I does not take a share because I is not survived by issue.*

Summary of Distribution to A's Issue

J = 1/4

F = 1/4

H = 1/4

K and L =1/8 each

3. Per Capita at each Generation (UPC!)

- Divide property into equal shares at the first generation where there is a ______________________________ member.
- Instead of passing a deceased member's share by representation, however, this method ______________________________ the remaining shares after each generation.
- Pooled shares are divided equally at the next generation.

Example 6:

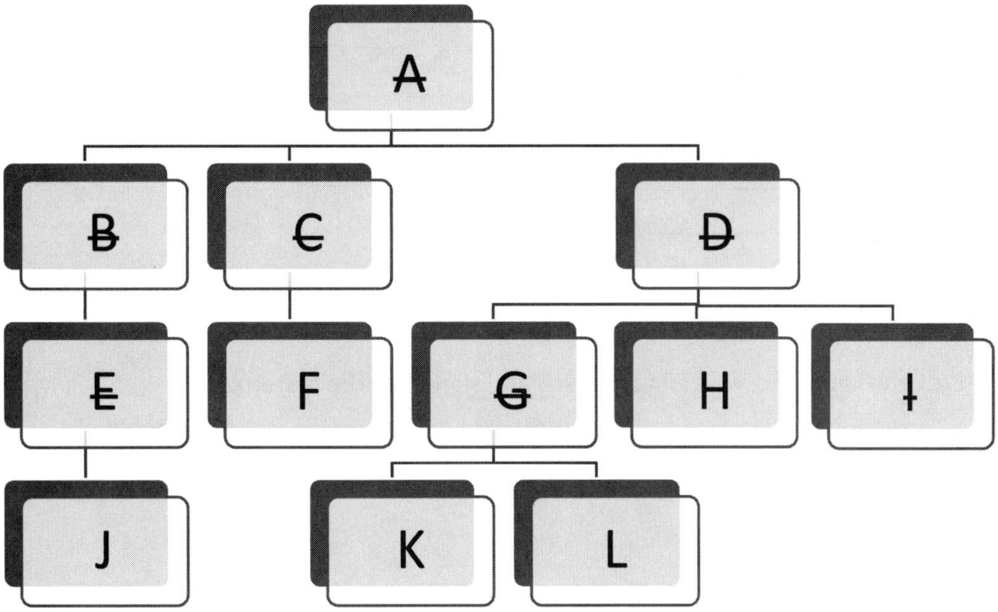

Step 1: *We start at E's generation, dividing the estate into four shares (E, F, G, and H). F and H take 1/4 each (we disregard I because I was not survived by issue).*

Step 2: *The remaining shares (2/4 or 1/2) are then pooled together and divided equally among the next generation (J, K, and L), giving them 1/6 each.*

Summary of Distribution to A's Issue

F = 1/4

H = 1/4

J, K, and L = 1/6 each

- Illustration:

  Decedent dies intestate, leaving an estate worth $525,000. Decedent is survived by Spouse. Decedent and spouse have two children, A and B. B predeceases Decedent, leaving two surviving children, X and Y. Spouse also has another child, Z, from a prior marriage. How is the estate divided among Decedent's family members?

  Spouse takes $________________________________ [Note: This is case 3 above.]

  A takes $________________________________.

CHAPTER 3: EXECUTION OF WILLS

A. Formal Wills

Exam Tip 1: Bar examiners love this topic. Highly tested.

Three formal execution requirements:

- Signed ______________________________;
- ______________________________; and
- Testamentary ______________________________.

1. Writing Signed by Testator

- Entire will must be written (or typed) and signed by the testator.

Note 4: The UPC does not permit ______________________________ wills. This includes audio and video recordings.

- Location of Signature
  - In some states, the signature must be at the ______________________________ of the document.
  - In other states (and the UPC), the signature can be located on ______________________________ of the will. What is important is whether the testator ______________________________ her name to be her signature.

Note 5: Under the second rule, if the signature is not at the bottom of the document, any words after the signature ______________________________ be given effect.

Example 7: *Instead of signing your will at the bottom, you sign halfway to the top. Under the first rule, your signature is no good and your will is invalid. Under the second rule, the will is valid, but any words after your signature are invalid.*

- Capacity: Testator must be at least 18 years of age and of sound mind.
- Form of Signature
  - A ______________________________ signature is not required.
  - The signature must indicate testator's desire to sign.

Example 8: *Terrance Taylor signs his will "T-Bone," his usual nickname. This should suffice, provided he intends for it to serve as his signature.*

2. Witnesses (Attestation)

a. Presence

- Most states require that the will be signed in the ______________________________ of at least ______________________________ witnesses.

Exam Tip 2: The bar examiners love "presence." It is a highly tested topic.

- Witnesses must also sign document, though not necessarily at the same time.
    - *Most* jurisdictions:
        - Testator must sign or acknowledge the will *in the presence* of the witnesses; and
        - Witnesses must sign *in the presence* of the testator.
    - UPC: Witnesses must sign within a ______________________________ time of the original signature by the testator.

Exam Tip 3: This means that the signatures do not have to be in the presence of witnesses or testator. Great example of how UPC makes it easier to execute a will.

- Two views of "in the presence":
    - ____ (Traditional approach)
        - Witness and testator must observe or have the opportunity to observe the signing of the will.
        - I.e., they are both in the same room.
    - ____ (Modern Approach)
        - Witness or testator must be ______________________________ the act is being performed, even if she cannot see it.

Note 6: The UPC adopts Conscious Presence **only** for the situation where the will is signed by another on behalf of the testator.

b. Interested witnesses

- Interested witness has a direct financial interest in the will.

Example 9: *T-Bone Taylor executes a will that is witnessed by Amy and Bethany. The will gives Amy $10,000 and nothing to Bethany. Amy is an interested witness.*

- Common Law: Interested witness was not ______________________________ to witness the will
- Purge Theory: Many states have adopted this theory.
    - If a witness (or witness's spouse) has a direct financial interest under the will, it does not affect the ______________________________ of the will.
    - BUT, probate court will ______________________________ any gain in excess of what the witness would take under intestate succession.
    - Exceptions: Do not purge gain if:
        - There were two other disinterested witnesses; OR
        - Interested witness would take a share under intestate succession AND interested witness takes the lesser of intestate share or bequest.

> ***Example 10:*** *T-Bone Taylor executes a will that is witnessed by Amy and Bethany. The will gives Amy $10,000 and nothing to Bethany. If the will is not admitted to probate, Amy, as T-Bone's heir, would take $100,000. Can Amy take under T-Bone's will? ______________________________. Amy is not really an interested witness, because her share under intestate succession would be much higher.*

- UPC: Abolished the interested witness doctrine
  - *What does this mean?* UPC reasons that this purge business is too difficult and it risks trapping innocent interested witnesses.
  - *So what do you do if there is funny business?* There are other ways of going after a problematic witness (e.g., undue influence or fraud).

3. Present Testamentary Intent

Testator must have the ______________________________ intent to make a testamentary transfer.

> ***Example 11:*** *As he is signing his will, T-Bone says to his attorney that he would "like to have a week to go over the will to make sure I am happy with it." Is there present testamentary intent? ______________________________.*

> ***Example 12:*** *Although the document says "Last Will and Testament" at the top if it, T-Bone thinks he is signing a real estate contract. He voluntarily signs. A court may refuse to admit T-Bone's will for lack of testamentary intent because he did not know he was executing a will.*

4. Competency

A testator must be at least ______________________________ years old and of sound mind.

> **Note 7:** Competency is measured at the time of the ______________________________. Subsequent incompetence will NOT invalidate a will.

5. Failure to Satisfy Formalities

- Common Law (majority rule): ______________________________ compliance with will formation formalities

  > ***Example 13:*** *T-Bone's will was typed in full, properly signed at the bottom, and signed by witness Amy. Bethany was supposed to sign the will as a second witness, but accidentally forgot to sign her name. Under the common-law view, this will is invalid.*

- Modern View (UPC and minority rule):
  - ______________________________ compliance with statutory formalities

- Even if formality is not met, a court will nevertheless admit a will to probate if there is ______________________________ evidence that the decedent intended the document to serve as his will.

__Example 14:__ T-Bone Taylor neglected to sign his will. He's easily distracted. The will was otherwise witnessed by two witnesses and it was typed in full, with "T-Bone Taylor's Last Will and Testament" typed at the top. He had also revised the will several times with the help of his lawyer. A court, following the substantial compliance doctrine, may recognize this document as T-Bone's will.

B. Other Documents

1. Holographic Wills

- An informal, handwritten will;
- Need not be ______________________;

__Example 15:__ On a napkin, T-Bone Taylor writes, "I leave everything to my wife, Charlene Taylor," and signs it "Terrance Taylor." This is a holographic will.

- To be valid, must be ______________________;
- How much writing?
  - Some jurisdictions: ______________________ markings not in the testator's handwriting invalidate the will
  - UPC: Only requires that ______________________ provisions be in the testator's handwriting
- Intent:
  - Look for words or phrases that suggest intent.

__Example 16:__ On a piece of stationery, T-Bone Taylor writes out how he wants his property to be divided upon his death. He uses words like "bequeath" and "inherit," which are evidence of testamentary intent.

  - UPC expressly authorizes looking to extrinsic evidence to establish intent.

Exam Tip 4: If you see a person handwriting something about their property, go into a holographic analysis. Intent is very important.

2. Codicils

______________________ a will; does not replace the underlying will

__Example 17:__ T-Bone Taylor's will gave everything to his wife, Charlene. Later, T-Bone executes a codicil to give half his estate to his best friend, Hank Mardukas. Thus, Charlene and Hank will each take half of T-Bone's estate. The prior will is not REVOKED; it is just AMENDED or SUPPLEMENTED.

Exam Tip 5: A codicil must be executed with the same formalities as a will. Formal codicils must be signed, witnessed, etc. Holographic codicils must be in writing.

Exam Tip 6: A formal will can be amended by holographic codicil, just as a holographic will can be amended by an attested codicil.

C. Will Substitutes (Non-Probate Transfers)

A decedent can avoid probate by transferring property via a will substitute, including:

- **Joint Tenancy:** Avoids probate because it has a right of ______________________________;
- **Revocable Trust:** Avoids probate because it is an inter vivos transfer;
- **Pour-Over Will:** Avoids probate because it distributes property under a trust;
- **POD Contract:** Avoids probate because it distributes by an ______________________________ transfer;

> ***Example 18:*** *T-Bone Taylor takes out a life insurance policy, naming his wife Charlene as the beneficiary. On T-Bone's death, the proceeds of the policy are not part of T-Bone's probate estate, because they were payable on death (POD).*

- **Deed:** Avoids probate because it is an ______________________________ transfer.

CHAPTER 4: REVOCATION OF A WILL

A. Nature of Wills

1. Ambulatory

Wills can be altered or revoked at any time up until the testator's ______________________________.

> ***Example 19:*** *You make a will. Life happens, things change, and you want a new will. We follow the later will, because it is a better indication of your intent.*

2. A will can be revoked in ______________________________ or in ______________________________.

B. Three Ways to Revoke a Will:

- Subsequent ______________________________;
- Physical ______________________________;
- Operation of ______________________________.

1. Subsequent Instrument

a. Express revocation: A later writing expressly revokes a prior will.

> ***Example 20:*** *T-Bone Taylor validly executes Will 1. Later, T-Bone executes Will 2, which includes the following clause: "Will 1 is hereby revoked." Will 2 is now the operative document.*

Example 21: *T-Bone Taylor validly executes Will 1. A year later, T-Bone calls his lawyer and requests that that the lawyer "revoke the first will; it's garbage." Is this valid revocation? ______________________________. Oral revocation is not enough to revoke.*

b. Implied revocation (i.e., inconsistency)

- Later writing is inconsistent with prior will(s).
- So long as it is validly executed, a ______________________________ document controls.

Example 22: *In his will, T-Bone Taylor gives his estate to his wife Charlene. Later, T-Bone executes a will giving his wife Charlene $50,000, and the residue of his estate to his best friend, Hank Mardukas. Because the later writing has a residuary gift (the gift to Hank M.), it revokes the first will by inconsistency.*

> **Exam Tip 7:** You must be able to distinguish between a codicil and a new will. A helpful way to do this is to look for a residuary gift:
>
> Original will has a residuary gift and later writing does not = later writing is probably a ______________________________.
>
> Original will does not have a residuary gift and later writing does = later writing probably a ______________________________.

2. Physical Act

A testator may also revoke a will in part or in its entirety by engaging in a physical act of destruction, such as tearing, ______________________________, or crossing stuff out.

> **Exam Tip 8:** To revoke a will, the testator must ______________________________ for the physical act to revoke the will.

Example 23: *Clumsy T-Bone Taylor accidentally set fire to his will as he was trying to light a cigar. This is not a valid revocation because T-Bone did not intend to revoke.*

a. Destroying specific language

- Majority: The particular language in question must be destroyed.
- UPC: Only requires that destructive act affect some part of the will.

b. Lost wills

- We know a will exists, but cannot find it at the testator's death
- Creates a ______________________________ presumption that the testator revoked the will by physical act
- Burden is on the ______________________________ to show will's existence by ____ evidence

Exam Tip 9: Duplicate originals can be admitted; copies cannot be admitted. A duplicate original is another version of the original (signed and attested).

Example 24: *After executing his will at his lawyer's office, T-Bone Taylor wanted to keep the original under his bed at home. The lawyer kept a photocopy on file. At T-Bone's death, the will cannot be located. This creates a rebuttable presumption that T-Bone revoked the will by physical act. Although T-Bone's estate can try to rebut the presumption, the photocopy may not be admitted to probate in place of the original will.*

3. Operation of Law

- In most jurisdictions, ______________________________ revokes all will provisions in favor of the former spouse.
- Exception: There is evidence that testator wanted the will to survive

Example 25: *A statement in the will suggesting that the testator still wanted the divorced spouse to take a share.*

Note 8: The UPC goes a step further, invalidating gifts not just to the ex-spouse, but to the ex-spouse's relatives as well.

Note 9: Separation does not affect the rights of a spouse.

- By contrast, a subsequent ______________________________ does not revoke a will because a surviving spouse is entitled to take an elective share.

C. Special Issue 1: Third-Party Revocation

A third party can revoke on behalf of a testator if:

- At the testator's ______________________________; and
- In the testator's conscious ______________________________.

Example 26: *T-Bone calls his lawyer, asking her to "rip up my will." The lawyer shreds the will. Is this valid revocation? ______________________________.*
Not in conscious presence.

D. Special Issue 2: Revoking Codicils

- By revoking a will, the testator also revokes any ______________________________ attached to the will.

Example 27: *T-Bone Taylor executed a will giving his estate to his wife Charlene. Later, T-Bone executed a codicil that gave his best friend Hank Mardukas half of his estate. If at some later point T-Bone revokes the original will, this also revokes the gift to Hank Mardukas.*

- But! The opposite is not true. If a testator revokes a codicil, the underlying will is ______________________________ in its original form.

E. Special Issue 3: Revival

1. Republication

UPC (majority rule) does not recognize automatic revival of a revoked will.

> ***Example 28:*** *T-Bone Taylor executes a will giving his estate to his wife, Charlene. Later, T-Bone executes a new will, which not only splits his estate between Charlene and his best friend Hank Mardukas, but also expressly revokes the first will. T-Bone and Hank have a falling out and T-Bone revokes the second will. Revocation of the second will does NOT automatically revive the first will. For the testamentary gift to Charlene to be admitted to probate, T-Bone will need to ______________________________ the first will.*
>
> *If T-Bone does not re-execute, he will die without a will, and his estate will be distributed through the rules of ______________________________ succession.*

> **Note 10:** Full disclosure: This rule can get a little picky. Refer to the Wills outline if you want the itty, bitty, picky details.

2. Dependent Relative Revocation (DRR)

- DRR provides a safety valve for testators who revoke a will on the basis of a ______________________________.
- The mistake can be grounded in law or in fact.
- DRR invalidates the mistaken revocation and revives the earlier revoked will.

> ***Example 29:*** *T-Bone Taylor executes a will giving his entire estate to his best friend, Hank Mardukas. After T-Bone gets word that Hank has died, he executes a new will giving his entire estate to his wife Charlene. If it turns out that Hank is in fact alive and well, Hank can seek to have DRR applied to undo the revocation of the first will, on the theory that the revocation of the first will was conditioned on a mistake of fact (i.e., Hank's death).*
>
> ***Example 30:*** *T-Bone Taylor executes a will giving his entire estate to his best friend, Hank Mardukas. T-Bone attempts to create a second will and writes on the first will that "this will is revoked because I have made a new will, /s T-Bone Taylor." If it turns out that the second will is not valid, Hank can seek to have DRR applied to undo the revocation of the first will, on the theory that the revocation of the first will was conditioned on a mistake of law (i.e., valid execution of the second will).*

> **Exam Tip 10:** If you see revocation based on a mistake, do a DRR analysis. Focus on the idea that but for the mistake, the testator would not have revoked the first will. Buzzwords: "revocation," "mistake," "causation," and "safety valve."

CHAPTER 5: CONSTRUCTION OF WILLS

A. Construction (Interpretation)

1. Plain Meaning Doctrine

- Courts tend to give the words in wills their plain meaning.
- We assume the testator meant the plain meaning of what he said, even if the testator meant something else.
- Exception: The will states otherwise (e.g., by defining terms).

2. Incorporation by Reference

- Will refers to a document outside the will itself.
- A will may incorporate an extrinsic document that is not testamentary in nature, if:
  - The document is in ______________________________ at the time of execution;

    Note 11: The UPC will waive this rule if the document disposes only of personal property.

  - The testator ______________________________ the document to be incorporated into the will; and
  - The document is ______________________________ in the will with sufficient certainty to permit its identification.

    Example 31: *A clause in T-Bone Taylor's will provides, "This will makes bequests in accordance with the list provided in my sketchbook, which I keep in the bottom drawer of my desk." This document is incorporated into the will.*

3. Acts of Independent Significance

A testator can dispose of property based on some act or event that is ______________________________ to the execution of the will.

Example 32: *T-Bone's will provides, "I devise my stamp collection to my daughter-in-law at the time of my death." T-Bone may or may not have a daughter-in-law at the time he writes the will. The stamp collection goes to his daughter-in-law at the time he dies.*

Note 12: This doctrine applies to acts that occur in the future (i.e., after the execution of the will). That makes it different from both incorporation by reference and republication by codicil.

4. Lapses and the Anti-Lapse Statute

- Common Law: A testamentary gift would ______________________________ (i.e., fail) if an intended beneficiary did not survive the testator.
- Failed gifts would be dumped into the ______________________________ gift.

__Example 33:__ T-Bone devises "my car to my best friend Hank Mardukas." Hank dies before T-Bone. Thus, the gift to Hank lapsed at common law and would go to the residue.

- Anti-lapse statutes: Provide an alternative disposition for lapsed gifts.
  - The statute prevents certain gifts from lapsing.
  - Requirements:
    - Protected relationship
      - Lapsed gift was intended for a relative of the testator

__Example 34:__ The testator's child, grandchild, great-grandchild

- Survived by ______________________________

__Example 35:__ T-Bone Taylor's will provides, "$10,000 to my son, Alex." Alex predeceases T-Bone and is survived by a son, Anton.

__Step 1:__ The gift to Alex is a covered relationship (T's son).

__Step 2:__ Although Alex predeceased T-Bone, Alex is survived by issue, Anton.

Because Alex and T-Bone are in a protected relationship, and because Alex is survived by Anton, the statute prevents the gift from lapsing. Thus, Anton takes the gift.

- If these requirements are not met, the common law rule applies and the gift goes to the residuary.

- Special rules for class gifts:
  - Common Law: Exception to the lapsed gifts rule
    - If a member's gift lapses, the rest of the class share that member's gift.

Note 13: Keep this in mind if you get a question with a class gift and the lapsed recipient is not protected by the anti-lapse statute.

- If the lapsed member is covered by an anti-lapse statute, that rule controls.
- If the lapsed members is NOT covered by an anti-lapse statute, the rest of the class members share the lapsed member's gift.

5. Abatement

- If the estate does not have sufficient funds to pay debts or make gifts, the gifts will be abated, or reduced, in a specific order.
- Types of testamentary gifts:
  - Specific gift: A gift of a ______________________________ piece of property

__Example 36:__ T-Bone devises "my stamp collection to Hank Mardukas."

- General gift: A gift of property satisfied from general _______________ of estate

  Example 37: *T-Bone devises "$10,000 to my nephew Alex."*

- Demonstrative gift: A general gift from a particular _______________

  Example 38: *T-Bone devises "$10,000 to my daughter Bonnie from my Bank USA account, but if the funds are insufficient, then from the estate's general assets."*

- Residuary gift: Left over

  Example 39: *T-Bone devises "the rest of my property to X."*

- Abatement hierarchy:
  - _______________ property (first to be reduced);
  - Residuary gift;
  - _______________ gifts;
  - Specific gifts (last thing to be reduced, most protected).

  > **Exam Tip 11:** If they can be satisfied, demonstrative legacies are treated as _______________ gifts. Otherwise, they are treated as _______________ gifts.

6. Ademption

a. Ademption by extinction

- A will makes a specific devise of property, but the specific piece of property is no longer in the estate at the testator's death.
- Traditional Rule: The devise is _______________ and the devisee takes nothing.
  - Often called the _______________ theory
- UPC: Takes a different approach, the _______________ theory
  - Look to the testator's intent at time she disposed of the property.
  - Look for facts that suggest the testator intended the ademption.

  > **Exam Tip 12:** UPC tries to avoid ademption. The UPC provides for the beneficiary to take replacement property on a specific gift.

  Example 40: *T-Bone Taylor devises his cherished stamp collection to his son, Harvey. When he made the will, T-Bone owned the stamp collection. Later, however, T-Bone sold the stamps. With the money he made on the stamps, T-Bone bought a rare picture of Elvis playing racquetball, which he owned at his death. Under the UPC, Harvey could receive the photo as replacement property.*

b. Ademption by satisfaction

- Applies when a testator satisfies a specific or demonstrative gift, either in whole or in part, by an ______________________________ transfer.
- Requirements:
  - The testator must ______________________________ for the gift to adeem; and
  - Intent must be supported by a ______________________________.

B. Ambiguities and Mistakes

1. Ambiguities

- Types: Latent and patent

  Example 41: *T-Bone's will devises "my stamp collection to my brother." T-Bone has two brothers, Arnold and Bernie.*

  - This is a ______________________________ ambiguity. We cannot see it on the face of the will.

  Example 42: *T-Bone's will devises some real estate to his brother. At one point in the document, it lists the address as "1122 Boogie Boogie Avenue," while in another spot in the document, it lists the address as 2211 Boogie Boogie Avenue.*

  - This is a ______________________________ ambiguity. It appears on the face of the document.

- Traditional Rule:
  - ______________________________ ambiguities had to be resolved without looking to extrinsic evidence;
  - Extrinsic evidence was admissible to resolve ______________________________ ambiguities.
- Modern Rule: Most courts allow both ambiguities to be resolved with extrinsic evidence.

  Example 43: *The brothers could introduce evidence showing which brother preferred stamps. They could also introduce evidence of the real address.*

2. Mistakes: Courts tend to be less forgiving when it comes to mistakes.

Example 44: *In drafting his will, T-Bone accidentally gave his stamp collection to Arnold instead of giving it to Bernie, an avid stamp collector. Even if Bernie can prove the mistake, courts are likely to leave the provision as executed.*

CHAPTER 6: POWER TO TRANSFER

- This section concerns limits on the testator's power to transfer property.
- Three situations:
  - Rights of the testator's ______________________________;
  - Gifts to the testator's ______________________________;
  - Bars to succession: ______________________________ statutes and disclaimer.

A. Rights of the Surviving Spouse

A surviving spouse is entitled to a number of means of support:

- Social security and pension plans;
- Homestead exemption;
- Personal property set asides;
- Family ______________________________ for reasonable living expenses during probate; and
- ______________________________ share.

1. Elective Share

- A surviving spouse can elect to take a ______________________________ share.
- The spouse's elective share will change the gifts to other beneficiaries.
- Amount:
  - UPC: Forced share is ______________________________% of the decedent's *augmented* estate.

> **Note 14:Augmented Estate:** The UPC subjects property acquired before the marriage, as well as property acquired during the marriage, to the elective share. The elective share under the UPC is broader than a community property share.

- Purpose: The law does not want the decedent to disinherit the surviving spouse, particularly when the surviving spouse is the "non-earner."

2. Waiver

Surviving spouse can waive the right to an elective share, if:

- The waiver is in ______________________________ after a **fair disclosure** of its contents; and
- The spouse is represented by ______________________________ legal counsel.

B. Gifts to Testator's Children

1. Advancements

- A lifetime gift to a child that is treated as satisfying all or part of the child's ______________________________ share.

Exam Tip 13: Operates like ademption by satisfaction (testate), except advancements deal with intestate succession.

- Two views on advancements:
  - Common Law:
    - Any lifetime gift is ______________________________ to be an advancement of that child's intestate share.
    - The child had the burden to show that an item was an outright gift.
  - UPC: A gift is an advancement **only if**:
    - The decedent declared in a ______________________________ writing that the gift was an advancement (or the heir acknowledged as such in writing); **or**
    - A writing indicates that the gift should be taken into account in computing the division of property of the decedent's estate.
- Calculating effect of advancement: "Hotchpot" analysis
  - **Add** the value of the advancements back into the intestate estate.
  - **Divide** the resulting estate by the number of children taking.
  - **Deduct** the child's advancement from the child's intestate share.

Example 45: *The decedent dies intestate, leaving three children—A, B, and C—and an intestate estate worth $50,000. A received an advancement worth $8,000 and B received an advancement worth $2,000. C did not receive an advancement.*

Step 1: *Add the advancements back into the estate ($50,000 + $8,000 + $2,000 = $60,000)*

Step 2: *Divide into equal shares ($60,000 ÷ 3 = $20,000 each)*

Step 3: *Deduct the advancement from the child's share*

A: $20,000 – $8,000 =	*$12,000*
B: $20,000 – $2,000 =	*$18,000*
C: $20,000 – $0 =	*$20,000*
Total	***$50,000***

2. Omitted Children

a. Intentional disinheritance

A parent can intentionally disinherit his children.

Example 46: *T-Bone's will provides, "I have intentionally not made any gifts to my child, Bernard, for he is a rotten child and unworthy of my love or money."*

b. Unintentional disinheritance

The testator has a child after executing a will and dies without amending the will.

- If the testator had no other children when the will was executed, then omitted child takes her ______________________________ share.
- If the testator had at least one child at the execution of the will, and the will devised property to at least one of those children, then the omitted child takes an ______________________________ share from the portion of the property already devised to the other child.

C. Bars to Succession

1. Slayer Rule

- A beneficiary who murders the decedent is barred from taking under the decedent's will.
- A beneficiary who murders the testator is treated as if he ______________________________ the testator.

> **Exam Tip 14:** Courts have not applied the Slayer Rule in involuntary manslaughter and self-defense cases. Thus, murder must be intentional and felonious (i.e., we're talking murder).

- UPC: Allows the killer's issue to take, when relevant (i.e., anti-lapse statute or intestate succession distribution)

2. Disclaimer

- A person may disclaim a testamentary gift.
- Requirements: The disclaimer must:
  - Be:
    - In writing, ______________________________, and filed with court; OR
    - ______________________________ to the person in charge of distributing the estate; AND
  - Identify the decedent, describe the interest being disclaimed, and define the ______________________________ of the disclaimer.
- Timing: Must disclaim within ______________________________ months of the decedent's death

3. Elder Abuse

Someone who is convicted of financial exploitation, abuse, or neglect of a person under her care is prohibited from inheriting from that person.

CHAPTER 7: WILL CONTESTS

- Objections to the validity of a will
- Only an ______________________________ party has standing to challenge a will.
- Interested party is someone who would:
  - Receive a financial benefit under the will; or
  - Take under intestate succession but does not take under the will.
- Interested party must file a contest claim within ______________________________ months after the will is admitted to probate.

A. Testamentary Capacity

Basic Rule: To execute a will, a testator must be:

- Of age (at least 18 years old); and
- Of sound ______________________________.

1. General Testamentary Capacity

- The person challenging the will ("the contestant") bears the burden of proving that the testator lacked the requisite mental capacity at the time of the ______________________________ of the will — "The When Question".
- Whether the testator had the ability to know:
  - The nature of the act — "The Why Question;"
  - The nature and character of her property — "The ______________________________ Question;"
  - The natural objects of his bounty — "The Who Question;" and
  - The plan of the attempted disposition — "The ______________________________ Question."

Exam Tip 15: The issue is NOT whether testator actually knew these things; it is whether the testator had the **ability** to know them.

Example 47: *T-Bone has a bit of a drinking problem, and occasionally suffers from memory lapses. This does not by itself mean that T-Bone lacks capacity to make a will; it does not mean that he lacked capacity at the time he executed the will.*

Example 48: *T-Bone suffered from intermittent bouts of dementia. While he was meeting with his lawyer to execute his will, T-Bone became disorientated and could not remember the names and faces of his two children, Bonnie and Clyde, who were the sole beneficiaries of his will. At that point in time, it is questionable whether T-Bone was able to know the natural objects of his bounty.*

Example 49: *Same facts as above, except T-Bone could recognize Bonnie and Clyde, but he could not remember where he was or who his lawyer was, and could not remember how much property he actually had. It is likely that T-Bone lacked general capacity, as he did not know what he was doing at the time.*

2. Insane Delusion

- A ______________________________ belief to which the testator adheres in spite of all reason and evidence to the contrary.
- The testator has general capacity, but has an insane delusion as to some belief.
  - Objective test:
    - Measure the testator's insane delusion against the actions of a ______________________________ person in the testator's position.
    - A belief is an insane delusion if the rational person could not have reached the same conclusion.
  - Causation: The contestant must show that the insane delusion was a ______________________________ cause of the testamentary disposition.

Example 50: *T-Bone Taylor was convinced that his wife Charlene was cheating on him. So convinced of this fact, T-Bone would sit on the couple's stoop and confront men who walked by, accusing them of having sex with his wife. He would not permit Charlene to be home alone because he was worried that her paramours would visit her while he was away from the house. Charlene vehemently denied the allegation. T-Bone's will provides, "I leave nothing to my wife because of her rampant pattern of adultery." In this case, Charlene would have a good case to challenge on insane delusion grounds.*

Exam Tip 16: Causation is the key here. Make sure to discuss whether the insane delusion caused the property distribution.

B. Undue Influence

1. In General

- A ______________________________ relationship
- The contestant alleges that a ______________________________ effectively controlled the testator's decision-making process.

2. Required Proof: The contestant bears the initial burden of showing:

- The beneficiary received a ______________________________ benefit under the will;
- The beneficiary had a ______________________________ relationship with the testator; and

Note 15: The confidential relationship is often professional (i.e., doctor, lawyer, therapist) or familial in nature.

- The testator had a weakened ______________________________ at the time of execution.

3. **Burden Shift**

- If the contestant meets the burden, it creates a presumption of undue influence.
- The burden shifts to the proponent (i.e., the third party) to show by a ______________________________ of the evidence that there was no undue influence.

4. **Consequences**

- The beneficiary is treated as if he predeceased the testator to the extent that the gift is in excess of the beneficiary's intestate share.

> **Exam Tip 17:** Like with an insane delusion, causation matters a great deal. The idea is that the suspect beneficiary exerted influence that caused the strange property division.

C. Fraud

The contestant bears the burden of showing that the beneficiary engaged in an unlawful ______________________________ at the time of the conveyance.

1. **Elements: Beneficiary made misrepresentation with:**

- The ______________________________ to deceive the testator; and
- The ______________________________ of influencing the testamentary disposition.

2. **Kinds of Fraud**

- Fraud in the Inducement: The misrepresentation causes the testator to make a different will than the testator would have otherwise made.

> ***Example 51:*** *T-Bone's sole heir, Bonnie, convinces T-Bone not to execute a will in favor of his best friend Hank Mardukas by promising that she will convey the property to Hank after T-Bone is dead. At the time, Bonnie has no intention of conveying to Hank. This is fraud in the inducement.*

- Fraud in the Execution: A misrepresentation as to the character or ______________________________ of the will.

> ***Example 52:*** *Knowing that T-Bone has poor eyesight and cannot read his will, Bonnie promises T-Bone that his will transfers all his property to his best friend Hank Mardukas. The document actually transfers the property to Bonnie and her brother Clyde, in equal shares. T-Bone signs the will. This is fraud in the execution.*

3. **Remedy**

A ______________________________ is the most common remedy for fraud.

> **Exam Tip 18:** Undue influence and fraud require an act by some third party, while insane delusion arises in the mind of the testator.

D. Forfeiture Clauses

- In Terrorem: A ______________________________ clause designed to dissuade a beneficiary from suing about his share.
- Rule: Under the UPC, the clause is ______________________________ if the beneficiary had probable cause to challenge.
- So...if the beneficiary **did not** have probable cause (i.e., the claim is groundless) the forfeiture clause **is** enforceable.

CHAPTER 8: THE PROBATE PROCESS; POWERS OF APPOINTMENT

A. Probate and Administration

1. The Probate Process

- The first thing you should do in any given estate problem is ______________________________ each piece of property as either probate or non-probate.
- Probate property passes by will or intestate succession.
- Non-probate property transfers by an instrument other than a will, such as:
  - ______________________________;
  - Trust;
  - Joint tenancy (with right of survivorship);
  - POD Contract.

> **Exam Tip 19:** Don't forget about intestate succession. If the decedent does not have a will or if the testator's will is invalid, probate property will pass by intestate succession.
>
> If you determine that a will is invalid in whole or in part, do not forget to discuss intestate succession.

2. Why Probate

- Primary purpose: Orderly administration of a decedent's estate
- Includes:
  - Protecting and satisfying ______________________________;
  - Quieting contested titles, and transferring titles to rightful holder;
  - Protect testator's interest (e.g., against fraud and undue influence);
  - Efficiently handling will contests.

> **Note 16:** Only those who stand to benefit financially under a will have standing to contest a will (intended beneficiaries or heirs).

3. Checklist

- Identify property as probate or non-probate.

        - Non-probate property: Figure out who takes it.
        - Everything else is probate property; it will pass either by testate or intestate succession.
    - Is there a will? If so, is it valid? Who are the intended beneficiaries?
        - Remember: Any property not specifically ______________________________ will pass by intestate succession.
    - No will: All property will pass by intestate succession.

B. Filing under UPC

- Probate proceedings must be brought within ______________________________ years of death, after which there is a presumption of intestacy.
- A party requesting probate can choose to have it occur through informal (ex parte) or formal probate (notice).

C. Creditors

- Non-claim statute
    - Bars a creditor from making a claim on the decedent's estate after a certain time period has elapsed
    - If a claim is not brought within that window, the claim is ______________________________.
    - The exact timeline is based on the statute.
- The personal representative must provide ______________________________ to the creditors of the estate.
- Seven classes of creditors (from most important to least important):
    - Administrative expenses;
    - Medical and ______________________________ expenses;
    - Family allowances;
    - ______________________________;
    - Secured claims;
    - Judgments against the decedent;
    - All other claims.

D. Personal Representative

- The person who acts on behalf of estate during probate process
- What do we call this person?
    - If appointed by the court: ____;
    - If named in the will: ____.
- Duties of Personal Representative
    - Inventory and appraise the estate;

- Locate and contact interested parties, including ______________________________;
- Satisfy debts, including taxes, burial expenses, and support;
- Close the estate.

- Duties owed by Personal Representative
  - The personal representative is a fiduciary, owing duties of ______________________________ and ______________________________.
  - The personal representative cannot engage in self-dealing.

> ***Example 53:*** *Decedent is an art collector. She appoints her best friend, also an art collector, to serve as the administrator. The best friend wants to buy a piece of art from the estate. This is not appropriate, as this is self-dealing.*

- The personal representative gets paid from the estate.

E. Choosing a Personal Representative

If the will does not name a personal representative. Who can serve? The following priority applies:

- A surviving spouse who is a devisee;
- Other surviving devisee;
- Surviving spouse (if not a devisee);
- Other heirs of the decedent;
- ______________________________ days after decedent's death, any creditor.

F. Power of Appointment

- Describes the ability of the decedent (______________________________) to select an individual (______________________________) to dispose of certain property under the will
- Power is ______________________________ to the donee (only the donee can appoint)
- Two Types: General and special

1. General

- No conditions or restrictions on the donee's power
- The donee can appoint herself or one of her creditors as the owner of the property.
- If the donee fails to exercise the power, the property reverts back to the donor's estate.

2. Special

- The donor can specify certain individuals or groups as the objects of the power.
- In doing so, the donor limits the donee's power.

> ***Example 54:*** *T-Bone gives power of appointment to his best friend, Hank. The power of appointment is exclusive to the extent that neither Hank nor his family can be appointed to the property. What type of power is this? A ______________________________ power.*

Example 55: T-Bone gives a power of appointment to his best friend, Hank, to give the property to his nieces and nephews. This is a non-exclusive power of appointment, because Hank is not able to exclude particular nieces and nephews.

G. Powers of Attorney

- An authority to act on another's behalf in a legal or business matter
- Principal/agent relationship
- To be valid, it must be:
  - In ________________________;
  - ________________________; and
  - ________________________.
- Three Types: General, Special, Advance Health Care Directives

1. General

Covers all affairs during a person's period of ________________________.

2. Special

Limits the authority to specific subject matters (i.e., resolving a particular business deal).

3. Advance Health Care Directives

a. Living will

- Dictates the care the individual wants in the event the individual is not able to make those wishes known.
- The agent's job is to see that the directive is ________________________.

b. Durable power of attorney for health care

- Appoints an agent in the event the principal becomes incapacitated and is unable to make medical decisions.
- Allows the agent to stand in the principal's shoes and ________________________ for her.

General Advice:

- Study your way—don't worry about others
- Stress is not a bad thing—let it motivate you
- Be a human—eat, rest, take a break!

[END OF HANDOUT]

Themis
Bar Review

Themis
Bar Review

MEE (MULTISTATE ESSAY EXAMINATION) ESSAY WRITING WORKSHOP

CHRISTOPHER IDE-DON, UC DAVIS SCHOOL OF LAW

CHAPTER 1: INTRODUCTION

A. The Bar Exam

- **Multistate Essay Exam** (MEE)—Six 30-minute questions
- **Multistate Performance Test** (MPT)—Two 90-minute questions
- **Multistate Bar Examination** (MBE)—Two hundred multiple-choice questions, six total hours

B. Exam Schedule

	Day 1	**Day 2**
AM	Either MPT or MEE (3 hours)	100 MBE questions (3 hours)
PM	Either MPT or MEE (3 hours)	100 MBE questions (3 hours)

C. Overall Exam Scoring

Essays: 30%	**MPT (Performance Test): 20%**	**MBE: 50%**
Six 30-minute essays	Two 90-minute MPTs	200 MBE questions, six total hours (175 scored & 25 experimental)

D. Essay Subjects

Civil Procedure (FRCP)
Constitutional Law
Contracts
Criminal Law
Criminal Procedure
Evidence (FRE)
Real Property
Torts

Business Associations *
Conflict of Laws
Family Law
Secured Transactions
Trusts and Decedent's Estates

* *(Includes Agency, Corporations, and Partnerships)*

E. Written Exam Scoring

- Point Sheets provided by the NCBE—visit website for past essays and point sheets
  - Point Sheets provide a score value for each major issue
- National substantive law (majority or otherwise generally accepted law)
- Instructions:

> "Demonstrate your ability to reason and analyze. Each of your answers should show an understanding of the facts, a recognition of the issues included, a knowledge of the applicable principles of law, and the reasoning by which you arrive at your conclusions. The value of your answer depends not as much upon your conclusions as upon the presence and quality of the elements mentioned above."

- Perfection is not required to pass.

F. Multiple-Choice Exam (MBE) Scoring

- 200 multiple-choice questions (175 are graded and 25 are pre-test questions)

G. Overall Scoring

- 50% Written + 50% Multiple Choice
- Your overall score determines whether you pass—you can "pass" one part and "fail" the other part and still pass the overall exam.

H. The Overall Bar Study Experience

- Marathon, not a sprint!
- 7–10 hours a day, consistency is the key
- Daily Schedule—Lecture; Review Law; Practice (or flip the day)
- Merge the processes of practice and review.
- Do the work—Completion = Passing

CHAPTER 2: ESSAY WRITING STRATEGIES

A. Preparing for the Essay Exam

- Practice!
- Open book, untimed → open book, timed → closed book, timed
- Read, outline and/or issue spot as many questions as possible to learn how the bar examiners like to test issues.

B. Organization

1. IRAC

- Issue
- Rule
- Analysis
- Conclusion

2. IRAirac

- Issue
- Rule
- Analysis
  - sub-issue #1 (element #1)
  - sub-rule
  - analysis
  - conclusion

  - sub-issue #2 (element #2)
  - sub-rule
  - analysis
  - conclusion

  - sub-issue #3 (element #3)
  - sub-rule
  - analysis
  - conclusion
- Conclusion

3. Example of IRAirac

- **Issue:** Negligence
- **Rule:** Duty, Breach, Causation, Damages
- **Analysis:**
  - **Sub-issue #1:** Duty
  - **Sub-rule:** Reasonable person
  - **Analysis:** *Facts from Exam Question*
  - **Conclusion:**

  - **Sub-issue #2:** Breach
  - **Sub-rule:** Failure to act as a reasonable person
  - **Analysis:** *Facts from Exam Question*
  - **Conclusion:**

                ▪ **Sub-issue #3:** Causation

                    • **Sub-issue:** Actual Cause
                    • **Sub-rule:** "But for" D's actions...
                    • **Analysis:** *Facts from Exam Question*
                    • **Conclusion:**

                    • **Sub-issue:** Proximate Cause
                    • **Sub-rule:** D's actions were foreseeable cause of P's injuries
                    • **Analysis:** *Facts from Exam Question*
                    • **Conclusion:**

                ▪ **Sub-issue #4:** Damages
                ▪ **Sub-rule:** P suffered actual damages
                ▪ **Analysis:** *Facts from Exam Question*
                ▪ **Conclusion:**

            - **Conclusion** (for the entire Negligence issue):

C. Reading and Outlining the Exam Answer

- Six questions: Read all six, or read one at a time.
    - 30 minutes per question
    - **Finish** each question
- Read the call of the question carefully and look for limitations or other instructions.
- Why you need to outline your answer
    - Organization
    - Prevents missed issues
    - Time Management—Finish!

D. Issue Spotting

- Bar Exam v. Law School Exam; All facts are relevant
- Read the call of the question first—specific questions will be presented.
- Engage the question: circle or highlight important facts, dates, or numbers in the question, and note first impressions in the margin as you read the fact pattern.
- The facts will dictate if an issue is BIG or small. The more facts provided for an issue, the bigger the issue. The more ambiguous the facts provided, the bigger the issue.
- Learn which issues are important, and how to distinguish between big, small, and non-issues.

E. Writing the Exam

1. Issue Statements

- Use headings and subheadings
- Use short paragraphs; discuss each issue separately
- Save time by making your heading the issue statement, or use "Was, Whether, Did"

2. Rule Statements

- **Big issues**—break down each element of the rule and analyze each part under separate headings.
- **Small issues**—state the rule, and then discuss in one short paragraph
- MBE vs. Essay
- Concise rule statements
- Running out of time?
- If you do not remember the rule...

3. Analysis

- Bar Exam v. Law School Exam; No case law
- Use the exact facts in your analysis. You do not have to write out an entire sentence of facts, just the key facts from the sentence.
- Argue both sides whenever there are facts or law to support a counter-argument. If the facts or law clearly favors one side, you do not have to spend time on a counter-argument.
- Be careful about writing a fact without providing an explanation of the meaning of the fact. In other words, why is the fact relevant here, why does it tend to show that the rule/element is met or not met.
- After you write a sentence out, ask if you can add any explanation or discussion to the sentence. A simple way to do this is to ask "so what?" after you have written the sentence. If you can provide further explanation, you should do so.
- Always finish your answer—no points awarded for outlining an issue.

FACT → ISSUE → RULE → ANALYSIS

"It's a funny thing, the more I practice the luckier I get." – Arnold Palmer

[END OF HANDOUT]

Themis
BarReview

AGENCY & PARTNERSHIPS ESSAY WORKSHOP

PROFESSOR CHRISTOPHER IDE-DON

UC DAVIS SCHOOL OF LAW

CHAPTER 1: AGENCY—ISSUES TESTED

A. Approach to Agency Essay Questions

- Identify whether an agency relationship exists
- Discuss whether the principal is liable for the agent's actions

> **Exam Tip 1:** Agency questions typically ask whether the principal is liable to third parties for actions taken by an agent.

B. Agency Relationship

1. **Principal—typically an employer, such as a corporation or a partnership**

2. **Agent—typically an employee**

C. Principal's Contractual Liability

- Principal's liability depends on whether the agent acted with authority

> **Exam Tip 2:** You should discuss all theories of authority in your exam answer to earn full credit. Spend more time on the theory(s) of authority that are relevant, based on the exam facts.

1. **Actual Authority (Express or Implied)**

   a. **Express Actual Authority**

   Principal directly tells the agent that he has the authority to take certain actions

   b. **Implied Actual Authority**

   Based on the agent's reasonable understanding of the principal's instructions

2. **Apparent Authority**

   - Based on the principal's manifestations to the third party
   - If the third party reasonably believes the agent has authority to act (based on the principal's conduct), the agent will have the power to bind the principal.

   > **Note 1:** If the principal is undisclosed, there cannot be apparent authority.

3. **Estoppel**

   - Principal is prevented from denying liability if he failed to take reasonable steps and use ordinary care to inform a third party of the lack of authority

> ***Example 1:*** *P has two co-agents, A and B. P learns that B, acting without actual or apparent authority, is informing P's neighbors that A has the authority to sell P's ring, which P has specifically forbidden A from doing. P's next-door neighbor purchases P's ring from A, in justifiable reliance on B's representation as to A's authority. P, in her suit to rescind the sale, may be estopped (prevented) from denying B's authority to make the representation as to A's authority.*

4. **Termination of Authority**

    - Principal has the power to terminate the agency relationship at any time
        - Actual authority—simply tell the agent that authority is revoked
        - Apparent authority—must tell the third party that authority is revoked

5. **Ratification**

    - A principal can ratify (affirm) an act performed by an agent, even if the agent did not have authority to act
    - Ratification requires that:
        - The principal ratify the entire contract;
        - The principal and third party have legal capacity to contract;
        - The ratification occurs before the third party withdraws from the contract; and
        - The principal know the material facts of the transaction.

CHAPTER 2: PARTNERSHIPS—ISSUES TESTED

A. Formation

- Requires an association of two or more persons to carry on a for-profit business as co-owners
- Requires sharing of profits
- No intent requirement
- No formal agreement or writing required

> **Note 2:** Repaying a loan with business profits does not necessarily make the lender a partner.

B. Relationships of Partner with Partnership and Between Partners

1. **Fiduciary Duties**

    Partner owes the partnership and the other partners fiduciary duties of loyalty and care

    a. **Duty of Loyalty**

    - Must not compete with the partnership
    - Must not advance an interest adverse to the partnership
    - Must not ***usurp a partnership opportunity***

- Cannot take a business opportunity that the partnership could have profited from
- Can present the opportunity to the partnership first, and if the partnership declines, the partner can take it without violating the duty of loyalty

b. Duty of Care

- Required to act as a reasonable partner
- Cannot engage in grossly negligent or reckless conduct, intentional misconduct, or a knowing violation of the law

c. Obligation of Good Faith and Fair Dealing

Must act fairly and in good faith

2. Profits and Losses

Absent a partnership agreement, each partner will share profits and losses equally

3. Transfer of Financial Interest

- Partner can transfer the right to receive distributions from the partnership to a third party
- Partner is still a partner with remaining rights and obligations
- Third party does not become a partner, but can seek judicial dissolution of the partnership
- A creditor of a partner can enforce a judgment against the partner's financial interest.

4. Property Ownership

Property acquired by the partnership must be used for the benefit of the partnership.

5. Management Rights

- Each partner has equal rights in the management and conduct of the partnership.
- A majority of the partners can make a decision as to ordinary business matters.
- All partners must consent to a matter outside the course of ordinary business.

6. Access to Records

Must provide partners with access to records during business hours

C. Relationships with Third Parties

Note 3: A partner is an agent of the partnership

1. Partnership's Contractual Liability

a. Express Actual

Express authority can arise from the partnership agreement or authorization by partners.

b. Implied Actual

Based on partner's reasonable belief that an action is necessary to carry out his express authority

c. **Apparent Authority**

Exists when a partner acts in the ordinary course of partnership business and the third party reasonable believes the partner has authority to act

2. **Partnership's Tort Liability**

Liable for a partner's tortious acts, including fraud, committed in the ordinary course of partnership business or with partnership authority

3. **Partners' Liability**

A judgment creditor of an individual partner may not attach and execute upon partnership real estate

4. **Liability to Third Parties**

- As a separate entity, a partnership is subject to a lawsuit for its obligations.
- Partners are also jointly and severally liable for all partnership obligations
- Partnership creditor must exhaust the partnership's assets before taking the partner's individual assets

D. Partnership Changes and Termination

1. **Dissolution**

- Any partner can choose to dissociate from the partnership by giving notice.
- Partnership may dissolve when a partner dissociates, but dissociation does not necessarily cause dissolution

2. **Winding Up**

A partnership that is dissolved only continues to exist to "wind up" its business.

a. **Assets:** Creditors have priority over partners to the partnerships' assets.

b. **Obligations:** Partnership assets are first applied to pay off obligations to creditors (creditors may include partners who made loans to the partnership) before being distributed to the partners.

E. LLP—Limited Liability Partnerships

- Partners' personal liability for partnership obligations is eliminated
- Individual partners are liable for their own torts.

1. **Formation**

- Requires filing a statement of qualification with the state
- Failure to form an LLP will typically result in a general partnership

2. **Limited Partners**

- Partners are agents of the LLP

- Not personally liable for LLP obligations

F. Transition from General Partnership to LLP

- If a general partnership incurs liability and then becomes an LLP, the LLP is liable for those obligations.
- If an individual partner in a general partnership is liable, and then an LLP is formed, the partner is still liable for that obligation.
- A new partner admitted to the LLP is not liable for pre-transition obligations.

G. LP—Limited Partnerships

- Formed by 2 or more people—at least one general partner and one limited partner
  - Limited partner's liability is limited to amount contributed to LP
- Formation—must file a certificate with the state
- Access to Records—limited partners have a right to inspect and copy records upon reasonable demand
- Liability—limited partner not liable for partnership obligations
  - Can be liable if the limited partner participates in control of the partnership
  - Removing a general partner does not amount to "control" of the partnership
  - Only liable to third parties who reasonably believe the limited partner is a general partner

CHAPTER 3: PRACTICE QUESTION

February 2005, Question 7 [ID 361]

For many years, Ruth owned and operated a restaurant as a sole proprietorship doing business as (d/b/a) Ruth's Family Restaurant. In 2001, Ruth sold the assets of the restaurant to Scott. Ruth and Scott agreed that: (1) the restaurant would operate under the name "Ruth's Family Restaurant" (2) Ruth would manage the restaurant for Scott but would have no ownership interest in the restaurant; (3) all necessary licenses would remain in Ruth's name; and (4) Ruth would hire all employees, but only on an at-will basis (as is customary in the restaurant business). No one other than Ruth and Scott was aware that Scott had bought the restaurant.

Prior to Scott's purchase of the restaurant, Ruth had purchased supplies from Wholesale Restaurant Supply Co. (Wholesale), always signing the contracts as "Ruth, d/b/a Ruth's Family Restaurant." Following Scott's purchase of the restaurant, Scott instructed Ruth in very clear terms not to make any purchases of restaurant supplies from Wholesale in the future. Ruth complied with this instruction for the next several months.

In 2003, Ruth hired Nora, her niece, as assistant manager of the restaurant under a written employment contract for a 20-year term. Ruth signed the contract as "Ruth, d/b/a Ruth's Family Restaurant."

Soon after Nora was hired, she pointed out to Ruth that Wholesale's prices were generally less than those of the other local supply company. Despite Scott's clear prohibition, Ruth resumed buying supplies from Wholesale, again signing all contracts as "Ruth, d/b/a Ruth's Family Restaurant."

When Scott discovered what Ruth had done, Scott took over management of the restaurant, discharged Nora and Ruth, and refused to pay thousands of dollars of invoices from Wholesale for restaurant supplies delivered to the restaurant.

Wholesale has sued Scott to recover on the outstanding invoices. Nora has sued Scott for breach of the employment contract.

Under agency law:

1. Is Scott liable to Wholesale? Explain.

2. Is Scott liable to Nora? Explain.

SAMPLE ANSWER

An agency relationship is created when a principal manifests assent to an agent, the agent acts on the principal's behalf, the agent's actions are subject to the principal's control, and the agent manifests assent or otherwise consents. A principal is an undisclosed principal if the third party has no notice of the principal's existence.

Here, Ruth and Scott formed an agency relationship with Scott as the principal and Ruth acting as the agent. Ruth and Scott agreed that Ruth would manage the restaurant on Scott's behalf but would have no ownership interest in the restaurant. Scott controlled Ruth's conduct by specifically instructing her not to enter into contracts with Wholesale and giving her the power to hire all employees only on an at-will basis. Scott's existence, however, was not known to any parties other than Ruth and Scott. Therefore, Scott is an undisclosed principal in the agency relationship.

1. Although Ruth did not have actual or apparent authority to bind Scott to the contract with Wholesale, Scott might be held liable to Wholesale on a theory of estoppel. (60%)

A principal is subject to liability on a contract the agent enters into on the principal's behalf if the agent has the power (authority) to bind the principal to the contract. An agent has the power to bind the principal to a contract when the agent has actual or apparent authority, or the principal is estopped from denying the agent's authority.

<u>Actual authority</u>

Actual authority may be either express or implied. Express actual authority can be created by specific detailed terms and instructions. Here, Scott specifically instructed Ruth not to enter into any contracts with Wholesale. While Ruth initially complied with this instruction, she later disobeyed it by entering into contracts with Wholesale. Ruth did not have actual authority to enter into these contracts because Scott specifically prohibited her from doing so. Thus, Scott is not liable on the contract with Wholesale on a theory of actual authority.

<u>Apparent authority</u>

Apparent authority derives from the reasonable reliance of a third party on that party's perception of the level of authority granted to the agent by the principal. Apparent authority is based on the principal's manifestations to the third party. There can be no apparent authority created by an undisclosed principal. Here, Scott was an undisclosed principal; Wholesale was not aware of his existence when it entered into contracts with Ruth. As a result, Ruth could not have apparent authority because Scott made no manifestations to Wholesale that Ruth was his agent or had the authority to enter into contracts on his behalf. Scott's existence was never divulged by Ruth. She signed all contracts as Ruth, d/b/a Ruth's Family Restaurant. Therefore, Scott is not liable to Wholesale on a theory of apparent authority.

<u>Estoppel</u>

A person who has not represented that an individual is authorized to act as an agent may be estopped from denying the existence of an agency relationship or an agent's authority with respect to a transaction entered into by the agent. An undisclosed principal may not rely on instructions given to an agent that qualify or reduce the agent's authority to less than the authority a third party would reasonably believe the agent to have under the same circumstances if the principal would have been disclosed.

Here, Ruth was acting as restaurant manager. In this capacity, Ruth was given the general power to manage the business and was authorized to purchase restaurant supplies. However, she was specifically instructed by Scott not to enter into contracts with Wholesale. Ruth did not follow the instructions and continued to enter into contracts with Wholesale. She decided to do so after being notified by Nora that Wholesale's prices were less than other suppliers. In making the contracts with Wholesale, Ruth was acting in Scott's best interest, despite being instructed not to do so. Scott's limiting instruction reduced Ruth's authority, as restaurant manager, to less than the authority Wholesale could reasonably believe Ruth to have under the same circumstances if the principal had been disclosed. It was reasonable for Wholesale to believe Ruth was authorized to make the contracts in her capacity as restaurant manager. Therefore, Scott might be held liable on the contract based on an estoppel of undisclosed principal theory.

2. Ruth had no authority to enter into the employment contract with Nora and therefore Scott is not liable to Nora. (40%)

<u>Actual Authority</u>

Actual authority may be either express or implied. Express actual authority can be created by specific detailed terms and instructions. Here, Scott and Ruth agreed that Ruth could hire employees but only on an at-will basis. Ruth's employment contract with Nora, for a term of 20 years, clearly violated this instruction. Therefore, Ruth did not have actual authority to enter into the contract with Nora and Scott is not bound by it under a theory of actual authority.

<u>Apparent Authority</u>

Apparent authority derives from the reasonable reliance of a third party on that party's perception of the level of authority granted to the agent by the principal. Apparent authority is based on the principal's manifestations to the third party. There can be no apparent authority created by an undisclosed principal. Here, only Scott and Ruth were aware of Scott's existence as principal. Scott made no manifestations to Nora that could cause her to believe Ruth had the authority to enter into the employment contract for such a term. Thus, Ruth did not have apparent authority to make the employment contract with Nora.

<u>Estoppel</u>

A person who has not represented that an individual is authorized to act as an agent may be estopped from denying the existence of an agency relationship or an agent's authority with respect to a transaction entered into by the agent. An undisclosed principal may not rely on instructions given to an agent that qualify or reduce the agent's authority to less than the authority a third party would reasonably believe the agent to have under the same circumstances if the principal would have been disclosed.

Here, Scott specifically limited Ruth's authority to hiring employees on an at-will basis. Although restaurant managers can hire and fire employees, at-will employment contracts are the norm in the restaurant industry. The creation of a 20-year employment contract would not fall within the authority that Ruth, as restaurant manager, would have had if the principal had been disclosed. Scott's instruction did not give Ruth less authority than a restaurant manager under similar circumstances would have; rather, it was exactly the type of hiring authority other restaurant managers had. Therefore, Nora cannot rely on a theory of estoppel of an undisclosed principal to hold Scott liable.

(Editor's Note: The foregoing model answer was drafted in accordance with the NCBE Grading Guidelines for this question. The analysis is illustrative of the discussions that might appear in a high passing answer and addresses all legal and factual issues the drafters intended exam candidates to raise. When self-grading, refer to the NCBE's weighting of each issue, which is indicated in parentheses for your reference.)

[END OF HANDOUT]

Themis
Bar Review

CIVIL PROCEDURE ESSAY WORKSHOP

PROFESSOR CHRISTOPHER IDE-DON

UC DAVIS SCHOOL OF LAW

CHAPTER 1: ISSUES TESTED (PART 1)

A. Summary of the Issues Tested

1. **Subject Matter Jurisdiction (SMJ)**
2. **Personal Jurisdiction (PJ)**
3. **Venue**
4. **Erie**
5. **Pleadings**
6. **Discovery**
7. **Summary Judgment**
8. **Trial Procedure**
9. **Post-Trial Procedure**

B. Subject Matter Jurisdiction (SMJ)

1. **Federal Question Jurisdiction**
   - The federal issue must be presented in the plaintiff's well-plead complaint
   - A federal defense is not sufficient
2. **Diversity Jurisdiction**

   a. **Diversity**
      - Must be complete diversity between the parties
      - Citizenship of the parties:
        - Individuals—domiciled where they are present with intent to remain indefinitely
        - Corporations—domiciled where incorporated ***AND*** where the principal place of business is located

   b. **Amount in Controversy**
      - Must exceed $75,000, plead of the complaint
      - Injunctive relief—can have monetary value assigned
      - Multiple Defendants—can aggregate dollar amounts if jointly liable

3. Supplemental Jurisdiction

- Court may exercise supplemental jurisdiction over additional claims so long as the claims arise out of a common nucleus of operative fact as the original claim

a. Federal question jurisdiction

1) Plaintiff can bring state law claims that are related to the federal claim
2) An additional plaintiff can bring a state law claim against the defendant if related to the original plaintiff's federal claim
3) A defendant can bring a cross-claim against another defendant so long as the claim is related to the original plaintiff's federal claim

b. Diversity jurisdiction

1) Plaintiff can bring any state law claim related to the basis of the original claim
2) An additional plaintiff can bring a related state law claim against the defendant so long as the plaintiff does not destroy diversity
3) A defendant can bring a cross-claim against another defendant so long as it is related to the original claim

c. Rejection of Supplemental Jurisdiction

- Courts have discretion to reject supplemental jurisdiction if:
  a) The claims are complex or predominate the lawsuit;
  b) The federal law claims are dismissed; or
  c) There are any other compelling reasons to decline jurisdiction.

4. Removal

- Plaintiff files in state court and a defendant seeks to remove to federal court
- Defendant may remove so long as the federal court can exercise SMJ over the case
- Additional removal factors:
  - Diversity Jurisdiction—no defendants can be citizens of the state in which the claim was originally filed
  - Motion for removal must be filed within 30 days of receiving the complaint
  - All defendants must join in or consent to removal

C. Personal Jurisdiction (PJ)

1. Traditional Bases

a. Service while voluntarily present

b. Domicile

c. Consent

2. Long-Arm Statute

> **Exam Tip 1:** On the exam, most statutes allow the exercise of PJ to the extent allowed by the Constitution

a. Due Process

1) Minimum contacts

   a) Purposeful availment (reasonably foreseeable to be sued in the state)

   b) Relatedness (defendant's conduct in relation to the action)

      i) Specific Jurisdiction (action arises out of the defendant's conduct)

      ii) General Jurisdiction (defendant is essentially "at home" in jurisdiction)

         (a) Corporation is "at home" where incorporated and where its principal place of business is located

2) Fairness (Fair play and substantial justice)

   - Interest of the forum state in adjudicating the matter;
   - Burden on the defendant of appearing in the case;
   - Interest of the judicial system in efficient resolution; and
   - Shared interests of the states in promoting common social policies

CHAPTER 2: ISSUES TESTED (PART 2)

A. Venue

1. Appropriate Venue

- Which federal district can the original action be filed in?

1) A district in which any defendant resides if all defendants reside in the state where the district is located;

> **Editorial Note 1:** To clarify, if all defendants reside in the same state, venue is appropriate in any district in which any of the defendants reside.

2) Where a substantial part of the events or omissions occurred, or where the property is situated; or

3) If neither of the above apply, venue is proper in a judicial district where any defendant is subject to PJ

2. Transfer of Venue Analysis

1) Is there personal jurisdiction?

2) Is there subject matter jurisdiction?

3) Is venue appropriate in the new district?

4) Is transfer to the new venue in the interest of justice?

B. The Erie Doctrine

> **Exam Tip 2:** Look for the fact pattern to present a state law in a federal court case.

1. Federal Question Jurisdiction

Federal substantive and procedural law will control.

2. Diversity Jurisdiction

- Court applies state substantive law and federal procedural law

a. Substance v. Procedure

- A state law that alters the calculation of damages is a substantive law under *Erie*
- A state law regarding a statute of limitations is substantive under *Erie*
- State laws that create evidentiary privileges are substantive under *Erie*

Example 1: *In a federal case based on diversity jurisdiction, the federal law does not recognize physician-patient privilege. However, state law recognizes a physician-patient privilege. The court must use the state law and apply the privilege.*

C. Pre-Trial Injunctions

1. Temporary Restraining Order (TRO)

- Party seeks to maintain the status quo prior to a hearing for a preliminary injunction
- Must show:

1) Immediate and irreparable injury would occur absent the TRO; and

2) An effort was made to give notice to the opposing side (or the reason notice should not be required)

- Court may grant TRO without the opposing party present

2. Preliminary Injunction

- Requires notice to the opposing party and a hearing

- Plaintiff must show:
    1) Likely to succeed on the merits;
    2) Likely to suffer irreparable harm in absence of injunction;
    3) Balancing the equities favors granting; and
    4) Injunction is in the best interests of the public

CHAPTER 3: ISSUES TESTED (PART 3)

A. Pleadings

1. Rule 4 Service of Process

- Corporations—service may be made on an officer, managing agent, general agent, or agent appointed or authorized by law

Exam Tip 3: Rules governing service of process are considered procedural.

2. Rule 12 Motions Against the Complaint

- Rule 12(b) Motion to Dismiss—lack of SMJ, lack of PJ, improper venue, etc.

a. Timing

- Lack of SMJ—can be raised at any time, even on appeal
- Lack of PJ, improper venue, and insufficient process—must be raised at the first opportunity (the first pre-answer motion or, if none, the answer)
    - Failure to raise these defenses in a timely manner will waive the defense
- Failure to state a claim or failure to join a necessary party under Rule 19—may be raised in any pleading, in a motion for judgment on the pleadings, or at trial.

3. Rule 15 Amendments (Relation Back)

- Plaintiff may amend its pleading once as a matter of right within 21 days after service on the defendant
- Otherwise, party may seek leave of court or written consent from opponent

a. Adding a new claim—permitted if:

- The original complaint was timely; and
- The new claim arises out of the same transaction or occurrence as the original claims

b. Adding a new defendant—permitted if:

- The claim arose out of the same conduct, transaction or occurrence;
- The new defendant received notice of the action within 90 days of the original complaint; and

- The new defendant knew or should have known that but-for a mistake, he would have been part of the original complaint

4. Rule 11 Standards for Filing

- When an attorney (or unrepresented party) submits a pleading, motion or other signed document, he certifies that the documents are filed in good faith.
- If challenged, must withdraw or revise the document
- May be subject to sanctions for violation of this Rule

B. Multiple Parties and Claims

1. Compulsory Joinder of Parties (Rule 19)

> **Exam Tip 4:** Look for facts in which the defendant claims that the plaintiff's lawsuit cannot proceed without adding another party.

- Requirements:

  1) The party must be necessary

  2) There must be PJ over the new party

  3) There must be SMJ (adding the party cannot destroy diversity)

     - If adding the party would ruin diversity, the court must decide whether the party is indispensable (dismiss the case) or not (proceed without the party)

a. Necessary Party if:

- Court cannot afford complete relief without the party;
- There is a danger that the party would be harmed without joining; or
- There is a risk of an inconsistent judgment or double liability

b. Factors to determine whether the new party is indispensable:

1) Extent to which judgment would prejudice the parties in the person's absence;

2) Extent to which prejudice could be reduced or avoided by protective provisions;

3) Whether a judgment rendered would be adequate; and

4) Whether the plaintiff would have an adequate remedy if action were dismissed for nonjoinder

2. Joinder of Claims

a. Cross-claims (Rule 13)

Example 2: *A plaintiff sues two defendants. The issue is whether Defendant 1 can sue Defendant 2.*

- Can bring a cross-claim so long as it arises out of the same transaction or occurrence as the plaintiff's original claim

- Must have SMJ over the cross-claim (federal question, diversity, or supplemental)

b. Impleader (Rule 14)

Example 3: *The defendant tries to pull a third party into the lawsuit.*

- Impleaded claim must relate to the original claim between the plaintiff and the defendant
- Must have SMJ over the impleaded claim (federal question, diversity, or supplemental)

c. Intervention (Rule 24)

Example 4: *A nonparty is seeking to join the lawsuit.*

1) Intervention as of right if:

   a) Nonparty has an interest in the subject matter of the action;

   b) The action may affect their interest; and

   c) The nonparty's interest is not adequately represented by the existing parties

2) Permissive intervention allowed if:

   a) Nonparty is granted a conditional right under federal statute; or

   b) Nonparty has a claim or defense related to the original cause of action

CHAPTER 4: ISSUES TESTED (PART 4)

A. Discovery (Rule 26)

1. Scope of Discovery

- Parties may discover any nonprivileged matter that is relevant to a claim or defense.
- Court may limit discovery if unduly expensive or burdensome
- Does not need to be admissible evidence in order to be subject to discovery
- A party may not discover privileged information.

a. Work product privilege

- Protects materials prepared by a party ***in anticipation of litigation***
- Exception:

   a) Information is not reasonably available by other means; and

   b) The party would be substantially prejudiced if not allowed to access the materials

Example 5: *Defendant interviews various witnesses prior to trial, and all of those witnesses have died. Plaintiff can argue that he cannot obtain the information another way and the case would be substantially prejudiced.*

- A party can never discover the mental thoughts and opinions about the case

2. **Expert Reports**

- o Expert not called as a witness—reports only accessible in exceptional circumstances

3. **Duty to Preserve Electronically Stored Information in Anticipation of Litigation**

- o Must take reasonable steps to preserve or could be subject to sanctions
- o Court may presume that the lost information was unfavorable to the party that failed to preserve it
- o Court may also dismiss the case or enter default judgment

4. **Physical and Mental Exams**

- o Can compel a mental or physical exam of a party if that party's mental or physical condition is at issue

5. **Depositions**

- o A party can depose another party or a nonparty
- o To depose a nonparty, must serve a subpoena
- o Can also request that a nonparty produce documents by serving a subpoena duces tecum

B. Adjudication Without Trial

1. **Summary Judgment Motion (Rule 56)**

- o Asserts that there is no genuine dispute as to any material fact and the party is entitled to judgment as a matter of law

> **Exam Tip 5:** If the fact pattern contains conflicting facts presented by the parties, that is a genuine dispute of fact. As long as it is a material fact, summary judgment is inappropriate.

C. Trial Procedure

1. **Jury Trial**

- o Seventh Amendment—right to jury trial when damages exceed $20
- o Must demand jury trial within 14 days after service of last pleading

2. **Judgment as a Matter of Law (Directed Verdict)**

- o Motion made by either party at the close of plaintiff's evidence or the close of all evidence
- o Granted if no reasonable person could differ as to the outcome

3. **Renewed Motion for Judgment as a Matter of Law (JNOV)**

- o Motion for judgment as a matter of law is denied and the issue goes to the jury
- o The jury deliberates and delivers a verdict
- o Renewed motion for judgment as a matter of law asks the court to override the jury's verdict
- o Can only "renew" this motion if it was made earlier

D. Post-Trial Procedure

1. Appeals

- Generally, there must be a final judgment
- Interlocutory appeal allowed after the denial or grant of an injunction

2. Claim Preclusion (Res Judicata)

> **Exam Tip 6:** Typically see a plaintiff attempting to asserting claim preclusion against a defendant who lost an earlier case

- Three requirements:

  1) The same plaintiff and the same defendant from lawsuit #1;
  2) Lawsuit #1 ended in a valid final judgment on the merits; and
  3) Claimant is asserting the same claim as in Lawsuit #1

> **Exam Tip 7:** Claim preclusion rarely applies on the exam because the question does not involve the same plaintiff or defendant in the second lawsuit.

3. Issue Preclusion (Collateral Estoppel)

> ***Example 6:*** *Plaintiff 1 sues Defendant and Plaintiff 1 wins an issue of fact or law. Plaintiff 2 brings a second lawsuit against the same Defendant and asks the court to preclude the Defendant from relitigating the issue.*

- Issue preclusion has four requirements:

  1) Same issue was actually litigated;
  2) Final valid judgment on the merits;
  3) Issue was essential to the judgment; and
  4) The party against whom issue preclusion is asserted must have been a party in the prior lawsuit or represented in that lawsuit (a successor-in-interest)—must be fair for new plaintiff to assert same issue (prior law required a mutuality of parties)

CHAPTER 5: PRACTICE QUESTION

July 2010, Question 7 (ID 301]

Until recently, Paul had always lived in State A. Last year, he decided he would move to State B for at least one year and, after a year, decide whether to remain in State B or return to State A. Six months ago, Paul moved to State B, rented an apartment, and took a job as a temporary employee. Paul has enjoyed living in State B so much that he recently left his temporary job and accepted a position as a permanent employee at a law firm in State B.

Shortly after he moved to State B, Paul bought a vacation home in State A, which he visits about once a month for two or three days. To pay for the vacation home, Paul obtained a loan from Credit Union in State A. Credit Union is incorporated in and chartered by State A. Its only office, located in State A, is both its corporate headquarters and the place where it transacts business with its customers. Ninety-five percent of Credit Union's customers are State A residents who do business with Credit Union in person at its State A office.

Paul's loan agreement with Credit Union provides that he will repay the loan in monthly installments over a 30-year period. Credit Union has a mortgage on Paul's vacation home to secure the debt. The loan paperwork lists Paul's State B address as his mailing and home address. The loan agreement also contains a privacy provision whereby Credit Union agrees not to disclose Paul's personal information to any third party without Paul's written permission. Credit Union sends a loan statement and payment coupon to Paul's State B address each month, and Paul returns the payment coupon with a check for the payment amount.

After the loan closed, a Credit Union employee mailed copies of all the loan paperwork to Paul. Unfortunately, the employee misread Paul's address in State B and sent the paperwork to an incorrect address. Several months later, Paul discovered that someone had gotten his loan paperwork and had used the information (including Paul's Social Security number and credit card numbers) to steal his identity. The identity thief had quickly accumulated $150,000 in unpaid bills in Paul's name. Paul's credit rating was ruined, and no one would extend him new credit.

Paul has sued Credit Union in the United States District Court for the District of State B for breach of the privacy provisions of the loan contract. The parties have stipulated that Paul's actual loss was $80,000. Paul's suit seeks $240,000 in damages, plus attorney's fees, pursuant to a State A statute that entitles victims of identity theft to recover treble damages and attorney's fees from anyone who wrongfully discloses their personal information. Paul's complaint also asserts that a federal statute restricting damages in state-law identity-theft cases to actual damages is unconstitutional and therefore does not preempt the treble damages provisions of the State A statute. The complaint asserts that the State B federal court has both diversity and federal-question jurisdiction over the case.

The long-arm statute of State B extends personal jurisdiction as far as the Constitution allows.

1. May the United States District Court for the District of State B exercise personal jurisdiction over Credit Union? Explain.

2. Does the United States District Court for the District of State B have diversity jurisdiction over the case? Explain.

3. Does the United States District Court for the District of State B have federal-question jurisdiction over the case? Explain.

SAMPLE ANSWER

1. The U.S. District Court for the District of State B may properly exercise specific personal jurisdiction over the nonresident defendant Credit Union because Credit Union engaged in contacts with the forum state that demonstrated purposeful availment and that gave rise to Paul's claims. (35%)

Under the Federal Rules of Civil Procedure, a federal district court may exercise personal jurisdiction to the same extent as a court of general jurisdiction of the state in which the federal district court sits. A state court of general jurisdiction may exercise personal jurisdiction over a nonresident defendant to the extent authorized by that state's long-arm statute and the Due Process Clause of the Fourteenth Amendment. Here, State B's long-arm statute extends personal jurisdiction as far as the Constitution allows.

Under the Due Process Clause, a nonresident defendant is subject to personal jurisdiction when its contacts with the forum state demonstrate purposeful availment of the benefits of the forum state and/or render it foreseeable that the defendant may be taken to court in the forum state. Here, Credit Union entered into a long-term contract with Paul knowing that he lived in State B and would be performing his contractual obligations (making payments) from State B. Credit Union also mailed several payment statements to Paul in State B. Credit Union, thus, purposefully availed itself of the benefits of State B and could foresee being brought into court in that state on matters related to the contract with Paul.

The Supreme Court has held that even when minimum contacts have been shown with a forum state, personal jurisdiction should not be extended if inconsistent with traditional notions of fair play and substantial justice. Here, it seems unlikely that Credit Union could show that it would be "unfair" for it to be brought into court in State B. It is a large corporation. While 95 percent of its business is done in State A, it was well aware that Paul lived in State B when it entered into the loan agreement. In addition, modern transportation and communication would minimize any burdens on Credit Union's participation in the case in State B. Thus, the exercise of personal jurisdiction by the courts of State B does not seem to offend notions of fairness.

2. The U.S. District Court for the District of State B has diversity jurisdiction over the case if Paul is a domiciliary of State B. (35%)

Under federal law, a U.S. District Court has diversity jurisdiction over a matter if no plaintiff shares the state of citizenship of any defendant and the amount in controversy in the case exceeds $75,000. A corporation is a citizen of the state in which it is incorporated and of the state in which it has its principal place of business. Here, Credit Union is both incorporated in and has its principal place of business in State A.

For an individual, citizenship is determined by domicile. In general, a person is a domiciliary of the state in which he is present and intends to reside for an indefinite period. Domicile is determined at the time the action is commenced. Here, Paul recently moved from State A to State B. He now resides most of the time in State B, returning for short visits periodically to his vacation home in State A. While he initially was unclear as to whether he would return to State A permanently after a year in State B, he recently accepted a permanent job in State B, which suggests that he intends to remain indefinitely in State B. Assuming that he is determined to be a domiciliary of State B, complete diversity of citizenship would exist, as Paul would be from a different state than Credit Union. If he were found to be a domiciliary of State A, though, complete diversity would not exist with Credit Union, and the court would not have diversity jurisdiction.

Amount in Controversy: With regard to the requirement that the amount in controversy exceed $75,000, in general, a plaintiff's good-faith assertion in the complaint that the action satisfies the amount-in-controversy requirement is sufficient, unless it appears to a legal certainty that the plaintiff cannot recover the amount alleged. Here, Paul's claim of $240,000 appears to satisfy the amount-in-controversy requirement. Note that even if the State A treble damages statute is preempted by federal law, the stipulation of $80,000 of actual loss would still satisfy the statutory threshold for diversity jurisdiction.

3. The U.S. District Court would not have federal question jurisdiction in this case because Paul's complaint does not state a federal claim. (35%)

Under the "well-pleaded complaint" rule, federal question jurisdiction exists only when the federal law issue is presented in the plaintiff's complaint. The determination of jurisdiction must be made by considering only the necessary elements of the plaintiff's cause of action, and not potential defenses. It is not sufficient to establish jurisdiction that a plaintiff alleges some anticipated federal law defense. Here, Paul's contract claim is created by state law and therefore would not fall within the court's original federal question jurisdiction. The only federal issue is whether Paul's cause of action is preempted by federal law. Paul's assertion of a defense to the possible applicability of a federal statute would not create federal question jurisdiction.

(Editor's Note: The foregoing model answer was drafted in accordance with the NCBE Grading Guidelines for this question. The analysis is illustrative of the discussions that might appear in a high passing answer and addresses all legal and factual issues the drafters intended exam candidates to raise. When self-grading, refer to the NCBE's weighting of each issue, which is indicated in parentheses for your reference.)

[END OF HANDOUT]

Themis
Bar Review

CONFLICT OF LAWS ESSAY WRITING WORKSHOP

PROFESSOR CHRISTOPHER IDE-DON
UC DAVIS SCHOOL OF LAW

CHAPTER 1: CONFLICT OF LAWS

Editor's Note 1: The Professor refers to specific page numbers throughout this lecture. The content does not always match these references due to formatting changes.

Note 1: Conflict of Laws is not tested in stand-alone questions. It is "embedded" in questions testing other subject areas including Civil Procedure, Family Law, and Decedents' Estates.

Transactions or events that give rise to legal disputes can have connections to two or more legal jurisdictions. The laws of such jurisdictions may differ with regard to the resolution of such disputes. Courts have developed legal doctrines and rules to determine which law to use.

A. Domicile

- If a person is domiciled in a particular state, then the person will be subject to personal jurisdiction in that state's courts whether or not the person can be found and personally served process.
- Ordinarily, the determination of a person's domicile is a question of fact.

1. Domicile of Individuals

Individuals can have more than one residence at a time, but they can have only one domicile at a time, which can be acquired either by choice or by operation of law.

a. Domicile by Choice

In general, domicile will be where the person is **present with the intent to remain** for an unlimited time and when he abandons any prior domicile. Thus, courts will look at the person's physical presence and intent to determine a person's domicile.

1) Physical presence

Actual physical presence in the location is required to establish the location as the person's domicile. The person, though, need not be present for any specific amount of time to establish domicile, so long as the amount of time is coupled with the intent to establish domicile.

2) Intent

In addition to physical presence in a location, the person must have the intent to make the location his home for the time being, or the absence of an intent to go elsewhere.

Presence under compulsion, such as a person in prison, will not establish domicile by choice.

Permanency is not required, but the intent to remain must be bona fide. In general, the person's actions and statements are used to establish intent. Ownership of real estate, voting, payment of taxes, having a bank account, or registration of an automobile are all factors that could be used to establish intent; however, none of these factors is conclusive.

Exam Tip 1: When analyzing a party's intent to remain in a location, you should discuss all relevant facts that either show his intent to remain or his intent to not remain.

2. Domicile of Corporations

A corporation's domicile is always the **state where it is incorporated**.

3. Continuity of Domicile

Once established, a domicile is **presumed to continue until a new domicile is acquired**. The burden of showing a change in domicile is on the party that asserts it. Temporary or even prolonged absences will not, by themselves, result in a change of domicile. Thus, a domiciliary of one state can live in another state for years and retain his domicile in the original state, so long as he intends to return to that state.

4. Change of Domicile

A change of domicile takes place when a person with capacity to change his domicile is physically present in a place and intends to make that place home, at least for the time being. The physical presence and the intent must be at the same time (concur).

B. Choice of Law

- When a cause of action involves contacts with more than one state, the forum court must determine which state's law is to be applied to decide the issues in the case.
- State choice-of-law rules generally have three sources: (i) specific choice-of-law statutes, (ii) contractual choice-of-law agreements, and (iii) general choice-of-law rules governed by forum state common law.

1. Constitutional Limitations

a. Due process

Under the Due Process Clause of the Fourteenth Amendment, the U.S. Supreme Court has held that a **forum state may apply its own law** to a particular case **only if it has a significant contact** or significant aggregation of contacts with the state such that a choice of its law is neither arbitrary nor fundamentally unfair.

b. Full faith and credit

The Full Faith and Credit Clause requires a forum state to apply the law of another state when the forum state has no contacts with or interest in the controversy, but it does not prevent the **forum state** from applying its own law when the forum **has** such **contacts or interest in the controversy**. However, it does not require a state to apply another state's law in violation of its own legitimate public policy.

C. Party-Controlled Choice of Law (recently tested)

Most courts will enforce a contractual choice-of-law provision if it is:

- A valid agreement with an effective choice-of-law clause;
- Applicable to the lawsuit under the terms of the contract;
- **Reasonably related to the lawsuit** (i.e., the law to be applied is from a state with connections to the parties or the contract); **and**
- Not in violation of the public policy of the forum state or another interested state.

D. Approaches to Choice of Law—In General

Courts generally approach choice-of-law questions using one of three different approaches:

- The **vested-rights** approach of the Restatement (First) of Conflict of Laws;
- The **most-significant-relationship** approach of the Restatement (Second) of Conflict of Laws **and**
- The **governmental-interest** approach.

A state may use different choice-of-law approaches for different substantive areas of the law.

> ***Example 1:*** *A state might use the vested-rights approach for contract cases, while applying the most-significant-relationship approach for tort matters.*

1. Vested-Rights Approach

This approach looks to the jurisdiction where the parties' rights are vested, meaning where the act or relationship that gives rise to the cause of action occurred or was created. Generally, this approach looks for the location where the **last liable event took place**.

In determining where vesting occurred, the forum court will first characterize the issues in the cause of action. Initially, this involves a determination of whether the issue is substantive or procedural.

- If the issue is **procedural**, then the forum court will apply its own procedural rules.
- If the issue is **substantive**, then the court must identify the substantive area of the law involved.

After characterizing the issue in the cause of action, the forum court will then determine what the forum state's choice-of-law rules require with regard to the characterized issue. For example, if the issue has been characterized as a substantive tort issue, then the law of the forum state may require that the law of the place of the injury apply.

2. Most-Significant-Relationship Approach

The Restatement (Second) of Conflict of Laws applies the law of the **state with the most significant relationship to the issue in question**.

When determining which state has the most significant relationship, the forum court generally considers the contacts that link each jurisdiction to the case, as well as the seven policy principles that are set forth in the Restatement (Second) of Conflict of Laws (see outline).

> **Exam Tip 2:** The Restatement (Second) of Conflict of Laws includes specific presumptive rules for several different substantive areas of the law that are discussed below. These specific presumptive rules have been recently tested.

3. Governmental-Interest Approach

Under the governmental-interest approach, it is **presumed that the forum state will apply its own law**, but the parties may request that another state's law be applied. If a party makes such a request, then that party must identify the policies of competing laws.

If there is a false conflict (i.e., the forum has no interest in the litigation), then the court applies the law of the state that does have an interest in the case. **If there is a true conflict** (i.e., the forum state and another state both have an interest in the litigation), **then the forum state will review its own policies to determine which law should apply**. If the conflict cannot be resolved, then the law of the forum state is applied.

E. Conflict-of-Laws Rules in Federal Diversity Cases (recently tested)

In federal diversity cases, the federal district court is generally required to apply the conflict-of-laws rules of the state in which it sits.

However, if a diversity case was transferred under federal venue law from a federal court in one state to a federal court in a different state, then the **first state's choice-of-law rules will be applied**.

> ***Example 2:*** *(Based on a recent exam question): O files a lawsuit in federal court in State A based on diversity jurisdiction. The federal court must use State A's choice of law rules. If the case is then transferred under federal venue rules to a federal court in State B, the federal court in State B must use State A's choice of law rules.*

CHAPTER 2: RULES FOR SPECIFIC ACTIONS

A. Rules for Specific Areas of Substantive Law

> **Exam Tip 3:** The exam question will typically tell you which area(s) of law applies and which approach the state takes to choice of law.

> ***Example 3:*** *(From a recent exam question): B files an action against C alleging unfair competition, a tort claim, in State A. To address choice of law problems, State A follows the "most significant relationship approach".*

1. **Torts**

   a. **Vested-rights approach**

   Under the vested-rights approach a tort case will be governed by **the law of the place where the wrong was committed** (i.e., *lex loci delicti*). This means the place where the last event necessary to make the actor liable for the tort took place (generally the place where the person or thing that is injured is situated at the time of the wrong).

   b. **Most-significant-relationship approach**

   Under the most-significant-relationship approach the court considers **four important contacts**: (i) the place of the injury, (ii) the place where conduct causing injury occurred, (iii) the domicile, residence, place of incorporation, or place of business of the parties, and (iv) the place where the relationship is centered.

   c. **Governmental-interest approach**

   Under the governmental-interest approach, the forum state generally looks to its own law, so long as that state has a legitimate interest in applying its own law.

2. **Contracts**

   a. **Express choice of law of the parties**

   If there is an express choice-of-law provision in the contract, then that law will govern unless:

   - It is contrary to public policy;
   - There is no reasonable basis for the parties' choice; **or**
   - There was fraud or mistake and true consent was not given.

   b. **Vested-rights approach**

   Under the vested-rights approach, certain contractual issues are deemed to vest in the location where the contract was executed, while others are deemed to vest in the location where the contract was to be performed.

   The law of the place **where the contract is executed** will apply to the following issues:

   - Validity of the contract;
   - Defenses to formation of the contract; **and**
   - Interpretation of the contract.

   The law of the location **where the contract was to be performed** will apply to:

   - Details of performance such as time and manner of performance;
   - The person who is obligated to perform and the person to whom performance is to be made;
   - Sufficiency of performance; **and**

- Excuses for nonperformance.

c. **Most-significant-relationship approach**

Under the most-significant-relationship approach, the following factors are considered, in addition to the seven policy factors (in the outline):

- The **location of the contracting, negotiation, and performance**;
- The **place where the contract's subject matter is located**; **and**
- The **location of the parties' domiciles**, residences, nationalities, places of incorporation, and places of business.

Generally, when the location of negotiation and performance are the same, the forum court will apply the law of that state.

d. **Default rules**

There are also default rules that apply to certain kinds of contracts. These default rules will generally apply **unless** another state is found to have a more significant relationship with regard to the issue.

- **Land contracts** are controlled by the **law of the state of the situs (location) of the land**.
- **Personalty** (personal property) **contracts** are controlled by the **law of the state where the place of delivery** is located.

3. **Property**

a. **Tangible personal property**

The UCC generally governs most issues involving the sale of (or security interests in) tangible personal property. Under the UCC, the parties may stipulate to the applicable law that will govern the transaction or, in the absence of such stipulation, the forum state will apply its version of the UCC "to transactions bearing an appropriate relation to" the forum state.

- **Secured Transactions:** Under the UCC, the law governing the perfection, nonperfection, and priority of security interests in tangible and intangible collateral is generally the **law of the state in which the debtor is located**.

b. **Transactions not covered by the UCC**

1) Vested-rights approach

The creation and transfer of interests in tangible personal property are governed by the law of the **state in which the property was located at the time of the transaction** at issue. This rule controls even when the property at issue may have been taken to another state without the permission of the owner.

2) Most-significant-relationship approach

Under the most-significant-relationship approach, the **law of the situs (location) of the tangible personal property at the time that the relevant transaction took place** generally determines the choice of law. However, if it is determined that another state has a more significant relationship to the transaction, then that state's law will apply.

c. **Real Property**

1) Vested-rights approach

The **law of the situs of the real property** governs legal issues concerning the title and disposition of real property and whether any interests in the property can be gained or lost. The forum state will refer to the law of the situs state even with regard to the choice-of-law rules.

2) Most-significant-relationship approach

Under the most-significant-relationship approach, the **law of the situs of the real property** is generally presumed to be most significant.

4. **Inheritance (recently tested)**

There are many questions that may arise when determining the law that governs inheritance. These questions include the validity of the will, the rights of nonmarital or adopted children to inherit property, and the marital rights of the surviving spouse.

a. **Personal Property**

Questions regarding the validity of a decedent's will regarding personal property and the transfer of personal property from someone who dies intestate or who has a will are governed by the **law of the deceased's domicile at the time of death**.

b. **Real property**

Questions regarding the validity of a decedent's will regarding real property and the transfer of real property from someone who dies intestate or who has a will are governed by the **law of the situs**.

Example 4: *(Based on a recent exam question): Z died a domiciliary of State A. At his death, he owned a house in State A. H also owned a farm in State B and had a savings account at a bank in State B. Z left a will leaving his entire estate to "University."*
State A law will determine the validity of Z's will regarding Z's house (real property) and his savings account (personal property), even though the account is located in State B. State A law will also govern the transfer of these two items.
State B law will determine the validity of Z's will in regard to Z's farm in State B. State B law will also govern the transfer of Z's farm.

5. **Family Law (recently tested)**

a. **In general**

Marriages are valid where they took place and are recognized in all other states. If a marriage violates a particularly strong public policy of the domicile of either party, however, it will be invalid. Such policies can include bigamy and incest.

> **Exam Tip 4:** A common law marriage that is valid where contracted is also valid in a state that does not permit common law marriage unless it violates a strong public policy of the domicile of either party.

b. **Divorce and marital property (recently tested)**

Questions of law relating to the **grounds for divorce** are controlled by the law of the **plaintiff's domicile** in a divorce matter.

In determining the enforceability of a premarital agreement:

- **Most states** apply the **law of the state with the most significant relationship** to the matter at hand.
- **Some states** apply the **law of the state in which the premarital agreement was executed.**

CHAPTER 3: DEFENSES; RECOGNITION OF FOREIGN JUDGMENTS

A. Introduction

There are generally three arguments against the application of foreign law (law from another state), that the law to be applied is:

- **Procedural**, rather than substantive;
- **Against public policy; or**
- A **penal law.**

B. Substance/Procedure Distinction

If the foreign law sought to be applied is **procedural**, then the forum state's law will **always** govern.

The forum state's law is applied to determine whether a law is substantive or procedural, so long as the result is not arbitrary or so unreasonable as to constitute a denial of due process or full faith and credit.

1. **Procedural**

Questions about the following matters are generally considered procedural and are controlled by the law of the forum state:

- The proper court in which to bring an action;
- The sufficiency of the pleadings;
- The proper or necessary parties to an action;

- Venue;
- The rules of discovery;
- Service of process;
- Others (see outline).

2. Federal diversity cases (recently tested)

Under the *Erie* doctrine, **in diversity jurisdiction cases, federal district courts must apply the substantive law of the state where the court sits.**

The *Erie* doctrine does not require that the forum state's procedural laws be applied, however, and if a Federal Rule of Civil Procedure addresses the procedural issue at hand, then that rule will be applied.

If no federal rule applies, then the district court must follow state law with regard to substance, but it can choose to ignore state law with regard to procedure, under certain circumstances.

To determine whether a given law is substantive or procedural, the court considers whether the failure to apply state law would lead to different outcomes in state and federal courts. If the answer is yes, then the court will generally apply state law.

> **Exam Tip 5: A state's choice of law rules are considered to be substantive law.** Therefore, a federal court with diversity jurisdiction must use the choice of law rules of the state that it is located in.

Example 5: *(Based on a recent exam question): O files a lawsuit in federal court in State A based on diversity jurisdiction. The federal court must use State A's choice of law rules because they are substantive in nature.*

C. Laws Against Public Policy

Both the Restatement (First) of Conflict of Laws and the Restatement (Second) of Conflict of Laws provide that if a foreign law violates the public policy of the forum state, then the forum court may refuse to apply that law.

D. Penal Laws

Both the Restatement (First) of Conflict of Laws and the Restatement (Second) of Conflict of Laws provide that a forum state will not enforce another state's penal laws.

E. Recognition of Divorce Judgments (recently tested)

Divorce decrees from other states are entitled to full faith and credit as long as the original state had jurisdiction to issue the decree and the decree is valid in the original state. Decrees have proper jurisdiction if at least one person resides where the decree was issued.

1. **Bilateral Divorce**

   If the court has personal jurisdiction over both spouses and at least one spouse is domiciled in the state, then the divorce judgment will be a valid bilateral divorce and will be entitled to full faith and credit.

2. **Ex Parte Divorce (recently tested)**

   Personal jurisdiction over both spouses is not necessary to dissolve a marriage. If the plaintiff spouse seeking divorce is domiciled in the forum state, the courts of that state have jurisdiction to dissolve the plaintiff's marriage (despite the lack of personal jurisdiction over the other spouse).

   However, the court may not issue a binding order affecting personal rights of the spouses such as property rights, alimony, and child custody unless the other spouse who is not domiciled in the state agrees to the order.

3. **Child Custody**

   There is a reciprocal statute in all 50 states that governs child custody: the Uniform Child Custody Jurisdiction and Enforcement Act (UCCJEA). Under the UCCJEA, a court can make **initial custody decisions if it is in the child's home state**, and all other states must give full faith and credit to such decisions.

   Other states cannot modify these custody decrees unless the original court has no significant connection to the child or parents anymore (i.e., neither the child nor the parents reside in that state anymore).

CHAPTER 4: PRACTICE QUESTION

February 2009, Question 5 [ID 304]

Bearco is a corporation incorporated under the laws of State A. Bearco maintains its corporate and administrative offices in State A; its factories are located in State B. Bearco's popular stuffed toy bear, "Griz," is sold throughout the United States. Bearco has registered the trademark "Griz" with the United States Patent and Trademark Office.

Copyco is a corporation incorporated under the laws of Country X, a foreign country, where Copyco has its manufacturing facilities and corporate offices. Copyco sells a line of toy bears called "Griz," which look remarkably similar to the Bearco "Griz" bears. Copyco sells its bears to consumers throughout the United States. However, it sells only on the Internet, using a parcel delivery service to deliver the bears to consumers. The Copyco website does not list a telephone number, street address, or post office box for the company. It lists only an e-mail address and an Internet address.

Bearco has filed an action against Copyco in the United States District Court for State A, properly invoking the court's federal question and diversity jurisdiction. Bearco alleges both trademark infringement (a federal law claim) and unfair competition (a tort claim that, in the United States, is based on state law).

State A and State B have materially different unfair-competition laws. Unfair competition is not actionable under the law of Country X.

To address choice-of-law problems, State A follows the "most significant relationship" approach of the Restatement (Second) of Conflict of Laws. State B applies the "vested rights" approach of the Restatement (First) of Conflict of Laws. Country X's choice-of-law methodology is unknown.

Bearco has been unable to determine Copyco's street address or post office box address either in the United States or in Country X and has filed a motion requesting that the district court authorize service of the summons and complaint by e-mail. There are no international agreements that affect the court's resolution of the issues in this case.

1. If the United States District Court for State A permits service of process on Copyco by e-mail, would such e-mail service be consistent with the Federal Rules of Civil Procedure and the United States Constitution? Explain.

2. Which jurisdiction's law should the United States District Court for State A apply to resolve Bearco's unfair-competition claim? Explain.

Sample Answer

1.a. E-mail service would be consistent with the Federal Rules of Civil Procedure under these circumstances. (20-30%)

The Federal Rules of Civil Procedure allow service of process on a corporation outside the United States to be made using any methods available for service of an individual outside the United States, except personal delivery. These methods include service in any manner, internationally agreed upon, which is reasonably calculated to give notice. If no international agreement exists, service may be effected by any method ordered by the court that is not prohibited by the law of the foreign country. Here, the facts indicate that no treaty applies, so the court can likely authorize service by e-mail, so long as laws of Country X do not specifically prohibit such service. Given the fact that the defendant's street address cannot be determined and the defendant's business conduct shows a preference for Internet communication, service by e-mail would seem reasonably calculated to give notice in this case.

1.b. E-mail service would be consistent with the United States Constitution under these circumstances. (20-30%)

Even if the Federal Rules of Civil Procedure allow a certain method of service, the method must be constitutional to be employed. To meet the Constitution's due process requirements, a litigant must be given reasonable notice of the action, under all the circumstances, so as to apprise him of the pendency of the action and allow an opportunity to object. Copyco does not list a street address or post office box and only lists its e-mail address on its website. Under these facts, service by e-mail may be the most likely to reach Copyco and would therefore comport with due process.

2. The federal court should apply State A's law to determine the unfair-competition claim. (40-60%)

The Supreme Court has held that a federal court exercising diversity jurisdiction over non-federal claims must apply the choice-of-law rule of the state in which it sits. Thus, here, the U.S. District Court sitting in State A should apply the choice-of-law rules followed by the courts of State A. The facts indicate that State A applies the Second Restatement's "most significant relationship" approach to conflicts of law. Under that approach, tort issues are governed by the law of the state that has the most significant relationship to the occurrence and the parties, based on several principles. Courts will consider several contacts with the state, including (i) the place where the injury occurred, (ii) the place where the conduct causing the injury occurred, (iii) the place of incorporation, and the place of business of the parties, and (iv) the place where the relationship, if any, between the parties is centered. In tort matters, the default rule is that the place of the injury controls, unless another state has a more significant relationship to the parties or to the occurrence of the tort.

Here, Bearco's injury, the loss of customers due to the Copyco knock-off bear, occurred in all 50 states, so those states have a significant relationship with the tort. Because there are so many states, the court should look to the other contacts to determine whether another state has a more significant relationship to the parties or the tort. Here, the wrongs were committed by Copyco either abroad or in all 50 states where it sells its competing product. There does not seem to be a relationship between the parties, so that contact is not significant. Thus, the most important contact appears to be where the parties are located. Copyco is a foreign corporation located in Country X. Bearco is incorporated and has its principal offices in State A. Although Bearco has factories in State B, it seems that State A has the most significant contacts with the tort of unfair competition.

If the court finds that Country X also has a significant interest in having its laws applied, the court must closely scrutinize the foreign law and the forum state's public policy. If the foreign law violates the public policy of the forum state, then the forum court may refuse to apply that law. Here, unfair competition is not actionable under the law of Country X. Country X likely has this policy to protect businesses and promote competition. State A's policy in allowing such actions is likely to protect State A businesses and promote fair business practices in State A. Because Copyco is actively conducting business in State A, it would violate State A's public policy to allow Copyco's alleged misconduct to continue without allowing a State A corporation to recover for that injury. Thus, the federal court will likely apply State A's unfair competition law.

(Editor's Note: The foregoing model answer was drafted in accordance with the NCBE Grading Guidelines for this question. The analysis is illustrative of the discussions that might appear in a high passing answer and addresses all legal and factual issues the drafters intended exam candidates to raise. When self-grading, refer to the NCBE's weighting of each issue, which is indicated in parentheses for your reference.)

[END OF HANDOUT]

Themis
Bar Review

CONSTITUTIONAL LAW ESSAY WORKSHOP

PROFESSOR CHRISTOPHER IDE-DON
UC DAVIS SCHOOL OF LAW

CHAPTER 1: SUMMARY OF ISSUES TESTED; SUBSTANTIVE LAW

A. Summary of Issues

1. Justiciability

- Standing
- Mootness
- Ripeness

2. Legislative Powers

- Commerce Clause
- Spending Power
- Delegation of Legislative Power

3. Executive Power

- Executive Order

4. State Powers

- Supremacy Clause
- Preemption
- Privileges and Immunities Clause
- 10th Amendment & Commandeering
- Dormant Commerce Clause

5. Takings

- Physical
- Regulatory
    - Total or Partial

6. Zoning

- Variance for conforming use

7. Procedural Due Process

8. Substantive Due Process

9. Equal Protection

10. Free Speech

- Symbolic Speech
- Vagueness & Overbreadth
- Prior Restraint
- Forum – Public, Limited Public, Non-Public
- Content Based v. Content Neutral
- Commercial Speech
- Obscenity

11. Freedom of Religion

- Establishment Clause
- Free Exercise Clause

B. Justiciability

1. Limitation—Eleventh Amendment

- Prohibits citizens from one state suing another state in federal court
- Abrogation—Congress may expressly repeal state immunity if acting to enforce rights under the 13th, 14th, and 15th Amendments
  - Congress may not abrogate state immunity by exercising Article I powers (such as the Commerce Clause).

2. Standing

a. Individual Standing

1) Injury in fact;

2) Causation; and

3) Redressability

b. Organizational Standing

1) Individual members have standing;

> **Exam Tip 1:** In addressing organizational standing, you must first analyze individual standing to meet the first requirement.

2) Claim is related to the purpose of the organization; and

3) The individual members are not necessary to adjudicate the claim

3. **Mootness**—must have a live controversy

4. **Ripeness**—injury must have occurred or not be speculative

C. Legislative Powers

1. Commerce Clause

- Congress has the power to regulate interstate commerce:

  1) Channels of interstate commerce

  2) Instrumentalities of interstate commerce

  3) Activities that have a ***substantial effect*** on interstate commerce

a. Substantial Effect

- Economic activity is presumed to have a substantial effect.
- Aggregation—can regulate economic activity that is intrastate if the activity as a whole has an effect on interstate commerce

Example 1: *Recall* Wickard v. Filburn, *in which a farmer was growing wheat on his land for purely intrastate purposes. Congress was authorized to* *regulate his wheat because it was an economic activity and the aggregate activity of all wheat farming had a substantial effect on interstate commerce.*

Example 2: *Congress passes legislation requiring all commercial buses to have seatbelts. Bus Company operates commercial buses only within the state of Columbia and claims that Congress does not have the power to regulate buses within Columbia if they do not cross state lines. Because commercial busing constitutes an economic activity,* ***Congress can aggregate the effects of all intrastate busing*** *within Columbia. Taken in the aggregate, there is an impact on interstate commercial activity.*

- Noneconomic activity cannot be aggregated; the activity itself must have a substantial impact on interstate commerce.

2. Spending Power

- Congress can condition federal funds to states and require states to implement certain regulations.

Example 3: *Congress requires states to pass seatbelt laws for all cars in order to receive federal money for highway construction. The condition of requiring seatbelts is related to the highways because seatbelts make travel on highways safer.*

- Permitted as long as the condition is related to the purpose of the funds
- **Commandeering**—states might claim that Congress is violating the 10th Amendment by forcing the state legislature to pass specific legislation
  - A valid exercise of the Spending Power ***does not*** violate the 10th Amendment

3. Delegation of Legislative Power

Congress may delegate its powers to an agency as long as it provides reasonably intelligible standards

D. Executive Powers

1. Issue Executive Orders

1. Domestic Affairs

President has appointment and removal powers, the pardon power, the commander in chief power, and the duty to execute the law

2. Foreign Affairs

President has the power to conduct foreign negotiations, to deploy troops overseas, and to make executive agreements

E. State Powers

1. Supremacy Clause

If state law conflicts with federal law, the federal law governs.

2. Preemption

a. Express Preemption

- The federal law explicitly states that it is the only law allowed in that area.
- Any state law addressing that issue is invalid.

b. Implied Preemption

1) Congress passes a federal law intending to "occupy the field"

2) The state law conflicts directly with federal law

1) The state law conflicts indirectly with federal law

> **Note 1:** A state can pass ***more*** stringent laws than the federal law, so long as they do not conflict.

3. Privileges and Immunities Clause

- Prohibits states from discriminating against nonresidents, unless it is necessary to achieve an important government interest
- This protection only applies to individual citizens; corporations cannot claim this clause

4. 10th Amendment & Commandeering

- All powers not expressly given to the federal government are reserved to the states.
- Federal government cannot "commandeer" state legislatures and force them to pass legislation.

> **Exam Tip 2:** This concept often arises with the Spending Power. The government cannot force the state legislature to enact specific laws, but it can condition federal funds to persuade the state legislature.

5. Dormant Commerce Clause

> **Note 2:** The Commerce Clause enables Congress to regulate interstate commerce.

- Under the Dormant Commerce Clause, a state may not discriminate against out of state commerce or in a way that unduly burdens interstate commerce.

> **Exam Tip 3:** A typical fact pattern will have a plaintiff who claims that a state's law is invalid under the Commerce Clause. This will require you to discuss the Dormant Commerce Clause and analyze whether the state has exceeded its powers by passing a law that negatively impacts interstate commerce.

a. Discrimination

- Can be discriminatory on its face or by its impact
- If a statute discriminates against out-of-state commerce, the state must show:

  a) It has an important state interest; and

  b) There is no other non-discriminatory means available to achieve that interest

- **Market Participant Exception**—can favor local business if state is acting as a buyer or seller

b. Unduly Burden Interstate Commerce

- If a statute is not discriminatory, the law may still be invalid if causes an "undue burden" on interstate commerce.
- A court will balance:
  - The purpose of the statute;
  - The burden on interstate commerce; and
  - Whether there are less restrictive alternatives

CHAPTER 2: SUBSTANTIVE LAW (CONT'D)—INDIVIDUAL RIGHTS

A. State Action

- The constitution protects against wrongful conduct by the government, not private parties.
- A private entity may be subject to the constitution if it is acting as if it is a state

  Example 4: *A private entity that is running a company town or significantly involved in a joint venture with the state*

F. 5th Amendment—Takings Clause

- Government may not take private property for public use without just compensation

1. Government Action

- Protects from government "taking" of private property
- Includes taking land and also regulatory takings by rezoning, prohibiting development, etc.

2. Private Property

- Usually involves land or other real property
- Can be other property such as contract and patent rights or trade secrets

3. Public Use

- Must be rationally related to a conceivable public purpose
- Includes health, safety, economic development, etc.

4. Type of Takings

a. Physical Taking

Government physically takes or occupies the land

b. Regulatory Taking

A law has the effect of decreasing the value of the property

1) **Total Taking**—the regulation leaves no economically viable use of the property
2) **Partial Taking**—the regulation affects some economic use of the land, but there is still some economic use available
    a) ***Economic impact***—how much value was lost due to the regulation;
    b) ***Reasonable expectations***—the owner's reasonable expectation of return on investment; and
    c) ***Character of the regulation***—does the regulation impact a few owners or the entire community?

a. Exaction

- Local government may exact promises from a developer in exchange for construction permits

    Example 5: *Requiring the developer set aside an easement over the developed land*

- Does NOT constitute a taking if there is:
    a) An ***essential nexus*** between legitimate state interests and the conditions imposed; and
    b) A ***rough proportionality*** between the burden on the owner and the impact on the community

5. Just Compensation

- Property owner is entitled to the fair market value of the property **at the time of the taking**
- Only a portion has been taken—owner entitled to compensation for land actually taken and any loss in value of the land still owned

> **Exam Tip 4:** In past exams, the plaintiff has asked for the fair market value of the land as if it had been developed. The plaintiff's recovery is limited to the value of the land at the time of taking.

6. **Zoning & Variances**

- Local governments have the power to pass zoning ordinances, so long as they are reasonably related to a legitimate government purpose (health, safety, morals, and general welfare).

  Example 6: *The plaintiff owns a restaurant in a commercial area. The city zones that area as residential and the restaurant must be converted to residential use. The plaintiff can seek a variance or bring a Takings Clause claim.*

b. **Variance**

- May be granted to allow the owner to continue the nonconforming use of the land
- The owner must show an undue burden if the variance is not granted.

c. **Takings Clause Claim**

- Must show that the zoning ordinance amounts to a regulatory taking

G. **Due Process**

> **Exam Tip 5:** The Due Process clause includes both procedural and substantive due process, which are often tested together.

1. **Procedural Due Process**

- The government shall not deprive a person of life, liberty, or property without due process of law.
- Process includes notice, a hearing, and a neutral decisionmaker

a. **Amount of Process Due—Factors:**

1) Interest affected—life, liberty (including fundamental rights), or property;

2) Value of additional safeguards; and

3) Burden or cost of additional process

2. **Substantive Due Process**

- Whether the government's action (such as a law or regulation) impermissibly infringes on an individual's rights

a. **Standard of Review**

1) Fundamental rights (life, liberty, property, voting, travel, privacy)

- **Strict scrutiny**—only valid if necessary to achieve a compelling governmental interest

2) Non-fundamental rights

- **Rational basis**—valid if rationally related to a legitimate government interest

H. Equal Protection Clause

Exam Tip 6: Involves treating classes of people differently

1. Discrimination requirement

- Discriminatory intent—strict or intermediate scrutiny (depending on classification)
- Disparate impact—rational basis review

Exam Tip 7: Determine whether the statute is facially discriminatory or impliedly discriminatory and whether there is a discriminatory intent. If the statute merely has a disparate impact, it is limited to rational basis review.

2. Standards of Review

Exam Tip 8: If the classification involves more than one category, different provisions in the statute may be evaluated under different levels of scrutiny.

Example 7: *A statute requires male students between the ages of 15–18 who are absent from school to attend a work camp in the wilderness. Forced work affects an individual's fundamental right of liberty and falls under strict scrutiny. Treating genders differently falls under intermediate scrutiny. Treating ages differently falls under rational basis review.*

a. Strict Scrutiny

- Applies to any law involving fundamental rights and classifications based on race, ethnicity, and national origin
- The **government** must show it is:

  a) The least restrictive means

  b) To achieve a compelling government interest

b. Intermediate Scrutiny

- Applies to laws involving gender and non-marital children born outside of marriage
- The **government** must show it is:

  a) Substantially related

  b) To an important government interest

- Gender discrimination—must also show an "exceedingly persuasive justification"
  - Must also show that facilities are substantially equivalent

c. Rational Basis

- Applies to all other rights and classifications
- Must be:

a) Rationally related

b) To a legitimate government interest

- The **plaintiff** bears the burden of showing the law is arbitrary or irrational.

> **Exam Tip 9:** Equal Protection and Due Process are often tested together in a fact pattern.

Example 8: *A statute requires male students between the ages of 15–18 who are absent from school to attend a work camp in the wilderness. Paul is a 16-year-old student who has been absent from school. He claims that the statute violated his Equal Protection and Due Process Rights.*

Equal Protection: The statute treats people differently as to a fundamental right (liberty), as to gender, and as to age.

Procedural Due Process: Determine whether Paul is given the amount of process that he is due because the statute infringes on his right to liberty.

Substantive Due Process: Determine whether the statute impermissibly infringes on a fundamental right (liberty).

B. Enabling Clause

Under the 14th Amendment, Section 5—Congress may pass legislation to enforce equal protection and due process rights (overriding state statutes)

CHAPTER 3: SUBSTANTIVE LAW (CONT'D)—INDIVIDUAL RIGHTS

I. Freedom of Speech

1. Symbolic Speech—Expressive Conduct

Example 9: *Someone burning a copy of the Constitution to show anger at the government.*

- Regulation is valid if:

  1) It furthers an important government interest;

  2) The interest is unrelated to the suppression of ideas; and

  3) The burden on speech is no greater than necessary

2. Overbreadth

A statute is impermissibly overbroad if it regulates more speech than necessary to protect a compelling government interest.

3. Vagueness

A statute is void for vagueness if it fails to provide a person of ordinary intelligence with fair notice of what is prohibited.

4. Prior Restraints

- A prior restraint prohibits speech before it occurs.

  Example 10: *A law requiring a license or a permit before engaging in speech or expressive conduct.*

- Prior restraints are generally not allowed unless specific procedural safeguards are in place
- Standards must be narrowly drawn, reasonable, and definite

5. Right Not to Speak

Protected by the First Amendment

Example 11: *The Supreme Court has held that a child in a public school has the right to not recite the Pledge of Allegiance.*

6. Content

Exam Tip 10: Start with the question: is this a content-based or a content-neutral restriction?

a. Content-based regulation (Strict Scrutiny)

- Government must show the regulation is:
  - a) Necessary to achieve;
  - b) A compelling governmental interest; and
  - c) Narrowly tailored to meet that interest

b. Content-neutral regulation (Intermediate Scrutiny)

- Government must show the regulation is:
  - d) Substantially related to;
  - e) An important government interest

c. Time, Place, and Manner Regulation

Validity depends on the type of forum

7. Less-Protected and Unprotected Speech

a. Less-Protected: Commercial Speech

- Commercial speech is protected unless it is false, misleading, or unlawful
- Protected commercial speech can only be regulated if:

a) The government interest is substantial;

b) The regulation directly advances the interest; and

c) The regulation is narrowly tailored

b. Unprotected: Obscenity, Incitement to Violence, Fighting Words

- Obscenity—the average person, applying contemporary community standards finds the speech:
  - Appeals to the prurient interest;
  - Depicts sexual conduct in a patently offensive way; and
  - Lacks serious literary, artistic, political, or scientific value
- Incitement to Violence—advocates use of force or unlawful action if:
  - Directed to inciting or producing imminent lawless action; and
  - Is likely to incite or produce such action (i.e., creates a clear and present danger)
- Fighting Words—by their very nature, likely to incite an immediate breach of the peace

c. Defamation

There are constitutional limitations on defamation actions when the plaintiff is a public official or public figure, or the speech involves a matter of public concern.

Note 3: These limitations are discussed further in the Torts materials.

8. Speech in a Government Forum

a. Traditional Public Forum

Example 12: *Sidewalks, streets, parks*

- Content-based regulations are subject to strict scrutiny.
- Content-neutral regulations are subject to the time, place, and manner test; must be:
  - Narrowly tailored;
  - To serve a significant government interest; and
  - Leave open ample alternative channels for communication

Example 13: *There is a statute that prohibitions distribution of flyers in a bus station but allows the plaintiff to hand out flyers on the sidewalk outside. This is an ample alternative channel for communication.*

b. Designated Public Forum

- Not historically used for speech-related activities but has been opened for such use
- Content-based regulations are subject to strict scrutiny.
- Content-neutral regulations are subject to the time, place, and manner test; must be:

- Narrowly tailored;
- To serve a significant government interest; and
- Leave open ample alternative channels for communication

c. Non-Public Forum

Example 14: *Government offices, schools, jails, military bases, sidewalks on postal office property, airport terminals*

Example 15: *Can also include privately owned areas that are held open to the public, such as a public lobby in a private building.*

- Government can regulate speech if:

  a) The regulation is viewpoint-neutral; and

  b) Reasonably related to;

  c) A legitimate government interest

- Government can regulate content in a non-public forum, so long as it is viewpoint neutral

Example 16: *A military base can ban speech about nuclear weapons completely, but it cannot allow only one side or the other.*

J. Religion

Exam Tip 11: There are two aspects to Freedom of Religion questions: The Establishment Clause and the Free Exercise Clause.

1. Establishment Clause

Prohibits the government from establishing a religion, preferring a particular religion over another, or preferring religion over non-religion

a. Facially Religious Preference

If statute shows a preference to one religion over another (or to religion over non-religion), strict scrutiny applies

b. Facially Neutral Statute

- A statute might have the **effect** of favoring religion
- Apply the *Lemon* test to determine whether the statute is constitutional:

  a) The law must have a secular purpose;

  b) The primary effect neither advances nor prohibits religion; and

  c) The law does not result in excessive government entanglement with religion

2. **Free Exercise Clause**

- Includes the freedom to believe and the freedom to act

  Note 4: Religion is protected, but philosophies and political beliefs are not.

- Must have a genuine belief in that religion

a. **Belief**

A person's beliefs are absolutely protected.

b. **Conduct**

- Laws that intentionally target religions conduct are subject to strict scrutiny.
- Laws that are generally applicable, but happen to impact religion are subject to the rational basis test

  Example 17: *A prison regulation states that prisoners may not use drugs of any kind. A prisoner practices a particular religion that involves the use of specific drugs. The regulation does not target a specific religion because it is a generally applicable law. So it is subject to mere rational basis review and is likely to be upheld.*

CHAPTER 4: PRACTICE QUESTION

July 2011, Question 8 [ID 2209]

There are two nursing schools in State A: Public Nursing School (Public) and Private Nursing School (Private). Public is an agency of the state government, and all its faculty and staff are state employees. Private is owned by a private corporation and receives no direct funding from the state. The State A Board of Education regulates the curriculum of each nursing school and certifies all graduates of the two nursing schools as eligible to become licensed nurses in State A.

Both Public and Private have a long-standing policy of restricting admission to women. Neither school has ever admitted a male applicant. There has been general discrimination against women in State A in the health care field. Historically, however, 95 percent of State A nurses have been female.

A male resident of State A wants to be a nurse. The man first applied to Private and was denied admission. His rejection letter from Private stated that he was "not eligible to enroll because Private was established as an all-female institution and does not admit or enroll male students."

The man next applied to Public and was again denied admission. His letter from Public stated that "you are not eligible to enroll because Public does not enroll male students. Mindful of the historical discrimination that women have faced in State A, our state has established Public to remedy this discrimination and provide opportunities for women who want to work in the growing field of health care as nurses." The letter continued, "Because your grades and test scores would have been sufficient to admit you if you were female, we offer you admission to our new Male Nursing Opportunity Program instead."

The Male Nursing Opportunity Program allows male residents of State A to become nurses by studying at a nursing school in an adjacent state. Graduates of the program are certified by the State A Board of Education as eligible to become licensed nurses in State A. However, the Male Nursing Opportunity Program facilities are not as modern as those at Public, the faculty is not as experienced, and graduates of the Male Nursing Opportunity Program do not enjoy the same employment opportunities as graduates of either Public or Private.

1. Has Private violated the man's rights under the Equal Protection Clause of the Fourteenth Amendment? Explain.

2. Has Public violated the man's rights under the Equal Protection Clause of the Fourteenth Amendment? Explain.

SAMPLE ANSWER

1. Private has not violated the man's rights under the Equal Protection Clause of the Fourteenth Amendment because its actions are not state actions. (30%)

The Equal Protection Clause of the Fourteenth Amendment applies only to government action. To trigger constitutional protections, state action is required. A private entity's conduct must constitute state action in order for these protections to apply. State action may be considered to exist when private parties carry out traditional governmental functions or if there is significant state involvement in the activities.

Neither exception would apply to Private. Running a school is not an activity traditionally performed exclusively by the state. To be considered significantly involved, the state must act affirmatively to facilitate, authorize, or encourage the private activity or must have intertwined its actions with those of the private entity to such an extent that the state and the private party mutually benefit from the involvement (e.g., a joint venture). Simply licensing or regulating a private party, as the State A Board of Education does here, does not amount to state involvement significant enough to trigger the protections of the Equal Protection Clause of the Fourteenth Amendment.

2.(a) Public has violated the man's rights under the Equal Protection Clause of the Fourteenth Amendment because it is a state actor discriminating based on gender and such gender discrimination cannot be justified under the intermediate scrutiny test absent an "exceedingly persuasive justification." (40%)

Public is the state nursing school and its action is therefore state action on its face. Denying the man admission to the State Nursing School based on his gender is presumed to be unconstitutional. Discrimination based on gender is discrimination based on a "quasi-suspect" classification and so is judged under the intermediate scrutiny standard. In applying this test, the burden is on the state to show that its different treatment of the sexes is substantially related to an important government interest and that an "exceedingly persuasive justification" exists for the distinction. The state here will need to show that the exclusion of males from its state nursing school serves an important governmental interest and provide "exceedingly persuasive justification" for excluding male applicants based on their gender.

The State would seem to have a difficult time in providing an "exceedingly persuasive justification" for denying the man admission to its nursing school based on his gender. Public's letter cites the historical discrimination women had faced in the healthcare field in State A, presumably to show that its exclusion of men is substantially related to the important governmental interest of redressing this historical wrong. However, the facts note that historically 95 percent of State A nurses have been female. Therefore, it is unlikely that excluding men would actually redress the general discrimination against women in the healthcare field. State can thus provide no persuasive justification for its exclusionary admissions policy and has violated the man's rights under the Equal Protection Clause.

2.(b) In providing the man with the opportunity for nursing education that is inferior to that offered to female students, the state has violated his rights under the Equal Protection Clause of the Fourteenth Amendment. (30%)

Different treatment of the genders by the government (for example separate sports facilities at state universities) does not violate the equal protection guarantee if the state can show that it has an "exceedingly persuasive justification" for the different treatment and that the separate facilities offered are "substantially equivalent."

As discussed above, the state is unable to provide exceedingly persuasive justification for the gender-separate nursing schools. Nor is Public able to show that the education offered by the two facilities is substantially equivalent. The two programs differ in that the Male Nursing Opportunity Program is clearly inferior. Its facilities are not as modern as those at Public, the faculty is not as experienced, and graduates of the Program do not have the same employment opportunities as graduates of either in-state nursing schools. Because Public has not shown substantial equality in the separate educational opportunities, the separate program for males violates the Fourteenth Amendment.

(Editor's Note: The foregoing model answer was drafted in accordance with the NCBE Grading Guidelines for this question. The analysis is illustrative of the discussions that might appear in a high passing answer and addresses all legal and factual issues the drafters intended exam candidates to raise. When self-grading, refer to the NCBE's weighting of each issue, which is indicated in parentheses for your reference.)

[END OF HANDOUT]

Themis
Bar Review

CONTRACTS & SALES ESSAY WORKSHOP

PROFESSOR CHRISTOPHER IDE-DON

UC DAVIS SCHOOL OF LAW

Editor's Note 1: The Professor refers to specific page numbers throughout this lecture. The content does not always match these references due to formatting changes.

ISSUE CHECKLIST

A. Applicable Law

B. Formation of Contract

1. Offer

- Unilateral/Bilateral
- Irrevocable Offers
- Termination of Offer
  - Revocation of Offer
  - Rejection by Offeree
  - Counter-Offer by Offeree
  - Lapse of Time
  - Death

2. Acceptance

- Unilateral/Bilateral
- Manner of Acceptance
- Counter-Offer
- Mailbox Rule

3. Consideration

- Adequacy of Consideration
- Gifts
- Moral Consideration
- Preexisting Duty Rule
- Past Consideration
- Promissory Estoppel (Consideration Substitute)

4. Defenses to Formation and Enforcement

- Defenses to Formation

- Mistake – Mutual & Unilateral
- Misrepresentation
- Undue Influence
- Duress
- Capacity

- Defenses to Enforcement
  - Statute of Frauds
    - Exceptions
  - Illegality
  - Unconscionability

C. Terms of the Contract

1. Modification – UCC/CL

2. Accord & Satisfaction

3. Parol Evidence Rule

- Integration
- Exceptions
  - Ambiguity
  - Collateral Deal
  - Condition Precedent

D. Performance of the Contract

1. Promises

- Standard of Performance

2. Conditions

- Express/Implied
- Satisfaction
- Excuse of Conditions
  - Waiver
  - Wrongful Interference
  - Estoppel

3. Discharge of Duty to Perform

- Impracticability
- Impossibility
- Frustration of Purpose

E. Third Party Beneficiary Contracts

F. Assignment/Delegation

G. Breach of Contract

1. Anticipatory Breach/Repudiation

- Retraction
- UCC Request Assurances

2. Material Breach

3. Minor Breach

H. Remedies

1. Legal Remedies

- Expectation Damages
  - Partial Performance
- Consequential Damages
  - Foreseeability
  - Causation
  - Certainty
- Incidental Damages
- Mitigating Damages
  - Cost of Cover
- Reliance Damages
- Quasi-Contract

2. Equitable Remedies

- Restitution Damages
- Specific Performance
  - Laches
  - Unclean Hands

3. UCC Remedies

- Buyer's Remedies
- Seller's Remedies

CHAPTER 1: ESSAY APPROACHES

Exam Tip 1: Always start by discussing the applicable law in the question.

A. Applicable Law

- The UCC governs all contracts involving the sale of goods, and common-law rules govern contracts involving services.
- **Mixed Contract**: When a contract includes both goods and services, whichever one predominates will determine the governing law.

> **Exam Tip 2:** Look for facts in the question that involve both goods and services. Explain why the UCC and the Common Law (CL) could both apply, then determine whether the goods or services are the main point of the contract.

- Merchants
    - Special rules apply to merchants under the UCC.
    - A merchant includes not only a person who regularly deals in the type of goods involved in the transaction or otherwise by his occupation holds himself out as having knowledge or skill peculiar to the practices or goods involved in the transaction, but also in some instances any businessperson when the transaction is of a commercial nature.

> **Editor's Note 2:** While at least one key UCC rule regarding the terms of an offer ("battle of the forms") does apply only if both parties are merchants, there are many other UCC rules that apply to a party who is a merchant, even if the other party is not, such as the warranty of merchantability.

B. Formation of Contract

> **Exam Tip 3:** If the question states that there is a valid written contract, do not spend time analyzing whether a contract was formed. Focus on the other contracts-related issues in the question.

A valid contract requires offer, acceptance, and consideration.

1. Offer

> **Exam Tip 4:** If the question is testing formation of contract, you should discuss each potential offer in chronological order, until you find the actual offer. Do not omit the analysis of potential offers!

- An offer requires a promise, terms, and communication to the offeree.
    - **Promise:** A promise a statement indicating a present intent to enter into a contract.
    - **Terms**
        - CL—all essential terms must be provided (parties, subject matter, price, quantity)
        - UCC—the essential terms are the parties, subject matter, and quantity; a court will "gap fill" any other missing terms.

- **Communication:** The offer must be communicated to the offeree (i.e., he must know of the offer).

> **Exam Tip 5:** Advertisements are generally not offers, unless they are specific and limit who may accept the offer. If an ad is presented in the facts, you must discuss it as a potential offer.

a. Unilateral or Bilateral Offer

After you find the actual offer, discuss whether the offer is for a bilateral or unilateral contract.

- Bilateral contract—one in which parties exchange promises; it can be accepted by a promise OR by the beginning of performance
- Unilateral contract—one in which the offeror makes a promise and the offeree must perform; it can only be accepted by complete performance

> **Exam Tip 6:** Look for exam facts that indicate a unilateral contract. The offeree must perform the contract with the intent to accept the contract, otherwise there will not be an acceptance. For example, if the party does not know about the offer, or believe the offer, her performance will not be an acceptance.

b. Irrevocable Offers

Offers are generally revocable. However, an offer can be irrevocable under certain circumstances.

- **Common Law, Option Contract:** An offer where the offeror promise to hold the offer open for a certain period of time. The offeree must pay consideration to the offeror to hold the offer open.
- **UCC Firm Offer:** An offer in writing where the offeror is a merchant and promises to hold the offer open for a certain period of time (maximum time is 90 days). No consideration is required!

> **Editor's Note 3:** The UCC Firm Offer Rule only applies if the offeror is a merchant and the assurance that the offer will remain open is contained in a signed writing from the offeror. If offeror is not a merchant or the assurance is oral, this rule does not apply even though the contract is governed by the UCC.

c. Termination of Offer

1) Revocation of Offer

   - An offer can be terminated if the offeror revokes the offer prior to acceptance.
   - Revocation is effective when received (a mailed revocation is not effective until received).
   - Offers can be irrevocable in certain circumstances:
     - Option/Firm Offer (see above)

- Unilateral Contract: If the offeree has started to perform in a unilateral contract, the offeror cannot revoke the offer (the offeree must be given a chance to complete the performance).

2) Rejection by Offeree

3) Counter-Offer by Offeree

- If the offeree counter-offers with different terms, the original offer will be deemed to be terminated.
- A "mere suggestion" of a different term or a "mere inquiry" about changing the terms is not a counter-offer and will not terminate the original offer.

4) Lapse of Time

5) Death of the offeror

2. Acceptance

Acceptance is the objective manifestation by the offeree to be bound by the terms of the offer.

a. Bilateral or Unilateral contract

- Bilateral contract—can be accepted by a promise OR by the beginning of performance
- Unilateral contract—can only be accepted by complete performance

b. Manner of Acceptance

- Any reasonable means of acceptance is allowed; unless the offer limits the means of acceptance
- Silence is generally not acceptance, unless the offeree has reason to believe that silence will constitute an acceptance.

c. Counter-Offers and Mirror Image Rule

1) Mirror Image Rule (Common Law)

- The acceptance must mirror the terms of the offer; any changes/additions to the terms constitute a rejection of the original offer and a counter-offer.

Note 1: Recall that a "mere suggestion" or a "mere inquiry" is not a counter-offer and will not terminate the original offer.

2) UCC (no Mirror Image Rule)

- If any party is a non-merchant:
  - An acceptance from the offeree with changes or additions will be a valid acceptance.
  - However, the contract **will not** include the changes or additions unless the offeror agrees to them.

- If both parties are merchants:
    - An acceptance from the offeree with changes or additions will be a valid acceptance.
    - The contract **will** include the changes or additions unless: (i) they materially alter the terms of the original offer; (ii) the original offer limits acceptance to the terms of the offer, **or** (iii) the offeror has previously objected, or objects to the changed or new terms.

d. Mailbox Rule

- Under the mailbox rule, an acceptance is valid when placed in the mail.
- **Exception:** If there is an option contract or firm offer, the acceptance is valid when received and must be received before the offer expires.
- **Special Issue:** If a party mails a rejection of an offer and then mails an acceptance to the offer, the first communication to be received is effective. The recipient of the communication does not have to read the communication for it to be effective!

3. Consideration

Consideration requires a bargained-for change in the legal position between parties. Most courts find consideration if there is a detriment to the promisee, regardless of the benefit to the promisor. A minority of courts look to either a detriment or a benefit, not requiring both.

- Legal Detriment: A legal detriment can take the form of a promise to do/not do something, or performance/refraining from performance.
- Adequacy of Consideration: A court will not look at the adequacy of the consideration (e.g., the monetary value of the items being exchanged).

Consideration-Related Issues:

a. Gift: A gift from one party is not supported by consideration (the receiving party is not suffering a legal detriment).

b. Preexisting Duty Rule: A promise to perform a preexisting legal duty will not qualify as consideration because the promisor is already required to perform (no additional legal detriment is being incurred) by the promisor.

Example 1: *Bob and Owen enter into a valid contract for Bob to build Owen's house. Bob is required to perform a duty (build the house). Owen is an anxious person, and one week later offers to pay additional money to Bob to ensure that the house is completed on time and Bob agrees. There will not be any consideration on Bob's behalf because Bob has a preexisting duty to build the house on time and he is not suffering an additional legal detriment.*

c. Past Consideration

- Under the common law, a legal detriment incurred in the past does not constitute consideration because it was not bargained for and it was not in exchange for a legal detriment in return.
- Moral Consideration (modern trend): A promise not supported by consideration may be enforceable if it is made in recognition of a significant benefit previously received by the promisor from the promisee.
  - This rule does not apply if the promisee conferred the benefit as a gift to the promisor.
  - The court may also reduce the amount of money owed under the promise if it is disproportionate to the benefit conferred by the promisee.

d. **Promissory Estoppel** (consideration substitute)

- If a promise is made by a party, but there is not consideration provided by both sides, the promise will still be enforceable if certain conditions are met.
- The promise will be binding if:
  - The promisor should reasonably expect the promise to induce action or forbearance;
  - The promise actually induces action or forbearance; and
  - Injustice can be avoided only by enforcement of the promise.
- The damages awarded under promissory estoppel are usually limited to reliance damages (money spent on reliance of the promise).

  Example 2: *Tom promises to give Dave his car as a gift for his Dave's birthday. In reliance on this, Dave builds a garage for the car and sells his old car. Tom decides to keep his car. Dave sues Tom for the car, but Tom argues that there is no consideration because he was making a gift of the car to Dave. Under Promissory Estoppel, even if there is no consideration (the car was a gift), the court may enforce Tom's promise to avoid injustice.*

CHAPTER 2: DEFENSES TO FORMATION AND ENFORCEMENT

A. Defenses to Formation

> **Exam Tip 7:** When a party asserts a defense to formation of the contract, she is asking the court to find that no contract was formed between the two parties at all.

c. **Requirements**: There must be a writing signed by the person to be charged (the person against whom enforcement is sought) that contains the essential terms of the deal.

1) Writing

- The writing does not have to be a formal contract (it can be in the form of letters or receipts) and multiple writings can be put together to meet the requirements, as long as they reference each other.
- UCC sale of goods for $500 or more: The writing need not contain all the terms of the contract, but the contract is not enforceable against the party beyond the quantity of the goods shown in writing.

2) Signature: A document on company letterhead may be enough to constitute a signed writing as long as the party to be charged intended to authenticate the writing as that of the signer to adopt the document.

> **Note 3:** The writing does not have to exist at the time of the promise. It can be created after the promises are made and still meet the SOF.

d. **Exceptions:** If the SOF is not met, a court will still enforce the contract in limited situations.

> **Exam Tip 10:** Discuss all potential exceptions to the SOF that are relevant based on the facts.

1) Contracts (usually for services) that cannot be performed within one year of making

Full performance has occurred by the party seeking to enforce the contract.

2) UCC Sale of Goods for $500 or more

a) If **full performance** has occurred by the party seeking to enforce the contract (the goods have been full delivered or fully paid for), the contract will be fully enforceable.

b) If **part performance** has occurred (part of the purchase price has been paid), the contract will be enforceable to the extent that the money has been paid.

c) No writing required if the contract involves **specially manufactured goods** for the buyer.

d) Letter or Memorandum of Confirmation

If **both parties are merchants** and a party sends a confirmatory letter/memo that meets the SOF to the other party and the other party knowingly receives the memo and **does not object in writing within 10 days**, the contract is enforceable against the receiving party, even though the receiving party did not sign the memo.

3) Sale of Land—Part Performance: If the contract involves the sale of land, the contract will be enforced if at least two of the following three acts have occurred:

- The purchaser pays part or all of the purchase price;

- The purchaser takes possession of the land; or
- The purchaser substantially improves the property.

4) Estoppel (applies to all contract types): If a party reasonably and detrimentally relies on a promise made by the party to be charged, a court may enforce the contract, despite the failure to meet the SOF requirement.

2. Illegality

A court will not enforce a contract that has involves illegal consideration or performance.

3. Unconscionability

A court will not enforce a contract that is so unfair, no reasonable person would agree to it. If a court finds unconscionability, it can refuse to enforce the entire contract, or strike the unconscionable portion of the contract, or limit the unconscionable terms.

- Procedural Unconscionability—occurs when the bargaining process leading to the formation of the contract is unfair (e.g., if a party is in a superior position and takes advantage of this position).
- Substantive Unconscionability—occurs when the actual terms of the contract are unfair; there must be a significant showing of unfairness in the contract to find this.

CHAPTER 3: TERMS OF THE CONTRACT

A. Modification

After a valid contract has been formed, any change to the terms of the contract is a modification. Both parties must agree to the modification.

1. Common Law: Under the common law, a modification must be supported by consideration.

a. Pre-existing Duty Rule

- Watch out for exam facts where a party offers to pay more money to the other party to guarantee completion of the contract on time. Under the Preexisting Duty Rule, there is no additional consideration here because the other party already has a duty to perform the contract on time. The modification (additional money) will not be enforceable.
- If a party agrees to pay more money in exchange for earlier performance of the contract, there will be consideration. The parties are changing their duties.

b. Statute of Frauds: If the modified contract falls within the Statute of Frauds, it must be in writing (unless an exception applies, see the exceptions to the SOF, above).

> **Note 4:** Under the common law, a provision requiring a modification to be in writing even though the modification would not otherwise fall within the Statute of Frauds is not enforceable.

2. **UCC**

- A modification **does not** require additional consideration, as long as the modification is entered into in good faith by both parties.
- Statute of Frauds: If the modified contract falls within the Statute of Frauds, it must be in writing (unless an exception applies, see the exceptions to the SOF, above).

> **Note 5:** A provision prohibiting oral modifications to a sales contract even though the modification would not otherwise fall within the SOF is valid under the UCC!

B. Accord and Satisfaction

When there is a dispute over the validity of the contract or the amount owed, a party can agree to accept a different performance from what was agreed upon in the contract.

- Accord—the new agreement where a party agrees to accept a different performance than what was agreed upon.
- Satisfaction—occurs when the different performance is completed by the other party, which discharges the original contract duties and the accord agreement duties.
- Consideration is found to support this type of agreement as follows:
  - The party performing the different performance is incurring a legal detriment.
  - The party that is agreeing to accept the different performance is giving up the right to dispute the original contract and sue for breach.

C. Parol Evidence Rule

Under the Parol Evidence Rule (PER), extrinsic evidence of oral or written communications prior to the written contract are generally inadmissible for contradicting the terms of the contract.

> **Exam Tip 11:** Look for facts involving a party that is seeking to introduce evidence of prior negotiations or discussions that occurred before a valid written contract was formed. If a valid written contract exists, the PER will generally bar any evidence of the prior negotiations or discussions.

1. **Integration**

First a court will ask if the writing in question was intended to be the final agreement (does it integrate) the terms of the contract.

- If the contract is not an integration (not a final agreement), the PER does not apply.
- Determining Total or Partial Integration:
  - The court will look at the words in the contract to determine if the parties intended for it to be a total or partial integration.
  - Merger clause: If the contract has a "merger" clause stating that the contract is the final and complete understanding of the parties, it is likely to be a total integration.
  - Total Integration: If the writing contains all of the terms of the agreement, it is a total integration and no parol evidence is admissible.

- Partial Integration: If the writing contains some of the terms of the agreement, it is a partial integration, parol evidence is admissible and the writing may be supplemented by additional terms, as long as they are **consistent** with the writing (and do not contradict any of the terms).

2. **Exceptions:** Parol evidence will be admissible in limited situations:

   a. **Timing:** The Parol Evidence Rule does not prohibit evidence of modifications or statements made **after** the contract was written.

   b. **Ambiguity and Interpretation:** Evidence is admissible for purposes of interpreting or clarifying an ambiguity in the contract.

   c. **Collateral Deal:** Evidence of a separate deal between the parties is admissible, if the deal is not part of the written contract.

   d. **UCC:** Evidence of usual performance and dealing between parties is admissible.

   e. **Condition Precedent:** Evidence of a condition precedent to the existence of the contract is admissible.

> ***Example 3:*** *If a party claims that a condition precedent was agreed upon in the discussions prior to the writing of the contract, evidence of this condition precedent is admissible as an exception to the PER.*

CHAPTER 4: PERFORMANCE OF THE CONTRACT

A. Performance of the Contract

After determining the existence of a contract and the terms of the contract, the next issue is the performance of the contract.

Promise or Condition: When discussing the performance of the contract, determine whether the contract involves promise(s) and/or condition(s). When a contract is unclear, a court will usually find a statement to be a promise.

> **Exam Tip 12:** Most Contracts essays involve promises between parties. Conditions are created by words such as "on condition that."

1. **Promises**

   In a contract, parties may exchange promises which require them to act or refrain from acting.

   a. **Standard of Performance**

      1) Common Law

         - Under the common law, a party has a duty to **substantially perform** his part of the contract.

- A party who substantially performs may recover on the contract even though that party has not rendered full performance.
  - A delay in performance does not necessarily constitute a failure to substantially perform.
- A party who has not substantially performed generally cannot recover damages based on the contract, but she may be able to recover through restitution.
- A party who fails to substantially perform is in material breach (see "Breach of Contract," below).

2) UCC

- Under the UCC, there must be **"perfect" tender** of the goods.
  - The buyer has a right to inspect the goods, and once he accepts them, he has an obligation to pay.
  - If a buyer rejects goods as nonconforming and time still remains to perform under a contract, the seller has a right to cure and tender conforming goods.
- Breach of Contract: If a party fails to meet the standard of performance, it will be in breach of contract. (See "Breach of Contract," below).
- Installment Contracts (UCC)

  Under the UCC, an installment contract is defined as one in which the goods are to be delivered in multiple shipments, and each shipment is to be separately accepted by the buyer.

  - Parties cannot vary or contract out of this definition.
  - Payment by the buyer is due upon each delivery, unless the price cannot be apportioned.

  i) Nonconforming shipment (also known as a "segment")

  If the seller makes a nonconforming tender or tenders nonconforming goods under one segment of an installment contract, the buyer can reject only if the nonconformity substantially impairs the value of that shipment to the buyer and cannot be cured.

  If the seller makes adequate assurances that he can cure the nonconformity, then the buyer must accept the shipment.

  ii) Remaining segments (shipments)

  When there is a nonconforming tender or a tender of nonconforming goods under one segment of an installment contract, the buyer may cancel the entire contract only if the nonconformity substantially impairs the value of the entire contract to the buyer.

2. Conditions

A condition is an event that must occur before a party's contractual rights or obligations are created, destroyed, or enlarged.

> **Editor's Note 6:** While a condition affects a party's contractual rights or obligations, it does not affect the "degree of performance" a party must render.

a. Express or Implied

- Express: Conditions expressed in the contract itself. Look for words such as "on condition that."
- Implied: A condition not written in the contract or otherwise specifically agreed to by the parties, but which a court may find exists.

Example 4: *A court may imply that a builder has to substantially perform before the owner has duty to pay.*

b. Satisfaction of Conditions

1) Timing of Conditions

   - Condition Precedent—the condition must occur before the other party has an obligation to perform
   - Condition Subsequent—if the condition occurs, the duty to perform will then be excused

2) Standard of Performance

   - Express conditions—must be met perfectly
   - Implied conditions—require substantial performance

c. Excuse of Conditions

1) Waiver: A party can waive a condition by words or conduct, as long as the condition is not material to the contract. The waiving party would then have a duty to perform, because it waived the condition.

2) Wrongful Interference: If a party hinders the other party's performance and interferes with the occurrence of the condition, the condition will be excused, and the wrongful party will have duty to perform.

3) Estoppel: If a party indicates that it will not enforce a condition, and the other party reasonably relies on this, the party will be estopped from later enforcing the condition.

Example 5: *(Promise): Harold Homeowner asks Bob to build a house. Bob promises to install bamboo wood flooring. If Bob fails to use bamboo flooring, but uses a similar wood, he has substantially performed the contract and is entitled to payment from Harold.*

__Example 6:__ (Condition): Harold Homeowner asks Bob to build a house. Harold expressly conditions payment for the house on the installation of bamboo wood flooring. If Bob fails to use bamboo flooring, the condition has not been met and Harold's duty to pay Bob for house has not been triggered.

Note 6: The result of a failed condition can be harsh (as seen in this hypo), so courts are hesitant to find a condition if the contract is unclear.

3. Discharge of Duty to Perform

In certain circumstances, a promisor party's duty to perform will be discharged, regardless of whether there is a promise or condition involved. All relevant theories for discharging a promisor party's duty to perform should be discussed.

a. Impracticability

- An unforeseeable event occurs (such as a natural disaster) making the performance of the contract extremely difficult;
- The nonoccurrence of the event was a basic assumption at the time of the contract; and
- The party seeking discharge was not at fault.

Note 7: Non-extraordinary increases in the cost of performance are not a sufficient basis for this defense.

b. Impossibility: An unforeseeable event occurs, making it objectively impossible for the party to perform.

c. Frustration of Purpose

- If an unexpected event arises that destroy the party's purpose for entering the contract, the party will be entitled to rescind the contract, even if the performance is still possible.
- Similar to impracticability, the nonoccurrence of the event must have been a basic assumption at the time of the contract and the party seeking discharge was not at fault.

__Example 7:__ (Frustration of Purpose): Gina agrees to rent an apartment in San Francisco for one day, so she can watch the Giants' victory parade after winning the World Series. On the day of the parade, an earthquake occurs and the parade is canceled. Gina's performance may be excused (paying rent) because the purpose of renting the apartment has been frustrated, even though she could still pay the rent.

B. Third-Party Beneficiary Contracts

- A third-party beneficiary contract results when the parties to a contract intend that the performance by one of the parties is to benefit a third person who is not a party to the contract.
- When a contract benefits persons other than the parties to the contract, a third party can enforce the contract if the third party is an intended beneficiary. Otherwise, the third party is an incidental beneficiary who cannot enforce the contract.

C. Assignment of Rights and Delegation of Duties

"Assignment" is the transfer of rights under a contract, and "delegation" is the transfer of duties and obligations under a contract.

1. Assignment of Rights

- Almost all contract rights can be assigned. Partial assignments are permissible, as is the assignment of future or unearned rights.
- Assignments are not allowed when they materially increase the duty or risk of the obligor or materially reduce the obligor's chance of obtaining performance.
- No formalities are needed for an assignment, but there must be a present intent to transfer the right immediately. No consideration is needed.
- An assignee takes all of the rights of the assignor as the contract stands at the time of the assignment, but she takes subject to any defenses that could be raised against the assignor.

2. Delegation of Duties

- Generally, obligations under a contract can be delegated.
- Delegation is not permitted when the other party to the contract has a substantial interest in having the delegating individual perform (e.g., in a personal services contract involving taste or a special skill), or the delegation is prohibited by the contract.
- When obligations are delegated, the delegator is not released from liability, and recovery can be had against the delegator if the delegatee does not perform, unless the other party to the contract agrees to release that party and substitute a new one (a novation). Merely consenting to a delegation does not create a novation.

CHAPTER 5: BREACH OF CONTRACT; REMEDIES

A. Breach of Contract

- If a duty to perform does exist and has not been discharged, a party's non-performance is a breach.
- If a party indicates prior to the time of performance that it intends to breach; this is an anticipatory breach/repudiation. Otherwise, when a party fails to perform on the date of performance, it will be in breach of contract.

1. **Anticipatory Breach/Repudiation** (frequently tested)

Anticipatory breach or repudiation occurs when a promisor party indicates that it will not perform prior to the date that performance is due that it will not perform.

a. Common Law

- The promisor party clearly and unequivocally indicates through words or acts that it will not perform.

- The nonbreaching party can:
  - Treat the repudiation as a breach of contract and sue immediately;
  - Suspend its own performance and demand performance from the promisor;
  - Cancel the contract; or
  - Wait for the date of performance, and then sue for breach.
- Retraction: The promisor party can retract its repudiation of the contract until/unless the other party acts in reliance on the repudiation, accepts the repudiation, or has already filed an action for breach of contract.

b. UCC

- A buyer/seller unequivocally refuses to perform, or fails to provide adequate assurances within a reasonable time (must not exceed 30 days) of the other party demanding them.
- Requesting Assurances
  - Either party can demand assurances if it has reasonable grounds to be insecure about the other party's ability to perform and may suspend performance until it receives assurances.

  Editor's Note 7: Although the lecturer states that a demand for assurances can be made by phone, the UCC 2-609(1) requires that the demand be made in writing.

  - A failure to provide reasonable assurances within a reasonable time (must not exceed 30 days), can be treated as a repudiation.
  - The nonbreaching party can:
    - Treat the repudiation as a breach of contract and sue immediately;
    - Suspend its own performance and demand performance from the promisor;
    - Cancel the contract; or
    - Wait for the date of performance, and then sue for breach.
- Retraction: The promisor party can retract its repudiation of the contract until/unless the other party has cancelled the contract, materially changed position on the basis of the repudiation, or otherwise indicated that he considers the repudiation to be final.

2. Material Breach

- A material breach occurs when the nonbreaching party does not receive the substantial benefit of the bargain.
- The nonbreaching party can withhold any promised performance and pursue remedies for breach.

3. Minor Breach

- A minor breach occurs when the breaching party has substantially performed, but not fully performed.
- The nonbreaching party is entitled to pursue remedies for the minor breach, but it still must perform under the contract.

> **Exam Tip 13:** If the facts are not clear on whether a material or minor breach occurred, you should discuss both issues/rules and present the arguments that the parties would make for both theories. Remember, you are not being scored on your conclusions, but rather your analysis!

B. Remedies

1. Legal Remedies

Remedies typically compensate the nonbreaching party for actual economic losses.

> **Exam Tip 14:** Discuss all relevant remedies, based on the facts presented in the question.

a. Expectation Damages

- Expectation damages are damages directly resulting from the breach of the contract. They are intended to put the injured party in the same position as if the contract was performed.
- Expectation damages must be foreseeable and the nonbreaching party must be able to prove the amount of damages with reasonable certainty.
- Amount: Calculating the amount of damages depends on the facts. Generally, the amount of damages will be based on the contract price for performance and the fair market value of performance.

__Example 8:__ B builds a house for O. O refuses to pay. B is entitled to the amount agreed upon in the contract.

__Example 9:__ B contracts with O to build O a house for $200,000, which is below the market value for a new house. B breaches and does not build the house. O finds another builder and pays $300,000 (fair market value) for a house to be built. O is entitled to $100,000 from B.

- Diminution in value (economic waste)
  - If the award of expectation damages would result in economic waste, then courts may instead award damages equal to diminution in value.
  - Economic waste occurs when the amount of damages owed is disproportional to any economic benefit or utility gained as a result of the award.

__Example 10:__ (from outline): Landowner grants Mining Company a five-year license to remove coal from his property. In return for the license, Mining Company agrees to restore the property to its original state at the end of the *five-year period. After five years, Mining Company refuses to restore the land. The restoration work would cost $29,000, but, if completed, it would result in only a $300 increase in the property's value. The court may elect to award only $300 in damages, instead of the usual $29,000 expectation award.*

Note 8: If the breach is willful, and only completion of the contract will give the nonbreaching party the benefit of its bargain, then a court may award expectation damages even if that award would result in economic waste.

Exam Tip 15: When discussing damages, you should use the specific dollar amounts provided in the facts and show the calculations that lead to the ultimate amount of damages awarded. The calculations are the same as analysis and they earn you points on the exam.

b. Consequential Damages

- Consequential damages are reasonably foreseeable damages other than expectation damages that are related to the breach of the contract (e.g., loss of profit).

  Example 11: *Restaurant enters a contract with Fisherman for the delivery of 1,000 pounds of crab for $10 per pound every week. Fisherman catches the crab but decides to sell it to another buyer instead. After a one month delay, Restaurant is able to find another source for the crab for $12 per pound. Restaurant seeks expectation damages for the increased cost of the crab $2 per pound and consequential damages for lost business profits during the one month when it did not have crab on the menu.*

- In order to recover consequential damages, three elements must be met:
  - Foreseeability: The damages must be natural and probable consequences of the breach or contemplated by the parties at the time the contract was formed.
  - Causation: The plaintiff must show that the damages were caused by the defendant's breach; if the damages would have occurred without the defendant's breach, there can be no recovery.
  - Certainty: The plaintiff must prove the dollar amount with reasonable certainty. When the amount of money is too speculative (e.g., a new business), the court will not award consequential damages.

c. Reliance Damages

- Damages that the nonbreaching party incurs in reasonable reliance upon the promise that the other party would perform.

  Note 9: A party cannot recover reliance and expectation damages; it must choose between reliance or expectation damages. You should discuss both items of damages on the exam.

  Example 12: *Tom enters into a contract to buy Dave's antique car. Tom tells Dave that he intends to enter the car in a contest. In reliance on the contract,*

Tom pays an entry fee to enter the car into the contest. Dave sells the car to another buyer. Tom can seek reliance damages for the contest entry fee.

d. Incidental Damages

- Damages that arise when the nonbreaching party is trying to remedy the breach (e.g., in a commercial contract, the cost of finding a replacement seller of goods).

e. Mitigating Damages

- The nonbreaching party has duty to avoid or mitigate its damages, to the extent possible, by seeking replacements/substitutes for goods and/or services.
- The nonbreaching party will be held to a standard of reasonable conduct.
- A failure to mitigate damages will reduce the damages recovered by the nonbreaching party.

Example 13: *Betty enters a contract to buy a freezer from Sally, with delivery of the freezer due April 1. On March 15, Sally informs Betty that she will not be able to deliver the freezer on April 1 (anticipatory breach/repudiation). On March 31, Betty orders a freezer from Adam, which included a $500 fee for one day delivery on April 1. Sally then sues Betty for the non-delivery of the freezer and seeks damages including the $500 delivery fee. Betty would have a strong argument that, with regard to the delivery fee, Sally did not mitigate her damages because she waited until 1 day before she needed the freezer to purchase it.*

2. Equitable Remedies

a. Restitution

Restitution allows nonbreaching and breaching parties to recover damages under an unjust enrichment theory (i.e., not based on the contract).

1) Nonbreaching Party

- Restitution usually arises when the nonbreaching party has partially performed the contract and other party then breaches. The nonbreaching party will then seek restitution damages for the benefit conferred to the breaching party. If the breaching party does not pay restitution damages, it will have been unjustly enriched by the nonbreaching party's performance.
- A nonbreaching party cannot seek restitution if it has performed all of its duties and the only performance due from the other party is the payment under the contract. The nonbreaching party must seek expectation damages instead.
- A nonbreaching party can seek damages based on the value of the benefit conferred on the other party.

- The amount is measured by the reasonable value of what it would cost the breaching party to obtain the benefit from another source, or the increase in the breaching party's wealth (example increase in value of land) from having received the benefit.

2) Breaching Party

- If a party has not substantially performed, it will be in breach of contract, and cannot recover under the contract.
- However, if the nonbreaching party has benefited from the breaching party's performance, the breaching party can recover for the benefit conferred minus the damages the nonbreaching party is entitled to.

b. Quasi-Contract (Implied-in-Law Contract)

- In certain situations, where there is no enforceable contract, or a contract does not exist at all, a court will award restitution damages on the basis of quasi-contract.
- The elements are:
  - The plaintiff must confer a measurable benefit on the defendant;
  - The plaintiff acted without gratuitous intent (i.e., he intended to be paid); and
  - It would be unfair to let the defendant retain the benefit because the defendant had an opportunity to decline the benefit but did not do so, or the plaintiff had a reasonable excuse for not giving the defendant such an opportunity (e.g., an emergency arose and the plaintiff could not consult with the defendant).

c. Specific Performance

Under the remedy of specific performance, the nonbreaching party can ask a court to order the breaching party to perform the contract. The following elements must be met:

- There must be a valid contract: This requires you to discuss whether a valid contract (offer, acceptance, consideration) exists.
- The terms of the contract must be certain/clear enough to allow a court to make an order.
- The nonbreaching party has satisfied any conditions precedent (or the condition has been excused), so the breaching party's performance is now due.
- Money damages are inadequate (this usually means the item(s) involved in the contract are unique.

  Example 14: *Land, pieces of art, antique cars.*

- It is feasible for the court to enforce and supervise the breaching party's performance.
  - Courts will not grant specific performance if it will be required to supervise the performance for a long period of time, or if it will be difficult to enforce.

- Specifically, courts will not require people to perform service contracts (e.g., employment) because it is not feasible to enforce/supervise a person's service and forcing a person to work can rise to the level of indentured servitude under the Thirteenth Amendment.

- No defenses exist: A court will not grant specific performance if the breaching party can assert defenses of laches or unclean hands.

  - Laches: If the nonbreaching party waited an unreasonably long time to seek specific performance and the delay prejudiced the breaching party, the court may deny specific performance.
  - Unclean Hands: If the nonbreaching party itself engaged in unethical or immoral acts relating to the contract, the court may deny specific performance.

3. Remedies under the UCC

a. **Buyer's Remedies** (see outline for more information)

Under the UCC, the buyer has several alternative remedies if the **seller fails to tender the goods**.

1) Damages

   - The buyer may recover the market price minus the contract price. The market price is the price that existed at the time of the breach at the place where tender was to occur under the contract.
   - The UCC also permits recovery for incidental and consequential damages resulting from the seller's breach.

2) Cover

   - The buyer may purchase similar goods elsewhere and recover the replacement price minus the contract price.

3) Specific performance

   - The buyer may demand specific performance for unique goods or if the buyer is unable to cover.

Under the UCC, if **either the tender or the goods are nonconforming**, then the buyer has the right to accept or reject all or part of the goods.

4) Express Warranties

   - Under the UCC, any promise, affirmation, description, or sample that is part of the basis of the bargain is an express warranty, unless it is merely the seller's opinion or commendation of the value of the goods. If the seller tenders goods that do not meet the express warranty(s) in the contract, they will be deemed to be nonconforming.

Editor's Note 8: Although the lecturer characterizes an express warranty as "something said out loud as part of the deal," an express warranty need not be made orally, but can arise in other ways such as from a writing, a model, or a sample.

- The buyer has the right to inspect the goods before deciding whether to accept or reject. Payment does not constitute acceptance if there is no right of inspection before payment.

5) Rejection

A valid rejection requires that the buyer give notice to the seller within a reasonable time, before "acceptance."

a) "Acceptance" under the UCC

Under the UCC, the buyer accepts goods by expressly stating acceptance, or using the goods, or failing to reject the goods.

b) Revocation of "Acceptance" under the UCC

A buyer may revoke an acceptance of goods if there is a defect that substantially impairs their value to the buyer and:

- The buyer accepted the goods on the reasonable belief that the seller would cure the defect, but the seller has failed to do so; or
- The buyer accepted the goods without discovery of the nonconformity, and such acceptance was reasonably induced either by the difficulty of discovering the nonconformity before acceptance or because the seller gave assurances that the goods were conforming.

Note 10: The failure to meet an express warranty set forth in a contract will constitute a "defect" or "nonconformity" for purposes of this rule.

The buyer must inform the seller of its decision to revoke within a reasonable time after the nonconformity is discovered or should have been discovered by the buyer.

6) Right to Cure

The seller has a right to cure a defective tender if:

- The time for performance under the contract has not yet elapsed; or
- The seller had reasonable grounds to believe that the buyer would accept despite the nonconformity.

b. Seller's Remedies (see outline for more information)

1) Wrongful rejection

If the buyer wrongfully rejects a tender of goods, then the seller has three alternative remedies and would also be entitled to incidental damages:

- Collect damages

  The seller would ordinarily be entitled to the contract price minus the market price at the time and place for tender, together with any incidental damages, less any expenses saved as a result of the buyer's breach.

- Resell the goods

  If the seller elects to resell and sue for the contract price minus the resale price, then the resale must be (i) only of goods identified in the contract and (ii) commercially reasonable. However, if the seller wishes to resell the goods in a private sale, the seller must first give the buyer reasonable notice of his intent to resell.

- Recover the price

  The seller can recover the price after rejection only if the seller is unable to sell the goods at a reasonable price after a reasonable effort or circumstances indicate that such an effort will not yield a sale.

CHAPTER 6: CONTRACTS QUESTION

July 2009, Question #5 [ID 267]

Sam was walking down the sidewalk when he heard shouts coming from a burning house. Sam immediately called 911 on his cell phone and rushed into the house. Inside the house, Sam discovered Resident trying to coax Resident's frightened dog from behind a couch. Sam, at great risk to his safety, crawled behind the couch and pulled the dog from its hiding place. Sam, carrying the dog, and Resident then safely made their way outside.

Once outside, Resident thanked Sam and asked Sam about his work. Sam told Resident, "I was hoping to start training as a paramedic in the fall, but I don't think I'll be able to afford the cost of the program."

Resident responded, "We need all the good paramedics that we can get! If you are going to start paramedic training, I want to help you. Also, my dog means everything to me. I want to compensate you for your heroism. Give me your address, and I will send you a check for a thousand dollars."

Sam said, "Thank you so much! Here is my address. I'll apply to the paramedic program tomorrow."

Sam applied to the paramedic training program but was denied admission. Sam then applied for and was accepted into a cosmetology training program and owes that program $1,000. Sam cannot pay the

$1,000 he owes because when Resident learned Sam was not attending the paramedic program, he refused to give Sam the $1,000.

Sam sued Resident to recover the $1,000.

What theories could Sam assert to recover all or some portion of the $1,000, and what is the likelihood of success on each theory? Explain.

SAMPLE ANSWER

1. Consideration (35%)

The issue is whether the agreement between Sam and Resident was supported by consideration, such that Sam could sue to enforce the agreement as a contract.

It is axiomatic that a purported contract is invalid unless it is supported by valuable consideration on both sides of the exchange; that is, each party must bargain for a change in the legal position of the other party. Under common law, consideration provided before the bargain is not adequate to support a contract, as the promisor must both seek and receive something of value at the time the contract is executed.

Sam will likely argue that he has provided consideration in one of two ways: either in his rescue of the dog or in his promise to apply for training as a paramedic. However, both of these arguments are likely to fail. Resident's promise to pay Sam $1,000 was not made in exchange for Sam's rescue of the dog; rather, it was made *in thanks* for those prior actions. Additionally, Sam's promise to apply for paramedic training does not constitute consideration because Resident did not seek that promise in exchange for his own promise to pay $1,000. There has not been an exchange between the parties, and so the contract is not supported by consideration.

2. Moral Consideration (25%)

The issue is whether the "moral consideration" rule provides a means for Sam to obtain recovery.

While no exceptions to the past consideration rule are recognized under common law, there is a modern trend to recognize the existence of consideration when a promise is made after the other party confers a significant benefit. The instant case is a clear example of such a situation: Resident promised to give Sam $1,000 in recognition of Sam's efforts to save Resident's dog. Consequently, if the applicable jurisdiction recognizes consideration based on a moral obligation, Sam may argue that the deal between him and Resident was indeed supported by consideration.

However, an important exception exists to the moral-consideration rule: the promise is not enforceable if the *promisee* conferred the benefit as a gift. Additionally, the promise is not enforceable to the extent that the value of the promise is disproportionate to the benefit conferred. The application of these two rules is a fact-specific inquiry, and the court would need to determine Sam's intent at the time he rescued Resident's dog. Furthermore, even if the court determines that Sam expected payment for his services, it may restrict the amount of recovery to less than the full $1,000 to the extent that it determines that $1,000 is disproportionate to the value of Sam's rescue effort.

3. Promissory Estoppel (40%)

The issue is whether the doctrine of promissory estoppel provides a means for Sam to obtain recovery.

Noncontractual promises may be enforced through the doctrine of promissory estoppel. Courts will invoke the doctrine to treat a promise as binding if (i) the promisor should reasonably expect it to induce action or forbearance on the part of the promisee or a third person, (ii) the promise does induce such action or forbearance, and (iii) injustice can be avoided only by enforcement of the promise.

Sam can argue convincingly that he relied on Resident's promise in incurring the $1,000 debt and that when Resident told Sam, "If you are going to start paramedic training, I want to help you," Resident should have expected Sam to act in reliance on that statement. However, in response, Resident would surely argue that Sam's reliance was not reasonable, because he ultimately incurred the debt by enrolling in a cosmetology program and not in a paramedic training program. The fact-finder will decide which argument prevails; the decision will likely be a close call.

Resident had also told Sam, "I want to compensate you for your heroism," and Sam could reasonably interpret that remark as indicating that Resident's promise to give him $1,000 was intended to compensate him for rescuing Resident's dog and was not specifically to induce him to enroll in paramedic training. Therefore, Sam may argue that he would suffer injustice if the court does not enforce Resident's promise (or a portion thereof).

(Editor's Note: The foregoing model answer was drafted in accordance with the NCBE Grading Guidelines for this question. The analysis is illustrative of the discussions that might appear in a high passing answer and addresses all legal and factual issues the drafters intended exam candidates to raise. When self-grading, refer to the NCBE's weighting of each issue, which is indicated in parentheses for your reference.)

[END OF HANDOUT]

Themis
Bar Review

CORPORATIONS ESSAY WORKSHOP

PROFESSOR CHRISTOPHER IDE-DON

UC DAVIS SCHOOL OF LAW

CHAPTER 1: ISSUES TESTED (PART 1)

A. Summary of the Issues Tested

1. **Formation**
   a. **Pre-Incorporation Contracts**
      - Promoter Liability
      - Novation and Adoption

   b. **Corporation Formation**
      - De Jure
      - Ultra Vires
      - De Facto
      - Corporation by Estoppel

2. **Securities (Stock)**
   - Value
   - Federal Causes of Action

3. **Shareholders**
   - Voting
   - Proxy Voting
   - Shareholder Agreements
   - Shareholder Actions
   - Piercing the Corporate Veil
   - Controlling shareholders

4. **Board of Directors**
   - Removal
   - Voting
   - Fiduciary Duties
     - Duty of Care
     - Duty of Loyalty

5. **Officers**
   - Authority (Agency)

6. **Dissolution and Winding Up**

7. **Limited Liability Companies (LLCs)**
   - Liability
   - Duties
   - Actions
   - Dissociation
   - Dissolution

B. Formation

1. Pre-Incorporation Transactions

- **Promoter**—enters into contracts securing capital to bring the corporation into existence
  - Personally liable for a contract entered into pre-incorporation, even after the corporation comes into existence
  - **Exceptions:**
    a) Novation—the corporation and the third party contract agree to substitute the corporation for the promoter

    b) Adoption—the corporation takes the benefits of the contract

2. Incorporation

- Must file articles of incorporation with the state
- **Ultra Vires Act**—occurs when a corporation has a narrow purpose and acts outside the scope of that purpose
  - A shareholder can file a suit to enjoin the action or take action against the officer, director, or employee who engaged in the act.
- **De Jure Corporation**—exists when the statutory requirements for incorporation are met
- A good faith attempt to incorporate can still invoke corporate protections if:
  1) **De Facto Corporation**—attempted to incorporate and ran business believing it was incorporated

  2) **Corporation by Estoppel**—a third party entered into a contract with the corporation as though it was properly incorporated; the third party is estopped from asserting that the corporation was not formed appropriately

     Example 1: *Based on a past bar essay: L and M improperly file articles of incorporation. They acted in good faith and they are now operating "Data, Inc." as a business, believing it is incorporated. L and M obtain a business loan from Big Bank who looks at the Data, Inc.'s business records prior to issuing the loan. L and M's business eventually fails and is unable to repay the loan. Big Bank will be estopped from arguing that Data, Inc. is not a corporation because it dealt with Data, Inc. as if it were a corporation and had an opportunity to discover that is was not actually incorporated. Big Bank will not be able to recover from L and M as individuals.*

C. Securities (Stock)

- Issuance of stock must be authorized by the board of directors.

1. Valuation

- Board of directors must determine whether the value paid for the stock is adequate
- **Par Value Stock**—corporation assigns a minimum value to its stock
  - If sold for less than the par value, the board is liable
  - Shareholder may also be liable if had knowledge of par value

2. Federal Causes of Action for Improper Sale of Securities (Stock)

- Rule 10b-5; and
- Section 16(b)

> **Exam Tip 1:** These causes of action are not frequently tested issues. See the outline for more information.

CHAPTER 2: ISSUES TESTED (PART 2)

A. Shareholders

1. Meetings

- Required to hold an annual shareholders meeting
- The primary purpose is to elect directors.

2. Right to Inspect Corporate Records

- Restricted to normal business hours
- Requires five days' notice
- Must state a proper purpose

3. Right to Vote

- To select the board of directors
- To approve fundamental corporate changes (e.g., merger, sale of corporation)

a. Proxy Voting

- Proxy—written agreement to allow a person to vote on behalf of the shareholder
- Revocable unless otherwise stated (irrevocable proxy is allowed)

4. Power to Amend Corporate Bylaws

- Can amend or repeal existing bylaws
- Can pass new bylaws
- Can limit the board of director's ability to change the bylaws

5. Shareholder Agreements

May enter into an agreement to vote their shares together

6. Right to Sue the Corporation

> **Exam Tip 2:** If the prompt simply asks whether a shareholder can sue the corporation, discuss the possibility of a direct action ***AND*** a derivative action.

a. Direct Action

- Suing the corporation for their own benefit (i.e., to remedy a wrong personal to the shareholder)
- Usually arises when the shareholder is denied voting rights, the board failed to declare a dividend, or the board failed to approve or deny a merger

b. Derivative Action

- Suing on behalf of the corporation
- Usually against a director or officer
- Any recovery goes to the corporation
- **Standing**—any person who is a shareholder at the time of the bad act or omission (and at the time the action is filed)
- **Demand upon the board**—required to demand action by the board
    - Board has 90 days to act before filing derivative action (unless demand is rejected, or irreparable harm would occur)
    - **Futility exception**—no demand is required if it would be futile

    Example 2: *If the shareholder is accusing the board of directors of wrongdoing, it would be futile to demand that the board bring a suit against itself.*

- **Board dismissal**—can bring motion if the action is not in the corporation's best interest
    - Can be challenged if board was not disinterested or not acting in good faith

7. Shareholder Liability—Piercing the Corporate Veil

- Generally, not personally liable for corporate acts
- Court may "pierce the veil" and hold shareholders personally liable
- Based on totality of circumstances, including the following factors:
    - Undercapitalization of the corporation at the time of formation
    - Disregard of corporate formalities (not holding annual meetings or holding votes)
    - Use of corporate assets as a shareholder's own assets
    - Self-dealing with the corporation
    - Siphoning corporate funds or stripping assets

> **Exam Tip 3:** On the exam, discuss each fact that supports or negates the contention that the shareholder is abusing the protections of the corporation.

8. Shareholders' Fiduciary Duty

- "Controlling" shareholders have a duty to not abuse their power to disadvantage minority shareholders.
- Controlling shareholder—someone who owns more than 50% of a corporation or otherwise controls voting power

CHAPTER 3: ISSUES TESTED (PART 3)

A. Board of Directors

- Manage and direct the corporation's business and affairs
- Selected by the shareholders at the annual shareholder's meeting

1. Removal

- Shareholders may remove for breach of fiduciary duty (common law); or
- Without cause (modern trend)

2. Voting

- Must have a quorum of directors present to hold a vote (generally a majority)

  Example 3: *If there are 10 directors on the board, must have 6 directors present to have a valid vote.*

- Presence—can include phone call so long as the director can hear and participate

3. Special Meetings

- Requires notice at least two days before meeting
- Notice must include the date, time, and place of meeting
- A director who did not receive proper notice can object
  - But, if the director attends the meeting and fails to object to lack of notice, the objection is waived

4. Fiduciary Duties

Exam Tip 4: A director's fiduciary duties are frequently tested.

a. Duty of Care

- Must act as an ordinarily prudent person
- Includes the duty to investigate and ask questions
- Can rely on reports and outside experts

Exam Tip 5: After discussing whether the director met the duty of care, discuss the business judgment rule.

1) Business Judgment Rule

- A rebuttable presumption that a director reasonably believed his actions were in the best interest of the corporation.
- Protects a director from liability for breaching the duty of care if he acted in good faith
- To overcome the presumption, one of the following must be shown:
  - The director did not act in good faith;
  - The director was not informed to the extent reasonably necessary;
  - The director did not show objectivity and had a material interest in the decision;
  - The director failed to timely investigate after being alerted to a significant matter; or
  - Any other failure to act as a reasonable director.

b. Duty of Loyalty

- Must act in the best interest of the corporation
- Violated if the director engages in:
  - Self-dealing; or
  - Usurping a corporate opportunity

1) Self-Dealing

- Engaging in a transaction with the corporation that benefits the director or a close family member
- Includes transactions with another business entity that the director is associated with

a) **Safe Harbor Rules**—Transaction can be protected if:

- The interested director discloses all material facts to the board of directors and receives approval by a majority of disinterested board of directors;
- The interested director discloses all material facts to shareholders and receives approval by a majority of disinterested shareholders; or
- The transaction is fair to the corporation substantively and procedurally

b) **Remedies**—Transaction can be enjoined or rescinded and the corporation can seek damages from the interested director

2) Usurping a Corporate Opportunity

- Taking an opportunity that the corporation would be interested in without offering it to the corporation first
- Director must present the opportunity to the corporation first

- If the corporation declines the opportunity, the director may take it without violating the duty of loyalty.

B. Officers

- Elected by the board of directors to run day-to-day operations
- Typical officers—president, secretary, and treasurer
- Act as agents of the corporation

> **Exam Tip 6:** Can raise Agency issues regarding whether the officer (as an agent) had authority to bind the corporation (the principal) to a contract with a third party

- An officer can act with actual express authority, actual implied authority, and apparent authority.

C. Dissolution and Winding Up

- A corporation may voluntarily terminate its status.
- Winding Up—corporation exists for the limited purpose of winding up its affairs and liquidating its business
- Order of distribution:

  1) Creditors of the corporation

  2) Shareholders of stock with preferences in liquidation

  3) Other remaining shareholders of stock

CHAPTER 4: ISSUES TESTED (PART 4)

A. Limited Liability Companies (LLCs)

- Has the tax advantages of a partnership and the limited liability of a corporation
- **Formation**—requires filing articles of organization
- Members can be individuals or corporations
- **Management**—can be member-managed or manager-managed
- **Authority**—members of a member-managed LLC have authority to bind the LLC

1. Liability

- Members are generally not liable for LLC obligations
- **Piercing the veil**—members can be liable for LLC obligations

2. Duties

- Members owe fiduciary duties to each other and to the LLC

a. Duty of loyalty (member-managed LLC)

- Must account to the LLC for any profit or benefit
- Must refrain from dealing with the LLC on behalf of an adverse interest
- Must refrain from competing with the LLC

> **Note 1:** From a recent question: An LLC had two corporate members. The question was whether a corporate member had a duty to bring a derivative action on behalf of the LLC against itself.

b. Duty of care

- Must act reasonably
- Actions are subject to the business judgment rule

3. Member Actions

a. Direct Action

May bring suit against LLC or other members to enforce the member's rights

b. Derivative Action

May bring a derivative action on behalf of the LLC against other members (or even against themselves)

4. Dissociation

- A member can withdraw at any time and for any reason
- Must provide notice (not necessarily written)

5. Dissolution

- Can occur if all members agree, if there are not enough members remaining, or any other reason stated in the operating agreement
- **Involuntary dissolution**—a member can ask for a court order to dissolve the LLC
    - Must show that a controlling member has acted oppressively and harmed the member seeking dissolution
- **Winding up**—must pay off debts to creditors before distributing assets to members

CHAPTER 5: PRACTICE QUESTION

July 2008, Question 5 [ID 273]

Cal is the CEO and chairman of the 12-member board of directors of Prime, Inc. (Prime). Three other members of Prime's board of directors (the Board) are also senior officers of Prime. The remaining eight members of the Board are wholly independent directors.

Recently, the Board decided to hire a consulting firm to help Prime market a new product. The Board met to consider whether to hire Wiseman Consulting (Wiseman) or Smart Group (Smart). The Board first heard from a representative of Wiseman. The Wiseman representative described some of the projects Wiseman had completed for other clients and outlined the work it proposed to do for Prime for $500,000. The Board then heard from a representative of Smart, another consulting firm. The Smart representative described a similar work plan and stated that Smart's proposed fee was $650,000. Either of these amounts would be a significant outlay for Prime.

After the Board heard both presentations, Cal disclosed to the Board that he had a 25% partnership interest in Smart. Cal stated that he would not be involved in any work to be performed by Smart for Prime. He knew but did not disclose to the Board that Smart's proposed fee for this consulting assignment was substantially higher than it normally charged for comparable work. The Board did not ask about the basis for Smart's proposed fee.

After receiving all of this information, and no other information, the Board discussed the relative merits of the two proposals for 10 minutes. The Board then voted unanimously (Cal abstaining) to hire Smart, even though hiring Smart would cost Prime approximately 30% more than hiring Wiseman. Cal was present throughout the meeting but did not participate except to the extent indicated above.

1. Did Cal violate his duty of loyalty to Prime? Explain.

2. Assuming Cal breached his duty of loyalty to Prime, does he have any defense to liability? Explain.

3. Did the directors of Prime, other than Cal, violate their duty of care? Explain.

SAMPLE ANSWER

1. The issue is whether Cal violated his duty of loyalty to Prime by not making full disclosures to the Board regarding a partnership in which he has interest which Prime is considering for hire. (15%)

Directors of a corporation have a duty of loyalty to act in a manner that the director reasonably believes is in the best interest of the corporation. A director breaches this duty of loyalty by placing his own interest before those of the corporation. If a director profits at the corporation's expense, it is a breach of the duty of loyalty.

In this case, Cal is the CEO and chairman of the board of Prime and therefore has a fiduciary duty of loyalty to Prime. Since Cal is a partner in Smart, Cal may have breached that duty because he stands to benefit personally if Smart is hired. As a partner of Smart, Cal will be entitled to a share of any profits derived from Smart's work for Prime. Cal did not make full disclosures to the Board of Prime because he did not disclose to the Board that Smart's proposed fee for this consulting assignment was substantially higher than it normally charged for comparable work. This information would be relevant for the Board of Prime to consider prior to entering into a transaction with Smart. Thus, Cal violated his duty of loyalty by not fully disclosing all relevant information to the Board of Prime.

2. The issue is whether Cal has any defenses to a breach of loyalty claim. (45%)

A director who breaches his duty of loyalty has three safe harbor defenses: approval by disinterested directors, approval by shareholders, or fairness.

Disinterested Directors: A director is protected from liability if he made a disclosure of all material facts to the disinterested board of directors and the majority of the board approved the transaction. Under these facts, it appears that the Prime board, except for Cal, did not have a personal interest in this matter. Thus, the transaction was approved by a majority of the disinterested board. However, Cal is not protected under this safe harbor because Cal did not make adequate disclosures to the Board of Prime. Cal did not inform the Board that the fee charged by Smart was substantially higher than would ordinarily be expected for work like this. Therefore, Cal is not protected from liability under this safe harbor.

Shareholder Approval: A director is protected from liability if he made a disclosure of all material facts to disinterested shareholders and the majority of the shareholders approved the transaction. It appears that the shareholders were not involved in the approval of the Smart consulting contract, thus Cal is not protected from liability under this safe harbor.

Fairness: A director is protected from liability if he could provide proof that the transaction was fair at the time of commencement. In this case, the fact that Smart's proposed fee is substantially higher than what it normally charges for comparable work suggests that the transaction is not substantively fair. Accordingly, Cal likely is not protected from liability under the fairness safe harbor.

Cal does not have any defenses to a breach of loyalty claim because the safe harbor defenses are inapplicable in his case.

3. The issue is whether members of Prime's board of directors (other than Cal) violated their duty of care by approving the Smart consulting contract without more information. (40%)

Directors owe a duty of care to a corporation. Directors must act with the care of an ordinary prudent person in a like position and similar circumstances, including being informed before making a business decision. Directors are protected by the business judgment rule which presumes that in making a business decision, the directors of a corporation acted in the best interests of the corporation. The party attacking a board decision must rebut the presumption that its business judgment was an informed decision.

In this case, there is no evidence that the directors did not have an honest belief that they were acting in the best interests of Prime. Additionally, at least eight directors were entirely disinterested. However, a court could find that the directors did not act on an informed basis before approving the Smart consulting contract. Due to the price discrepancy between the Smart and Wiseman proposals, one would expect the directors to investigate why Smart's rates were significantly higher. Additionally, the fact that the Board only discussed the two proposals for 10 minutes suggests that the Board did not act with the care that an ordinarily prudent person would have in similar circumstances. Therefore, it is likely that a court would find that the Board violated its fiduciary duty of care by approving the contract with Smart.

(Editor's Note: The foregoing model answer was drafted in accordance with the NCBE Grading Guidelines for this question. The analysis is illustrative of the discussions that might appear in a high passing answer and addresses all legal and factual issues the drafters intended exam candidates to raise. When self-grading, refer to the NCBE's weighting of each issue, which is indicated in parentheses for your reference.)

[END OF HANDOUT]

Themis
Bar Review

CRIMINAL LAW ESSAY WRITING WORKSHOP

PROFESSOR CHRISTOPHER IDE-DON

UC DAVIS SCHOOL OF LAW

ISSUE CHECKLIST

A. Party liability

- Principal
- Accomplice
- Accessory after the fact

B. Responsibility

- Insanity—M'Naghten, irresistible impulse, Durham, & MPC
- Intoxication—voluntary and involuntary

C. Homicide

- Causation: Actual/but for and proximate cause
- Common law
    - Intent to kill
    - Intent to inflict great bodily injury
    - Reckless indifference to unjustifiably high risk to human life
    - Felony murder
- 1st degree—deliberate and premeditated
- 2nd degree—statutorily created category & common-law murder
- Voluntary manslaughter—provocation; time to cool off
- Involuntary manslaughter—criminal negligence or unlawful act

D. Other Crimes Against the Person

- Criminal battery, criminal assault, kidnapping, false imprisonment, rape

E. Crimes Against Property

- Larceny, embezzlement, larceny by false pretenses, robbery, burglary

F. Inchoate Crimes

- Conspiracy
- Attempt

G. Defenses

CHAPTER 1: ESSAY APPROACHES

A. Party liability

1. Principal

The person who actually commits the actus reus of the crime

2. Accomplice

- A person who aids or abets the principal prior to or during the crime
- Must intend to help the principal commit the crime and intend that the principal commit the crime that is charged

> **Note 1:** Mere knowledge that another person intends to commit a crime is not enough to make a person an accomplice. The accomplice must act with the intent that the principal commit the crime that is charged.

a. Accomplice Liability for Other Crimes

The accomplice is liable for any crimes that are the natural and probable consequence of the accomplice's conduct.

> ***Example 1:*** *The accomplice lends his truck to the principal to commit a burglary. During the burglary, the principal commits a battery against a security guard. The accomplice may be liable for the burglary and also the battery if it is a natural and probably consequence.*

b. Withdrawal

To legally withdraw (and avoid liability for the substantive crime), the accomplice must:

1. Repudiate prior aid;
2. Do all that is possible to countermand prior assistance; and
3. Do so before the chain of events is in motion and unstoppable.

3. Accessory After The Fact

A person who aids a felon to avoid apprehension after the felony is committed. To be guilty the person must know the felony was committed.

> **Note 2:** See outline for other general principles, such as actus reus, mens rea, and jurisdiction.

B. Responsibility

1. Insanity

> **Note 3:** All four of these approaches requires a mental disease or defect.

a. M'Naghten Rule

The defendant is not guilty if, because of a mental disease or defect, the defendant did not know either (i) the nature and quality of the act, **or** (ii) the wrongfulness of the act.

b. **Irresistible Impulse Test**

The defendant is not guilty if a mental disease or defect prevented him from being able to conform his conduct to the law.

c. **Durham Rule**

The defendant is not guilty if the crime would not have been committed but for the mental disease or defect.

d. **Model Penal Code Test**

The defendant is not guilty if a mental disease or defect either prevents the defendant from knowing the wrongfulness of the conduct or prevents the defendant from being able to conform his conduct to the law.

2. **Intoxication**

a. **Voluntary Intoxication**

- Involves the voluntary ingestion of an intoxicating substance
- It is a defense to specific intent crimes if the intoxication prevents the formation of the required intent.
- Voluntary intoxication is not a defense to crimes involving malice, recklessness, or negligence, or for strict-liability crimes.

b. **Involuntary Intoxication**

- Unknowingly or forced to ingest an intoxicating substance
- It is a defense to both general and specific intent crimes, as well as malice crimes when the intoxication serves to negate an element of the crime

C. **Homicide**

1. **Killing a person**

A living person must die.

2. **Causation**

> **Exam Tip 1:** Causation only needs to be discussed in depth if there is some ambiguity.

a. **Actual Cause**

- The victim would not have died but for the defendant's act
- When there are multiple causes, the defendant's act must be a substantial factor in causing the death

b. **Proximate Cause**

It is foreseeable that the defendant's actions would cause the victim's actions

1) Intervening Causes

- Actions by a third party that occur between the defendant's conduct and the victim's injury

2) Superseding Causes

- Actions by a third party will relieve the defendant of liability if they are unforeseeable
- Negligence is generally foreseeable (i.e., the doctor negligently treating the victim)

D. Types of Murder

1. Common-Law Murder

At common law, murder is the unlawful killing of a human being committed with malice aforethought. "Malice aforethought" includes the following mental states:

- Intent to kill
- Intent to inflict serious bodily injury
- Reckless indifference to an unjustifiably high risk to human life (depraved heart)
- Intent to commit certain felonies (felony murder)

> **Exam Tip 2:** If common law murder is tested, you should always discuss the intent to kill, intent to inflict serious bodily injury, and reckless indifference theories. Felony murder should only be discussed in certain situations (see notes below).

2. Felony Murder Rule (FMR)

> **Exam Tip 3:** You should only discuss the felony murder rule if the facts present a killing that occurs during an inherently dangerous felony.

- Under the FMR, a defendant can be found guilty for the unintended but foreseeable killing that is proximately caused by or during the commission or attempted commission of an inherently dangerous felony.
- Traditionally, burglary, arson, robbery, rape and kidnapping are considered to be inherently dangerous felonies.

> **Exam Tip 4:** To earn full credit, you must state the underlying felony that occurred and analyze the elements of the felony. Then analyze the felony murder rule.

a. Defenses to Felony Murder

- If the death was unforeseeable the FMR will not apply
- Point of Safety: If the felony is complete and the defendant has reached a place of safety, the FMR will not apply.

b. Death of a bystander (Majority Rule)

A defendant will not be liable for the death of a bystander caused by a police officer or as a result of resistance by the victim of the felony because neither person is the felon's agent.

c. Death of a co-felon

A defendant will not be liable for the death of a co-felon if a victim or police officer kills the co-felon.

3. First-Degree Murder

> **Exam Tip 5:** Remember to use common law murder unless the prompt tells you that the jurisdiction uses first and second-degree murder.

a. Premeditated

A murder is premeditated if the defendant had enough time to plan and reflect on the idea of the killing. The amount of time needed for premeditation may be brief, a mere second of reflection is sufficient.

b. Deliberate

The defendant made the decision to kill in a cool and dispassionate manner

4. Second-Degree Murder

> **Exam Tip 6:** Second-degree murder is the statutory version of common law murder.

- Second-degree murder is a homicide committed with the necessary malicious intent:
  - The intent to kill;
  - The intent to do great bodily injury; or
  - Depraved-heart murder

5. Voluntary Manslaughter

> **Note 4:** First degree murder can be mitigated down to voluntary manslaughter.

- Voluntary manslaughter is murder committed in response to adequate provocation.

a. Provocation

- Objective Element: A reasonable person would have been provoked by the victim's actions.
  - Words are generally not enough provocation
  - Sufficient provocation—discovery of adultery, a serious battery
- Subjective Element: The defendant must also have actually been provoked.

b. Time to Cool Off

- Objective: There must not have been sufficient time for an ordinary (reasonable) person to cool off.
- Subjective: The defendant also must not have actually cooled off.

6. Involuntary Manslaughter

Involuntary manslaughter is an unintentional homicide committed with criminal negligence or during an unlawful act.

a. Criminal Negligence

- Grossly negligent action (or inaction when there is a duty to act) that puts another person at a significant risk of serious bodily injury or death
- Model Penal Code: In addition to grossly negligent action, the defendant must also have been actually aware of the risk his conduct posed.

b. Unlawful Act

- The defendant commits an unlawful act that does not rise to felony murder and a death occurs as a result

E. Other Crimes Against the Person

1. Criminal Battery

The intentional unlawful application of force to another person that causes bodily harm to that person, or constitutes an offensive touching

2. Criminal Assault

An attempt to commit a battery, or intentionally placing another in apprehension of imminent bodily harm

3. Kidnapping

The unlawful confinement of a person against that person's will coupled with either movement or concealment of that person

4. False Imprisonment

The unlawful confinement of a person without consent

5. Rape

Unlawful sexual intercourse with a person against his/her will by force or threat of immediate force.

CHAPTER 2: ESSAY APPROACHES (CONT'D)

A. Crimes Against Property

1. Larceny

- The trespassory taking and carrying away of the personal property of another, without consent, with the specific intent to permanently deprive the owner of the property at the time of the taking
  - Taking and carrying away can be met by the slightest movement.
  - Intent to permanently deprive must be present at the time of the taking.

2. Embezzlement

The fraudulent conversion of the property of another by a person who is in lawful possession of the property

3. False Pretenses

- Occurs when the defendant obtains title to the property of another person through reliance of that person on a false representation of material fact made by the defendant with the intent to defraud
  - False Representation: The representation must be false and must be of a material past or present fact.
    - An opinion, sales talk or puffing, a prediction, or a false promise is not sufficient.
  - Reliance: The victim must rely upon the false representation, and that reliance must cause the victim to pass title to the defendant.
  - Intent to Defraud: The defendant must know that the representation is false and specifically intend to defraud.

4. Robbery

A larceny by force or intimidation when the taking of property is from the victim or in his presence

5. Burglary

- Burglary is the breaking and entering of the dwelling of another at nighttime with the specific intent to commit a felony therein.
  - Breaking: the slightest push can be sufficient
  - Entering: merely crossing the threshold can be sufficient
  - Specific intent to commit a felony: At the time of the breaking and entering, the defendant must have the intent to commit a felony (e.g., larceny, robbery, rape, murder) inside the dwelling.

- A defendant who fails to commit the underlying felony may nevertheless be guilty of burglary and attempt to commit the underlying felony.

> **Note 5:** See outline for other crimes against property (such as larceny by trick, forgery, extortion, arson, and receipt of stolen property).

B. Inchoate Crimes

1. Conspiracy (Majority Rule)

- An agreement between two or more people to accomplish an unlawful purpose;
- With specific intent to agree and commit the criminal objective; and
- An overt act in furtherance of the conspiracy

> **Exam Tip 7:** A defendant can be convicted of conspiracy to commit a crime and the underlying crime itself (as well as any crimes committed in furtherance of the conspiracy). There is no merger doctrine with regard to conspiracy.

Example 2: *A defendant can be liable for conspiracy to commit robbery and robbery itself (and any other crimes in furtherance of the conspiracy).*

a. Liability for co-conspirator crimes

A conspirator is liable for the conspiracy and all the crimes of a co-conspirator committed in furtherance of the conspiracy.

b. Withdrawal (Majority Rule)

After there has been an agreement but before an overt act has been committed, a person may avoid criminal liability for conspiracy.

2. Attempt

Attempt requires a substantial step toward the commission of a crime coupled with the specific intent to commit the crime. Mere preparation is not enough.

> **Exam Tip 8:** If a person succeeds in committing the crime, he will not be liable for the attempt and the crime itself. The doctrine of merger applies.

a. Abandonment

- At common law, once the defendant has taken a substantial step toward the commission of the offense, the defendant may not legally abandon the attempt to commit the crime.
- Some states do recognize voluntary abandonment as a defense to attempt. Abandonment is not voluntary if it is motivated by a desire to avoid detection.

> **Note 6:** See outline for the discussion of merger and solicitation.

C. Defenses

1. Self-defense

- Self-defense is the use of reasonable force to protect oneself at a reasonable time.

    - Deadly force may only be used to protect against the use of deadly force.
- Unreasonable use of force can be used as imperfect self-defense. Too much force for the circumstances may mitigate a murder charge down to voluntary manslaughter.

2. **Duress**
   - A third party's unlawful threat causes a defendant to reasonably believe that the only way to avoid death or serious bodily injury to himself or another is to violate the law, and that causes the defendant to do so
   - Under the majority rule, duress is not a defense to intentional homicide, but it is available for criminally negligent homicide

CHAPTER 3: PRACTICE ESSAY

SAMPLE CRIMINAL LAW ESSAY [ID 2277]

When Suspect returned from 10 months of overseas military duty, he was distraught to learn that his girlfriend, Judy, had married Suspect's best friend, Victor. One afternoon, Suspect saw Judy and Victor walking arm in arm in a shopping center. He approached them waving his clenched fist, angrily called Victor a traitor, and threatened Victor and Judy that he would beat them up "when you least expect it." Victor said, "You don't scare us." Suspect then shoved Victor and Judy and pushed his way past them.

The next day, Suspect took out his army pistol, muttering to his roommate, "I'm going to shoot a couple of rats." At about noon, armed with the pistol, Suspect climbed quietly through an open window at Victor's house at a time when he knew both Victor and Judy were there. Suspect confronted Victor and Judy in the living room and, pointing the pistol at Victor, said, "You stole my lady. Now you're going to pay the price. But first, take that gold watch off your wrist and give it to me." After Victor complied, Suspect shot and killed Victor.

Suspect then grabbed Judy and dragged her kicking and screaming into an upstairs bedroom. He forced her to undress and had sexual intercourse with her. He then pointed the pistol at her head and pulled the trigger. The pistol failed to discharge. Suspect then placed the pistol at Judy's neck and said, "You'd better not tell the police about any of this. If you do, I'll come back and finish the job." He then fled and was later arrested.

With what crimes can Suspect be charged? Explain fully, including an explanation of how the facts establish each element of each crime charged.

SAMPLE ANSWER

1. First encounter

Battery

Battery is the unlawful application of force to another person that causes bodily harm or constitutes an offensive touching. At the first encounter, Suspect shoved and pushed past Judy and Victor. This created the unlawful touching and the pushing would have been offensive to Judy and Victor. Therefore, Suspect could be charged with battery.

Assault

Assault is either an attempt to commit a battery or intentionally placing another in apprehension of imminent bodily harm. Prior to the shoving, Suspect had said he would beat up Judy and Victor at a later time. As Suspect said he would beat up Judy and Victor at a later time, there was no threat of imminent harm, and therefore no assault. Further, actual apprehension is a necessary component. Here, Victor said, "You don't scare us", so there was no actual apprehension of imminent harm. Therefore, Suspect could not be charged with assault.

Editor's note: Neither Victor nor Judy need to be fearful of contact threatened by Suspect in order to be apprehensive of such contact. But here, neither was apprehensive of imminent harm.

2. Second encounter

Robbery

Robbery is larceny by force or intimidation when the taking is from the person or presence of the victim. Larceny is the trespassory taking and carrying away of the personal property of another with the intent to steal. Here, Suspect took and carried away Victor's watch - his personal property- without permission and intended to keep the watch. Therefore, he could be charged with larceny. Suspect committed the larceny while holding Victor at gunpoint, which would be the threat of force. Therefore, Suspect could be charged with robbery.

Burglary

Under the common law, burglary is the breaking and entering of the dwelling of another at nighttime with the specific intent to commit a felony therein. Here, Suspect did not commit a breaking because he climbed through an open window at Victor's house and did not open or enlarge it. Also, he entered Victor's house in the daytime, which would not meet the nighttime element of burglary. Suspect did enter Victor's house and likely had the intent to commit the felony of robbery or murder, but the other elements are not met, so he cannot be charged with burglary.

3. Murder

Murder is the unlawful (i.e. without a legal excuse) killing of a human being committed with malice aforethought. Malice aforethought includes the mental state of intent to kill. When Suspect left his roommate, he said that he was going to "shoot a couple of rats". Assuming the rats he was referring to were Judy and Victor, his statement shows intent to kill them. Suspect then shot and killed Victor with his army pistol. One can infer intent to kill if the defendant uses a deadly weapon in the commission of the crime. Therefore, Suspect could be charged with murder.

4. Voluntary Manslaughter

Voluntary manslaughter is murder committed in response to adequate provocation, i.e., in the heat of passion. Whether or not one acts in the "heat of passion" in response to adequate provocation is subject to the reasonable person standard. Discovery of adultery by a spouse may constitute sufficient provocation that would cause a reasonable person to momentarily act out of passion rather than reason, but encountering a former girlfriend and her new husband holding hands while walking down the street does not appear to rise to that level of provocation. Further, if there was sufficient time between the "provocation" and the killing for a reasonable person to cool off, murder is not mitigated to manslaughter. Here, a day passed between the encounter and the killing. Therefore, the elements of murder are established and are not likely to be reduced to voluntary manslaughter.

5. Rape

Rape is unlawful sexual intercourse with a person against his/her will by force or threat of immediate force. Here, after killing her husband, the armed Suspect dragged Judy "kicking and screaming" upstairs and forced sexual intercourse upon her. Though most statutes have removed the force requirement, under these facts, the requisite force was applied and the elements of rape are established.

6. Attempted murder

To constitute attempt, there must be a substantial step towards commission of a crime coupled with intent to commit the crime. Suspect had stated to his roommate while he taking out his army pistol that he intended to kill some rats. He then went to Judy and Victor's home and killed Victor. It is therefore probable that the "rats" Suspect was referring to were both his former girlfriend and her husband. He thus had the requisite intent. The substantial step Suspect took was to point his army pistol at Judy's head and pull the trigger. Though Suspect did not actually kill Judy because the gun failed to discharge, he did threaten to "finish the job" if she told police. The elements of the crime of attempted murder are therefore established under these facts and Suspect could be charged with attempted murder.

7. Kidnapping

Kidnapping is the unlawful confinement of a person against that person's will coupled either with the movement or the hiding of that person. Here, Judy was confined in her home by gunpoint and then compelled by force to move to the bedroom. The fact that she was kicking and screaming along with the fact that Suspect was armed indicates that the move and confinement were against her will. The elements of the crime of kidnapping are established.

8. Assault

Assault is either an attempt to commit a battery or intentionally placing another in apprehension of imminent bodily harm. Here, after the pistol failed to discharge, Suspect placed the pistol at Judy's neck and said, "You'd better not tell the police about any of this. If you do, I'll come back and finish the job." Suspect's statement to Judy was a conditional threat of future harm to her, so it would not place her in imminent apprehension of harm. Suspect could not be charged with assault for his statement to Judy.

[END OF HANDOUT]

Themis
Bar Review

CRIMINAL PROCEDURE ESSAY WORKSHOP

PROFESSOR CHRISTOPHER IDE-DON
UC DAVIS SCHOOL OF LAW

CHAPTER 1: ISSUES TESTED (PART 1)

A. Summary of Issues Tested

1. **4th Amendment**
   - Government conduct/State Action
   - Reasonable expectation of privacy
   - Seizure of persons
   - Warrant requirement
   - Exceptions to warrant requirement
     - Stop and frisk
     - Search incident to lawful arrest
     - Automobile exception
     - Plain view
     - Exigent circumstances
     - Consent
   - Exclusionary rule—Fruit of the poisonous tree & exceptions
1. **5th Amendment**—Miranda Rights and Custodial Interrogation
2. **6th Amendment**—Right to Counsel
2. **Due Process Clause**—Line-ups
3. **Trial Considerations**
   - Burden of proof
   - Sentencing enhancements
4. **Post-Trial Considerations—Double Jeopardy**
5. **Additional Issues**
   - Confrontation Clause
   - Guilty Pleas
   - Right to Discharge Attorney & Substitute a New Attorney
   - Right to Represent Oneself
   - Right to a Separate Trial from Co-defendant
   - Right to a Speedy Trial
   - Right to Testify at Trial

B. 4th Amendment

- Prohibits unreasonable searches and seizures

3. **Government Conduct**
   - Must show some government or police agency action
   - Does not protect against private actors
4. **Standing**
   - Defendant must have a reasonable expectation of privacy as to the places searched or items seized

> **Exam Tip 1:** A typical Crim Pro question will start with a seizure of a person, and then a search will occur. A good answer will walk through each government action chronologically.

5. Seizure of a Person

- By means of physical force ***OR*** show of authority, a person's freedom of movement is restrained
- **Test**—under the totality of circumstances, would a reasonable person not feel free to leave
- Types of Seizure—Arrest, stop and frisk, police checkpoints, and traffic stops

a. Arrest

- Generally, requires an arrest warrant
- Warrantless arrest allowed if an officer has ***probable cause*** to believe that a felony has been committed

b. Terry Stop (Investigatory Stop) and Frisk

Valid when an officer has ***reasonable suspicion*** that someone is engaged in criminal activity

c. Police Checkpoint

- Valid if:
  - Done in a non-discriminatory manner; and
  - There is an automobile-related reason for the checkpoint

Example 1: *A DUI checkpoint is legal because it is done for the purpose of preventing drunk driving (so long as it is conducted in a non-discriminatory manner).*

d. Traffic Stop

Valid if the officer has ***reasonable suspicion*** or ***probable cause*** that a traffic law has been violated

> **Exam Tip 2:** A recent question provided a statute that allowed an officer to arrest a person for a traffic violation if the officer had probable cause to believe the person had violated the statute.

6. Search

- Occurs when government conduct violates the defendant's reasonable expectation of privacy

a. Valid Search Warrant

- A search conducted pursuant to a valid warrant is generally constitutional
- To be valid, the warrant must:

a) Be issued by a neutral magistrate;

b) Be based upon ***probable cause***; and

c) Describe with particularity the places to be searched and the items to be seized

b. Execution of Search Warrant

- Knock and announce—police must knock and announce their presence
- Defective warrant—police execution in good faith will not result in a violation

c. Exceptions to the Warrant Requirement

1) Terry Stop and Frisk

- Can stop a person based on ***reasonable suspicion*** that the person is engaged in a criminal activity
- Frisk—officer can pat down the outer clothing of the defendant for officer safety
    - **Plain feel**—can seize an item if it is immediately obvious that the object is contraband
- Automobile Frisk—allowed after a valid stop if:
    - The officer has a reasonable belief there is a weapon in the car; and
    - The search is limited to those areas that may contain a weapon
- Finding contraband during the frisk can give rise to probable cause to arrest

2) Search Incident to Lawful Arrest

- May search arrestee within a reasonable scope
- **Lawful arrest**—requires probable cause
- **Scope**—defendant and the immediate area (i.e., wingspan)
    - In arrestee's home—can search areas within reach or where others may be hiding
    - In a vehicle—can search glove compartment if within reach of defendant or if it is reasonable that evidence of the offense of arrest may be found

3) Automobile Exception

- If police have ***probable cause*** to believe a vehicle contains evidence of a crime, can search ***any*** part of the car believed to have contraband

4) Plain View

- Requirements:
    - Police are ***lawfully present***; and
    - Incriminating nature of the item is ***immediately apparent***

5) **Exigent Circumstances**

- Several circumstances can satisfy the exigency requirement, for example:
  - Hot pursuit of a fleeing felon
  - Danger of destruction of evidence
  - Police or public safety

6) **Consent**

- Cannot exceed scope of consent
- Must be voluntary (no threats, compulsion, or false assertion of lawful authority)

d. Exclusionary Rule

- Excludes evidence obtained as a result of the government's violation of the 4th Amendment
- Also excludes "fruits of the poisonous tree"—other evidence obtained as a result of the violation

Example 2: *A police officer illegally searches Defendant and finds a gun. The officer takes the gun but releases Defendant. Later, the officer discovers the gun had been stolen and obtains an arrest warrant. Defendant is arrested one day later for the stolen gun. At the time of arrest, Defendant is searched, and the officer finds cocaine in Defendant's pocket.*

Exam Tip 3: A typical question will ask whether the gun and/or the cocaine should be excluded from evidence.

Defendant can move to exclude the gun because it was obtained by an illegal search. Defendant can also move to exclude the cocaine as fruit of the poisonous tree because the arrest that justified the search was illegal (i.e., the arrest warrant was based entirely on the gun, which was unlawfully obtained evidence).

e. Exceptions to the Exclusionary Rule

1) Inevitable Discovery Rule

2) Independent Source Doctrine

3) Passage of Time (Attenuation)

4) Good Faith Reliance

CHAPTER 2: ISSUES TESTED (PART 2)

A. 5th Amendment

- Provides that no person shall be compelled in a criminal case to testify against himself
- Often called the right against ***self-incrimination***

- Applies to testimonial evidence coercively obtained by police

1. *Miranda* Warnings

- Required to give warnings prior to ***custodial interrogation***
- **Custody**—defendant reasonably believes he is not free to leave or is otherwise deprived of freedom
- **Interrogation**—police expressly question defendant ***OR*** police words or actions are likely to elicit an incriminating response

Example 3: *If an officer is not directly questioning the defendant but makes a statement to another officer that they know is likely to elicit a response from the defendant, that situation likely amounts to an interrogation.*

> **Exam Tip 4:** Government informants—if the defendant does not know that he is speaking to an informant, there is no custodial interrogation under the 5th Amendment.
>
> **Exam Tip 5:** Police line-up—if the defendant is placed in a line-up, that is not a custodial interrogation under the 5th Amendment.

2. Waiver of *Miranda* Rights

- Must be ***knowing*** and ***voluntary***
    - Voluntary—cannot be the result of government coercion
- Silence is not sufficient to invoke or waive *Miranda* rights
- Must make an affirmative statement

3. Uncoerced (voluntary or spontaneous) Statements

- After a defendant receives *Miranda* warnings and does not invoke the right to remain silent, the defendant might decide to make an uncoerced statement to police
- This constitutes a waiver of *Miranda* rights
- Police have no obligation to inform the defendant that his attorney is trying to reach him

4. Invoking *Miranda* Rights

a. Right to counsel

- Must ***unambiguously assert*** the right to counsel
    - Police cannot question the defendant any further
- Not offense specific—once the right is invoked, police cannot question the defendant about any crimes
- Ambiguous statement—police are under no duty to clarify or provide counsel
- A subsequent voluntary statement can be admissible

b. Right to remain silent

Must ***unambiguously assert*** the right to remain silent

c. Re-approaching the defendant

- After invoking rights, police may not re-approach the defendant later
- **Exception**—if there is a break in custody for 14 days or more, police may re-approach the defendant, give fresh *Miranda* warnings, and attempt to get a waiver

Editorial Note 1: To clarify, the 14-day break applies only to re-approaching a suspect who has invoked the right to counsel. There is not a specific amount of time that must elapse before police may re-approach a suspect who has invoked the right to remain silent.

5. Standing

- Defendant may only assert his own *Miranda* rights

Example 4: *If there are two defendants (Co-Defendant A and Co-Defendant B), Co-Defendant A cannot object to a violation of Co-Defendant B's* Miranda *rights.*

6. Exclusion of Statements

- **Voluntary confession**—not protected by *Miranda*
- **Involuntary confession**—inadmissible for any purpose
- Based on the totality of the circumstances:
  - Police conduct
  - Defendant's characteristics (age, education, experience)
  - Timing of statement

a. Second confession

- Arises when a confession is obtained in violation of *Miranda*, then later the rights are read, and the defendant waives and confesses again
- May be admissible if the initial confession was the result of a good faith mistake

b. Voluntary statement in violation of *Miranda*

- Excluded as substantive evidence
- Admissible as impeachment evidence if inconsistent with later testimony

c. Physical evidence

Any physical fruits of a ***voluntary*** confession can be admissible evidence.

B. 6th Amendment—Right to Counsel

- Automatically applies at all ***critical stages*** of prosecution after formal proceedings begin
- Formal proceedings—indictment or formal charge

> **Exam Tip 6:** Critical stages include: ***post-charge in person line-ups*** and questioning by a ***government informant*** (even if the defendant is not aware).

- **Offense specific**—does not prevent the police from questioning the defendant about other crimes that have not been formally charged
- **Waiver**—must be ***knowing*** and ***voluntary***

C. Line-Ups under the Due Process Clause

- Must not be conducted in a manner that is impermissibly suggestive or provides a substantial likelihood of misidentification

> ***Example 5:*** *If the defendant is the only male and the other people in the lineup are female, this is impermissibly suggestive.*

D. Trial Considerations

1. Due Process Clause—Burden of Proof

Prosecution must prove ***all elements*** of the crime ***beyond a reasonable doubt***

> ***Example 6:*** *From a recent question: a jury instruction told the jurors to presume that an element of the offense had been met. This took the burden of proof away from the prosecution and violated the Due Process Clause.*

2. Sentencing

Any fact, other than a prior conviction, that is used to increase the sentence beyond the statutory maximum, must be charged and proved beyond a reasonable doubt.

> **Editorial Note 2:** This rule applies when the fact could increase the sentence beyond the ***maximum*** prescribed by statute.

E. Post-Trial Considerations

1. Double Jeopardy

- Provides protections against:
  1) Prosecution for the same offense after acquittal;
  2) Prosecution for the same offense after conviction; and
  3) Multiple punishments for the same offense
- **Same v. separate offenses** (*Blockburger* test)—each crime must require proof of an element that the other does not to be considered a separate offense

> **Exam Tip 7:** This may arise when you are given two statutes. You have to make sure that each requires an element that the other does not. If this standard is not met, they may be viewed as the same offense and subject to a Double Jeopardy objection.

- Prohibits multiple prosecutions of greater and lesser-included offenses
  - Permissible to charge a defendant with a greater and lesser-included offense ***in the same action***

    Example 7: *May charge the defendant with felony murder (greater offense) and robbery (lesser-included offense).*

F. Additional Issues

Exam Tip 8: These issues have been tested but not frequently.

- Confrontation Clause
- Guilty Pleas
- Right to Discharge or Substitute an Attorney
- Right to Represent Oneself
- Right to a Separate Trial from Co-defendant
- Right to a Speedy Trial
- Right to Testify at Trial

CHAPTER 1: PRACTICE QUESTION

July 2008, Question 8 [ID 282]

On April 10, a convenience store was robbed by someone carrying a gun. The store's video camera caught the robbery on tape. The tape was shown on the evening news.

On April 11, an anonymous caller contacted the police saying, "I saw that tape of the robbery. The robber kind of looks like Student. He's an 18-year-old student at the high school."

On April 12, two police officers took the tape to the high school and showed it to the principal, who said, "It could be Student. It's hard to tell because the tape is not clear." The tape was also shown to Student's homeroom teacher, who said, "It might be him, but I couldn't say for sure."

Later that day, the police officers went to the store where Student works after school. They asked the manager if they could talk with Student, who was called to the manager's office. The police introduced themselves to Student and said, "We'd like to talk to you." They walked with Student into the manager's office and shut the door. One police officer sat behind the manager's desk; the other, in full uniform with his revolver visible, sat near the door. Student sat between them. The manager's office measures eight feet by ten feet.

The police officers told Student they wanted to ask him some questions about the convenience store robbery on April 10. Student said he knew nothing about a robbery. He continued to deny that he had any knowledge of the robbery for about 20 minutes. Student did not ask to leave, and neither police officer told Student he was free to leave.

After about 20 minutes, the police officers told Student that they had a videotape of the robbery and that they had shown it to three people, all of whom positively identified Student as the robber.

Student said nothing for a few minutes. One of the police officers then said, "You know, if we can tell the prosecutor that you cooperated, she might go a lot easier on you. I'd hate to see you end up doing a long stretch in prison. Let's just say it's not a nice place." Student then blurted out, "I did the robbery. I used a little air gun."

Immediately after Student made that statement, the police officers informed Student that he was under arrest for the robbery of the convenience store. They read him his *Miranda* rights. Student stated he understood his *Miranda* rights and told the police officers that he was not going to say anything more to them. The police officers placed Student in handcuffs and took him to the police station where he was booked for armed robbery.

Student had had two earlier brushes with the law. When he was 16, he had been found delinquent in juvenile court for auto theft and had been placed on supervision for one year. When he was 17, he had received a ticket for underage drinking and had paid a fine of $150. He is a "C" student, but his teachers believe he is an "underachiever."

Student's defense attorney has filed a motion to suppress Student's statements on three grounds:

Student's statements were obtained in violation of Student's Fourth Amendment rights.

Student's statements were obtained in violation of his *Miranda* rights.

Student's confession was not voluntary.

How should the trial court rule on each of the grounds in the motion to suppress? Explain.

SAMPLE ANSWER

<u>1. Student's Fourth Amendment Rights</u> (30%)

Seizure: The issue is whether the police interview of Student violated Student's Fourth Amendment right to be free from unreasonable seizure such that Student's statements should be suppressed.

A person has a Fourth Amendment right to be free from unreasonable seizure. A person is seized by the police when the officer, by means of physical force or show of authority, terminates or restrains freedom of movement in such a way that a reasonable person would believe that he was not free to leave. In this case, Student was taken into his manager's office for 25 minutes with two officers, one of whom had a visible weapon. The door was closed, and one officer sat between Student and the door. Student was not told that he was free to leave. Under these circumstances, a reasonable person in Student's position would have believed that he was not free to leave until given permission by the police officers, therefore Student was seized.

Reasonable Suspicion: Assuming there was a seizure, the next issue is whether the seizure violated Student's Fourth Amendment rights.

The Fourth Amendment permits detention of an individual for a brief period of time if the police have a reasonable suspicion based on articulable facts that the individual in question has been recently involved in criminal activity. Whether reasonable suspicion exists is based on the totality of the circumstances. In this case, three people stated that the person on the tape of the convenience store robbery looked like Student. These identifications gave the police officers sufficient facts to form the basis of a reasonable suspicion that Student was the robber. Accordingly, Student's Fourth Amendment rights were not violated, and his statements should not be suppressed.

<u>2. Miranda Rights</u> (40%)

Interrogation: The issue is whether Student's statements should be suppressed because the police failed to read Student his *Miranda* rights when they questioned him in the manager's office.

Any statement obtained as the result of custodial interrogation may not be used against the suspect at a subsequent trial unless the police provided procedural safeguards effective to secure the privilege against self-incrimination.

An interrogation refers not only to questioning, but also to any words or actions that the police know or should know are likely to elicit an incriminating response. In this case, the police officers asked Student several questions regarding the robbery. Additionally, the police officers' statements regarding prison time and positive identifications would likely elicit an incriminating response. Thus, Student was subject to an interrogation.

Custody: Assuming there was an interrogation, the next issue is whether Student was in custody.

A person is in custody when he is not free to leave or is otherwise deprived of his freedom in any significant way. In this case, Student was questioned in the manager's office. Student was outnumbered two to one, and one officer with a visible firearm sat between Student and the door. Although police did not tell Student that he was free to leave, Student was probably not in custody. The police officers did not tell Student that he was under arrest until the end of the interview. During the interview, Student was not under any restraints. While Student may not have felt that he was free to leave, a reasonable person would not have believed he had been arrested or otherwise taken into formal custody. Thus, Student was not in custody, and there should be no suppression for a *Miranda* violation.

<u>3. Voluntariness of Confession</u> (30%)

The issue is whether Student's confession following police interrogation was voluntary or involuntary.

Voluntary confessions are not protected by *Miranda*. A confession is involuntary only if the police coerced the defendant into make the confession. Whether a statement is voluntary or coerced is determined based on the totality of the circumstances, including facts such as the conduct of the police, the characteristics of the defendant, and the time of the statement.

Here, Student is a high-school senior with minimal experience with the criminal justice system. The police questioned Student in a small, closed room. The police outnumbered Student two against one, and one of the police officers had a visible firearm. The police did not tell Student that he could leave and did not tell him that he was not obligated to answer their questions. Additionally, the police lied to Student about the positive identifications made regarding the robbery. Furthermore, the police made a veiled threat about what would happen to Student in prison if he did not confess. Thus, a court could find that Student's confession was involuntary based on the totality of the circumstances.

However, most courts would likely consider Student's statement to be voluntary. Student is an adult with average intelligence and some experience with the juvenile justice system. The interview in the office lasted only 25 minutes. Although the officer's statements about the identifications were not completely true, the fact that Student was deceived does not render a statement involuntary. The statement by police officers about prison time and prison conditions could be perceived as general observations. Accordingly, most courts would likely consider Student's statement voluntary, and the confession should not be suppressed.

NCBE EDITOR'S NOTES FOR THIS ESSAY QUESTION

Credit should be given for reasonable arguments on either side of the issue for points 2 and 3.

(Themis Editor's Note: The foregoing model answer was drafted in accordance with the NCBE Grading Guidelines for this question. The analysis is illustrative of the discussions that might appear in a high passing answer and addresses all legal and factual issues the drafters intended exam candidates to raise. When self-grading, refer to the NCBE's weighting of each issue, which is indicated in parentheses for your reference.)

[END OF HANDOUT]

Themis
Bar Review

EVIDENCE ESSAY WRITING WORKSHOP

PROFESSOR CHRISTOPHER IDE-DON

UC DAVIS SCHOOL OF LAW

SUMMARY OF ISSUES TESTED

Editor's Note 1: The Professor refers to specific page numbers throughout this lecture. The content does not always match these references due to formatting changes.

A. Purpose

1. **Logical relevance**
2. **Legal relevance**
3. **Character evidence**
    a. **Civil**
    b. **Criminal**
        1) D's character—specific rules for prosecution, D, and when D "opens the door"
        2) V's character—specific rules for prosecution and D
    c. **Prior bad acts**
        1) Not admissible to show D's criminal propensity to prove D committed the crime in question unless MIMIC evidence (**m**otive, **i**ntent, absence of **m**istake, **i**dentity or **c**ommon plan)
4. **Habit evidence**
5. **Sex-offense cases**

B. Witnesses

1. **Competence**
2. **Opinion testimony**—rules for lay opinion and expert witnesses
3. **Recollection refreshed**
    a. **Present recollection refreshed**
    b. **Past recollection recorded**

4. **Impeachment**

   a. **W's character for truthfulness**—opinion/reputation testimony admissible to attack W's character for truthfulness (can only bolster credibility after it's directly attacked and cross-examination rules

   b. **Criminal conviction**—can be used to impeach witness's character for truthfulness

   c. **Prior inconsistent statements**

   d. **W's bias or interest**

   e. **Impeachment of hearsay declarant**

   f. **Rehabilitation of W**

C. **Tangible evidence**

   1. **Authentication**

D. **Privileges**

   1. **Spousal immunity and confidential marital communications**

   2. **Public policy exclusions**

      a. **Subsequent remedial measures**

      b. **Compromise offers and negotiations**

      c. **Offers to pay medical expenses**

      d. **Liability insurance**

E. **Hearsay**

   1. **Assertive Conduct**

      a. **Laughing, crying, gestures**

   2. **Non-Hearsay Use**

      a. **Effect on the listener/reader**

      b. **Circumstantial evidence of state of mind**

      c. **Legally significant verbal act**

   3. **Double Hearsay**—hearsay within hearsay

   4. **Non-hearsay**

      a. **Opposing party's statement**—judicial/adoptive admissions or vicarious statements

      b. **Prior statements**—consistent/inconsistent or identifications

5. **Hearsay Exceptions**

   a. **Declarant unavailable**

      1) Dying declaration

      2) Statement against interest

      3) Former testimony

   b. **Declarant availability not at issue**

      1) Present sense impression

      2) Excited utterance

      3) Business and public records

      4) Statement of mental/emotional/physical condition

      5) Statement made for medical diagnosis/treatment

      6) Recorded recollection

      7) Judgments of previous convictions

F. **Constitutional Limitations**—the Sixth Amendment Confrontation Clause

CHAPTER 1: ESSAY APPROACHES

A. Purpose

1. **Logical Relevance, FRE 401**

   Evidence is relevant if it has a tendency to make a fact more or less probable than it would be without the evidence and the fact is of consequence in determining the action.

   > **Exam Tip 1:** When analyzing the logical relevance of an item of evidence, be sure to clearly explain how the evidence is helpful for determining the outcome of the dispute.

2. **Legal Relevance, FRE 403** (Exclusion of Logically Relevant Evidence)

   Relevant evidence may be excluded if its probative value is substantially outweighed by the danger of unfair prejudice, confusing the issues, misleading the jury, undue delay, wasting time, or needlessly presenting cumulative evidence.

3. **Character Evidence, FRE 404**

   a. **Character Evidence—Civil Case**

      In a civil case, character evidence is not admissible to prove that a person acted in accordance with that character or trait on a particular occasion.

However, character evidence (reputation, opinion, and specific acts) is admissible when character is an essential element of a claim or defense, such as: defamation, negligent hiring or entrustment, and child custody.

Note 1: This exception is rarely used.

b. Character Evidence—Criminal Case

In a criminal case, the prosecution is not permitted to introduce bad character evidence about a defendant in order to prove he has the propensity to commit crimes, thus he is likely to have committed the crime in question.

1) Defendant's Character

A defendant may introduce evidence of his own good character (reputation or opinion) to show that it is inconsistent with the crime charged.

Note 2: Reputation evidence refers to the defendant's reputation in the community at large, not just his friends. Opinion evidence refers to the testifying witness's personal opinion of the defendant, not the opinions of others.

If the defendant "opens the door", the prosecution may:

- Call a witness to rebut and attack the defendant's claims of good character with reputation or opinion based evidence, or
- Cross-examine the defendant's character witness and ask about the defendant's reputation, opinion, or specific bad acts by the defendant

Note 3: The prosecution can only "ask" about specific bad acts, it cannot enter extrinsic evidence.

2) Victim's Character

A defendant may introduce reputation or opinion evidence of the victim's character trait if it is relevant to the defense asserted (for example, if the defendant is charged with assault and battery and claims self-defense, he can introduce evidence that the victim has a violent character).

If the defendant "opens the door," the prosecution may:

- Introduce rebuttal (reputation or opinion) evidence of the victim's character trait, or
- Attack the defendant's character regarding the same trait that the defendant attacked of the victim

Exam Tip 2: If the facts involve a criminal case, read carefully to see if the defendant has "opened the door" by presenting evidence about his character or the victim's character, which would then allow the prosecution to rebut this with evidence attacking defendant or rehabilitating victim.

c. Specific Bad Acts, FRE 404(b)

Evidence of a crime, wrong, or other act is not admissible to prove a person's character in order to show that on a particular occasion the person acted in accordance with the character.

However, evidence of prior bad acts may be admissible for another purpose, such as proving motive, opportunity, intent, preparation, plan, knowledge, identity, absence of mistake, or lack of accident. This is sometimes referred to as the MIMIC rule, which refers to **M**otive, **I**ntent, absence of **M**istake, **I**dentity, or **C**ommon plan. Modus operandi can be used as identity evidence.

> **Exam Tip 3:** If a specific bad act is introduced as evidence, consider arguments for any non-character uses of the evidence.

4. Habit Evidence, FRE 406

Evidence of a person's habit or an organization's routine practice may be admitted to prove that on a particular occasion the person or organization acted in accordance with the habit or routine practice. The court may admit this evidence regardless of whether it is corroborated or whether there was an eyewitness.

5. Sex-Offense Cases, FRE 412

In civil or criminal cases involving alleged sexual misconduct, evidence of the victim's sexual conduct or predisposition is generally barred.

Exception: In a civil case, the court may admit evidence offered to prove a victim's sexual behavior or sexual predisposition if its probative value substantially outweighs the danger of harm to any victim and of unfair prejudice to any party.

B. Witnesses

1. Witness Competence, FRE 601

A non-expert witness must have personal knowledge of a matter in order to testify about it.

2. Lay Opinion, FRE 701

A lay opinion is admissible if it is rationally based on the witness's perception, helpful clearly understanding the witness's testimony or to determining a fact in issue; and not based on scientific, technical, or other specialized knowledge.

> **Exam Tip 4:** Lay witnesses are qualified to give testimony about the speed of a vehicle—this has been tested on past essay exams.

3. Expert Testimony, FRE 703

- The subject matter of expert testimony must be scientific, technical or some other specialized knowledge that will help a trier of fact understand evidence or determine a fact at issue that focuses on the relevance of testimony.

- A witness must be qualified as an expert by knowledge, skill, experience, training or education.
- The testimony must be based on sufficient facts or data and the product of reliable principles and methods.
- Finally, the witness must apply these principles and methods reliably to facts of the case.

a. Present Recollection Refreshed, FRE 612

A witness may examine any item to refresh his present recollection, and his testimony must be based on his refreshed recollection (he may not read from the refreshing document itself). The item itself is not entered into evidence unless the adverse party introduces it into evidence.

> **Note 4:** When the item used to refresh a witness's recollection is a document, the adverse party is entitled to have the document produced, to inspect the document, to cross-examine the witness about it, and to introduce any relevant portion of the document into evidence.

b. Past Recollection Recorded, FRE 803

A memorandum or record about a matter the witness once had knowledge of but now has insufficient recollection of to testify that was made or adopted by the witness when it was fresh in the witness's memory and is accurate may be read into evidence under the recorded recollection hearsay exception.

> **Note 5:** The memo or record itself may be admitted into evidence if the adverse party introduces it into evidence.

4. Impeachment, FRE 607–609

> **Exam Tip 5:** An item of evidence may be inadmissible under the Character Evidence Rule, but still admissible for impeachment purposes.

A witness may be impeached by calling into question her credibility.

A witness's credibility can be attacked by:

- Opinion/reputation testimony from another witness, FRE 608

> **Note 6:** Evidence of truthful character is admissible only after the witness's character for truthfulness has been attacked.

- Specific instances of conduct, FRE 608
  - Generally (see below for Criminal Conviction exception), extrinsic (outside) evidence is not admissible to show specific instances of witness's conduct relating to truthfulness.
  - However, on cross-examination, a witness can be asked about specific instances of his conduct to attack or support the witness's credibility.

- Exception to specific instances of conduct rule: Criminal convictions, FRE 609
  - Extrinsic evidence of a criminal conviction for crimes involving dishonesty/false statements (e.g., perjury or fraud) must be admitted.
  - Extrinsic evidence of a criminal conviction for a crime not involving dishonesty/false statement (e.g., assault) if the crime was punishable by death or imprisonment for more than one year (a felony):
    - If the conviction is being used in a civil or criminal case against a witness who is *not* a defendant, the evidence is admissible subject to a Rule 403 analysis (i.e., is the probative value substantially outweighed by the danger of unfair prejudice or other factors) to determine admissibility.
    - If the conviction is being used in a criminal case against a witness who is the defendant, the evidence will be admissible only if the probative value outweighs the prejudicial effect to the defendant.
  - 10-year rule: If more than 10 years has passed since the conviction or release (whichever is later), the evidence of the conviction will only be admissible if the probative value substantially outweighs the prejudicial effect and the proponent gives reasonable notice of the intent to use it.
- Prior inconsistent statements, FRE 613
  - A witness's prior statement that is inconsistent with the witness's current testimony is admissible to impeach the witness.
  - Extrinsic evidence of the prior statement can be admissible for purposes of impeachment.
- Bias or interest
  - Extrinsic evidence is admissible to show that the witness is biased and may not be testifying truthfully is admissible.
- Sensory competence
  - Extrinsic evidence showing that a witness is physically or mentally impaired and is therefore not a credible witness is admissible.

    Example 1: *Grandmother testifies that she was in her house and witnessed D shoot V in a parking lot that is 100 yards from her house. Defense enters evidence that Grandmother is unable to see more than 25 yards.*
- Impeachment of a hearsay declarant, FRE 806
  - If a hearsay statement is admitted into evidence, the declarant who made the original statement can be impeached as if the declarants/he was a testifying witness.

__Example 2:__ Wife (witness) testifies about a statement made by her husband (the declarant who made the original statement). The opposing side enters evidence that husband (declarant) was convicted of perjury one year ago. The conviction would be admissible to impeach the husband (declarant).

- Rehabilitation of a witness
  - If a witness is impeached, the witness may be rehabilitated by the introduction of rebuttal evidence, including:
    - Explanation or clarification during redirect examination;
    - Reputation or opinion evidence about the witness's character for truthfulness; or
    - A prior consistent statement.

CHAPTER 2: TANGIBLE EVIDENCE; PRIVILEGES; HEARSAY

A. Tangible Evidence

1. Authentication, FRE 901–02

All tangible evidence must be authenticated. To authenticate an item, the proponent must produce sufficient evidence to support a finding that the thing is what its proponent claims it is.

> **Exam Tip 6:** Look for facts indicating that the authenticity of the evidence could be in question, for example handwriting or the sound of a person's voice may be in dispute. A lay person can testify about the authenticity of handwriting and a person's voice if they have prior knowledge.

2. Best Evidence Rule, FRE 1001–08

The best evidence rule requires that the original document or a reliable duplicate be produced in order to prove the contents of a writing, recording, or photograph, including electronic documents, X-rays, and videos. This rule applies only when the contents of the document are at issue or a witness is relying on the contents of the document when testifying.

B. Privileges and Other Policy Exclusions

1. Privileges

a. Spousal Testimonial Privilege

The testifying spouse can assert the privilege and refuse to testify against another spouse; it only applies if there is a valid marriage in existence.

b. Confidential Marital Communications

Both spouses can assert the privilege and prevent the other spouse from testifying about confidential communications made during the marriage. This privilege continues even if the marriage has ended (marriage ends upon divorce).

> **Note 7:** If a spouse breaks confidentiality and discloses information to a third party, the spouse may not be able to assert this privilege.
>
> **Exam Tip 7:** The spousal testimonial privilege and confidential marital communications privileges are often tested together. If there are facts about spouses or ex-spouses testifying, you should discuss both issues.

2. Public Policy Exclusions

a. Subsequent Remedial Measures, FRE 407

Evidence of subsequent remedial measures taken by the defendant that would have made an earlier injury or harm less likely to occur are admissible for purposes such as impeachment or to show ownership or control, but not to show negligence.

b. Settlement Offers and Statements Made During Negotiations, FRE 408

Settlement offers and statements made during settlement negotiations are excluded. The settlement offer must be made in response to a disputed claim. If there is no disputed claim and a settlement offer is made, it is not barred.

c. Offers to Pay Medical Expenses, FRE 409

Offers to pay medical expenses are inadmissible to prove liability.

d. Evidence of Liability Insurance, FRE 411

Evidence of liability insurance is not admissible to show liability, but is admissible to prove agency, ownership, control, or the witness's bias or prejudice.

C. Hearsay

1. Hearsay Approach

- Write the "hearsay" heading and rule
- Explain why item could be hearsay—used for the truth of the matter asserted
- Look for non-assertive conduct—the hearsay rule only applies to assertive conduct
- Look for non-hearsay uses—such as the effect on the listener or reader
- Look for double hearsay—hearsay within hearsay
  - If you see double hearsay, define the two levels and discuss both levels separately
- Discuss all relevant non-hearsay "exceptions"
- Discuss all relevant hearsay exceptions

2. Hearsay, FRE 801(c)

Hearsay is an out-of-court statement that is offered to prove the truth of the matter asserted. If offered to prove something other than the truth of the matter asserted, then the statement is not hearsay.

3. Assertive Conduct

Assertive conduct is treated as a statement and is subject to the hearsay rules. Assertive conduct such as gesturing (e.g., nodding one's head to indicate "yes") or pointing a finger in a direction to indicate a direction of travel (e.g., right, left, or forward) will be treated as a statement. Laughing or crying may or may not be assertive conduct, depending on the circumstances.

4. Non-Hearsay Use

If a statement is used to show something other than the truth of the matter asserted, it will not be hearsay. For example, a statement can be used to show the effect on the listener or reader, or as circumstantial evidence of the declarant's state of mind.

> **Exam Tip 8:** An example of a non-hearsay use of evidence is a mechanic telling a defendant that his car's brakes are bad. The non-hearsay use of this statement is to show the effect on the listener—it has the effect of putting the listener-defendant on notice that he has bad brakes.
>
> **Exam Tip 9:** Before discussing hearsay exceptions, look for any non-hearsay uses of the evidence and discuss them. Then, even if you find a non-hearsay use for the evidence, proceed to discuss the hearsay exceptions that might apply.

5. Double Hearsay, FRE 805

Hearsay within hearsay is not excluded by the rule against hearsay if each part of the combined statements conforms with an exception to the rule.

> **Exam Tip 10:** Read the facts carefully and look for items of evidence that contain two layers of hearsay. For example, a written police report containing a statement made by a witness to a car crash would present two levels of hearsay. The written police report is hearsay and contained within it is the statement made by the witness, which is also hearsay. In order to admit the report and the statement within it, both levels of hearsay must be admissible.

6. Non-Hearsay Exceptions to consider, FRE 801(d)

a. Prior statements

- Prior inconsistent statements
- Prior consistent statements
- Prior statements of identification

b. Opposing party's statement

- Party opponent—anything the party opponent says is admissible, it does not have to be against her interest
- Adoptive admission
- Vicarious statements—look for statements made by an employee that can be attributed to an employer

7. **Hearsay Exceptions**

   a. **Declarant unavailable as witness, FRE 804**

      1) Former testimony

      2) Dying declaration

      3) Statement against interest—not the same as an opposing party's statement! This applies to any declarant who is unavailable to testify that makes a statement against her (criminal or civil) interest

      4) Statement of personal or family history

      5) Statement against party that caused declarant's unavailability

   b. **Declarant's availability as a witness immaterial, FRE 803**

      1) Present sense impression

      2) Excited utterance

      3) Statement of mental, emotional, or physical condition

      4) Statement made for medical diagnosis/treatment

      5) Recorded recollection (witness no longer able to testify)

      6) Business records

      7) Public records

      8) Learned treatises

      9) Judgment of previous conviction

D. Constitutional Limitations—The Sixth Amendment Confrontation Clause and Hearsay Statements

The Sixth Amendment Confrontation Clause gives a defendant in a criminal case the right to be confronted by the witnesses against him.

The admission of out of court "testimonial" statements (such as hearsay statements) violates a defendant's right to confrontation if (i) the witness is unavailable to testify at ta trial and (ii) the defenses has not had a prior opportunity to cross-examine the witness.

"Testimonial" definition: Statements made to police officers in the course of an interrogation are generally testimonial. However, when the primary purpose of the questioning is to enable police assistance to meet an ongoing emergency, the statements are not testimonial. If the emergency is over, the statements made during interrogation are testimonial.

> **Note 8:** If the statements are admitted for a non-truth purpose (declarant's state of mind), the Confrontation Clause does not bar them.

CHAPTER 3: PRACTICE ESSAY

Evidence Question, February 2008, Question 4 [ID 286]

Victor was taken by ambulance to a hospital. Standard hospital practice requires the admitting nurse in the emergency room to record all information provided by a patient about the cause of the patient's illness or injury. Following that practice, the admitting nurse, Nurse, asked Victor: "What happened?" Victor responded: "I was stabbed with a big knife. Dan did it." Nurse immediately wrote Victor's statement in the appropriate place in the hospital record.

One week after his hospital admission, Victor unexpectedly died as a result of the stab wound. Dan was charged with Victor's murder.

When Victor's wife, Wife, heard of Dan's arrest, she was shocked. She told Friend, "When Victor and I were alone together in the hospital, he told me who stabbed him, and it wasn't Dan!" But Wife refused to tell Friend whom Victor had identified as his assailant.

During the trial, in order to prove that Dan stabbed Victor, the prosecutor offered the hospital record made by Nurse that contained Victor's statement that Dan stabbed him. The prosecutor cannot locate Nurse to testify at trial. Defense counsel objected to admission of the hospital record and the statements in it, but the court overruled the objection.

During the presentation of Dan's case, defense counsel suggested that Victor had been attacked by Stepson, Wife's child by a previous marriage. Defense counsel called Wife as a witness and questioned her concerning Victor's statement to her about the identity of his assailant. Wife refused to answer on the basis of the marital privilege. The prosecutor objected to the questions directed to Wife on the grounds that they sought to elicit hearsay. The court sustained both Wife's claim of privilege and the prosecutor's hearsay objection.

1. Did the trial court err in admitting into evidence the hospital record containing Victor's statement? Explain.
2. Did the trial court err in sustaining Wife's claim of privilege? Explain.
3. Did the trial court err in sustaining the prosecutor's hearsay objection to Wife's testimony? Explain.

SAMPLE ANSWER

1. Admissibility of Hospital Record

(a) Hearsay within Hearsay (20%)**:** At issue is whether the hospital record itself and Victor's statement within the hospital record each must fall within a hearsay exception. Hearsay is an out-of-court statement offered to prove the truth of the matter asserted and is inadmissible unless it falls within an exception. Hearsay within hearsay (double hearsay) is admissible as long as each level of hearsay falls within a hearsay exception.

Here, the hospital record is double hearsay. The hospital record itself is the first level of hearsay. The hospital record is hearsay: it is an out-of-court statement offered by the prosecutor to prove that Victor told Nurse that Dan stabbed him. Victor's statement is also hearsay it was made out of court and is being offered to prove the statement is true (i.e., that Dan committed the crime).

Thus, the issue is whether a hearsay exception applies to the hospital record or Victor's statement.

(b) Business Records Exception (25%)**:** A record or other writing of any act or event made in the course of regularly conducted business is admissible under the business-records exception to the hearsay rule. To be admitted, the custodian of the record or other qualified witness must establish that the record was made (i) at or near the time of the event, (ii) by a person with knowledge of the event and under a duty to report it, and (iii) as part of a regular practice of making the kind of entry in question during the regular course of business.

Here, Nurse had personal knowledge of what Victor said, and she wrote down his statements near the time of the event and near the time when he made them. Additionally, the facts state that it was standard hospital practice for the admitting nurse to record all information provided by a patient about the cause of the patient's injury. However, the facts do not indicate whether the hospital record was properly authenticated. Therefore, if the custodian of the record or another qualified witness established the requirements for admission, the hospital record satisfies the business-records exception to the hearsay rule and is admissible.

(c) Statement Made for Medical Diagnosis or Treatment (25%)**:** A statement that is made for the purpose of describing medical history or past or present symptoms, pain, or other sensation is admissible if it is made to a physician or other medical personnel for the purpose of medical diagnosis or treatment. A statement of the cause or source of the condition is admissible if it is reasonably pertinent to diagnosis or treatment.

Here, Victor's statement to Nurse that he was stabbed with a knife is pertinent to treatment for the injury being treated. However, statements of fault ordinarily are not admitted under this exception because the identity of the person who was at fault in causing the injury is not pertinent to the treatment that is to be given. Thus, Victor's statement that Dan stabbed him is inadmissible.

2. Confidential Marital Communications (20%)

At issue is whether a spouse may assert the confidential marital communications privilege to avoid testifying with respect to communications with a deceased spouse. The confidential marital communications privilege provides that communications made between spouses while they were married are privileged if the communication was made in reliance on the sanctity of marriage. The privilege protects communications made during the marriage, even if the marriage no longer exists or if one of the parties to the marriage is dead. Under the majority view, both spouses hold the privilege for all communications between them. When one spouse has revealed the content of those communications to a third party, then confidentiality no longer exists and the privilege should not apply.

Here, Wife could invoke this privilege because Victor's statements were statements of one spouse to another in private. However, some courts hold that only the communicating spouse can assert the privilege. Thus, Wife could not assert the privilege in a minority of states. However, it could be argued that Wife will not be allowed to invoke the confidential marital communications privilege because she broke confidentiality by telling a third party a portion of what her husband told her. Accordingly, Wife might be required to testify to the fact that she revealed to Friend that Victor told her that he was attacked by someone other than Dan.

3. Impeachment of Hearsay Declarant (10%)

At issue is whether an inconsistent hearsay statement is admissible to impeach a hearsay declarant. Once a hearsay statement is admitted into evidence, the hearsay declarant's credibility may be attacked by any evidence that would be admissible if the declarant had testified as a witness. Any inconsistent statement, even a hearsay statement, made by the hearsay declarant may be admitted to impeach the declarant's credibility.

Here, the court admitted Victor's statement to Nurse that Dan attacked him. Victor's statement to Wife that Dan was not his assailant is hearsay because it was an out-of-court statement and was offered to prove the truth of the matter asserted. Victor's statement to Wife is admissible to impeach Victor's credibility because any inconsistent statement made by the hearsay declarant may be admitted to impeach the declarant's credibility. Thus, if the hospital record is admitted to prove that Victor identified Dan as his assailant, then Victor's statement to Wife is admissible to attack Victor's credibility.

NCBE EDITOR'S NOTES FOR THIS ESSAY QUESTION

- *Other hearsay exceptions are also inapplicable to Victor's identification of his assailant. Although Victor died a week after making the statement, the statement would not be admitted as a dying declaration or statement made under belief of impending death. The exception requires that the declarant believe that death is imminent at the time of the making of the statement. Victor died unexpectedly; thus, there is no indication that he had the necessary expectation of impending death at the time the statement was made.*

Fed. R. Evid. 804(b)(2). The exception for an "excited utterance" probably would not apply because the facts do not show that Victor was still under the "stress of excitement" of the stabbing when he made the statement to Nurse. See Fed. R. Evid. 803(2).

(Editor's Note: The foregoing model answer was drafted in accordance with the NCBE Grading Guidelines for this question. The analysis is illustrative of the discussions that might appear in a high passing answer and addresses all legal and factual issues the drafters intended exam candidates to raise. When self-grading, refer to the NCBE's weighting of each issue, which is indicated in parentheses for your reference.)

[END OF HANDOUT]

Themis
BarReview

FAMILY LAW ESSAY WORKSHOP
PROFESSOR CHRISTOPHER IDE-DON
UC DAVIS SCHOOL OF LAW

CHAPTER 1: GETTING MARRIED AND DIVORCED

A. Common-Law Marriage

1. Elements

- **Capacity**: mental and legal capacity to marry
- **Present agreement** both parties must intend to presently be married
- **Cohabitation**: the parties must live together
- **Holding out a marital relationship** to the community: hold themselves out as "spouses"

Note 1: Most states do not recognize common law marriage.

2. Conflict of laws

A marriage (including a common law marriage) valid in one state will be valid in another state **unless** it violates a strong public policy of the other state.

B. Divorce and Separation

1. Grounds for no-fault divorce

- Every jurisdiction has a unilateral no-fault ground for divorce, requiring neither fault nor consent of the other spouse.
- Generally requires that the marriage be irretrievably broken with no prospect of reconciliation (often using the term "irreconcilable differences")
- No attempt at reconciliation required

2. Separation

- Some states require a minimum period of separation before a divorce will be granted.
- The separation does not have to be agreed to by both spouses.
- A spouse can unilaterally move out and start the separation period.

3. Mediation

- Mediation is sometimes used to facilitate the separation and divorce process.
- The mediator must follow a code of conduct. Duties include that the mediator must:
  - Be **impartial** and **disclose any conflicts of interest** he may have;
  - Clearly **explain** and **control the mediation process** and ensure that the parties have the information to make an informed decision; and
  - ***Not coerce or improperly influence*** a party to make a decision.

Exam Tip 1: Mediator misconduct may be grounds for not enforcing a separation agreement or a property settlement.

C. Division of Property at Divorce

1. Community property

- Only used in nine states: Arizona, California, Idaho, Louisiana, Nevada, New Mexico, Texas, Washington, and Wisconsin
- Generally requires an equal division of the marital property

2. Equitable distribution

- Majority rule
- Requires an **equitable**, or **fair** distribution of all marital property, **not necessarily an equal 50/50 division**
- Takes into consideration all of the circumstances between the parties

3. Marital property (MP) and separate property (SP)

- MP is divided between spouses, but SP generally remains the property of the owning spouse.
- SP includes assets acquired during marriage by gift, descent, or devise. SP also includes anything acquired before marriage.
- MP is all property/assets acquired during marriage by any means other than gift, descent, devise.

  Example 1: *Wages earned by spouses.*

- SP can be transformed into MP if marital funds or efforts by owner-spouse enhance its value/or build equity during marriage.

  Example 2: *A spouse purchases a house before marriage, making the house Separate Property. After marriage, the spouse uses Marital Property funds to pay the mortgage on the house. At divorce, the other spouse is entitled to a share of the value of the home.*

- **Specific types of marital property include:**
  - **Future retirement/pension benefits:** If a spouse works during the marriage and creates or earns profits or benefits that will not be received until after divorce, the profits will be considered MP.
  - **Professional licenses/degrees:** Most courts do not treat these as MP, but may award reimbursement for a spouse's actual contribution to educational and living expenses.
  - **Personal injury claim proceeds:** There are two approaches to personal injury awards, and you should discuss both:
    - **Approach 1:** If the cause of action accrues during marriage, even if the spouses are separated, all proceeds are treated as MP

- **Approach 2:** Damages are divided between MP and SP by type
    - Compensatory damages (e.g., pain, suffering, disability) are SP of the injured spouse
    - Consortium loss damages are SP of the non-injured spouse
    - Lost wages, lost earning capacity and medical expenses are MP

4. Modification of a property division award

- A property division is not modifiable after the fact because it is based on the parties' assets at the time of divorce.
- Changes in the parties' circumstances after divorce do not affect the award.

CHAPTER 2: FINANCIAL SUPPORT OF SPOUSES AND CHILDREN

A. Spousal Support

- Spousal support, also referred to as spousal maintenance or alimony, is the obligation of one party to provide the other with financial support.
- The majority of jurisdictions consider various factors when determining the support award. These factors include:
    - Financial resources of both parties
    - Standard of living during marriage
    - Time it will take for receiving spouse to find employment
    - Length of marriage
    - Contributions to marriage
    - Age and health of both parties
    - Marital misconduct ***(only in some states)***

1. Types of support

- **Permanent alimony** is an award for the remainder of the dependent spouse's life (generally only appropriate after long marriages).
- **Limited-duration alimony** is typically awarded when the marriage was of short duration (making permanent alimony inappropriate).
- **Rehabilitative support** *(recently tested)* is for a limited period of time, such as until the spouse receives education or employment.

    Example 3: *A spouse may be required to pay rehabilitative alimony for a period of four years while a dependent spouse attends college, at which point the support obligation will automatically terminate.*

- **Reimbursement alimony** *(recently tested)* compensates a spouse for financial sacrifices made during the marriage that resulted in a reduced standard of living to secure an enhanced standard of living in the future.

Example 4: *A spouse worked two minimum wage jobs and did not pursue a higher degree during marriage so that the other spouse could go to school and obtain an advanced degree or professional license. The working spouse may receive reimbursement alimony due to her past contribution to the marriage.*

2. Modification of support

- In general, spousal support may be modified.
- The party seeking modification of spousal support has the burden of establishing **a significant change in circumstances** that warrants the modification.
- A party's voluntary reduction in income will generally not reduce support payments.
- A court may consider new obligations that arise for the spouse who is paying support.

  Example 5: *If a spouse remarries and has children with his new spouse, his ability to pay may be decreased.*

- In most jurisdictions, if the receiving spouse remarries, then spousal support may be terminated.

  Exam Tip 2: When discussing a party's action for modification of spousal support, analyze the facts carefully and discuss both parties' arguments regarding the significant change in circumstances.

3. Support during marriage

In most jurisdictions, spouses have a duty to support each other equally under family expense statutes. If a creditor provides a "necessary" item (such as medical care) to one spouse, it can sue the other spouse for payment if the purchasing spouse does not pay.

B. Jurisdictional Issue: Divisible (Ex Parte) Divorce

- A court hearing a family-related dispute must generally have both subject-matter jurisdiction and personal jurisdiction.
- A state court **may grant a divorce to one spouse**, even if it does not have personal jurisdiction over the other spouse.
- However, if there is no personal jurisdiction over the absent spouse *(see UIFSA)*, the state does not have jurisdiction to address **property division**, **spousal support**, or **child support**.

  Exam Tip 3: Look for situations when spouses now live in separate states, and a spouse who has met a residency requirement in one state wants a divorce or support from the other spouse. These situations often trigger this issue.

C. Child Support

1. Child's right to support from parents

- Both parents are legally required to support their minor children.
- Parents cannot bargain away child-support payments and cannot agree to any release or compromise that would negatively affect the child's welfare.

2. Uniform Interstate Family Support Act (UIFSA)

- The UIFSA governs when a state has **personal jurisdiction over an out-of-state parent** in an action to establish or enforce child support, or establish paternity.
- A court will be found to have personal jurisdiction over an out-of-state parent in various situations, including when the out-of-state parent:
  - Is personally served within the state or consents to jurisdiction;
  - Resided with the child in the state in the past; or
  - Engaged in sexual intercourse in the state, and the child may have been conceived by that act of intercourse *(recently tested).*
- See Family Law Outline III.C.4. for other bases of personal jurisdiction under the UIFSA.

3. Amount of child support

- Child-support awards are typically based on income received by the obligor (paying) parent.

> **Editor's Note 1:** Most jurisdictions have adopted an income-shares model, which uses the combined net income of **both** parents to determine the child support amount.

- Other factors may include:
  - Best interests of child
  - Age
  - Special needs
  - Assets of both parties
  - Standard of living during marriage

> **Editor's Note 2:** All jurisdictions have adopted child support guidelines. There is a **rebuttable presumption** that the amount calculated pursuant to the child-support guidelines is correct, but if the court decides to deviate from that amount, the court will consider other factors in determining the amount and set forth specific findings explaining and supporting the deviation.

4. Modification

- In general, child support modifications are permissible when there is a **substantial change in circumstances** regarding the child's needs or the parents' financial situation.
- The party seeking the modification of child support bears the burden of showing a substantial change in circumstances.
- Circumstances may include a parent's change in occupation, remarriage of a parent, or an increase or involuntary decrease in income by either parent.
  - A court will only modify child support amounts prospectively.
  - A court will not reduce the amount of child support retroactively.

5. **Termination**

- A parent's obligation to pay support usually ends when the child reaches the age of majority (typically 18 years of age).
- Some jurisdictions have the authority to order support beyond the age of majority when the child is in college.
- Reasonable parental demands *(recently tested)*: An employable child's right to support is contingent on compliance with reasonable parental demands; an employable child who fails to comply, even if attending college, risks loss of parental support.

6. **Jurisdiction over existing child support obligations** *(recently tested)*

a. Modification

- Under the UIFSA, the state that issued the initial child support order has continuing exclusive jurisdiction to modify the child support order.
- **Exceptions:**
  - The parties (both parents) and the child no longer reside in the state; or
  - The parties expressly agree to permit another state to exercise jurisdiction.

b. Enforcement

- Under the UIFSA, the receiving parent may register a child support order from one state in another non-issuing state.
- The non-issuing state can then enforce the support order.

CHAPTER 3: CHILD CUSTODY

Having custody (i.e., control) of a child can mean having legal custody or physical custody, or both. Either or both of these types of custody can be shared under a joint custody arrangement.

- **Legal custody** is the right of a parent to make major decisions regarding the child.
- **Physical custody** is the right to have the child reside with a parent or guardian and the obligation to provide for routine daily care and control of the child.
- **Joint custody** generally requires that the parents are both willing and able to cooperate with respect to the wellbeing of the child; typically, neither parent has a superior right to make major decisions.

A. Uniform Child Custody Jurisdiction and Enforcement Act (UCCJEA)

The purpose of the UCCJEA is to prevent jurisdictional disputes with courts in other states on matters of child custody and visitation.

1. **Initial custody determination (home-state jurisdiction)**

   A court has subject-matter jurisdiction to preside over custody hearings and either enter or modify custody or visitation orders if the state is:

   - The child's home state and has been the home state for a period of **six months or since birth**, if the child is less than six months old; or
   - Was the child's home state **in the past six months**, and the child is absent from the state, but **one of the parents still lives there**.

2. **Significant-connection jurisdiction**

   A court can enter or modify an order if:

   - **No other state** has or accepts home-state jurisdiction;
   - The child and at least one parent have a **significant connection** with the state; and
   - There is **substantial evidence** in the state concerning the child's care, protection, training and personal relationships.

3. **Exclusive-continuing jurisdiction**

   Courts that make the initial ruling in a custody case have exclusive jurisdiction over the matter until the court determines that:

   - Both **parties no longer reside** in the state; or
   - The **child no longer has a significant connection to the state**, and any substantial evidence connected to the child's condition is no longer available in the state.

   > **Editor's Note 3:** The lecturer slightly misstates the rule above. Note that a new significant connection to another state is not sufficient to terminate exclusive-continuing jurisdiction.

B. Best Interests of the Child Standard

- The standard for determining child custody is the **best interests of the child.**
- Courts will consider the wishes of an older child if the court can determine that the child has sufficient maturity to express a preference. The court will look at the child's reasoning behind her preference.
- **Race or religion:** Courts generally will not use race or religion in determining custody.
- **Third party rights:** Legal parents are presumptively entitled to custody of their children in cases against third parties, including grandparents or stepparents.

> **Exam Tip 4:** A recent exam presented a statute that authorized a court to award custody of a child to her grandparents. The grandparents in the question filed a petition for custody of their granddaughter and the mother of the child objected. The statute would be unconstitutional because it did not have language requiring the court to give "**special weight to the parent's determination of her child's best interest.**"

C. Visitation and Parenting Time

- Generally, the noncustodial parent is allowed reasonable visitation (or "parenting time") with a minor child.
    - Parents have a constitutional right to have contact with their children.
- **Unwed biological fathers** *(recently tested)***:** An unwed father has a substantive due process right to have contact with his child, but only when the father demonstrates a **commitment** to the responsibilities of parenthood (e.g., participation in child rearing or providing financial support).

D. Modification of Custody Order

The burden is on the parent seeking modification to establish that the modification is warranted. Most jurisdictions require a substantial change in circumstances to modify the custody order.

1. Relocation *(recently tested)*

- In most jurisdictions, the custodial parent seeking relocation bears the burden of demonstrating that **the relocation is for a legitimate and reasonable purpose**, as opposed to restricting the noncustodial parent's visitation.

> **Editor's Note 4:** The lecturer slightly misstates the burden on parents seeking to relocate a child. If the custodial parent is proposing to relocate with the minor child in a way that impairs the noncustodial parent's ability to see the child under the court-ordered visitation schedule, the relocation will almost always constitute a substantial change in circumstances. However, prior to granting a modification to the order, the custodial parent must establish that the relocation is for a legitimate and reasonable purpose.

- In determining whether to modify the custody order and allow the parent to relocate, court will consider various factors, including:
    - The best interests of the child
    - The relationship of the non-relocating parent with the child
    - Age and needs of the child
    - The child's preference
    - The quality of life of relocating parent and child

CHAPTER 4: MARITAL AGREEMENTS AND RELATIONSHIPS BETWEEN THE FAMILY AND THE STATE

A. Marital Agreements

1. Premarital agreements

- A premarital (also known as "prenuptial" or "antenuptial") agreement is a contract made before the marriage, typically containing terms that relate to division of property or spousal support in the case of a divorce and at death.
- Clauses relating to child custody and support are unenforceable.

- A premarital agreement is enforceable if there has been full **disclosure**, the agreement is **fair and reasonable**, and it is **voluntary**.

  Editor's Note 5: Additionally, the agreement must be in **writing** and **signed** by the party to be charged.

- Under the Uniform Premarital Agreement Act (UPAA), to make an agreement unenforceable, a party must show *at least one of the following*:
  - **Involuntariness** (fraud, duress, coercion); **or**
  - **Unfairness or unreasonableness** together with **lack of reasonable knowledge or disclosure**.

  Editor's Note 6: The lecturer misstates this rule. Note that only one of these elements is required to invalidate a premarital contract, not both.

a. Voluntary

- Parties must enter into the contract voluntarily (i.e., free of fraud, duress, or coercion)
- Courts consider factors such as time-pressure and the opportunity to be represented by independent counsel.

  Exam Tip 5: The parties need not actually seek legal representation to make the agreement voluntary.

b. Fair and reasonable

- The court will look for factors such as duress, undue influence, misconduct by a mediator, and whether the party to be charged had independent representation.
- The courts will also consider the fairness of the terms themselves.
- Most courts evaluate fairness **at the time of execution** of the contract, and a minority of jurisdictions will also evaluate it at the time of enforcement.

  Editor's Note 7: The current trend is for courts to enforce contractual agreements that may not be fair as long as there has been fair disclosure.

c. Full disclosure

- Premarital agreements must provide full disclosure of financial status, including income, assets, and debts of all parties.

2. Separation agreements

- Separation agreements are made between spouses who are planning for divorce to define property division, spousal support, child support, custody, and visitation.
- Separation agreements may be invalidated in part or in whole if a party can show **unconscionability** or **fraud**.

3. Property-settlement agreement

- The purpose of a property-settlement agreement is to settle the economic issues of the marital estate. It is entered into by the parties before a divorce decree is issued.
- Property settlement agreements may be invalidated in part or in whole if a party can show **unconscionability** or **fraud**.

4. Conflict of laws

When determining the validity of a premarital agreement, states will apply the law of either:

- The state in which the **agreement was executed**; or
- The state with the **most significant relationship** to the parties and transaction.

B. Relationship between the Family and the State

Adoption is a statutory legal action in which the previous parent-child relationship is terminated and a new parent-child relationship is established.

1. Unwed fathers' rights *(recently tested)*

- Unwed fathers have protections under the 14th Amendment Due Process Clause if they have shown **commitment to being a parent**.
  - Includes the right to object to the termination of his parental right by an adoption
- Some states maintain a **putative father's registry** that allows unwed fathers to register themselves as the father of a child.
  - If registered, the father will receive notice and a hearing before rights are terminated

2. Legal effects of adoption

- Adoptive parents have all the rights and responsibilities that biological parents would have had.
- An adopted child has all the rights and responsibilities that a biological child would have had.

3. Limits on parental authority

- A parent has a right to make decisions about how to raise child, including religion, but courts may intervene in the best interest of the child.
- If medical treatment contradicts a parent's religious beliefs, courts can intervene to protect a child when necessary medical care is needed to prevent serious harm to the child's health.

CHAPTER 5: PRACTICE QUESTION

February 2008, Question #3 [ID 292]

Husband and Wife married 10 years ago. Shortly thereafter, Husband adopted Wife's two children, Amy, age 6, and Bert, age 9. Neither Amy nor Bert has ever had a relationship with their biological father.

One year ago, Husband and Wife were divorced. The divorce decree provided that:

(1) Husband shall pay Wife $1,000 per month in child support for Amy until Amy is 18 years old;

(2) Husband shall pay child support in the form of college tuition up to $20,000 per year for both Amy and Bert.

Three months ago, Husband stopped making support payments for Amy and college tuition payments for Bert. Husband stopped paying for two reasons:

First, Husband was disinclined to continue supporting Amy and Bert, now ages 16 and 19, respectively. Since the divorce, Husband has quarreled frequently with both children. Bert also disobeyed Husband and joined a rock band that plays at a local bar four nights per week. Since joining the band, Bert's college grades slipped from A's to C's, and he was arrested for driving while intoxicated. Bert has refused Husband's requests that he leave the band and devote more time to study.

Second, Husband, who formerly worked 40 to 60 hours per week, is now working only 10 to 20 hours per week so that he can finish writing a novel. Husband has worked on the novel sporadically over the past few years, but has not had time to complete it. Husband's current income is only 25% of what it was when he was employed full time.

Wife, who works full time at the job she has held since her marriage to Husband, has neither reduced nor increased her income since the divorce. Since Husband stopped paying support, she has been borrowing money to meet the family's expenses.

Wife recently filed a petition to obtain a judgment against Husband for the child-support arrears and Bert's tuition. Husband responded with a petition seeking:

(1) a dissolution of his adoption of Amy and Bert on the basis of irreconcilable differences;

(2) downward modification of all of his support obligations, on account of his reduced income, retroactive to the date on which Husband stopped making support and tuition payments; and

(3) a declaration that Husband need not pay Bert's college tuition so long as Bert continues to perform in a rock band.

The age of majority in the state is 18. The trial court entered judgment in favor of Wife and denied Husband's petition in all respects.

Did the trial court err? Explain.

Sample Answer

1. The issue is whether an adoptive parent may dissolve the adoption of a stepchild based on a quarrelsome relationship with the child.

Generally, an adoption may not be dissolved. Some states have permitted dissolution in limited circumstances including the discovery of an undisclosed mental or physical illness. In evaluating dissolution claims, courts typically look to the length of the relationship, the child's needs, and the parent's motives. In this case, the facts do not indicate that there was an undisclosed mental or physical illness. Additionally, Husband has been Ann and Bert's parent for a substantial amount of time. Husband appears to seek dissolution for financial reasons and because of disagreements he had with his children. The claim for dissolution is inadequate to justify a court to grant Husband's petition. Accordingly, the trial court did not err in denying Husband's petition to dissolve the adoption.

2. The issue is whether a support obligor can obtain retroactive modification of a support obligation.

Most jurisdictions permit an award of child custody to be modified. Federal law provides that a modification award is made retroactive to the date of service of the motion on the opposing party, but support obligations that have accrued prior to that date generally may not be modified. In this case, Husband petitioned to obtain downward modification of his support obligations retroactive to the date on which Husband stopped making support and tuition payments. Because retroactive modification of child support obligations is forbidden, the trial court did not err in refusing to retroactively modify Husband's support obligation.

3. The issue is whether a support obligor may obtain downward modification of his future support obligation based on a voluntary reduction of his income.

Modifications of child support obligations are permissible when there is a substantial change in circumstances regarding the child's needs or parents' financial situation. However, the amount of child support may not be reduced because the support obligor voluntarily quits his job or voluntarily reduced his own pay. In these cases, the obligor's earning capacity is considered by the court.

Here, Husband voluntarily reduced his own income by 75%. Husband's income reduction does not have any obvious end point. Husband intends to spend his time writing a novel, however Husband could easily defer his plan to write a novel or reduce his income much less drastically. In addition, Wife is having a difficult time making up the lost income. Wife works full time and is borrowing money in order to meet household expenses. The timing of Husband's decision to reduce his income suggests bad faith because it is at the very same time that he wanted to stop supporting Ann and Bert. Accordingly, the court probably did not err in denying Husband's petition to modify his future support obligation.

4. The issue is whether a divorced parent of a 19-year-old college student may refuse to support that student when the student has refused to obey reasonable parental commands.

Some jurisdictions have the authority to order child support beyond the age of majority when the child is in college. The support rights of an employed child are contingent on the compliance by the child with reasonable parental demands. In this case, Bert joined a rock band that plays at a local bar four times a week and his grades have fallen significantly. The facts indicate that Bert's job is preventing him from keeping up with his studying. In addition, Bert was arrested for driving while intoxicated, which indicates that he should not be working in a bar. In sum, the evidence suggests that the trial court erred in denying Husband's request for modification of his college tuition obligation to Bert.

[END OF HANDOUT]

Themis
BarReview

REAL PROPERTY ESSAY WORKSHOP

PROFESSOR CHRISTOPHER IDE-DON
UC DAVIS SCHOOL OF LAW

CHAPTER 1: SUMMARY OF ISSUES TESTED; SUBSTANTIVE LAW—OWNERSHIP

A. Summary of Issues Tested

1. **Ownership**
   a. **Present Estates**
      1) Fee simple absolute
      2) Fee simple determinable
      3) Fee simple subject to condition subsequent
      4) Life estate
      5) Restraint on Alienation
   b. **Co-tenancy**
      6) Types
         a) Tenancy in common
         b) Joint tenancy
      7) Severance
      8) Ouster
      9) Rights and Duties among Cotenants
   c. **Landlord-Tenant**
      10) Types of Leaseholds
      11) Landlord-Tenant Duties
      12) Assignment and Subletting
2. **Title**
   a. **Adverse possession**
   b. **Transfer by deed**
   c. **Title assurance systems**
      13) Recording acts (Notice, Race, and Race-Notice)
      14) Notice
3. **Rights in land**
   a. **Covenants & Equitable Servitudes**
   b. **Easements**
4. **Mortgages/security devices**
   a. **Mortgages and Deeds of Trust**
   b. **Foreclosure**

B. Ownership

1. **Present Estates**
   a. **Fee Simple Absolute**—absolute ownership
   b. **Fee Simple Determinable**
      - Ownership automatically terminates upon a condition and passes to grantor
      - Look for durational words: "as long as," "until"

c. **Fee Simple Subject to Condition Subsequent**

- When the condition occurs, the grantor can exercise a right of reentry
- Look for conditional words ("but if") and words such as "right to re-enter"

> **Exam Tip 1:** If the conveyance is ambiguous, discuss both fee simple determinable and fee simple subject to condition subsequent.

d. **Life Estate**—Ownership terminates upon the end of the measuring life

e. **Restraint on Alienation**

- A grantor can place a reasonable restraint on the grantee's ability to freely transfer
- If the restraint is unreasonable, a court will strike it from the conveyance

Example 1: *Grantor conveys his estate as follows: "to A so long as he does not make any transfer of Greenacre. In the event of such a transfer, Greenacre shall automatically revert back to Grantor." This is likely an unreasonable restraint on alienation and a court will strike it from the conveyance.*

2. **Concurrent Estates**

a. **Tenants in Common**

- Unified possession of estate—each tenant owns an undivided interest in the entire property
- No right of survivorship; interest is freely devisable or transferable
- In most states there is a presumption that a conveyance to two or more people is a tenancy in common

b. **Joint Tenancy with Right of Survivorship**

- Requires express language and the four unities (possession, interest, time, title)
- Right of survivorship—when one joint tenant dies, the interest goes to the other joint tenants

Example 2: *A and B are joint tenants with rights of survivorship. When B dies, his interest goes to A and A owns the entire estate in fee simple.*

1) **Severance**

If one joint tenant conveys his interest, it severs (destroys) the joint tenancy and creates a tenancy in common

Example 3: *A, B, and C are joint tenants with rights of survivorship. A sells his interest to D, severing A's joint tenancy. D is a tenant in common with B and C. B and C are still joint tenants with rights of survivorship. If B dies, B's interest goes to C through the right of survivorship. C now owns a 2/3 interest and D owns a 1/3 interest as a tenant in common.*

2) Mortgage as severance

- A joint tenant may grant a mortgage on his interest in the property.

Example 4: *A, B, and C are joint tenants with rights of survivorship. A grants a mortgage on his interest to Bank.*

- Majority (lien theory)—a mortgage is simply a lien and does not sever the joint tenancy
- Minority (title theory)—a mortgage is a transfer of title and severs the joint tenancy

c. Rights and Obligations of Co-Tenants

1) Possession—each cotenant has the right to possess the entire property

- Ouster—A cotenant who is being denied access can bring a court action to regain access to the property
- Adverse Possession—If one cotenant ousted the other, he can make a claim for adverse possession if he meets the requirements.

Example 5: *Cotenant #1 prevents Cotenant #2 from accessing the property. Cotenant #1 has ousted Cotenant #2. If Cotenant #2 does not bring a court action, Cotenant #1 may be able to acquire the entire property by adverse possession (if she meets all of the requirements).*

2) Rent

- A cotenant does not owe rent for his use of the property
- A cotenant must share rents received from a third party

3) **Operating Expenses** (e.g. taxes, mortgage payments)—a cotenant can generally collect expenses if he paid more than his share

4) Repairs and Improvements

- A co-tenant does not have a right to be reimbursed by other co-tenants for repairs, even if necessary.
- A co-tenant may only seek contribution for necessary repairs if the co-tenant gave notice of the need for repairs.

Editorial Note 1: The Professor may have oversimplified these rules. In general, a co-tenant is not entitled to reimbursement for repairs. However, most jurisdictions allow contribution for necessary repairs in actions for accounting or partition. In some jurisdictions, a co-tenant can maintain a separate action for contribution so long as the other co-tenants had notice of the necessary repairs.

C. Landlord and Tenant

1. Types of Leaseholds

a. **Tenancy for Years**—created by express agreement for fixed period of time

b. **Periodic Tenancy**—repetitive, ongoing estate measured by set periods that automatically renew (e.g., month-to-month)

c. **Tenancy at Will**—parties must expressly agree, no fixed period of time, may be terminated by either party at any time

d. **Tenancy at Sufferance**—a tenant wrongfully holds over past the expiration of the lease, lasts until eviction or converts into a periodic tenancy

2. Landlord and Tenant Duties

a. **Tenant's Duties**—pay rent, avoid waste, and make reasonable repairs

- **Withholding or Deducting Rent**

  a) If landlord breaches the covenant of quiet enjoyment, can terminate lease and stop paying rent

  b) If the landlord violates the implied warranty of habitability (residential only), can terminate lease and stop paying rent OR deduct from the rent

- **Avoid Waste**—tenant cannot damage the property and must repair damages he causes
- **Pay Rent**—if fails to pay rent, landlord can sue for damages and eviction
  - Surrender—tenant transfers lease back, and landlord accepts, tenant no longer obligated to pay rent
  - Abandonment—if the tenant abandons the property, landlord can accept as an offer of surrender
- **Termination**—occurs automatically at the end of the lease term OR if surrender occurs

b. **Landlord's Duties**

1) **Duty to Repair**—landlord must repair damages under ***residential*** leases, unless the tenant caused the damages

2) **Implied Warranty of Habitability**

- Only applies to ***residential*** leases
- Landlord must maintain the property such that it is reasonably suited for residence

> **Exam Tip 2:** Look for failure to provide heat, electricity, running water, or plumbing. These would render a property unfit for residential use.

- Tenant must give ***notice*** to the landlord and ***reasonable opportunity*** to repair
- If the landlord fails to make repairs, the tenant may:

i) Stay in the property and deduct rent until the repair occurs;

ii) Stay in the property, pay for repairs, and deduct the cost from rent; or

iii) Terminate the lease and move out

3) Covenant of Quiet Enjoyment

- Applies to ***residential*** and ***commercial*** leases
- The landlord cannot disrupt the tenant's possession or enjoyment of the property

a) Constructive Eviction:

i) Landlord substantially interferes with the tenant's use and enjoyment of the land;

ii) Tenant gives notice of the problem and reasonable time for the landlord to repair, but the landlord does not repair; and

iii) Tenant vacates the premises in a reasonable amount of time

3. Assignment and Sublease

- **Assignment**—a transfer of the tenant's entire remaining lease to a new party
- **Sublease**—a transfer of a portion of the tenant's lease (less than the remainder of the lease)

a. Liability

- Original tenant remains liable to landlord for lease obligations under privity of contract
- Assignee is liable to landlord for rent and covenants that run with the land under privity of estate
- Subtenant is not liable to landlord because not in privity of contract or estate

b. Prohibition Clauses

- Allowed to prohibit assignment or sublease
- If the lease prohibits only assignment, the tenant may still sublease
- If the tenant violates the prohibition, the landlord can terminate the lease
    - Waiver—if the landlord accepts payment from the new tenant, he waives the right to enforce the prohibition clause
- Consent—some clauses allow assignment or sublease only with landlord's consent
    - The landlord can only withhold consent on a commercially reasonable ground

4. Duty to Mitigate

- Landlord has duty to make reasonable efforts to re-rent the property
- The duty applies even if the tenant improperly breached the lease
- If a tenant moves out early and the landlord has multiple vacant apartments, the landlord is not obligated to prioritize the tenant's vacant apartment.

CHAPTER 2: SUBSTANTIVE LAW (CONT'D)—TITLE

A. Adverse Possession

- Allows a person to obtain ownership of property by meeting the elements

1. Elements

a. **Continuous**—possession must be continuous and uninterrupted through the statutory period

- Tacking—allows subsequent possessors to "tack on" to prior possession periods

Example 6: *Adverse Possessor #1 occupied the property for 5 years. Adverse Possessor #2 obtains the property from Possessor #1 and occupies for another 5 years. At this point, Adverse Possessor #2 can show 10 years of adverse possession by tacking.*

- Requires some type of privity (e.g., blood, contract, deed, will)

b. Actual—adverse possessor must have actual possession of the land

c. Open and Notorious—must make use of the land as a reasonable owner would

d. Hostile—must be without the owner's permission

e. **Exclusive**—must not share the land with the true owner

2. Scope of Possession

- Generally, only transfers title to the portion that was actually adversely possessed
- Color of title (i.e., enters pursuant to a deed or will that is not actually valid)—allows the possessor to obtain title to the whole property under constructive adverse possession
- Still subject to existing easements on the land

B. Deeds

1. Valid Deed Requirements

Must identify the parties, must be signed by the grantor, must include words of transfer, and must contain a reasonably definite property description

2. Intent to Transfer a Valid Deed

Grantor must intend to make a present transfer of the property interest to the grantee

a. Transfer to grantee—creates a presumption of intent to transfer

b. Transfer to Third Party Agents

1) To an independent third party for delivery to the grantee, but the grantor reserves the right to take the deed back—not deemed delivered

2) If the grantor does not reserve the right to take the deed back, the grantor's intent to presently transfer the property is determined by the facts.

   a) If the grantor intended to presently transfer, he cannot void the gift later

   b) If the grantor did not intend to presently transfer, the transfer is not valid

3) Testamentary Transfer

   - If the grantor gives the deed to an independent third party for delivery upon the grantor's death, the grantor's intent to make a present transfer is determined by the facts.
   - If the grantor intended to transfer only upon his death, it is not a present intent to transfer; it is a testamentary transfer and is governed by the wills requirements

C. Types of Deeds

1. General Warranty Deed

- Contains six covenants (i.e., promises) relating to the conveyance

a. Three Present Covenants

- **Covenant of Seisin**—the grantor owns the land as described in the deed
- **Covenant of the Right to Convey**—the grantor has the right to transfer title
- **Covenant Against Encumbrances**—no undisclosed encumbrances
- Breach occurs at the time of conveyance
- Present covenants do not run with the land; a later grantee cannot sue the original grantor

b. Three Future Covenants

- **Covenant of Quiet Enjoyment**—the grantee's possession will not be interfered with by a third party's claim for title
- **Covenant of Warranty**—the grantor will defend against a third party's claim for title
- **Covenant of Further Assurances**—the grantor will do whatever is necessary to pass title to the grantee
- Breach occurs when there is interference with possession
- Future covenants run with the land; a later grantee can sue the original grantor

2. Quitclaim Deed

- Contains no covenants of title
- The grantee receives whatever interest the grantor possessed

3. New Homes—Implied Warranty of Fitness or Suitability

- Seller warrants he used adequate materials and workmanship
- Covers hidden (i.e., latent) defects and obvious (i.e., patent) defects

- The buyer has a duty to reasonably inspect the residence
- Buyer may sue for breach against the builder, developer, and contractors within a reasonable time after discovery of the defect

D. Recording Acts

- A valid deed does not need to be recorded to convey good title.
- Common law rule is "first in time, first in right"—the first person to obtain rights in the land is viewed as the true owner, regardless of later conflicting claims
- Modern recording acts establish who has priority over land when there are conflicting claims.

1. Types of Statutes

> **Exam Tip 3:** A typical essay will provide a statute. First determine which type of statute it is, then apply the statute to the facts.

a. Notice Statute—If a person purchases land without notice of a prior interest, the person will prevail in an ownership dispute against the prior interest

Example 7: *A sells land to B. B does not record his interest. A then sells the same land to C, who has no notice of B's ownership. C will prevail in an ownership dispute because she bought the land for value and without notice of B's prior claim.*

b. Race Statute—The first person to record their deed will prevail in an ownership dispute, regardless of knowledge.

Example 8: *A sells land to B. B does not record his interest. A then sells the same land to C, who knows that B already bought the same land. C records his interest in the land on Monday. B records his interest in the land on Tuesday. C will prevail in an ownership dispute because she recorded first.*

c. Race-Notice Jurisdiction—If a person purchases land without notice of the prior interest, and records first, the person will prevail in an ownership dispute against the prior interest.

Example 9: *A sells land to B. B does not record his interest. A then sells the same land to C, who has no notice of B's prior claim. C then records her interest on Monday. B records his interest on Tuesday. C will prevail in an ownership dispute because she bought the land without notice of B's prior claim AND she was the first to record her interest.*

> **Note 1:** Recording acts apply to all types of property interests, including easements, covenants, leases, mortgages, etc.

2. Bona Fide Purchaser (BFP)

- A BFP is a person who pays value for the property and takes it without notice of prior claims.
- Notice and Race-Notice Statutes protect BFPs.
- A BFP must pay value for the interest, it cannot be a gift

3. Shelter Rule

- BFPs who are protected by the recording act will "shelter" their grantees from prior claims.
- Applies when a subsequent grantee cannot qualify as a BFP in their own right

4. Adverse Possessors

- Recording acts do not protect BFPs from adverse possessors

> **Note 2:** The recording acts are meant to encourage owners to record their interests. The acts protect later grantees from prior claims that could have been recorded but were not. Because adverse possessors do not have documents describing their interest, they are not subject to the recording acts.

5. Notice

a. Actual—Actual knowledge

b. Inquiry—Reasonable investigation would have disclosed prior claims

c. Constructive—Grantees are on notice of all prior interests that were properly recorded

- Wild Deeds—recorded outside the grantor's chain of title; these do not provide constructive notice to a grantee

CHAPTER 3: SUBSTANTIVE LAW (CONT'D)—EASEMENTS, COVENANTS, AND SERVITUDES

A. Easements

- The right to use another's property for a limited purpose
- The servient estate is burdened by the easement
- The dominant estate benefits from the easement

1. Classification of Easement

- Appurtenant—attached to the land
- In Gross—specific to the person

2. Types of Easements

- Express Easement—created by the parties in a writing that complies with the Statute of Frauds
- Easement by Necessity—created when the dominant property is useless without the benefit of an easement across the neighboring servient property

  Example 10: *Property that is landlocked with no access to a road.*

- Easement by Implication—created when the owner of two parcels used one to benefit the other (i.e., a quasi-easement) and the parties intended the easement to continue upon the sale of the dominant parcel

- Requires that the prior use was continuous, apparent, and reasonably necessary to the dominant land's use and enjoyment

- Easement by Prescription—obtained like adverse possession (continuous, actual, open, and hostile for the specific period) except there is no exclusivity requirement.

3. Transfer of Easement

An easement appurtenant will usually continue after land is transferred.

4. Enforceability of Easement

> **Exam Tip 4:** Easements can be terminated or rendered unenforceable in a number of ways. The following are the more frequently tested methods.

a. Abandonment

- Occurs when the owner of the easement acts affirmatively to show a clear intent to relinquish the easement
- Mere non-use of the easement is not sufficient to terminate the easement.

b. Merger

Occurs when the owner of the easement becomes the owner of the servient estate in addition to the dominant estate.

c. Sale to a Bona Fide Purchaser

If a written easement has been granted but not recorded, it is not enforceable against a bona fide purchaser

B. Covenants

- Involve a promise to do or not do something in relation to land
- Land can be either benefitted or burdened by a covenant
- Covenants can exist between landowners and also between landlords and tenants

> **Exam Tip 5:** A frequently tested issue is whether a covenant is enforceable after the original parties sell their land.

Example 11: *Owner owns two parcels of land and sells one parcel to Buyer. Buyer intends to open a restaurant on the parcel, so Owner promises to not open a restaurant on his parcel. Buyer then sells his parcel to Chip. The issue is whether Chip, as a subsequent buyer, can enforce Owner's promise to not build a restaurant (i.e., can Chip benefit from the covenant).*

Example 12: *Owner owns two parcels of land and sells one parcel to Buyer. Buyer intends to open a restaurant on the parcel, so Owner promises to not open a restaurant on his parcel. Owner then sells his parcel to Eddy. The* *issue is whether Buyer can enforce the covenant against Eddy (i.e., is Eddy burdened by the covenant to not build a restaurant on the parcel).*

1. **Requirements for Covenant to "Run with the Land"**

   - In order for the benefit of a covenant to run with the land, there must be a writing, intent, touch and concern, and vertical privity.
   - In order for the burden of a covenant to run with the land, there must be a writing, intent, touch and concern, notice to the burdened party, horizontal privity, and vertical privity.

   a. **Writing**—must comply with the Statute of Frauds

   b. **Intent**—original parties must intend for the promise to run with the land

   c. **Touch and Concern**—must affect how both pieces of land are used

   d. **Notice—only required for burden to run**

   e. **Horizontal Privity—only required for burden to run**

   The original parties most have shared some interest other than the promise, such as grantor-grantee.

   Example 13: *A owned both parcels and sold one to B. The covenant was part of the sale to B.*

   f. **Vertical Privity**

   - Concerns the relationship between the original party and the successor party
   - Burden: for the burden to run with the land, the owner must transfer the entire interest

   Example 14: *A owns the land in fee simple absolute. A must convey a fee simple absolute in order for the burden to run.*

   - Benefit: the benefit will run if the successor takes any portion of the original estate (including a lease)

2. **Enforcement of Covenant**

   The injured party can sue for money damages.

C. **Equitable Servitude**

- Almost the same as a covenant except it is enforced by an injunction rather than money damages

1. **Requirements for Equitable Servitude to "Run with the Land"**

   a. **Writing**—must comply with the Statute of Frauds

   b. **Intent**—original parties must intend for the promise to run with the land

   c. **Touch and Concern**—must affect how both pieces of land are used

d. **Notice—only required for burden to run**

CHAPTER 4: SUBSTANTIVE LAW (CONT'D)—MORTGAGES AND DEEDS OF TRUST

A. Mortgages and Deeds of Trust

Exam Tip 6: A mortgage and deed of trust are treated very similarly on the exam.

- Mortgage—document that conveys a property interest in real property as security for an obligation
  - Typically, a borrower (mortgagor) conveys an interest in his land to a bank (mortgagee) in exchange for a loan.
  - If the mortgagor defaults on the loan, the house could be foreclosed and sold at public auction
- Deed of Trust—a writing grants an interest in property as security for an obligation, but the deed goes to a third party as trustee
  - If the borrower defaults, the deed of trust can be privately sold (potentially to the mortgagee)
- Purchase Money Mortgage—the borrower uses the loan in order to purchase the mortgaged property

  Example 15: *A home mortgage is usually a purchase money mortgage.*

  - A purchase money mortgage has priority upon foreclosure

B. Transfer of Mortgaged Property

- The original mortgagor remains personally liable on the mortgage even after selling the mortgaged property to a third property
- Assumption of the Mortgage—the buyer might assume the mortgage and become personally liable to the lender in addition to the original mortgagor

C. Foreclosure

- When the borrower fails to repay the loan, the lender can foreclose upon the property and sell it

1. Priority of interests

- Generally, the first mortgage gets priority over later mortgages
- **Exception 1**—when a state recording at applies
  - A later mortgage might have priority if it is protected by the recording act

Example 16: *Homeowner grants a mortgage to Bank 1 and then another to Bank 2. In a notice jurisdiction, if Bank 2 takes the mortgage without notice of the prior mortgage, Bank 2 will have priority*

- **Exception 2**—a purchase money mortgage will take priority over non-purchase money mortgages

2. **Future Advance Mortgage**

   - Arises when a borrower grants an interest in their property in exchange for the right to receive future payments (i.e., a line of credit)
   - A priority issue arises when the mortgage is granted but no amount is actually given on the loan

> ***Example 17:*** *Homeowner grants a future advance mortgage to Bank 1 but does not take any money immediately. Homeowner then grants a traditional mortgage to Bank 2 and receives the full amount of that loan from Bank 2. Bank 1 will generally have priority over Bank 2, even though it has not paid out any money.*

CHAPTER 5: PRACTICE QUESTION

July 2007, Question 6 [ID 320]

Owen owned vacant land (Whiteacre) in State B located 500 yards from a lake and bordered by vacant land owned by others. Owen, who lived 50 miles from Whiteacre, used Whiteacre for cutting firewood and for parking his car when he used the lake.

Twenty years ago, Owen delivered to Abe a deed that read in its entirety:

Owen hereby conveys to the grantee by a general warranty deed that parcel of vacant land in State B known as Whiteacre.

Owen signed the deed immediately below the quoted language and his signature was notarized. The deed was never recorded.

For the next eleven years, Abe seasonally planted vegetables on Whiteacre, cut timber on it, parked vehicles there when he and his family used the nearby lake for recreation, and gave permission to friends to park their cars and recreational vehicles there. He also paid the real property taxes due on the land, although the tax bills were actually sent to Owen because title had not been registered in Abe's name on the assessor's books. Abe did not build any structure on Whiteacre, fence it, or post no-trespassing signs.

Nine years ago, Abe moved to State C. Since that time, he has neither used Whiteacre nor given others permission to use Whiteacre, and to all outward appearances the land has appeared unoccupied.

Last year, Owen died intestate leaving his daughter, Doris, as his sole heir. After Owen's death, Doris conveyed Whiteacre by a valid deed to Buyer, who paid fair market value for Whiteacre. Neither Doris nor Buyer knew of the Owen-to-Abe deed. Both Doris and Buyer believed that Owen was the owner of

Whiteacre at the time of his death. Buyer promptly and properly recorded the deed from Doris and immediately went into possession of Whiteacre.

Last month Abe returned to State B. When he discovered Buyer in possession of Whiteacre, he sued Buyer for possession.

State B has enacted the following statutes:

1. Actions to recover possession of real property shall be brought within ten years after the cause of action accrues.

2. No conveyance or mortgage of real property shall be good against subsequent purchasers for value and without notice unless the same be recorded according to law.

Who is entitled to possession of Whiteacre? Explain.

SAMPLE ANSWER

1. The issue is whether Owen conveyed a fee simple absolute to Abe by the Owen-to-Abe deed (25-35%)

In order to be valid, a deed must identify the grantor and the grantee, describe the property, contain words of transfer, and be signed by the grantor. In this case, the Deed named the seller, described the land, included words of transfer, and was signed by Owen. However, the deed did not contain the grantee's name. Accordingly, the deed was not valid, and Owen did not effectively convey Whiteacre to Abe.

2. The issue is whether Abe acquired title to Whiteacre by adverse possession (35-45%)

The doctrine of adverse possession allows title to pass to a person who exercises exclusive physical possession of a piece of property for a certain amount of time. For adverse possession to occur, possession must be continuous, open and notorious, actual, exclusive, and hostile. Possession must be open and notorious such that a reasonable true owner would become aware of the claim. The applicable state law provides that a cause of action for possession is available for ten years after a possessor's entry.

In this case, Abe's acts of possession were open and notorious because a reasonable true owner would have become aware of Abe's claim. Although Abe did not build any structures or fence Whiteacre, he planted vegetables, cut timber, and parked vehicles on Whiteacre. Abe also paid taxes for Whiteacre. Abe used the land for eleven years, which is more than the time required to acquire title by adverse possession in State B. Abe permitted others to use the land which suggests exclusivity. Finally, Abe's hostile possession of Whiteacre is evidenced by his entry under an invalid deed. Accordingly, Abe acquired title to Whiteacre by adverse possession.

3. The issue is whether Buyer acquired title from Doris that was superior to Abe's title (30-40%)

If a person acquires title by adverse possession, that title is good as a title traceable to a period record owner. Thus, if Abe acquired title by adverse possession, he is entitled to recover possession from Buyer. The applicable law under State B is a notice statute which provides that a purchaser need only purchase without notice of the prior interest to prevail. The statute intends to protect subsequent purchasers against interest holders who could have, but failed to record documents describing their interests. However, interest holders who acquired title by adverse possession do not possess documents describing their interests that could be recorded.

As discussed above, if Abe acquired title to Whiteacre by adverse possession, then Abe did not possess documents that could have been recorded to describe his interests. Accordingly, Abe is entitled to recover possession from Buyer. If Abe did not acquire title by adverse possession, then Buyer acquired title to Whiteacre from Doris and Buyer would be entitled to possession because Buyer had no notice of Abe's interest in the land.

NCBE EDITOR'S NOTES FOR THIS ESSAY QUESTION

- *If an applicant does not know the rule that a deed must name the grantee, the applicant should conclude the Owen-to-Abe deed is valid. If the applicant wrongly concludes that deed is valid, then the applicant might either completely skip Point Two, or, in discussing Point Two, conclude that Abe did not acquire a title by adverse possession because Abe's possession was not hostile.*

(Editor's Note: The foregoing model answer was drafted in accordance with the NCBE Grading Guidelines for this question. The analysis is illustrative of the discussions that might appear in a high passing answer and addresses all legal and factual issues the drafters intended exam candidates to raise. When self-grading, refer to the NCBE's weighting of each issue, which is indicated in parentheses for your reference.)

[END OF HANDOUT]

Themis
Bar Review

SECURED TRANSACTIONS ESSAY WRITING WORKSHOP

PROFESSOR CHRISTOPHER IDE-DON

UC DAVIS SCHOOL OF LAW

CHAPTER 1: INTRODUCTION

Editor's Note 1: The Professor refers to specific page numbers throughout this lecture. The content does not always match these references due to formatting changes.

- I. In General
  - Definitions
- II. Attachment
  - Value, Rights in Collateral, Security Agreement
  - PMSI
- III. Perfection
  - Filing a Financial Statement
  - Control
- IV. Priorities
  - Creditors
  - Transferees
  - Other Secured Parties
- V. Default
  - Disposition
  - Proceeds

A. General Exam Approach

1. **Step 1:** For each party claiming an interest in the collateral (property), determine whether the secured interest has **"attached"** to the collateral in question.
2. **Step 2:** For each party claiming an interest, determine whether the secured interest has been **"perfected"**.
3. **Step 3:** If there is more than one party claiming an interest in the collateral, determine who has **priority**.
4. **Step 4:** If the collateral is disposed of (sold), determine which party(s) receives the **proceeds**.

B. Definitions

1. **Secured Transaction**—A secured transaction under Uniform Commercial Code (UCC) Article 9 involves a loan or purchase that is secured by collateral. The relationship typically involves two parties, a debtor and a creditor. The debtor gives the creditor a security interest in the debtor's specific property (collateral) to assure that the debtor will perform (repay the loan, pay the purchase price).

2. **Security Interest**—A security interest is an interest in personal property or fixtures that secures payment or performance of an obligation.

3. **Parties**—There are three types of parties with respect to a secured transaction: (i) a secured party, (ii) an obligor, and (iii) a debtor.

   a. **Secured Party**—A secured party is the person in whose favor a security interest is created under the security agreement. Usually, the secured party is the person who has loaned money or extended credit to the obligor. For example, a bank that loans money to a business is a typical secured party.

   b. **Obligor**—An obligor is a person who must pay (or otherwise perform) with respect to the obligation that is secured by a security interest in the collateral. For example, a business that receives a loan from the bank is a typical obligor.

   c. **Debtor**—A debtor is a person who has an interest, other than a security interest or other lien, in the collateral, such as the sole owner of the collateral. Although the debtor is usually also the obligor, the debtor need not be.

      Example 1: *(From outline): A loans money to B without seeking security from her. B's sister, C, cosigns the note and grants A a security interest in her car to secure the loan to B.*

      A is a secured party (loaned money to B, has a security interest in C's car).

      B is an obligor (must repay the loan to A, or else A can take C's car).

      C is both an obligor (C is also responsible for repaying the loan to A) and a debtor (C is the sole owner of the car, which is the collateral).

4. **Collateral**—Property subject to a security interest is called "collateral." The characterization of collateral can affect the validity of a security interest, the way in which a security interest can be perfected, and the rights of a third party in the collateral, such as a buyer of collateral.

   a. **Tangible Collateral: Goods**—"Goods" encompasses anything that is **"moveable at the time that a security interest attaches."** There are four classes of goods:

      1) **Consumer goods:** "Consumer goods" are those goods acquired primarily for personal, family, or household purposes.

         Example 2: *A bicycle or telescope purchased for home use.*

2) **Farm products:** "Farm products" are goods that are crops or livestock and include supplies that are used or produced in farming. For goods to be considered farm products, the obligor must be engaged in a farming operation.

3) **Inventory:** "Inventory" includes goods, other than farm products, that are held for sale or lease; are furnished under a service contract; or consist of raw materials, works in process, or materials used or consumed in a business. This term usually refers to goods that are consumed in a business

Example 3: *Gasoline used to run the machines in a factory.*

4) **Equipment:** "Equipment," a catchall class, consists of goods that are not consumer goods, farm products, or inventory. It usually refers to goods that are used or bought for use primarily in a business, such as employees' desks or machinery used in manufacturing.

Note 1: When the obligor uses the property for multiple purposes, the **principal use** to which the obligor puts the property determines the class of the goods.

Exam Tip 1: The most frequently tested Goods are Consumer Goods, Inventory, and Equipment. Also, a party may give a security interest in more than one type of Goods, for example "Inventory and Equipment".

b. Intangible Collateral—Intangible collateral includes nine classes of personal property. The more frequently tested types of intangible collateral are:

1) **Accounts:** "Accounts" include the right to payment for goods sold, property licensed, or services rendered. Also included is a right to payment for the issuance of an insurance policy, the use of a credit or charge card, or winning a lottery.

2) **Deposit account:** A "deposit account" includes a savings, passbook, time, or demand account maintained with a bank.

C. Eligible Transactions

1. General Rule

- Article 9 governs a transaction that creates, by agreement, a security interest in personal property or a fixture.
- In addition, a lease, consignment, agricultural lien, and even a purchase of personal property may be subject to Article 9.

2. Leases (recently tested)

- Leases are covered under Article 9 when the transaction, although in the form of a lease, is in economic reality or substance a secured transaction. It is generally determined on a case-by-case basis.

- There are several rules for when a lease can create a security interest. The most frequently tested rule is: "A transaction in the form of a lease creates a security interest if lease payments must be made for the full term of the lease and are not subject to termination and the lessee has an option to become the owner of the goods for nominal (a small amount of money) consideration at the conclusion of the lease agreement."

  Example 4: *(Based on a recent exam question): P enters into a "lease" agreement with L for the lease of a printing press. L maintains title of the printing press and P is required to pay $2,500 per month for five years for the use of the press. The agreement states that it cannot be terminated by P for any reason. At the conclusion of the lease, P had the option to return the printing press or purchase it for $10.*

  Note 2: Although the agreement is called a "lease" and L retained title of the printing press, the actual terms of the agreement created a sale of the printing press to P with a security interest retained by L. Watch out for "leases" and sellers that "retain title" of the goods!

CHAPTER 2: ATTACHMENT AND PERFECTION OF SECURITY INTEREST

A. Attachment

Generally, a security interest that is enforceable against the debtor with respect to the collateral is said to have "attached" to the collateral. For the security interest to be enforceable against the debtor, three conditions must coexist:

- **Value** has been given by the secured party;
- The **debtor has rights** in the collateral; and
- The debtor has authenticated a **security agreement** that describes the collateral, or the secured party has **possession** or **control** of the collateral pursuant to a security agreement.

  Exam Tip 2: You should always discuss whether a security agreement is enforceable and attached. Discuss all three conditions and use the facts provided in the question.

1. **Value Given**—The secured party must give value for the security interest. Value may be given:
   - By providing **consideration** sufficient to support a simple contract;
   - By **extending credit**, either immediately or under a binding commitment to do so;
   - By, as a buyer, **accepting delivery** under a preexisting contract, thereby converting a contingent obligation into a fixed obligation; or
   - In satisfaction of, or as security for, part or all of a preexisting claim.

   Example 5: *A typical exam question will present a bank that provides a loan to a business. The loan money would be considered the "value given".*

2. **Debtor's Rights in Collateral**—For the security interest to attach to the collateral, the **debtor generally must have rights in the collateral**. The basic rule is that a security interest attaches *only* to the rights that the debtor has. A debtor's limited rights in collateral are sufficient for a security interest to attach.

   Example 6: *A typical exam question will present a business that gives the bank an interest in the business' "Inventory and Equipment". The "Inventory and Equipment" would be the collateral and the business must actually have a right (usually takes the form of ownership) in the collateral.*

   a. **After-acquired collateral (recently tested)**

      - A security interest may apply not only to the collateral that the debtor owns at the time the security is granted, but also to collateral that the debtor acquires in the future.

        Example 7: *A business may give a bank an interest in "all Inventory* ***now*** *owned or* ***hereafter*** *acquired".*

      - **Exception:** An after-acquired clause is not effective if the collateral is consumer goods, unless the debtor acquires them within 10 days after the secured party gives value.

   b. **Proceeds from Collateral:** A security interest in collateral automatically attaches to identifiable proceeds from the sale, exchange, or other disposition of the collateral.

      Example 8: *(From outline): A secured party acquires a security interest in a debtor's inventory. The debtor sells items of inventory in exchange for checks. The secured party's security interest will attach to the checks if they are identifiable as proceeds.*

   c. **Accessions:** Accessions are goods that are physically united with other goods in such a manner that the identity of the original goods is not lost, such as memory installed in a computer, or tires installed on a car. A security interest that is created in collateral that becomes an accession is not lost due to the collateral becoming an accession.

3. **Security Agreement or Possession/Control of Collateral**

   - The debtor has authenticated a **security agreement** that describes the collateral, or the secured party has **possession** or **control** of the collateral pursuant to a security agreement.
   - The security agreement must meet the following requirements:
     - It must be in a record, such as a written or typed document,
     - Contain a description of the collateral (such as "all of debtor's equipment"; and
     - Be authenticated (typically signed) by the debtor.

   Exam Tip 3: In most exam questions, the facts will present a valid security agreement that is written, describes the collateral, and is signed by the debtor. You should quickly analyze these elements and move on to the other issues.

- **Purchase Money Security Interest** (recently tested)—A PMSI gives lenders a security interest in goods that have been purchased with funds borrowed from them or purchased on credit from them. A PMSI is subject to special rules with respect to perfection and priority (discussed later). A PMSI may exist only with respect to two types of collateral—goods (including fixtures) and software. A PMSI in goods exists when:
    - A secured party gave value (e.g., made a loan) to the debtor and the debtor uses the loan to acquire rights in or use of the collateral; **or**

      Example 9: *(From outline): A, an automobile dealer, sells B, the debtor, an automobile. B does not have the full purchase price of the automobile. B goes to C, a bank, and borrows money to purchase the automobile. In exchange for the loan, B gives C a security interest in the automobile (the collateral) that she is purchasing from A. Pursuant to the agreement with C, B is to make payments to C until the loan for the automobile has been paid in full. C has a PMSI in the automobile.*

    - A secured party sells the collateral to the debtor, and the debtor enters an agreement requiring it to pay the secured party all or part of the purchase price (i.e., a sale of goods on credit).

      Example 10: *(From outline): A, an automobile dealer, sells B, the debtor, an automobile and agrees to finance the automobile because B does not have the full purchase price. B, pursuant to the agreement, is to make payments on a monthly basis until the automobile has been paid in full and gives A a security interest in the automobile (the collateral). A has a PMSI in the automobile.*

B. Perfection of Security Interest

> **Exam Tip 4:** Perfection of a security interest is a frequently tested issue. After discussing whether a security interest has attached, you should always discuss whether the security interest has been perfected.

"Perfection" of a security interest is generally necessary for the secured party to have rights in the collateral that are superior to any rights claimed by third parties. A security interest is "perfected" upon attachment of that interest **and** compliance with one of the methods of perfection.

> **Note 3:** Perfection is not required for the secured party to have rights against the debtor. The secured party has rights against the debtor if the security interest has attached (see above). Perfection is relevant for determining a secured party's rights against third parties (such as other secured parties).

1. **Methods of Perfection**—Under Article 9, a secured party can perfect a security interest in the following ways:
    - **Filing** of a financing statement
    - **Possession** of the collateral
    - **Control** over the collateral

- **Automatic** perfection (either temporary or permanent)
- **Statute:** If there is another statute that governs perfection of a security interest, that statute may provide another method of perfection.

> ***Example 11:*** *(From a recent question): State A has a statute that provides "All security interests in a motor vehicle must be noted on the vehicle's certificate of title to be perfected." [This statute would govern the manner of perfection.]*

a. Filing a Financing Statement (most common)

- A security interest in any collateral, except a deposit account, money, or letter-of-credit rights that are not a supporting obligation, may be perfected by filing a financing statement. The primary objective of filing is to give interested parties notice of the existence of the security interest.
- A financing statement must contain the following information:
  - The **debtor's name**;
  - The **name of the secured party** or a representative of the secured party; **and**
  - The **collateral** covered by the financing statement.

1) **Timing**—The financing statement will be effective on the date of filing. A financing statement is generally effective for five years and may be continued for another five years by filing a continuation statement within six months prior to the expiration of the statement.

2) **Error in the debtor's name** (recently tested)

   - A financing statement that fails to accurately contain the debtor's name may be "seriously misleading" and therefore not effective to perfect the security interest.
   - **Exception:** When a standard search of the filing office records under the debtor's correct name would disclose the financing statement, the erroneous name does not make the financing statement seriously misleading and it will be valid.

> ***Example 12:*** *(From a recent question): Bank files a financing statement incorrectly naming the debtor as "Beagle Roofing". The actual name of the debtor is "Beagle Contracting".*

> **Note 4:** If a standard search of the filing office records under the actual name "Beagle Contracting" would disclose the financing statement for "Beagle Roofing", the incorrect name would not make the financing statement "seriously misleading" and it would be valid.

b. Control over the Collateral—A secured party may perfect a security interest in in investment property, deposit accounts, letter-of-credit rights, electronic chattel paper, or electronic documents by taking control of the collateral. The security interest remains perfected only while the secured party retains control.

1) **Deposit Account** (recently tested)—A security interest in a deposit account can be perfected only by control. A secured party has control of a deposit account if:

- The secured party is the bank with which the deposit account is maintained;
- The bank, secured party, and debtor agreed in writing to follow the instructions of the secured party; **or**
- The secured party becomes the bank's customer with respect to the deposit account.

c. **Automatic Perfection** (recently tested)

- Under some circumstances, a security interest is automatically perfected upon attachment.
- **PMSI** (Purchase Money Security Interest) **in consumer goods** (recently tested)
  - Remember, a PMSI gives lenders a special security interest in goods that have been purchased with funds borrowed from them or purchased on credit from them.
  - A PMSI in consumer goods is automatically perfected upon attachment. A secured party does not need to file a financing statement or have possession to have a perfected PMSI in consumer goods. A PMSI in other types of goods (e.g., inventory, equipment) or in automobiles is not automatically perfected.

> **Exam Tip 5:** Read the facts carefully to determine if the PMSI is in consumer goods, or other goods. If the PMSI is not in consumer goods, the secured party still must take steps to perfect the interest (filing a financial statement).

2. **Proceeds of Sale of Collateral**—If a security interest in collateral is perfected, and then the collateral is sold for cash proceeds (or checks or deposit account), the secured party will have a perfected security interest in the proceeds.

3. **Timing of Perfection**

   - A security interest is perfected upon (i) attachment of that interest and (ii) compliance with one of the methods of perfection (such as filing a financing statement).

> **Note 5:** Typically, the security interest attaches and is then perfected. It is possible for the secured party to take steps toward perfecting the security interest prior to attachment (example: filing a financing statement first). The security interest would then be perfected upon attachment.

   - In addition, a security interest that is perfected by one method and later perfected by another method without a lapse in perfection is continuously perfected despite the change in method. The date of perfection is the date on which the security interest first became perfected.

CHAPTER 3: PRIORITIES (FREQUENTLY TESTED)

Exam Tip 6: Priority problems are frequently tested and occur when two or more parties claim a right to the same collateral.

- The determination of priority involves two steps:
  - Identify the status of each claimant; then
  - Apply the appropriate priority rule.
- Potential Claimants
  - Creditors
  - Transferees/buyers
  - Other secured parties

A. Creditors

1. **General Creditor** (Unsecured)—A general creditor is one who has a claim, including a judgment, but who has no lien or security interest with respect to the property in question (i.e., the collateral). This type of creditor does not have a claim to particular property owned by the debtor. A secured party will always prevail over a general creditor with respect to the debtor's collateral.

2. **Judicial Lien Creditor**—A judicial lien creditor is a creditor who acquires a lien on the collateral by a judicial process, rather than by operation of law. A perfected security interest has priority over a judicial lien creditor, but the judicial lien creditor had priority over an unperfected security interest.

   Note 6: Even if the security interest is unperfected at the time the judicial lien comes into existence, the secured party will have priority if the only reason why it was unperfected was that the secured party had not yet given value.

   Example 13: *(From outline): On Day One, the debtor authenticates a security agreement, which describes the collateral. On Day Two, the secured party files a financing statement. On Day Three, the creditor acquires a judicial lien on the collateral. On Day Four, the secured party gives value. The secured party will have priority even though the security interest was unperfected on Day Three.*

B. Transferees

Transferees (frequently tested)—Transferees of the collateral are persons who obtain full title to the goods as a result of a transfer of the collateral from the debtor.

1. **Transferee versus secured party with a security interest**—If the collateral is transferred from the debtor to the transferee and the transferee is not a buyer, the security interest continues in the collateral unless the secured party authorized the transfer free of the security interest. In other words, the secured party still has a security interest in the collateral.

2. **Buyer versus secured party with an unperfected security interest**—A buyer, other than a secured party, of collateral that is goods, tangible chattel paper, tangible documents or a security certificate takes free of an unperfected security interest in collateral if the buyer:

   - Gives value; **and**
   - Receives delivery of the collateral;
   - Without knowledge of the existing security interest.

3. **Buyer versus secured party with a perfected security interest**—A buyer of collateral subject to a perfected security interest generally takes the collateral subject to that interest, unless the secured party has authorized its sale free of the security interest.

4. **Buyers in the Ordinary Course of Business** (BOCB) (frequently tested)—A buyer in the ordinary course of business (BOCB) takes the goods free of a security interest that the seller gave to the creditor in the goods, **even if the security interest is perfected and the buyer knows of its existence**. A BOCB is a person who:

   - Buys goods (not including farm products);
   - In the ordinary course of business;
   - From a merchant who is in the business of selling goods of that kind;
   - In good faith; **and**
   - Without knowledge that the sale violates the rights of another in the same goods.

> **Note 7:** The requirement that a BOCB take without knowledge means actual knowledge that the sale is in violation of another party's rights. Mere notice or reason to know is insufficient.
>
> **Exam Tip 7:** Remember that a person may have knowledge that there is a perfected security interest in goods when he purchases them and still qualify as a BOCB, as long as the elements of BOCB are met.

5. **Consumer Buyer** (frequently tested)

   - A consumer buyer of consumer goods takes free of a security interest, even if perfected, unless prior to the purchase, the secured party filed a financing statement covering the goods. A consumer buyer is a person who:
     - Buys consumer goods for value;
     - For his own personal, family, or household use;
     - From a consumer seller; **and**
     - Without knowledge of the security interest.
   - **Special Problem:** PMSI (Purchase Money Security Interest)
     - Remember, a PMSI gives lenders a special security interest in goods that have been purchased with funds borrowed from them or purchased on credit from them.

- A PMSI in consumer goods is automatically perfected upon attachment. Perfection through filing a financial statement is not required, but a party with a PMSI may still elect to file a financial statement.
- If a financial statement for a PMSI in consumer goods is not filed, and the consumer buyer does not know of the PMSI, then he will take free of the security interest.
- If the party holding the PMSI in consumer goods does in fact file, then his security interest will be good even against a consumer buyer.

Note 8: Secured parties with a PMSI in consumer goods should file a financial statement, to protect their interest against consumer buyers.

Example 14: *(Based on a recent question): Astronomy is a telescope store. A sells a telescope (a consumer good) to B on credit and completes the requirements for attachment, giving A a PMSI in the telescope (a consumer good). A does not file a financing statement. Because A's PMSI is in a consumer good, its interest is automatically perfected upon attachment and no financing statement is required to perfect its interest.*

Later, B (a consumer seller) decides to sell the telescope to C (a consumer buyer). C buys the telescope for his family to use at home and does not know about A's PMSI in the telescope. Because C did not know about A's PMSI in the telescope and A did not file a financing statement, C will take the telescope free of A's interest.

C. Priorities Among Secured Parties

1. **Perfected security interest versus perfected security interest**—When there are two or more perfected secured parties with rights in the same collateral, the first to party to either file a financial statement or perfect has priority.

Example 15: *(From a recent exam question): On March 1, Owner approaches Bank and starts discussions about obtaining a loan. On March 1, Bank files a financial statement and starts to process the loan, but does not complete the requirements for attachment.*

On March 2, Owner approaches Financing Company and discusses a loan. On March 2, Financing Company, completes the requirements for attachment, and files a financing statement, thereby perfecting its security interest.

On March 5, the Bank completes the requirements for attachment, thereby perfecting its security interest.

Here, both the Bank and Financing Company have perfected security interests. Because the Bank filed a financial statement first, it will have priority over Financing Company.

2. **Perfected security interest versus unperfected security interest**—If only one security interest is perfected and the other is not, then the perfected interest takes over the unperfected one.

3. **Unperfected security interest versus unperfected security interest**—If neither interest is perfected, then the first party to have attached their interest has priority.

4. **PMSI (Purchase Money Security Interest) Rules**

   - Preference is generally given to a PMSI over a non-PMSI security interest.

     - A PMSI in goods other than inventory or livestock prevails over all other security interests in the collateral, even if the other security interests perfected earlier, so long as the PMSI is perfected before or within 20 days after the debtor receives possession of the collateral.

   a. **A PMSI in inventory or livestock**—prevails over all other security interests in the same collateral, even if they were previously perfected, if (i) the PMSI is perfected by the time the debtor receives possession of the collateral, and (ii) the purchase-money secured party sends an authenticated notification of the PMSI to the holder of any conflicting security interest before the debtor receives possession of the collateral.

     - The notification must state that the purchase-money secured party has or expects to have a PMSI in the debtor's inventory or livestock and it must include a description

   b. **PMSI versus PMSI**—If there are two or more competing PMSIs, the first to party to either file a financial statement or perfect has priority.

   c. **Proceeds from a PMSI in goods**—The priority of a PMSI in goods generally extends to the identifiable proceeds of the original collateral, but only as to proceeds in which the security interest is perfected when the debtor receives possession of the collateral or within 20 days thereafter.

5. **Construction Mortgage** (recently tested)—A construction mortgage (i.e., a mortgage that secures an obligation incurred for the construction of an improvement on land, including the cost of acquiring the land, and that indicates it is a construction mortgage in the real property records) has priority over a subsequent security interest in a fixture, including a PMSI in a fixture. The construction mortgage must be recorded before the goods become fixtures, and it covers only goods that become fixtures before completion of the construction. UCC § 9-334(h).

6. **Proceeds**—Generally, the basic rules (e.g., first-to-file-or-perfect) govern priority if there are conflicting security interests and at least one of those interests is claimed as proceeds. The filing or perfection date for the original collateral is treated as the filing or perfection date for the proceeds.

CHAPTER 4: DEFAULT

- Generally, default will be the failure of the obligor to make timely payments to the secured party.
- Once a default has occurred, the secured party may:
  - Seek possession of the collateral and, in order to satisfy the obligor's outstanding obligation, either:
    - Sell the collateral; **or**
    - Retain it in full or partial satisfaction of the obligation;
  - Initiate a judicial action to obtain a judgment based on that obligation; **or**
  - Subject to statutory limitations, pursue any course of action to which the debtor and obligor have agreed.

A. Security Agreement Covering Fixtures (recently tested)

- When a security agreement covers fixtures, a secured party may proceed as to the fixtures in accord with the rights and remedies with respect to the real property.
- When a secured party's security interest has priority over owners and individuals who encumber real property, that secured party may remove the fixture from the real property. With respect to an owner or encumbrancer who is not the debtor, the secured party is liable for the cost of repairing any physical object damaged by the removal but not for any reduction in the value of the real property due to the removal.

B. Possession of Collateral—After default, a secured party is entitled to take possession of the collateral. Unless the security agreement provides otherwise, a secured party is not required to give notice of default, nor is he required to give notice of his intent to take possession of the collateral.

C. Disposition of Collateral—After default, a secured party may sell, lease, license, or otherwise dispose of all or any of the collateral. Within limits, the secured party may keep the collateral (strict foreclosure) in full or partial satisfaction of the obligation.

1. **Commercially Reasonable Standard for Disposition**—All aspects of the disposition of collateral (method, manner, time, and place) must be conducted in a commercially reasonable manner. A disposition is commercially reasonable when conducted:
   - In the usual manner on a **recognized market**, such as a stock exchange, that has standardized price quotations for fungible goods;
   - At the **price current** in any recognized market at the time of the disposition; **or**
   - Otherwise in conformity with **reasonable commercial practices** among dealers in the type of property that was the subject of the disposition.
2. **Price**—There is not a specific price that must be obtained by the secured party in disposing of the collateral. The mere fact that a higher price could have been obtained by disposing of the collateral in a different manner or at a different time does not establish that the disposition was

not commercially reasonable. A low price may trigger scrutiny by the court of the disposition and its reasonableness.

3. **Time of Disposition**—There is not a specific time in which a disposition must occur.

4. **Type of Disposition**

   - A secured party may dispose of the collateral publicly or privately.
   - A secured party may purchase the collateral at a public sale, but she cannot do so at a private sale unless the collateral is of a kind that is customarily sold on a recognized market (e.g., the New York Stock Exchange) or the subject of widely distributed standard price quotations. A secured party cannot purchase the collateral at a private sale when the prices are individually negotiated or when items are not fungible in a recognized market.

5. **Notice of Disposition**—A secured party is generally required to send an authenticated notification of disposition. The notification is required to be reasonable as to its content, the manner in which it is sent, and its timeliness.

   - Notification of disposition is required to be sent to (i) the debtor, (ii) any secondary obligor, and, in the case of non-consumer goods, (iii) any other secured party or lien holder who held a security interest that was perfected by filing or pursuant to a statute, and (iv) any other party from whom the secured party has received authenticated notice of a claim or interest in the collateral.
   - **Timeliness of notice:** In general, the test for the timeliness of a notification of a disposition is **reasonableness**. The notification should be sent sufficiently far in advance of the disposition to allow the notified party to act on the notification. In a transaction other than a consumer transaction, when a secured party sends a notification of disposition after default and at least 10 days before the earliest time for disposition set forth in the notification, the timeliness of the notice is reasonable, provided that the notice is sent in a commercially reasonable manner.

D. **Application of the Proceeds From a Disposition** (recently tested)

1. **Cash proceeds**—A secured party must apply, or pay over for application, cash proceeds of a disposition in the following order:

   - Reasonable expenses for collection and enforcement, including reasonable attorney's fees and other legal expenses; then
   - Satisfaction of obligations secured by the security interest; then
   - Satisfaction of any subordinate security interests, provided that the junior secured party made an authenticated demand for proceeds before distribution of the proceeds is complete; then
   - The remainder of the proceeds to the debtor.

2. **Treatment of a surplus or deficiency**

   a. **Surplus:** If, after the required payments and applications of proceeds have been made, there is a surplus, the secured party generally must pay the surplus to the debtor.

   b. **Deficiency:** If, after the required payments and applications of proceeds have been made, there is a deficiency, then the obligor generally is liable for the deficiency.

3. **Transferee's Rights**—A sale of the collateral gives the buyer at the sale all of the debtor's rights in the collateral. If the transferee/buyer acts in good faith (i.e., honesty in fact and the observance of reasonable commercial standards of fair dealing), then the disposition discharges the security interest being foreclosed and any subordinate security interests and liens. However, the transferee takes the collateral subject to any security interests that were senior to the security interest foreclosed.

CHAPTER 5: PRACTICE QUESTION

February 2011, Question #3 [ID 1953]

Astronomy Corporation (Astronomy) sells expensive telescopes to home stargazers. Astronomy has a long-term financing arrangement pursuant to which it borrows money from Bank. In a signed writing, Astronomy granted Bank a security interest in all its present and future inventory to secure its obligations to Bank under the financing arrangement. Bank filed a properly completed financing statement reflecting this transaction. The financing statement lists Astronomy as the debtor and Bank as the secured party. The financing statement indicates that the collateral is inventory.

Astronomy sells telescopes to some of its customers on credit. For a credit sale, Astronomy requires the customer to sign an agreement granting Astronomy a security interest in the purchased item to secure the customer's obligation to pay the balance of the purchase price.

Six months ago, Johnson, an amateur stargazer, went to Astronomy's showroom, saw a $3,000 telescope that he liked, and bought it on credit from Astronomy. Johnson paid $500 in cash and agreed to pay the $2,500 balance in installment payments of $100 per month for the next 25 months, interest free. Consistent with Astronomy's policy for credit sales, Johnson signed an agreement granting Astronomy a security interest in the telescope to secure Johnson's obligation to pay the balance of the purchase price. Astronomy did not file a financing statement with respect to this transaction. At the time of the sale of the telescope to Johnson, Johnson was unaware of the financial arrangement between Astronomy and Bank.

One month ago, Johnson sold the telescope for $2,700 in cash to his neighbor, Smith, another amateur stargazer. Smith had no knowledge of any interest of Bank or Astronomy in the telescope. Johnson then left the country without paying the remaining $2,000 owed to Astronomy and cannot be located.

One week ago, Astronomy defaulted on its obligations to Bank.

Both Bank and Astronomy have discovered that Johnson sold the telescope to Smith. Bank and Astronomy each have demanded that Smith surrender the telescope on the grounds that it is collateral for obligations owed to them.

1. Does Bank have a security interest in the telescope that is enforceable against Smith? Explain.
2. Does Astronomy have a security interest in the telescope that is enforceable against Smith? Explain.

Sample Answer

1.(a) The issue is whether Bank had a perfected security interest in the telescope before Astronomy sold it. (20%)

Inventory under UCC Article 9 includes goods, other than farm products, that are held for sale. Because Astronomy held the telescope for sale, it was inventory and covered by Bank's security interest. A security interest that is enforceable against the debtor with respect to the collateral is said to have attached to the collateral and three conditions must exist: (1) the secured party must give value, (2) the debtor must have rights in the collateral, and (3) the debtor must authenticate a security agreement that describes the collateral or else the secured party retains possession or control of the collateral.

Here, the three conditions are satisfied: Bank gave value by loaning money to Astronomy, Astronomy had rights in the inventory, and Astronomy signed a security agreement describing the collateral.

A security interest is perfected upon attachment and compliance with one of the methods of perfection. An interest in inventory can be perfected by filing a financing statement. Therefore, Bank perfected its security interest in the telescope when it filed the properly completed financing statement.

1.(b) At issue is whether the Bank's security interest continued after Astronomy sold the telescope. (30%)

A buyer of collateral subject to a perfected security interest generally takes the collateral subject to that interest, unless the secured party has authorized its sale free of the security interest. However, a buyer in the ordinary course of business (BOCB) takes free of a security interest created by the buyer's seller, even if the security interest is perfected and the buyer knows of its existence. A BOCB is a buyer who (i) buys goods, (ii) in the ordinary course of business, (iii) from a merchant in the business of selling goods of that kind, (iv) in good faith, and (v) without knowledge that the sale violates another's rights.

Here, Johnson qualifies as a BOCB because he bought the telescope from Astronomy, who is in the business of selling telescopes and in the ordinary course of that business. The facts do not suggest that Johnson acted in bad faith or knew the sale violated the rights of another. Thus Johnson, a BOCB, took the telescope free of Bank's security interest created by Astronomy, the seller. Because Johnson owned the telescope free of Bank's security interest, his sale to Smith would also be free of Bank's security interest.

2. (a) The issue is whether Astronomy had a perfected security interest in the telescope before Johnson sold it to Smith. (25%)

Astronomy's security interest attached because the three Article 9 requirements for attachment were fulfilled: (i) Value in the form of the telescope had been given by Astronomy, the secured party, (ii) Johnson, the debtor, had rights in the telescope, and (iii) Johnson had authenticated a security agreement granting Astronomy a security interest in the telescope.

A purchase-money security interest (PMSI) is a special type of security interest that exists when a secured party sold goods to the debtor, and the debtor incurs an obligation to pay the secured party all or part of the purchase price (a sale on credit). A PMSI in consumer goods is automatically perfected. A consumer good is acquired primarily for personal, family, or household purposes. Here, Astronomy had a PMSI because it sold the telescope to Johnson on credit. This interest was perfected automatically because it is a consumer good (Johnson obtained it for personal or household use). Thus, Astronomy had a perfected security interest in the telescope before Johnson sold it to Smith.

(b) The issue is whether Astronomy's security interest in the telescope was enforceable against Smith. (25%)

A consumer buyer of consumer goods takes free of a security interest unless, prior to the purchase, the secured party has filed a financing statement covering the goods. A consumer buyer is a person who: (i) buys goods for value, (ii) for his own personal, family, or household use, (iii) from a consumer seller, and (iv) without knowledge of the security interest. Here, Smith purchased the telescope for his own personal use from Johnson, a consumer seller, and without knowledge of Astronomy's security interest. Thus Smith is a consumer buyer. Because Astronomy did not file a financing statement, it cannot enforce its security interest against Smith.

(Editor's Note: The foregoing model answer was drafted in accordance with the NCBE Grading Guidelines for this question. The analysis is illustrative of the discussions that might appear in a high passing answer and addresses all legal and factual issues the drafters intended exam candidates to raise. When self-grading, refer to the NCBE's weighting of each issue, which is indicated in parentheses for your reference.)

[END OF HANDOUT]

Themis
BarReview

TORTS ESSAY WORKSHOP

PROFESSOR CHRISTOPHER IDE-DON
UC DAVIS SCHOOL OF LAW

CHAPTER 1: SUMMARY OF ISSUES; SUBSTANTIVE LAW—NEGLIGENCE

A. Summary of Issues Tested

1. Negligence

- Duty
- Breach
- Causation
  - Actual
  - Proximate
- Damages
- Defenses

2. Strict Liability

- Abnormally dangerous activities
- Animals—wild and domestic
- Strict Products Liability

3. Defamation

4. Invasion of Privacy

- Misappropriation
- Intrusion upon seclusion
- False light
- Public disclosure of private facts

5. Intentional Torts

- False imprisonment
- Battery
- Assault
- Intentional Infliction of Emotional Distress (IIED)
- Trespass to Chattels
- Conversion
- Nuisance

B. Negligence

> **Exam Tip 1:** Negligence is frequently tested. A good answer will touch on each element and emphasize the most relevant elements based on the facts.

1. Duty

a. Who is owed a duty?

- All foreseeable plaintiffs
- Majority view (Cardozo)—plaintiffs within the zone of foreseeable harm
- Minority view (Andrews)—anyone who is harmed

b. Affirmative duty to act

- Generally, there is no affirmative duty to aid or rescue someone.

- Assumption of duty—if someone starts to aid or rescue, must act with reasonable ordinary care to not increase the risk of harm
- Psychotherapists' duty to warn—if a patient makes credible threats of physical violence, under a duty to warn the intended victim

c. Standard of care

- To act as a reasonably prudent person under the circumstances

> **Exam Tip 2:** Apply the general standard of care unless a special standard applies (i.e. landowner, physician, etc.) or there is a statute (negligence per se).

2. Special Standards of Care

a. Possessors of land

- Modern Rule—must exercise reasonable care under the circumstances to all land entrants, except trespassers
- Traditional Approach

> **Exam Tip 3:** Under the traditional approach, first categorize the plaintiff as a trespasser, invitee, or licensee. Then analyze the standard of care owed to that person.

  - Trespasser—on the land without consent or permission
    - Duty: to refrain from willful, wanton, reckless, or intentional misconduct
  - Invitee—invited as member of the public or a business visitor
    - Duty: to inspect and discover unreasonably dangerous conditions and protect the invitee from them
  - Licensee—enters with express or implied permission for a specific purpose
    - Duty: to warn of concealed dangers that are known or should be obvious and use reasonable care in conducting activities

- **Attractive Nuisance**—involves injuries to trespassing children; liable if:
  - An artificial condition exists in a place where the owner knows or should know that children are likely to trespass;
  - The condition imposes and unreasonable risk of serious bodily injury;
  - The children cannot appreciate the danger due to their youth;
  - The burden of eliminating the danger is slight compared with the risk of harm; and
  - The land possessor failed to exercise reasonable care to protect children

b. Landlord duty to tenants

Protect from foreseeable attacks by third parties

c. Duties of children

- Duty to act as a reasonable child of the same age
- If engaged in an adult activity (e.g., driving a car), duty to act as a reasonably prudent adult

d. Custom

- Evidence of an industry or community custom is admissible as evidence of the relevant standard of care
- Evidence of custom is not conclusive

e. Professionals

Duty to perform at the same level as another practitioner in the same community

f. Physicians/Doctors

Duty to perform as an average doctor based on a national standard

3. Breach

- Occurs when the defendant fails to meet the applicable standard of care
- Modern factors for determining breach (cost-benefit analysis):

1) The foreseeability of harm;

2) The severity of harm; and

3) The burden on the defendant to prevent the harm

a. Res Ipsa Loquitur

- Arises when there is no direct evidence of the defendant's negligent conduct
- Allows the trier of fact to infer that there was negligent conduct
- The plaintiff must prove that:

a) The type of accident would not normally occur absent negligence;

b) The injury was caused by an agent or instrumentality within the exclusive control of the defendant; and

c) The injury was not due to the plaintiff's own actions.

b. Negligence Per Se—Alternative Duty and Breach Analysis

- Arises when there is a statute that imposes a specific duty
- Plaintiff must be within the class of persons the statute is meant to protect
- Plaintiff must suffer the type of harm the statute was meant to protect against
- Defendant's violation of the statute must be the proximate cause the plaintiff's harm

4. Causation

Exam Tip 4: Discuss actual and proximate cause under separate headings.

a. Actual Cause

- Plaintiff must show that but-for defendant's actions plaintiff's injury would not have occurred

1) Substantial Factor Rule
   - Arises when there are multiple causes of the harm and each alone would have been a factual cause of the injury
   - The conduct of each defendant is a cause in fact if it was a substantial cause of the injury

2) Alternative Causation
   - Arises when the plaintiff's harm is caused by multiple defendants (2–5) and each defendant's conduct was individually tortious
   - The burden of proof can shift to the defendants to prove that each was not the cause in fact

b. Proximate Cause

- Plaintiff must show that the injury was a foreseeable result of the defendant's conduct
- Intervening cause—an outside force that contributes to the plaintiff's harm ***after*** the defendant's act
  - If foreseeable, will not cut off defendant's liability
  - If unforeseeable, it is a superseding cause and cuts off the defendant's liability

5. Damages

- Plaintiff must prove actual injury, not just economic loss
- Eggshell-skull rule—arises when the plaintiff has a preexisting condition or vulnerability
  - Defendant is liable for the full extent of the plaintiff's injuries, even if the extent of the harm was not foreseeable

C. Negligent Infliction of Emotional Distress (NIED)

1. Zone of Danger

- Plaintiff must have been within the zone of danger of the threatened physical impact
- Must have some physical manifestation of the emotional distress

Example 1: *The plaintiff is almost hit by a car and suffers a heart attack as a result of the shock of the event. The plaintiff can claim NIED because he was in the zone of physical danger, he experienced emotional distress, and that distress was physically manifested as a heart attack.*

2. Bystanders

- A bystander who is outside the zone of danger may recover for NIED if the plaintiff:
  - Is closely related to a person harmed by the defendant's negligence;
  - Was present at the scene of the injury; and
  - Personally observed the injury.

> **Editorial Note 1:** For both zone of danger and bystander NIED claims, the plaintiff must experience emotional distress as a result of the defendant's negligence, and that distress must be manifested by physical symptoms.

D. Defenses to Negligence

1. Contributory Negligence (old rule)

If the plaintiff's negligence contributed to his harm, it was a complete bar to recovery.

2. Comparative Fault (modern rule)

- Pure comparative negligence (minority rule)—plaintiff's recovery is reduced by the amount of the plaintiff's fault, regardless of how at fault the plaintiff is

  Example 2: *If the plaintiff is 51% at fault for his own injuries, he can still recover 49% of the damages.*

- Modified or partial comparative negligence (majority rule)—plaintiff's recovery is reduced by the amount of the plaintiff's fault, but the plaintiff cannot recover if he is more at fault than the defendant

  Example 3: *If the plaintiff is 51% at fault, the plaintiff cannot recover from the defendant.*

3. Assumption of the Risk

Plaintiff's recovery may be barred or reduced if she voluntarily and knowingly assumed the risk of the behavior

CHAPTER 2: SUBSTANTIVE LAW (CONT'D)—STRICT LIABILITY

A. Abnormally Dangerous Activity

- A defendant engaged in an abnormally dangerous activity is subject to strict liability for personal injuries and property damage caused by the activity.
- Abnormally dangerous activity—high risk of harm, that is not commonly found in the community, which has a risk that cannot be eliminated with due care

  Example 4: *Explosives, fumigation, disposing of hazardous waste, storing chemicals*

1. **Causation**

> **Note 1:** The causation analysis is the same analysis as discussed above under negligence.

a. **Actual Cause**

Plaintiff must show that but for defendant's act, plaintiff's injury would not have occurred

b. **Proximate Cause**

Plaintiff must show that her injuries were the foreseeable result of defendant's conduct

2. **Damages**

Plaintiff must prove actual injury and not just economic loss

3. **Defenses—Assumption of the Risk**

Recovery may be barred or reduced if plaintiff voluntarily and knowingly assumed the risk.

B. **Wild Animals**

- Strict liability applies to wild animals (e.g., bear, tiger, etc.)
- Also applies to domestic animals if the owner knows or has reason to know of a dangerous propensity
- Plaintiff must also show causation and damages

C. **Strict Products Liability**

- Defendant in the business of selling a commercial product may be strictly liable for a defective product causing foreseeable injuries to a plaintiff

1. **Absolute Duty**

Proper defendant—includes manufacturer, distributor, and retailer

2. **Defective Product**

A product is defective when, at the time of the sale or distribution, it contains a manufacturing defect, a design defect, or inadequate instructions or warnings (i.e., failure to warn).

> **Exam Tip 5:** It is possible for a product to be defective based on more than one theory. You should discuss all defect theories that are raised by the facts.

a. **Manufacturing Defect**

- A deviation from what the manufacturer intended the product to be that causes harm to the plaintiff
- The test is whether the product conforms to the defendant's own specifications.

b. Design Defect

- Consumer-expectation test—plaintiff must prove that the product is dangerous beyond the expectation of an ordinary consumer
- Risk-utility test—plaintiff must prove that a reasonable alternative design that is economically feasible was available to defendant, and failure to use that design rendered the product unreasonably dangerous.

> **Exam Tip 6:** Look for facts in the exam question about the availability of alternative designs and the cost of these alternative designs.

c. Failure to Warn

Exists if there were foreseeable risks of harm, not obvious to an ordinary user of the product, which could have been reduced or avoided by providing reasonable instructions or warnings

> **Exam Tip 7:** Read the exam facts carefully. The defendant might provide a warning about one type of harm, but it is insufficient to warn about the type of harm that actually occurred.

3. Causation

a. Actual Causation

The product must have been defective when it left defendant's control and the defect was the actual cause of the harm.

b. Proximate Causation

- The defect causing the plaintiff's injuries occurred when the product was being used in an intended or reasonably foreseeable way.
- A defendant may still be liable if the plaintiff misuses the product, as long as the misuse is foreseeable.

4. Damages

Plaintiff must suffer personal injury or property damage

5. Defenses

a. Contributory Fault

- The plaintiff's contributory fault is generally not a defense to a strict products liability action.
- If the plaintiff knows of the defect and unreasonably uses the product anyway, contributory fault may be a defense to bar or reduce recovery.

b. Assumption of the Risk

Recovery may be barred or reduced if plaintiff voluntarily and knowingly assumed the risk of using the product

6. Negligent Products Liability

> **Exam Tip 8:** After you analyze strict products liability, you should always discuss negligent products liability. This analysis is the same as a typical negligence analysis in relation to the product.

D. Warranties

1. Express Warranty

- A promise or guarantee made by the defendant about the product
- If the product does not meet this warranty, the defendant has breached this warranty and plaintiff can recover damages.

2. Implied Warranty of Merchantability

A product that is sold is impliedly warranted to be reasonably useful and safe for average use.

3. Implied Warranty of Fitness for Particular Purpose

If a seller knows or has reason to know of a particular purpose for which some item is being purchased by the buyer, the seller is guaranteeing that the item is fit for that particular purpose.

CHAPTER 3: SUBSTANTIVE LAW (CONT'D)—DEFAMATION AND INVASION OF PRIVACY

A. Defamation

- A plaintiff may bring an action for defamation if the defendant's defamatory language:
  - Is of or concerning the plaintiff;
  - Is published to a third party who understands its defamatory nature; and
  - Damages the plaintiff's reputation.

1. Defamatory Language

The language diminishes the respect, esteem, or goodwill towards plaintiff.

2. Of or Concerning Plaintiff

A reasonable person must believe that the defamatory statement refers to this particular plaintiff and holds him up to scorn or ridicule in the eyes of a substantial number of respectable members of the community.

3. Publication

Statement must be communicated to a third party

4. Damage to Plaintiff's Reputation

- Libel (written statements)—general damages are presumed
- Slander (oral statements)—damages are not presumed

- Slander per se—damages are presumed when statements involve professional reputation, disease, crimes of moral turpitude, or unchaste behavior

5. Constitutional Defamation Requirements

- The Constitutional defamation requirements apply if:
  1) The plaintiff is a public official (e.g., politician) or public figure (e.g., celebrity); or
  2) The plaintiff is a private individual, but the statement involves a matter of public concern.

a. First Constitutional Requirement: Falsity

- Plaintiff must prove that the statement is false; and
- If plaintiff is a public official or figure, must also prove that the defendant acted with actual malice
  - Malice—defendant either had knowledge that the statement was false or acted with reckless disregard as to the truth or falsity of the statement
- If the plaintiff is a private individual and the defendant's statement involves a matter of public concern, the plaintiff is required to prove that the defendant acted with negligence **or** actual malice.

b. Second Constitutional Requirement: Limits on Damages

- A public official or figure or a private individual and matter of public concern—plaintiff must prove actual damages
- A private individual who can show actual malice may also recover punitive damages.

B. Defamation Defenses

1. Truth

Truth is an absolute defense to defamation.

2. Consent

Consent is an absolute defense as long as defendant did not exceed the scope of consent.

3. Absolute Privilege

- Used for remarks during judicial or legislative proceedings, between spouses, or in required publications
- Cannot be lost

4. Qualified Privilege

- Affects an important public interest or is in the interest of defendant or a third party
- Can be lost if exceeds the scope of the privilege or the speaker acted with malice

C. Invasion of Privacy Torts

1. Misappropriation

- The unauthorized use of plaintiff's name, likeness, or identity for defendant's advantage (commercial or otherwise)
- Plaintiff must prove lack of consent and injury.

> ***Example 5:*** *A celebrity's photo is used in an advertisement without being compensated and without the celebrity's permission.*

2. Intrusion upon Seclusion

Defendant's acts of intrusion into plaintiff's private affairs are objectionable to a reasonable person

3. False Light

Plaintiff must prove that defendant published facts about plaintiff or attributed views or actions to plaintiff that place him in a false light and are highly offensive to a reasonable person

> ***Example 6:*** *A newspaper using a photo of a celebrity and falsely stating that the photo was taken at an objectionable event.*

4. Public Disclosure of Private Facts

Actionable if the publication would be highly offensive to a reasonable person, and is not of legitimate concern to the public

CHAPTER 4: SUBSTANTIVE LAW (CONT'D)—INTENTIONAL TORTS AND VICARIOUS LIABILITY

A. Intentional Torts—Personal Injury

1. Battery

Requires harmful or offensive contact (objective standard) with the plaintiff's person (or anything connected to it), intent by defendant to cause the touching (transferred intent applies), and causation

> **Exam Tip 9:** The intent requirement is met if the defendant has the desire to bring about the harmful contact OR the defendant engaged in an action knowing that the harm was substantially certain to occur.

2. Assault

Requires an act or threat (mere words not enough) placing the plaintiff in in reasonable apprehension of imminent harmful or offensive contact with his person, intent by defendant to place plaintiff in apprehension (transferred intent applies), and causation

3. Intentional Infliction of Emotional Distress (IIED)

Requires extreme and outrageous conduct by the defendant causing severe emotional distress to plaintiff and intent by the defendant to cause distress.

a. Liability to third parties

- Defendant can be liable if he distresses a member of victim's immediate family
- Defendant can be liable if he distresses a bystander (not family) if the distress results in bodily injury to the bystander

4. False imprisonment

- The intentional confinement or restraint of plaintiff (e.g., physical barriers or force, threats, invalid use of legal authority, duress) for any amount of time.
- There must be no reasonable means of safe escape.
- Actual damages are not necessary if plaintiff was aware of confinement.

a. Shopkeeper's Privilege (Defense)

If a shopkeeper reasonably suspects plaintiff of stealing, he can detain the plaintiff for a reasonable amount of time in a reasonable manner.

B. Defense—Consent

- Must be voluntary
- Defendant will be liable if he exceeds the scope of plaintiff's consent

C. Intentional Torts—Harm to Property

1. Trespass to chattels (tangible personal property)

- An interference with the plaintiff's possession of her chattel
- Requires intent to perform the act that interferes with the possession (transferred intent applies), causation, and damages

2. Conversion

Requires <u>serious</u> interference with plaintiff's possession of her chattel, intent to perform the act that interferes with the possession (transferred intent does not apply), causation, and damages.

3. Trespass to land

The physical invasion of another's land and intent to enter the land or cause physical invasion

a. Private Necessity (Defense)

- Allows a person to enter plaintiff's land to protect her own person or property from harm
- Not liable for trespass but responsible for actual damages

b. Public Necessity (Defense)

- Allows a person to enter plaintiff's land to prevent an imminent public disaster
- Not liable for damage if actions were reasonable or had a reasonable belief that necessity existed, even if initial entry was not necessary

4. Nuisance

a. Private Nuisance

A substantial (offensive to a reasonable person) and unreasonable (balance the interests of the plaintiff and defendant) interference with another's use or enjoyment of his land

b. Public Nuisance

An unreasonable interference with a right common to the general public

c. Defenses

- Regulatory compliance is a partial defense if the defendant is following the law.
- Coming to the nuisance is a defense.

d. Remedies

Money damages and injunctive relief

e. Abatement (eliminating the nuisance)

1) Private Nuisance

- Reasonable force is permitted to abate the nuisance
- Plaintiff must give notice of the nuisance and defendant must refuse to act before action can be taken

2) Public Nuisance

- Absent unique injury, public nuisance may be abated only by public authority

D. Vicarious Liability

Exam Tip 10: Frequently arises in the context of an agency relationship

1. Employee v. Independent Contractor

- Determine whether the person who committed the tort is an employee or an independent contractor
- Generally, an employer is liable for the torts of an employee, but not for the torts of an independent contractor.
- The more control the employer exercises, the more likely the person is an employee

2. Liability

- Employer is liable for an employee's torts committed within the scope of employment

        - Can include intentional torts if within scope of employment
    - Employer is generally not liable for an independent contractor's torts
        - Might be liable for non-delegable duties or inherently dangerous activities

CHAPTER 5: PRACTICE QUESTION

February 2008, Question 2 [ID 1830]

Last month, Paul attended a fund-raising lunch at Library, where he purchased and ate a chicken salad sandwich. Later that day, he became severely ill and was diagnosed with food poisoning. As a result of the food poisoning, Paul developed a permanent digestive disorder.

Several other people also became sick after eating at the lunch, and the Health Department determined that the chicken salad was contaminated with salmonella bacteria. According to the Health Department, raw chicken often contains salmonella bacteria. Although the risk of salmonella contamination cannot be eliminated, proper preparation and cooking can ensure that the chicken is safe for eating. The chicken must be thoroughly cooked, and all utensils or surfaces that come in contact with raw chicken must be thoroughly cleaned with hot water and soap before further use.

The Reading Club had initiated and planned the Library's first and only fund-raising lunch. Ann, Bill, and Chuck independently volunteered to make the chicken salad. Each made a separate batch of salad, using their own recipes and working individually at their own homes. Another volunteer combined the three batches of salad at Library, and a Library employee sold sandwiches at the lunch. All lunch profits went to Library.

Ann, Bill, and Chuck each purchased their chicken from Supermarket. The chicken was contained in packages labeled with a prominent warning describing the risk of salmonella contamination and the precautions necessary to avoid those risks.

A Health Department spokesperson has said that "Someone who made the chicken salad did not take proper precautions." Ann, Bill, and Chuck all claim they took the proper precautions.

Paul has consulted an attorney about bringing a tort action against: 1) Library, 2) Supermarket, and 3) Ann, Bill, and Chuck. If Paul can prove only the facts outlined above:

1. Can Library be found liable to Paul under a strict liability theory? Explain.

2. Can Supermarket be found liable to Paul under a strict liability theory? Explain.

3. Can Ann, Bill, and Chuck be found liable to Paul under either a strict liability or negligence theory? Explain.

SAMPLE ANSWER

1. Paul v. Library (20%)

The issue is whether Library is a commercial seller. Under strict liability, the seller or other distributor of a defective product may be liable for any harm to persons or property caused by such product. To be subject to strict liability for a defective product, the defendant must be in the business of selling or otherwise distributing products of the type that harmed the plaintiff.

In this case, the chicken salad sandwich was a defective product because it contained salmonella bacteria. However, Library is not in the business of selling or distributing chicken salad sandwiches. Accordingly, Library cannot be strictly liable to Paul because it is not a commercial product seller.

2. Paul v. Supermarket (35%)

The issue is whether Supermarket is subject to strict liability for selling a defective product or for failure to warn. To be subject to strict liability for a defective product, the defendant must be in the business of selling or otherwise distributing products of the type that harmed the plaintiff. Included as a seller are the product's manufacturer, its distributor, and its retail seller. In this case, Supermarket is a retail seller of chicken. Accordingly, Supermarket may be found liable if the chicken it sold was defective.

A product is defective when, at the time of the sale or distribution, it contains a manufacturing defect, a design defect, or inadequate instructions or warnings. A defect for failure to warn exists if there are foreseeable risks of harm, not readily recognized by an ordinary user of the product, which risks could have been reduced or avoided by providing reasonable instructions or warnings.

In this case, the chicken sold by supermarket contained packages labeled with a prominent warning describing the risk of salmonella contamination and the precautions necessary to avoid those risks. The chicken did not contain either a manufacturing defect or a design defect because the risk of salmonella contamination is inherent in raw chicken. Accordingly, the chicken was not defective, and Paul cannot recover damages from Supermarket.

3. Paul v. Ann, Bill, and Chuck

<u>Negligence – Res Ipsa Loquitur</u> (30%): The issue is whether Paul may recover damages from Ann, Bill, or Chuck under res ipsa loquitur when he cannot show who was negligent and caused his injury. In general, a duty of care is owed to all foreseeable persons who may foreseeably be injured by the defendant's failure to act as a reasonable person of ordinary prudence under the circumstances. In this case, Ann, Bill, and Chuck owed a duty to Paul because it was foreseeable that Paul, as an attendee at the fund-raising lunch, would consume the chicken salad.

Under the doctrine of res ipsa loquitur, the trier of fact may infer the existence of negligence in the absence of direct evidence of such negligence. For the doctrine to apply, the plaintiff must prove that (i) the plaintiff's injury or damage was caused by an instrumentality or condition that was under the defendant's exclusive control or the defendant is responsible for all others in control at the relevant times, (ii) the plaintiff's harm would not have occurred if the defendant had used ordinary care while the instrumentality was under his control, and (iii) the plaintiff was not responsible for his injury.

In this case, the Health Department stated that someone who made the chicken salad did not take proper precautions because salmonella contamination does not occur when chicken is cooked and prepared properly. Paul cannot recover damages based on res ipsa loquitur because Paul cannot establish that any one defendant had exclusive control of the chicken salad. There were two other individuals who made batches of the chicken salad independently.

Additionally, a plaintiff may recover when two or more defendants are negligent and either individual could have caused the plaintiff's injuries. In this case, Paul cannot recover because he cannot show that Ann, Bill, and Chuck were all negligent. Accordingly, Paul cannot recover damages from Ann, Bill, or Chuck on a negligence theory because he cannot show which defendant was negligent.

<u>Strict Liability</u> (15%): The issue is whether Ann, Bill, or Chuck are subject to strict liability. Under strict liability, the seller or other distributor of a defective product may be liable for any harm to persons or property caused by such product. However, to be subject to strict liability for a defective product, the defendant must be in the business of selling or otherwise distributing products of the type that harmed the plaintiff. In this case, the chicken salad sandwich was a defective product because it contained salmonella bacteria. However, Ann, Bill, and Chuck are all volunteers engaged in fund-raising. None of them was in the business of selling or distributing chicken salad sandwiches. Accordingly, none of them would be subject to strict liability for a defective product.

NCBE EDITOR'S NOTES FOR THIS ESSAY QUESTION

- *An applicant could receive extra credit for noting that charitable immunity, which would probably have protected Library from liability in an earlier era, has been abrogated in virtually all jurisdictions.*

(Editor's Note: The foregoing model answer was drafted in accordance with the NCBE Grading Guidelines for this question. The analysis is illustrative of the discussions that might appear in a high passing answer and addresses all legal and factual issues the drafters intended exam candidates to raise. When self-grading, refer to the NCBE's weighting of each issue, which is indicated in parentheses for your reference.)

[END OF HANDOUT]

Themis
Bar Review

TRUSTS ESSAY WRITING WORKSHOP

PROFESSOR CHRISTOPHER IDE-DON

UC DAVIS SCHOOL OF LAW

Summary of Issues Tested

Editor's Note 1: The Professor refers to specific page numbers throughout this lecture. The content does not always match these references due to formatting changes.

A. General Considerations

1. Revocable/Irrevocable Trusts

2. Mandatory/Discretionary Trusts

3. RAP

4. Parties to a Trust

- Settlor; Trustee; Beneficiaries (Income and Remainder)

B. Express Trusts

1. Private Express Trusts—Elements

- Intent, Property, Valid Purpose, Ascertainable Beneficiaries

2. Types of Express Trusts

- Inter Vivos
  - Pour Over Will
- Testamentary

3. Charitable Trusts

- Cy Pres Doctrine

C. Remedial Trusts—Resulting Trust

D. Beneficiary/Creditor Rights to Distribution

- Income Beneficiaries; Remainder Beneficiaries
- Alienation
- Support Trusts
- Discretionary Trust
- Mandatory Trust
- Spendthrift Trust

E. Trust Modification and Termination

- Settlor's Power
- Beneficiaries
- Trustee

F. Future Interests

- Disclaimer
- Class Gifts
- Lapse/Anti-Lapse

G. Trustee's Powers, Duties, and Remedies for Breach of Duties

- Trustee Powers
- Duty of Loyalty
- Duty of Prudence
    - Prudent Investor Rule
    - Duty to Diversify
    - Duty to Make Trust Property Productive
    - Duty to be Impartial
- Duty to Disclose
- Duty to Account
- Remedies

CHAPTER 1: ESSAY APPROACHES

A. General Considerations

1. Revocable versus Irrevocable Trusts

A revocable trust can be terminated by the settlor at any time. An irrevocable trust usually cannot be terminated.

Majority rule—a trust is presumed to be irrevocable unless it expressly states otherwise.

Uniform Trust Code (UTC), and in a minority of jurisdictions—a trust is presumed revocable unless it expressly states that it is irrevocable.

> **Exam Tip 1:** Be on the lookout for facts that specify whether the trust is revocable or irrevocable.

2. Mandatory versus Discretionary Trusts

A mandatory trust requires the trustee to distribute all trust income. In a discretionary trust, the trustee is given the power to distribute income at his discretion. The trustee does not abuse his discretion unless he acts dishonestly or in a way not contemplated by the trust creator.

3. Rule Against Perpetuities

Trusts are subject to the Rule Against Perpetuities. Therefore, a trust may fail if all interests thereunder may not vest within the applicable period of perpetuities (usually a life in being plus 21 years). Some jurisdictions take a "wait and see" approach to the application of the rule, refraining from invalidating future interests until it is clear that they will not vest within the perpetuities period.

> **Exam Tip 2:** Not a frequently tested issue.

4. Parties to a Trust

- **Grantor/Settlor**—the creator of the trust.
- **Trustee**—holds legal interest or title to trust property.
- **Beneficiaries**—receive the benefit of the trust.
  - **Income Beneficiaries**—receive income from the trust (e.g., profits from a business held by the trust).
  - **Remainder Beneficiaries**—entitled to the trust principal upon termination of the trust.

B. Express Trusts

> **Exam Tip 3:** If the facts state that there is a valid trust, you do not have to analyze the elements of a trust.

1. Private Express Trust

A private express trust clearly states the intention of the settlor to transfer property to a trustee for the benefit of one or more ascertainable beneficiaries.

a. Intent

The settlor must intend to make a gift in trust. The settlor's intent may be manifested orally, in writing, or by conduct.

b. Trust property

A valid trust must contain some property that was owned by the settlor at the time the trust was created and was at that time transferred to the trust or to the trustee. Any property interest, including real property, personal property, money, intangibles, partial interests, or future interests (whether vested or contingent) are sufficient.

c. Valid trust purpose

A trust can be created for any purpose, as long as it is not illegal, restricted by rule of law or statute, or contrary to public policy. Terms that violate public policy will be stricken from the trust; the trust will not fail overall unless the removal of the terms is fatal.

(Recently tested): Trust provisions that restrain a first marriage have generally been held to violate public policy. However, a restraint on marriage might be upheld if the trustee's motive was merely to provide support for a beneficiary while the beneficiary is single.

d. Ascertainable beneficiaries

- The beneficiaries must be identifiable so that the equitable interest can be transferred automatically by operation of law and directly benefit the person.
- The settlor may refer to outside writings or acts to identify beneficiaries.
- Exceptions to Identifiable Beneficiaries:
  - **Indefinite Class:** A trustee can select a beneficiary from an indefinite class (such as "my friends"), unless the trustee must distribute equally to all members of the indefinite class (not valid).
  - **Unborn children:** Trusts for the benefit of unborn children are valid, even though the beneficiaries are not yet ascertainable at the time the trust is created.
  - **Class Gifts:** Trusts for a reasonably definite class (such as "my brothers", or "my grandchildren") will be upheld.
  - **Charitable trusts** (trusts that exist for the good of the public at large) must not have individual ascertainable beneficiaries.

2. Types of Private Express Trusts

a. Inter vivos trust

An inter vivos trust is a trust created while the trustor is living that transfers some or all of the trustor's property into a trust. The trustor can designate himself or a third party as the trustee.

- **Pour-Over Provision:** A pour-over is a provision in a will that directs the distribution of property to a trust upon the happening of an event, so that the property passes according to the terms of the trust without the necessity of the will reciting the entire trust.
- **(Recently Tested):** A will may "pour over" estate assets into a trust, even if the trust instrument was not executed in accordance with the Statute of Wills, as long as the trust is identified in the will, and its terms are set forth in a written instrument.
  - A later amendment to the trust will apply to the assets passed to the trust by the previously executed pour-over will.
  - The amendment does not have to be executed with formalities prescribed for the execution of a will. No witness or signature requirements!

b. Testamentary trust

A testamentary trust is created in writing in a will or in a document incorporated by reference into a will. The will containing the trust must meet the attested or holographic will requirements.

3. Charitable Trusts

For a trust to be considered charitable, it must have a stated charitable purpose and it must exist for the benefit of the community at large or for a class of persons the membership in which varies.

a. Charitable Purpose

Purposes considered to be charitable include the relief of poverty, the advancement of education or religion, and other purposes benefiting the community at large or a particular segment of the community.

b. Indefinite Beneficiaries

The community at large, or a class comprising unidentifiable members, not a named individual or a narrow group of individuals, must be the beneficiary of a charitable trust.

c. Rule Against Perpetuities

Charitable trusts are not subject to the Rule Against Perpetuities and may continue indefinitely.

d. Cy Pres Doctrine (Recently Tested)

A court may modify a charitable trust to seek an alternative charitable purpose if the original one becomes illegal, impracticable, or impossible to perform.

> **Exam Tip 4:** Look for facts indicating that a trust was created for the benefit of a charity that no longer exists (such as a retirement home, college or university, or zoo). There will usually be a similar charity that is in existence and it will ask the court to modify the trust and substitute it as the beneficiary of the trust.

- **Specific or General Intent:** To determine whether it should modify the trust, a court will analyze whether the trust has a specific intent to help one charity or a general intent to help charity.
  - If there is **specific intent**, the court may not modify the trust and the trust will be terminated and become a resulting trust (an implied trust that is held for the settlor or his/her heirs).
  - If there is **general intent**, the court will substitute a similar charity.
  - The modern approach is to presume a general intent and apply the cy pres doctrine.

> **Exam Tip 5:** To earn full credit on the exam, you must carefully analyze whether the trustor intended for the trust to only benefit one specific charity (such as one specific retirement home), or if the trustor intended to generally benefit charity (all retirement homes).

C. Remedial Trusts

1. Resulting Trust

When a trust fails in some way or when there is an incomplete disposition of trust property, a court may create a resulting trust requiring the holder of the property to return it to the settlor or to the settlor's estate. When a testamentary trust fails, the residuary legatee succeeds to the property interest. The purpose of a resulting trust is to achieve the settlor's likely intent in attempting to create the trust.

CHAPTER 2: BENEFICIARY/CREDITOR RIGHTS TO DISTRIBUTION; MODIFICATION AND TERMINATION

A. Beneficiary/Creditor Rights to Distribution

- **Income Beneficiaries:** Receive income from the trust (example, profits from a business held by the trust).
- **Remainder Beneficiaries:** Entitled to the trust principal upon termination of trust.
- **Creditors (Recently tested):** A beneficiary's creditors may reach trust principal or income only when such amounts become payable to the beneficiary or are subject to her demand.

1. Alienation

A beneficiary's equitable interest in trust property is freely alienable (it can be sold or used as collateral for a loan) unless a statute or trust instrument limits this right.

2. Support Trusts

A support trust directs the trustee to pay income or principal as necessary to support the trust beneficiary. Creditors cannot reach the assets of a support trust, except to the extent that a provider of a necessity to the beneficiary can be paid directly by the trustee.

3. Discretionary Trust

The trustee is given complete discretion regarding whether or not to apply payments of income/principal to the beneficiary.

If the trustee exercises his discretion to pay, then the beneficiary's creditors have the same rights as the beneficiary, unless a spendthrift restriction exists. If the discretion to pay is not exercised, then the beneficiary's interest cannot be reached by his creditors.

The beneficiary of a fully discretionary trust lacks standing to challenge the actions or inactions of the trustee unless there is a clear abuse of discretion.

4. Mandatory Trust

Trustee has no discretion; the trust governs when trust property is to be distributed.

5. Spendthrift Trust

A spendthrift trust expressly restricts beneficiary's power to voluntarily or involuntarily transfer his equitable interest (this is called a spendthrift clause).

Creditors usually cannot reach the trust interest, unless money is owed for child/spousal support, or to basic necessities providers, or tax lien holders.

B. Trust Modification and Termination

1. Settlor's Power to Revoke or Amend

If a settlor of a trust retains the power to revoke a trust, she also has a power to modify or amend the trust. In the absence of such a reservation, modification or termination can occur only with the consent of all beneficiaries and if the proposed change will not interfere with a primary purpose of the trust.

- Under the **majority rule**—a trust is presumed to be irrevocable unless it expressly states otherwise.
- Under the **Uniform Trust Code (UTC) and in a minority of jurisdictions**—a trust is presumed revocable unless it expressly states that it is irrevocable.
- An amendment to a trust does not have be executed with the formalities prescribed for the execution of a will. No witness or signature requirements!

2. Beneficiaries

- A trust terminates automatically only when the trust purpose has been accomplished.
- A trust may also terminate if the settlor is deceased/has no remaining interest, and all the beneficiaries (this includes the income beneficiaries and remainder beneficiaries) consent. However, a trustee can block a premature trust termination by the beneficiaries if the trust is shown to have an unfulfilled material purpose.
- The most common example of a trust that has an unfulfilled material purpose is one in which the settlor provided for successive interests, in which case both the present and the future beneficiaries must agree in order for the trust to be terminated prematurely.

3. Trustee

- **Trustee's Power to Terminate**—none, unless the trust contains express termination provisions.
- **Removal of Trustee**—a court can remove a trustee if the purpose of the trust would be frustrated by the trustee's continuance in office or if the trustee violated a duty.

CHAPTER 3: FUTURE INTERESTS; FIDUCIARY DUTIES

A. Future Interests

1. Disclaimer

Almost all states have enacted statutes that permit beneficiaries of trusts to disclaim their interest in the trust property. In most states, a disclaimer is not effective unless it is reduced to writing within nine months after the future interest would become "indefeasibly vested." If the income beneficiary of a trust disclaims her interest, then the trust principal becomes immediately distributable (accelerates) to the remainder beneficiaries of the trust if the remainder is vested. If the remainder is contingent upon a condition, the remainder will not accelerate.

> ***Example 1:*** *A testator creates a valid testamentary trust. Under the terms of the trust, all trust income would be paid to the testator's son during his lifetime, and upon his death, the trust assets would be distributed to the testator's grandson. The testator dies. One week later, the testator's son effectively disclaims his interest in the trust income.*
>
> *Analysis: Because the testator's son is the income beneficiary and effectively disclaimed his income interest, the trust principal is automatically distributable to the grandson (the remainder beneficiary) because the grandson's interest is vested (there is no contingency that must be met here).*

When the holder of a future interest effectively disclaims that interest, the disclaimant is deemed to have predeceased the life tenant.

> ***Example 2:*** *A testator creates a valid testamentary trust. Under the terms of the trust, all trust income would be paid to the testator's son during his lifetime, and upon his death, the trust assets would be distributed to the testator's grandson. The testator dies. Within nine months, the testator's grandson effectively disclaims his future interest in the trust principal.*
>
> *Analysis: The income from the trust is paid to the son for as long as he lives. When the son dies, because the grandson effectively disclaimed his interest, the trust principal reverts back to the testator's estate or, if the anti-lapse rules apply, the trust principal will go to the grandson's issue.*

2. Class Gifts

Class gifts are generally permissible. The settlor can make "my children" the beneficiaries of the trust.

Class Gifts to Surviving Children—see outline for details.

> ***Example 3:*** *A settlor placed his assets in a trust. The terms of the trust provided that the trust principal was to be paid on his death to his surviving*

children equally. At the time of the creation of the trust, the settlor had three children, A, B, and C. A predeceased the settlor, but was survived by a child. The settlor has recently died, survived by B, C, and D.

Analysis: Under common law, the trust principal would be divided equally between B and C because A predeceased the settlor. Under the UPC, the trust principal would be divided equally between B, C, and D because A had a child who survived the settlor.

3. Lapse of a Gift

In most states, anti-lapse statutes do not apply to nonprobate gifts, and, therefore, if a gift to "issue" fails by reason of the non-survival of the issue, then children and further descendants of the deceased issue will not take under the trust.

However, some states have enacted UPC § 2-707 or a similar statute, under which a substitute gift is created in the descendants of the deceased issue. When such statutes govern, even words of survivorship (e.g., "to those of my issue who are living") will not cut off this substitute gift.

B. Trustee's Powers, Duties, Remedies for Breach of Duties

1. Trustee Powers

The trustee has powers granted expressly in the trust, and powers necessary to act as a reasonably prudent person in managing the trust, including the implied power to contract, sell, lease, or transfer the trust property.

2. Duty of Loyalty

Duty to administer trust in good faith (subjective standard) and to act reasonably (objective standard) when investing property and otherwise managing the trust solely in the best interests of the beneficiaries.

a. Self-Dealing

- When the trustee personally engages in a transaction involving trust property, a conflict of interest arises between the trustee's duties to the beneficiaries and her own personal interest.
- **Prohibited transactions**—buying/selling trust assets, selling property between trusts that trustee manages, borrowing from or making loans to trust, using trust assets to secure personal loan, engaging in prohibited transactions with friends/relatives, or otherwise acting for personal gain through trustee position.
- There is an irrebuttable presumption that trustee breached duty of loyalty when self-dealing is an issue; no further inquiry into trustee's reasonableness or good faith is required because self-dealing is a per se breach.

- **Exceptions:** Even when self-dealing is authorized (by settlor, court order, or all beneficiaries), transaction must still be reasonable and fair to avoid liability for breach.
- **Remedy:** The beneficiaries can set aside the transaction or ratify the transaction and recover the profits from the transaction.

b. Conflict of Interest

- When a trustee invests trust assets in a corporation in which the trustee has an interest (for example, owns stock in the corporation) that might affect the trustee's judgment, a conflict of interest arises.
- There is a presumption of a breach of the duty of loyalty that can be rebutted by showing that the terms of the transaction were fair or that the transaction would have been made by an independent party.

3. Duty of Prudence

- General duty to act as a reasonably prudent person and treat the trust property as if it was his/her own.
- Duty to follow the trust directions and carry them out in accordance with the trust.
- **(Frequently Tested) Investments:**
    - **Prudent Investor Rule:** Requires trustee to act as a prudent investor would act when investing his own property (putting less emphasis on risk level); trustee must exercise reasonable care, caution, and skill when investing and managing trust assets.
    - **Duty to Diversify:** Trustee must adequately diversify the trust investments in order to spread the risk of loss under a total performance portfolio approach, but not if administrative costs would outweigh the benefits.
    - **Duty to Make Property Productive:** Pursue all possible claims, derive the maximum amount of income from investments, sell assets when appropriate, secure insurance, pay expenses, and act within a reasonable period of time in all matters.

      Example 4: *If the trust contains rental property, the trustee has a duty to try and rent the property; a failure to try and rent the property would be a breach of duty.*

    - **Duty to be Impartial:** Balance interests of the present beneficiaries (must not favor one of the present beneficiaries over the others, unless trust provides for it).

      Example 5: *Settlor's trust states that Trustee is to equally distribute the rent from an apartment to S's three children, A, B, and C. A suffers from a health condition and is unable to work. Trustee distributes 2/3 of the rent from the apartment to A and only 1/3 to B and C. Trustee has breached his duty of impartiality.*

- **Additional Duty to be Impartial:** The Trustee must balance the interests of the present and future beneficiaries by investing property so that it produces a reasonable income for the income beneficiaries while preserving the principal for the remainder beneficiaries.

  Example 6: *Settlor's trust states that A and B are to receive the income from the trust for life (A and B are therefore present income beneficiaries) and upon their death all of the trust assets are to go to C (C is a remainder beneficiary). Trustee invests the trust money into a high risk stock that pays frequent and substantial dividends (trust income), but the stock decreases in value by 50%. The present income beneficiaries, A and B, are receiving high income, but the remainder beneficiaries will receive a reduced principal; this would be a breach of duty of impartiality.*

4. Other Duties

- **Duty to Disclose:** Disclose complete and accurate information about nature and extent of the trust property, including allowing access to trust records and accounts.
- **Duty to Account:** Periodically account for actions taken on behalf of the trust so that trustee's performance can be assessed against the terms of the trust.
- **Remedies for Violation of Trustee's Duties:** Lost profits, interests, and other losses resulting from a breach of trust are trustee's responsibility; beneficiaries may sue the trustee and seek damages or removal of the trustee for breach of duties.

CHAPTER 4: PRACTICE QUESTION

July 2007, Question 6 [ID 3569]

In 1995, a man and his friend created a corporation. The man owned 55% of the stock, and the friend owned 45% of the stock. When the man died in 2005, he left all of his stock in the corporation to his wife.

In 2009, the wife died. Under her duly probated will, the wife bequeathed the stock her husband had left her to a testamentary trust and named her husband's friend as trustee. Under the wife's will, the trustee was required to distribute all trust income to the wife's son "for so long as he shall live or until such time as he shall marry" and, upon the son's death or marriage, to distribute the trust principal to a designated charity. The stock, valued at $500,000 at the wife's death, comprised the only asset of this trust.

In 2013, after the stock's value had risen to $1.5 million, the trustee's lawyer properly advised the trustee to sell the stock in order to comply with the state's prudent investor act. Because of this advice, the trustee decided to sell the stock. However, instead of testing the market for potential buyers, the trustee purchased the stock himself for $1.2 million. Thereafter, on behalf of the trust, the trustee invested the $1.2 million sales proceeds in a balanced portfolio of five mutual funds (including both stocks and bonds) with strong growth and current income potential.

Recently, both the son and the charity discovered the trustee's sale of the stock to himself and his reinvestment of the proceeds from the stock's sale. They learned that, due to general economic conditions, the stock in the corporation that had been purchased by the trustee for $1.2 million had declined in value to $450,000 and the value of the trust's mutual-fund portfolio had declined from $1.2 million to $1 million. Both the son and the charity have threatened to sue the trustee.

The son has also decided that he wants to get married and has notified the trustee that he believes the trust provision terminating his income interest upon marriage is invalid.

1. Would the son's interest in the trust terminate upon the son's marriage? Explain.

2. Did the trustee breach any duties by buying the trust's stock and, if yes, what remedies are available to the trust beneficiaries if they sue the trustee? Explain.

3. Did the trustee breach any duties in acquiring and retaining the portfolio of mutual funds and, if yes, what remedies are available to the trust beneficiaries if they sue the trustee? Explain.

Sample Answer

1. The issue is whether a trust condition providing for the termination of an income interest upon marriage is invalid as a matter of public policy. (30%)

A trust can be created for any purpose, as long as it is not illegal, restricted by rule of law or statute, or contrary to public policy. Trust provisions that restrain a first marriage have generally been held to violate public policy. However, a restraint on marriage might be upheld if the trustee's motive was merely to provide support for a beneficiary while the beneficiary is single.

Here, because the trust provides that the son's income interest would terminate upon his marriage no matter what the circumstances of that marriage, the provision appears to be void for public policy. There are no facts to suggest that the trust is only intended to support the son while he is single. On the contrary, this is a mandatory trust, so the trust income is payable to the son without considering how much financial support he needs.

Thus, the marital restraint is void as a matter of public policy, and the son's income interest should continue.

2. The issues are whether the trustee violated his duty of loyalty by purchasing the stock from the trust and, if so, what remedies are available. (35%)

A trustee is bound by a broad range of fiduciary duties, including a duty of loyalty. When a trustee personally engages in a transaction involving the trust property, a conflict of interest arises between the trustee's duties to the beneficiaries and her own personal interest. A trustee buying or selling trust assets is considered self-dealing, even if the transaction occurred at fair market value. When self-dealing is established, an irrebuttable presumption is created that the trustee breached the duty of loyalty. No further inquiry into the trustee's reasonableness or good faith will be required, because self-dealing is a per se breach of the duty of loyalty. When the duty of loyalty is breached, any beneficiary has standing against the trustee if his interests are violated, and he can choose either to set aside the transaction or to ratify the transaction and recover any profits therefrom.

Here, the trustee breached his duty of loyalty by purchasing stock from the trust because the purchase was an act of self-dealing. This is a per se breach of the duty of loyalty, and therefore, neither the reasonableness of the transaction nor the trustee's good faith are relevant. The trust beneficiaries may obtain an order setting aside the transaction or seek damages. Rescission would return the shares to the trust, but the trust would have to refund the purchase price to the trustee, leaving the trust with assets worth only $450,000. By seeking damages instead, the trust would collect $300,000, representing the difference between the value of the shares when purchased by the trustee and the purchase price.

Thus, the trustee has breached the duty of loyalty, and the trust beneficiaries should seek damages.

3. The issue is whether the trustee violated the prudent investor rule by retaining mutual fund investments after they declined in value. (35%)

The Uniform Prudent Investor Act (the "UPIA") requires the trustee to act as a prudent investor would when investing his own property. The trustee must exercise reasonable care, caution, and skill when investing and managing trust assets unless the trustee has special skills or expertise, in which case he has a duty to utilize such assets. Determinations of compliance under the UPIA are made with reference to the facts and circumstances as they existed at the time the action was made, and they do not utilize hindsight. Part of being prudent is taking care to make informed decisions regarding the investment scheme and/or delegating such decision-making to an expert. In assessing whether a trustee has breached this duty, the UPIA requires consideration of numerous factors, including (i) the distribution requirements of the trust, (ii) the general economic conditions, (iii) the role that the investment plays in relationship to the trust's overall investment portfolio, and (iv) the trust's need for liquidity, regularity of income, and preservation or appreciation of capital. Although the trustee must adequately diversify the trust investments to spread the risk of loss, investing in one mutual fund may be sufficient if the fund is sufficiently diversified.

Here, the trustee diversified the assets among five mutual funds when one may have been sufficient. Because growth funds are aimed at achieving principal appreciation and income funds at producing current income, the trustee also appears to have considered the needs of both the income beneficiary and remainderman. There are no facts to show any failure to monitor the portfolio.

Thus, there are no facts suggesting that the trustee breached any prudent investment duty with respect to the selection of the investments he made.

(Editor's Note: The foregoing model answer was drafted in accordance with the NCBE Grading Guidelines for this question. The analysis is illustrative of the discussions that might appear in a high passing answer and addresses all legal and factual issues the drafters intended exam candidates to raise. When self-grading, refer to the NCBE's weighting of each issue, which is indicated in parentheses for your reference.)

[END OF HANDOUT]

Themis
Bar Review

WILLS AND DECEDENTS' ESTATES ESSAY WORKSHOP

PROFESSOR CHRISTOPHER IDE-DON
UC DAVIS SCHOOL OF LAW

CHAPTER 1: INTESTACY

Editor's Note 1: The Professor refers to specific page numbers throughout this lecture. The content does not always match these references due to formatting changes.

- **Intestacy**
  - Spouses
  - Issue – Per Capita with Representation
- **Execution of Wills**
  - Capacity
  - Intent
  - Attested Will
  - Holographic wills
  - Codicils
  - Will Substitute – Deed
  - Choice of Law
- **Revocation**
  - Prior to death—subsequent instrument, physical act, operation of law
  - Revocation of Codicil
  - Revival
  - Republication
  - Dependent Relative Revocation (DRR) doctrine
- **Construction**
  - Integration
  - Incorporation by reference
  - Acts of independent significance
  - Specific v. General devises
  - Abatement
  - Ademption
  - Lapse & Anti-lapse
  - Ambiguities
- **Power to transfer**

- Surviving spouse rights
- Omitted spouse and children

- **Will contests**
  - Insane delusion
  - Undue influence
  - Fraud in the inducement

A. Intestacy

> **Exam Tip 1:** If a person dies without a will, or if a will is found to be invalid, the estate will be distributed following the intestacy rules below. A typical exam question will have a disputed will that might be valid. The question will usually ask you to discuss the distribution of assets if the will is valid and if the will is not valid.

1. Uniform Probate Code (UPC) Approach

- The surviving spouse gets 100% of the estate if the decedent's only surviving relatives are also surviving relatives of the surviving spouse (example: children that decedent and surviving spouse had together), and the surviving spouse does not have any other descendants.
- The surviving spouse gets $300,000 and 75% of the remainder of the estate if no descendant is alive at the time of decedent's death, but there is a surviving a parent of the decedent.
- The surviving spouse receives $225,000 and 50% of the remainder of the estate if all of the decedent's issue are also issue of the surviving spouse, and the surviving spouse has other issue.
- If the decedent has issue not related to the surviving spouse, then the surviving spouse receives $150,000 and 50% of the remainder of the estate.
- If the decedent has a spouse but no descendants or parents, then the surviving spouse takes the entire estate.

2. Community Property Rules—do not apply unless the exam question states that the jurisdiction applies Community Property rules.

a. Community Property

At death, the surviving spouse is entitled to 1/2 of the Community Property (CP). The surviving spouse of an intestate decedent is also entitled to the decedent's 1/2 CP and quasi-CP. Therefore, the surviving spouse will take 100% of the CP.

B. Surviving Spouses

- To be entitled to take under an intestacy statute, the surviving spouse must have been legally married to the decedent.
- **Putative spouses:** Even if a marriage is not valid, as long as one party believes in good faith in its validity, the spouses are termed putative and qualify as spouses for inheritance purposes.

- **Uniform Probate Code:** The surviving spouse must be legally married to the decedent at the time of death, and there must be clear and convincing evidence that he/she survived the decedent by 120 hours to take by intestacy.

C. Issue

Issue refers to lineal descendants of the testator, including children, grandchildren, and great-grandchildren.

1. Adoption

- Adoption curtails all inheritance rights between the natural parents and the child.
- Adopted children take the same as a natural child.

2. Non-Marital Children

- The common-law rule was that if a child was born out of wedlock (mother and father are not married when child is born), then she could not inherit from her natural father.
- The modern trend adopted by most jurisdictions is that an out-of-wedlock child cannot inherit from her natural father unless:
  - The father subsequently married the natural mother; or
  - The father held the child out as his own and either received the child into his home or provided support; or
  - Paternity was proven by clear and convincing evidence after the father's death; or
  - Paternity was adjudicated during the lifetime of the father by a preponderance of the evidence.

D. Calculating Share – Per Capita with Representation

> **Editorial Note 1:** For purposes of the MEE, examinees should be prepared to discuss all three approaches to intestacy: per stirpes, per capita with representation, and per capita at each generation (UPC). Although per capita with representation is an emerging trend, there is still no definitive majority approach. Please see the substantive Wills and Decedents' Estates Lecture for more details about these approaches.

1. **Per Capita**—If the surviving issue are all of equal degree of kinship (all the same level of relation to the decedent), the property passes equally to each person.

2. **Per Capita with Representation**—If the surviving issue are not of equal kinship, the property is divided at the first generation in which at least one member survives the decedent. The shares that would go to the member that predeceased the decedent would go to his/her issue.

   Example 1: *Decedent had two sons, A and B. He dies without a will. A survives the decedent (is still alive), but B died before Decedent. B is survived by two children, C and D (grandchildren of Decedent). Under Per Capita with Representation, the property would be divided between A and B because A is the first generation where issue is still living. A would get 1/2 of the estate. B is* *dead, so he would not get anything. Instead, B's children, C and D, would take B's share and split the other 1/2 of the estate equally and receive 1/4 each.*

3. **Ancestors and Remote Collaterals**—If no surviving spouse or issue exist, then the property may be distributed to the decedent's ancestors (e.g., parents, grandparents, great-grandparents) and more remote collateral relatives (i.e., those related to the decedent through a common ancestor, such as siblings, cousins, aunts, and uncles).

4. **UPC Approach**—If there is no surviving spouse or descendant, then the estate passes in the following order to the individuals designated below who survive the decedent:

    - To the decedent's parents equally if both survive, or to the surviving parent;
    - Then to the descendants of the decedent's parents;
    - Then the estate passes to the decedent's maternal and paternal grandparent, one-half to each, or to the descendants of the decedent's maternal and paternal grandparents if the grandparents are deceased;
    - Then the entire estate passes to the decedent's nearest maternal and paternal relative; and
    - If there are no surviving relatives, then the estate escheats to the state.

CHAPTER 2: EXECUTION OF WILLS

Exam Tip 2: If the fact pattern states that there is a valid will, you do not have to discuss the execution of the will. However, if the facts do not state that there is a valid will, you must discuss whether the will was validly executed. If there are multiple wills or codicils in the fact pattern, discuss each one in the order presented.

Exam Tip 3: You should always discuss Capacity and Testamentary Intent when analyzing whether a will was validly executed.

A. Capacity

The testator must be at least 18 years old and possess a sound mind. The testator lacks the requisite mental capacity if he, at the time of execution, did not have the ability to know the:

- Nature of the act;
- Nature and character of his property;
- Natural objects of his bounty; and
- Plan of the attempted disposition.

B. Testamentary Intent

The testator must understand he is executing a will and intend for it to have testamentary effect, and must generally know and approve of its contents.

C. Attested (Witnessed) Wills

1. **Writing & Signature:** The will must be in writing and signed by the testator (T), or by some other person in his presence and at his direction.

2. Witnesses

- **Majority view:** The will must be signed in the joint presence of and attested to by two witnesses.
- **UPC:** The witnesses do not have to be present at the same time. Also, the T does not have to sign in their presence, as long as he acknowledges his signature to them before they sign and they sign within a reasonable time.
- Each witness must be of sufficient mental capacity and maturity.

a. Interested Witness

- At common law, a witness who has a financial interest in the will is an "interested witness" and is not competent to be a witness to the will. If the interested witness is a necessary witness, the will has not been validly executed.
- Today, many states invalidate the portion of the will that provides an excess portion to the interested witness (any amount in excess of what the witness would otherwise have received).
- The UPC has now abolished the interested witness doctrine.

D. Compliance ("Substantial Compliance")

> **Exam Tip 4:** You should discuss "substantial compliance" if you determine that a will was not validly executed. Then, you should discuss the outcome if the will is treated as valid and the outcome if the will is not treated as valid.

- At common law, **strict compliance** with the formalities was required.
- Under the UPC, a will that is not executed in compliance with the law will treated as if it were valid if there is clear and convincing evidence that the testator intended for the document to serve as his will and he has **substantially complied** with the required formalities.

E. Holographic Wills

> **Exam Tip 5:** If you determine that a document does not meet the requirements of an attested will, you should consider whether there is a valid holographic (handwritten) will.

- T must handwrite the "material provisions" of a holographic will. "Material provisions" include the beneficiaries of the will and the items that they will receive. A preprinted will form can still be a valid holographic will, as long as the "material provisions" are handwritten.
- T must sign the instrument.
- **No witness requirement:** Although it need not be witnessed or dated, it must be clear that T intended the document to be a will.

F. Codicils

- A codicil is a supplement to a will that alters, amends, or modifies the will, rather than replacing it. Generally, a codicil must be executed with the same formalities as a will (can be attested or holographic).

Exam Tip 6: Be sure to clearly explain how the codicil is changing the terms of the original will AND whether the codicil was executed properly.

- **Republication Date:** A validly executed codicil republishes a will as of the date of the codicil.

  Example 2: *A will is created in 2000. A valid codicil to the will is executed in 2002. The date of publication of the will (including the codicil) will now be considered 2002.*

- **Cure Invalid Will:** A valid codicil executed after the original will may cures problems that existed at the execution of the will, such as an insufficient number of witnesses.

  Example 3: *T attempts to execute an attested will in 2000, but there is only one witness, so the will is not valid. T executes an attested codicil to will in 2002 that is properly witnessed by two people. If the codicil incorporates by reference the will from 2000, the will from 2000 will be valid and include the 2002 codicil.*

- **Attested Will and Holographic Codicil:** A valid attested will can be altered, amended, or modified by a holographic codicil.

  Example 4: *A valid attested will is executed in 2000 leaving $1 million dollars to C. In 2002, Testator crosses out the $1 million dollar amount and handwrites a statement on the will that he intends to leave $2 million dollars to C. Testator signs and dates below his statement. Under the UPC, Testator has met the formalities of a holographic codicil (signed writing, dated, testator's intent in his own handwriting, no witnesses required) and C is now entitled to $2 million dollars.*

G. Will Substitutes

1. Trusts

A trust may achieve the results of a will.

2. Pour-over Wills

A pour-over will includes a clause wherein some or all of the decedent's probate property is given to the trustee of the decedent's inter vivos trust.

3. Deeds

A deed of property can serve as a will substitute for transferring property upon the death of the landowner. If a grantor (owner of land) delivers a deed to a third party (agent) with instructions to give the deed to a person (grantee) upon the grantor's death, the deed will serve as a will substitute and the deed will be transferred to grantee upon the grantor's death.

H. Conflict of Laws

1. Personal Property

Questions regarding the validity of a decedent's will regarding personal property and the transfer of personal property from someone who dies intestate or who has a will are governed by the law of the deceased's domicile at the time of death.

2. Real property

Questions regarding the validity of a decedent's will regarding real property and the transfer of real property from someone who dies intestate or who has a will are governed by the law of the situs (location of the property).

> **Editor's Note 2:** This issue regarding a conflict of laws is discussed in the Conflicts of Law outline at II.C.4.

CHAPTER 3: REVOCATION AND REVIVAL

A. Revocation

> **Exam Tip 7:** A will or codicil may be revoked in whole, or in part, any time prior to death of the testator by a subsequent writing, physical destruction, or by operation of law.

1. Subsequent Instrument

A testator can revoke a will or codicil by executing a later valid will or codicil that partly or completely revokes the prior will or codicil. Oral revocations are not valid.

Partial or Complete Revocation: A revocation can be partial (part of the original will or codicil is revoked, but part of it is not) or complete (the entire original will or codicil is revoked).

> **Exam Tip 8:** When discussing revocation by will or codicil, carefully analyze and explain whether the original will or codicil is partially or completely revoked; consider both sides of the argument.

Express or Implied: The revocation can be express (the new will or codicil expressly states that it is revoking the prior will or codicil) or can be implied (the terms of the new will or codicil conflict with the terms of the prior will or codicil) by the terms of the subsequent instrument.

> **Exam Tip 9:** Implied revocation—be sure to explain why the new will or codicil conflicts with the prior will. For example, the original will gives testator's house to B. A subsequent codicil gives the house to C. The testator has impliedly revoked the gift of the house to B.

Inconsistencies: If there are inconsistencies between the prior will or codicil and the subsequent will or codicil, the later document controls and revokes the prior inconsistencies.

2. **Physical Destruction**

A will or codicil may be partially or completely revoked by destroying a portion of the will or codicil with the intent to revoke it. The act of destruction must occur with the intent to revoke (simultaneous act and intent).

Majority Rule: The majority rule is that an effective canceling of a will requires defacement of the language of the will (i.e., at least some of the language must be crossed out, including the signature).

UPC: rejects the majority rule; the destructive act must merely affect some part of the will.

If a will once known to exist cannot be found at the testator's death, or is found mutilated, then there is a rebuttable presumption of revocation. The presumption is inapplicable if a duplicate original is found. Extrinsic evidence is permitted to rebut the presumption.

Destruction of a signed original or duplicate original presumptively destroys all copies.

A third party can revoke through physical destruction of the will or codicil on behalf of the testator if it is requested by testator and destroyed in testator's presence.

3. **Revocation by Operation of Law – Divorce**

In most states, divorce revokes all will provisions in favor of the former spouse, unless it can be shown that the testator intended for the will to survive. Separation does not revoke the will provisions unless there is a separation agreement.

4. **Alteration**

A testator cannot increase a gift to a beneficiary by canceling words in his will, but he may be able to decrease the gift as long as the alteration is made to the existing language of the will rather than through the addition of new language.

5. **Holographic Wills**

A holographic will can be altered or revoked in whole or in part by holographic changes, but must be signed under the UPC.

B. **Revival**

Exam Tip 10: Look for fact patterns where there a valid will and a later will or codicil is created, revoking the original will. If the later will or codicil is subsequently destroyed, the original will may be revived.

1. **Republication**

Revocation of a later will or codicil that revokes the original will revives the original will if there is proof that the testator intended to revive the original will. If the later will or codicil is revoked by physical act, **extrinsic evidence** of testator's intent to revive the original will is admissible.

2. Dependent Relative Revocation (DRR)

> **Exam Tip 11:** DRR should be discussed when a testator revokes the original will under a mistaken belief of law or fact. DRR will revive the original will if the testator would not have revoked the original will but for the mistake of law or fact.

The doctrine of Dependent Relative Revocation (DRR) will allow a court to revive a revoked will when the testator revoked the will by subsequent instrument or physical act under a mistaken belief of law or fact. It must be shown that the testator would not have revoked the original will but for the mistaken belief.

> ***Example 5:*** *T creates a valid will giving B $10,000. Later, T attempts to create a second will giving B $20,000, but the testator does not know that the second will is actually invalid. T tears up the first will (physically revoking it), mistakenly believing that the second will is valid. T dies one year later. Because the second will is invalid and the first will was physically revoked, B would take nothing. However, applying DRR, a court will revive the first will because T mistakenly believed the second will was valid when he tore up the first will. B will take $10,000 under the first will.*

CHAPTER 4: CONSTRUCTION OF WILLS

A. Construction

Construction of a will requires a court to determine the terms of the will and how to distribute the estate.

1. Integration

Under the doctrine of Integration, the will consists of all pages that are present at the time of execution and that are intended to form part of the will, which can be shown by physical connection of the pages (stapled or paper clipped together) or by the ongoing nature of the language of the will (pages are not attached, but page numbers indicate that the pages follow each other).

2. Incorporation by Reference

> **Exam Tip 12:** Look for facts where a testator's will or codicil mentions or references a separate document. The separate document may be "incorporated" into the will or codicil and the terms of the document will be followed as if they were part of the will or codicil document.

A writing not executed with testamentary formalities may be incorporated by reference if it existed at the time the will was executed, is intended to be incorporated, and is described in the will or codicil with sufficient certainty.

UPC: The writing need not exist at the time the will was executed if it only disposes of the T's personal property (in other words, the testator can write a will referencing another document and then create the document later).

A validly executed codicil can incorporate an invalid will and make the terms of the will valid.

> ***Example 6:*** *T creates a typewritten will giving his house to J that is invalid because there are no witnesses. Later, T executes a valid typewritten and witnessed codicil stating that that he is now giving his house to B; he also states that everything else in his original will document is to be followed. T has executed a valid codicil and the terms of the original will document are now incorporated by his reference in the codicil (the terms of the original will are now valid).*

3. Acts of Independent Significance

A will can provide for designation of a beneficiary or amount of a disposition by reference to some unattested act or event occurring before or after execution of the will or the T's death, if the act or event has some significance apart from the will.

> ***Example 7:*** *Testator leaves his house "to the person that is my brother's spouse at the time of my death." T is designating the beneficiary who will receive his house by referencing the act/event of his brother getting married; getting married is an act/event with separate legal significance.*

B. Classification, Abatement, and Ademption

When distributing the real property (devise) and personal property (bequest or legacy) under a testator's will, an estate's assets may be insufficient to satisfy the gifts made under the will. In this situation, a court must determine the order of distribution and abatement (reduction or elimination of gifts) by classifying each gift.

> **Exam Tip 13:** Be sure to analyze each devise and legacy/bequest in the will and determine its classification.

1. Specific Gift

A specific legacy, devise, or bequest is a gift of property that can be distinguished with reasonable accuracy from other property that is part of the testator's estate (a specific car ("my car") or item of furniture).

2. General Gift

A general legacy is a gift of personal property (such as money) that the testator intends to be satisfied from the general assets of his estate (such as "$100,000 to John").

3. Demonstrative Gift

A testator intends that a demonstrative legacy be paid from a particular source, but if that source is insufficient, he directs that the legacy be satisfied out of the general assets of the estate.

> ***Example 8:*** *$100,000 to John from my Bank of Columbia account, but if funds are not sufficient, then the rest paid out of general funds.*

4. Residuary

A residual legacy is a legacy of the estate remaining when all claims against the estate and all specific, general, and demonstrative legacies have been satisfied.

> ***Example 9:*** *I give the rest and residue of my estate to Mark.*

C. Abatement

If the assets of the estate are insufficient to pay all debts of the testator and legacies, a court will "abate" or reduce the gifts to pay the debts. The court will abate the gifts in the following default order:

- Intestate property (property that has not been addressed in the will)
- Residuary bequests
- General bequests
- Specific bequests

(Demonstrative legacies are treated as specific legacies for abatement purposes to the extent that they can be satisfied, and otherwise as general legacies.)

In other words, specific gifts are the last items to be sold/reduced in order to pay off debts of the estate; intestate property is the first item to be sold/reduced.

D. Ademption by Extinction

> **Exam Tip 14:** When a specific gift in a will is no longer in the testator's estate at the time of the testator's death, discuss the rules of ademption.

- **Traditionally**, if the subject matter of a **specific gift** is missing, destroyed, or there is a substantial change in the form of the gift (the court can trace the gift it undergoes a minor change), the beneficiary takes nothing. This does not apply to general or demonstrative gifts, which can be satisfied from the general assets of the estate.
    - The beneficiary is entitled to whatever is left of the specifically devised property or balance of the purchase price owing from the purchaser of the property.
- **UPC approach:** The testator's intent at the time he disposed of the subject matter of the devise or bequest is examined.
    - If there is evidence that the testator intended for the beneficiary to receive the gift, despite ademption, the UPC permits a beneficiary of a specific extinct gift to inherit the property

acquired by the testator as replacement property or, if the testator is owed money relating to the extinction, the outstanding balance.

  - If neither the replacement property nor the outstanding balance doctrine applies, then the UPC provides that a beneficiary of a specific gift is entitled to money equivalent to the value of the specific property as of the date of disposition of the gift if ademption is inconsistent with the testator's Intent or Plan of Distribution.

    Example 10: *(From outline): X's will devises 123 Main St. to his son, Y. At the time of the will's execution, X owned the property, but he later sold the property and used the proceeds to buy bonds. X still owned the bonds at this death. Under the majority rule and common law, Y would not receive the bonds at death, as the specific devise of property was adeemed. Under the UPC, Y would receive the bonds under the replacement property exception.*

E. Special Problem: Stocks (Securities)

UPC: A bequest of a security (stocks) that was owned at the time the will was executed will include any additional shares of that stock or of another stock as long as the action was initiated by the corporate entity. A stock dividend is treated like a stock split instead of a cash dividend, so the beneficiary will also receive the stock dividends.

F. Special Problem: Life Insurance Contracts

If an insured dies while a life insurance policy is in effect, the policy proceeds are payable to the named beneficiary. Although the owner of a life insurance policy typically retains the right to change the named beneficiary without obtaining that beneficiary's consent, the owner must do so in accordance with procedures specified in the life insurance contract. Life insurance contracts almost never permit a change of beneficiary by will, and courts have almost invariably upheld such restrictions.

G. Lapse and Anti-Lapse

- Under the common law, if a beneficiary dies before the testator, the gift to the beneficiary lapses (fails).
- Under modern anti-lapse statutes, if the beneficiary was blood-related to the testator, the beneficiary's surviving issue (child, grandchild, etc.) will take in his/her place.
- **Class Gift Rule:** If the will beneficiaries are a class, such as "my brothers", the traditional rule is that only the members of the class who are alive at the time of the execution of the will receive the benefit of the will. However, under modern statutes, if an anti-lapse statute applies (because the predeceased class member was related to the testator), then the issue of the predeceased member also will take.

    Example 11: *T creates a will giving his property to "my brothers" upon his death. Upon T's death, his surviving brother A would receive a share of his estate. If his other brother, B, had already died, anti-lapse would apply and give B's share to B's issue (children).*

H. Ambiguities in the Will

Traditionally, there was a distinction between patent and latent ambiguities: patent ambiguities appeared on the face of the will and were required to be resolved within the four corners of the instrument but without extrinsic evidence; latent ambiguities were not apparent from a reading of the will and were allowed to be resolved by extrinsic evidence. Many states no longer distinguish between patent and latent ambiguities and allow both to be resolved by extrinsic evidence.

I. Mistakes

Extrinsic evidence is admissible to show a mistake in the execution of a will, such as when the testator is unaware that she was signing a will. Extrinsic evidence is not allowed if the mistake involves the reasons behind the testator making the will or a particular gift.

CHAPTER 5: POWER TO TRANSFER

A. Omitted Spouse

- **Omitted Spouse:** A marriage or domestic partnership is formed after the execution of testator's will and spouse is not mentioned in the will.
- An omitted spouse is entitled to an intestate share unless:
    - The omission was intentional;
    - The spouse was given property outside of the will in lieu of a disposition in the will; or
    - The spouse is party to a valid contract (prenuptial agreement) waiving her right to a share in the estate.

B. Omitted Children

Exam Tip 15: To earn full credit, you should discuss why the child qualifies as omitted child and then consider any limitations that may apply.

- **Omitted Children:** A child who is omitted from the will can force a share if certain requirements are met:
    - The child is born or adopted after the will is created, or the testator mistakenly believed the child was dead; and
    - The child is unintentionally omitted from the will.
    - **Limitations:** A share will not be forced if the child has been provided for outside of the will, or if the testator had other children at the time the will was executed and left substantially all of his estate to the omitted child's parent.
    - **Share:** If the testator had no other children when the will was executed, then the child takes her intestate share. If the testator has at least one other child living at the time of the execution of the will, and the will devised property to at least one of those children, then the omitted child's share is taken from that portion of property already devised to the other child, and it must equal the share the other child receives.

C. Bars to Succession

1. Homicide ("Slayer Statute)

A party cannot take property from a decedent when the party was responsible for the decedent's death. The UPC and the majority of jurisdictions treat the killer as if he had predeceased the decedent.

2. Disclaimer

Because acceptance of a testamentary gift is presumed, a party must actively disclaim if she wishes not to accept it. The disclaiming party is treated as if she had predeceased the decedent, and the property is distributed to the next eligible taker.

D. Will Contests

A will contest is an objection raised against the validity of a will, based on the contention that the will does not reflect the actual intent of the testator. The basis of a will contest is the assertion that the testator (i) lacked testamentary capacity, (ii) was operating under an insane delusion, or (iii) was subject to undue influence or fraud.

1. Capacity

The testator must be at least 18 years old and possess a sound mind. The testator lacks the requisite mental capacity if he, at the time of execution, did not have the ability to know the:

- Nature of the act;
- Nature and character of his property;
- Natural objects of his bounty; and
- Plan of the attempted disposition.

> ***Example 12:*** *Professor Ide-Don states that an individual must be over the age of 18 in order to execute a valid will. An individual who is 18 years of age or older may execute a valid will if the individual otherwise has capacity.*

2. Insane delusion

> **Exam Tip 16:** Similar to capacity, look for facts indicating that the testator is suffering from an insane delusion, such as mental illness and drug or alcohol abuse.

A belief is an insane delusion if a rational person in the testator's situation could not have reached the same conclusion.

If it is shown that the testator has an insane delusion, it must be also shown that but for this delusion, testator would not have disposed of his property in the manner he did. (In other words, the delusion must have caused the testator to make the disposition).

3. Undue influence

General Rule: Undue influence occurs when mental or physical coercion is exerted by a third party on a testator with the intent to influence the testator such that he loses control of his own judgment. If undue influence is shown, the will may be invalidated in whole, or in part.

Undue Influence – Majority View: A contestant must show four elements:

- **Susceptibility:** The testator was susceptible to being influenced.
- **Motive:** The influencer has reason to benefit.
- **Opportunity:** The influencer had opportunity to influence.
- **Causation:** The influencer caused an unnatural result.

4. Fraud

A will can be invalidated due to fraud. Fraud requires a misrepresentation made by a beneficiary with both the intent to deceive the testator and the purpose of influencing the testamentary disposition. The result must be a will that would not have been executed but for the fraud.

Fraud in the Inducement: A misrepresentation that causes the testator to make a different will that he otherwise would have made. It must be shown that the testator would not have made the gift if he had known the truth.

Fraud in the Execution: A misrepresentation as to the will itself or its contents (testator does not know he is creating a will or is not told the true content of the will).

CHAPTER 6: PRACTICE QUESTION

February 2004, Question 1 [ID 342]

In 1995, Testator, age 85, executed a will in the presence of two witnesses. Immediately before signing the document, Testator's attorney asked Testator if she declared the instrument to be her will. Testator responded: "You bet it is. I want Charity to have everything. My family has enough." Then the attorney had Testator sign the document on the line provided for her signature. The two witnesses signed immediately below Testator's signature without any further direction or comment from Testator.

When Testator executed this will, she was suffering from cancer and her medications made it very difficult for her to remember facts. For example, when she executed her will she knew, correctly, that her estate was worth $500,000 and that she had previously made large gifts to her child and some of her grandchildren. However, she could neither remember the name of her stockbroker nor recount the names of her stocks under her stockbroker's management. Also, she had no difficulty correctly naming her child and all of her grandchildren, but she could not recall that she had a great-grandchild. She also knew she owned both a home and a condominium but could not recall the precise street address for either residence.

Testator died in 2002 survived by her only child, Mary, and by three grandchildren and one great-grandchild, all of whom are descendants of Mary. Testator's will, which devised her entire estate to Charity, was timely offered for probate by Bank, the executor named in the will. Mary and one of her children, Grandchild, have initiated a timely contest of the will.

Governing state law provides that a will is properly executed if the testator signs the will in the presence of two witnesses after having (a) declared the instrument to be her will, and (b) requested the witnesses to act in such capacity.

1. Do Mary and Grandchild each have standing to contest Testator's will? Explain.

2. On what theory or theories, other than undue influence, might a person with standing contest Testator's will, what defenses might Bank, as executor, assert, and what is the likely outcome? Explain.

Sample Answer

1. The issue is whether either Mary or Grandchild has standing to contest Testator's will.

Only directly interested parties who stand to benefit financially may contest a will. Intestacy statutes generally favor the decedent's surviving spouse and issue. Under intestacy laws, an intestate's children take to the exclusion of their own descendants.

The facts indicate that Testator did not have a surviving spouse, but she was survived by her only child, Mary. Accordingly, if Testator's will were denied probate, Testator's entire estate would pass to Mary. Therefore, Mary would have standing to contest the will because she stands to benefit if Testator's will is denied probate. However, Grandchild does not have standing to contest the will because Grandchild would not be financially better off if the will were denied probate. Because an intestate's children take to the exclusion of their own descendants, Grandchild would not be entitled to anything if Testator's will was denied probate. Accordingly, only Mary has standing to contest Testator's will.

(2)(a) The issue is whether Testator's will can successfully be contested on grounds of lack of mental capacity.

In order to validly execute a will, Testator must have "mental capacity." A testator has mental capacity if she knows (1) the nature and extent of her property, (2) those persons who are the natural objects of the her bounty, (3) the disposition the testator is attempting to make, and (4) the interrelationship of these items in connection with the testamentary plan formulated in the will. All persons are afforded the presumption that they have mental capacity. The burden of proving that the testator lacks mental capacity rests on the contestant of the will.

Under these facts, it could be argued that Testator did not know the nature and extent of her property because she could not identify the stocks that she owned or name the stockbroker who managed them. Additionally, Testator could not recall the addresses of her residences. However, Testator knew what her estate was worth and knew she owned two residences. Because Testator understood the big picture about her financial affairs this would likely be a close case and difficult to successfully carry the burden of proof. Therefore, the court will likely find that the Testator had the mental capacity to execute a will.

It could also be argued that Testator could not identify all those who are the natural objects of her bounty. Although Testator could not identify her great-grandchild, that relationship is relatively remote and Testator could identify her more closely related relatives. Testator's failure to recall whether she had a great-grandchild probably would not be sufficient to overcome the presumption that she had mental capacity. Accordingly, Testator will likely be found to have the mental capacity to execute a will.

(2)(b) The issue is whether Testator's will can successfully be contested on grounds of lack of due execution.

At common law, strict compliance with the formal requirements of wills is required. Governing state law provides that a will is properly executed if the testator signs the will in the presence of two witnesses after having (a) declared the instrument to be her will, and (b) requested the witnesses to act in such capacity.

A minority of jurisdictions and the UPC have granted courts the power to probate a non-compliant will in situations when there is clear and convincing evidence that the decedent intended for the document to serve as her will and has substantially complied with the statutory formalities. Under this approach, if the execution of a will substantially complies with most of the formalities, or at least the most important of them, the will is valid.

Under these facts, the signing, witnessing, and declaration requirements were satisfied. However, the execution of the will did not strictly adhere to the required formalities because the Testator did not expressly request the witnesses to act in such capacity. Accordingly, the will could be successfully contested on grounds of lack of due execution, unless the court adopts the substantial compliance doctrine. In this case, Testator's statement that "My family has enough" and bequeathing all of Testator's property to Charity suggests a clear intent of Testator to make the document her will. Additionally, Testator substantially complied with the statutory formalities because she properly had her will signed, witnessed, and declared. Accordingly, the will could be successfully contested on grounds of lack of due execution, unless the court adopts the substantial compliance doctrine.

[END OF HANDOUT]